U.S.A. vs. E.S.A.
The Politically Incorrect Side
of the
Endangered Species Act of 1973

Thoughts, articles, and treatises on how the most draconian law in the history of the United States of America is destroying our economy and our personal freedoms

John Andre

Published by

John Andre
P.O. Box 520
Hamilton, MT 59840

October, 2011

e-mail: john@shoshonewilderness.com

ISBN-13: 978-1466431393

Cover Photo by Jeff Vanuga

To Anita.
Her love sustains me on a daily basis.

Contents

Introduction

> "How soon we forget history... Government is not reason. Government is not eloquence. It is force. And, like fire, it is a dangerous servant and a fearful master."
> George Washington

On December 28, 1973, President Richard M. Nixon signed into law, the Endangered Species Act of 1973. The bill had been introduced just six months earlier, on June 12, 1973. A mere 42 days after its introduction, the bill passed the Senate by a vote of 92-0. After coming out of conference committees, the bill passed the Senate by acclimation on December 20, 1973, and a day later, the House by a vote of 355-4. Here is what President Nixon said upon signing the bill:

"Nothing is more priceless and more worthy of preservation than the rich array of animal life with which our country has been blessed. It is a many-faceted treasure, of value to scholars, scientists, and nature lovers alike, and it forms a vital part of the heritage we all share as Americans. I congratulate the 93rd Congress for taking this important step toward protecting a heritage which we hold in trust to countless future generations of our fellow citizens. Their lives will be richer, and America will be more beautiful in the years ahead, thanks to the measure that I have the pleasure of signing into law today. "

> "There are more instances of the abridgment of the freedom of the people by gradual and silent encroachments of those in power than by violent and sudden usurpations."
> James Madison, Virginia Ratifying Convention, June 16, 1788

And thus it is with the Endangered Species Act of 1973. A law, passed with all good, nearly unanimous, intentions, that has become so perverted, so distorted, so abused, as to threaten the very "life, liberty, and pursuit of happiness", that was, and is, guaranteed to all Americans, by our Constitution.

> "Freedom is never more than one generation away from extinction. We didn't pass it on to our children in the blood stream. It must be fought for and protected and handed on for them to do the same. Or one day we will spend our sunset years telling our children and grandchildren what is used to be like in the United States when men were free."
> Ronald Reagan, 40th President of the United States of America

Introduction

Being against the Endangered Species Act, to the unitiated, is like being against Baseball, Mom, and Apple Pie. It's un-American, right? I urge the reader to read this book carefully, and put yourself into the place of the Americans this law has affected. Ask yourself, was this the intent of Congress, to give unlimited power to unelected bureaucrats? Would such an act, if that was truly the intent, sail through our Congress (however disfunctional you believe that body to be) by a vote of 447-4?

Over 200 years ago, Thomas Jefferson predicted the problem.

> "Experience hath shewn, that even under the best forms [of government] those entrusted with power have, in time, and by slow operations, perverted it into tyranny."
> Thomas Jefferson, Founding Father

Definition of "Tyranny": 1. cruel use of power: cruelty and injustice in the exercise of power or authority over others. 2. oppressive government*

It is time to repeal the Endangered Species Act of 1973. Not amend it. Not change it. Not massage it. Repeal it, and start over again, applying the lessons learned, so that similar mistakes and abuses of government power will not be endured by future Americans. There is no person on the planet that loves wildlife more than I do. But I love freedom, humanity, and my country, even more. And when rats, flies, lizards, bats, smelts, suckers and spiders take precedence over feeding and housing the American people, it is time to speak up, and for Congress to wake up.

> "When all government, domestic and foreign, in little as in great things, shall be drawn to Washington as the center of all power, it will render powerless the checks provided of one government on another and will become as venal and oppressive as the government from which we separated."
> Thomas Jefferson to Charles Hammond, 1821.

Decades ago, Rachel Carson's **Silent Spring** sounded the alarm about the abuses of industrialization and the deleterious effects on our streams, atmosphere, and wildlife. Generations of Americans, now and in the future, have her to thank for a much cleaner, healthier environ-

*www.merriam-webster.com/dictionary/tyranny

ment. The good that has been done by the environmental movement of the 1960s and 70s is unchallengeable. However, America governs by the swing of the pendulum, and that pendulum has swung too far. Now, the "Silent Spring" is the silence of American industry, the silence of American home builders, the silence of American tractors, and the silence of American hopes and dreams.

> "The time is near at hand which must determine whether Americans are to be free men or slaves."
> George Washington

This book is for my grandchildren: Johhny, Sophia, Olivia, Abigail, Simon, Rylan, and those yet to come, that they might enjoy the blessings of true liberty.

Chapter One

<u>Farmers vs. the Rats:</u> <u>Part One</u>
<u>The Domenigoni Family</u>

The Domenigoni Family-An Iconic California Family*

In 1874, Angelo Domenigoni, at the age of 23, immigrated to southern California, from his native homeland of Switzerland. He was so poor, that he had to leave his family behind, and had had to borrow the money for passage to America. Like so many immigrants of that time, Angelo came to America to seek his fortune, in a free nation, where hard work, diligence, innovation, industriousness, and perseverance would be rewarded. He epitomized "the American Dream." Working hard and saving, Angelo was able to bring his young wife and two children to California. They eventually raised seven children on their ranch, which grew to several thousand acres. They grew grain, raised cattle and dairy cows, and it required a team of 36 horses to pull the farm's combine. Angelo became the first U.S. Postmaster for the area, and their ranching and associated business interests thrived.

The Angelo Domenigoni
Family, circa 1880

Angelo Domenigoni,
family patriarch

Here is what Elsa Domenigoni Barton, granddaughter of Angelo Domenigoni, wrote in "The Friendliest Valley, Pioneers of Winchester" in 1971:

*Source: "The Friendliest Valley, Pioneers of Winchester"

"My three brothers and sister, and their families, still live in Winchester, carrying on their farming with the same high standards of the Domenigoni family. The fourth generation is "coming along." ...Four generations of the family, from immigrant to modern Americans of the 1970s with our ups and downs, our happy times and our tragedies, have contributed in a wholesome way, we hope, **to the America we love**."

"Two years after Elsa Domenigoni Barton penned those words, **"the America we love"**, on December 28, 1973,. Richard Nixon signed into law The Endangered Species Act of 1973. No one thought that a simple effort to preserve wildlife would become the most draconian law in the history of the United States. The law would eventually cost the Domenigoni family nearly a third of their farmland, hundreds of thousands of dollars, the homes of many of their neighbors, and very nearly their lives. The Endangered Species Act of 1973 has become the most anti-capitalist, anti-property rights, pro big government law ever enacted. And it passed the U.S. Senate by acclimation, so innocuous was it considered at the time.

The Domenigoni's Fight for Their Land
The following is a brief biography of Cindy Domenigoni, wife of Andy Domenigoni, great grandson of Angelo Domenigoni. Cindy is on the Chancellor's Advisory Committee for 2010-2011, for the University of California, Riverside.

"Partner
Domenigoni Brothers Ranch
Co-owner/Manager
Sky Canyon Enterprises, LLC

Cindy is the First Vice President of the Riverside County Farm Bureau and the President of the Winchester Homeowner's Association. She is also the past Chairman of the Riverside County Commission For Women. Cindy is the co-founder and director of the Domenigoni Ranch Poker Ride for Juvenile Diabetes Foundation. Cindy is a member of the Temecula Valley Chamber of Commerce and the Murrieta Chamber of Commerce as well as an appointee on the Riverside County Multiple Species Habitat Conservation Advisory Committee. Cindy and her husband Andy have been farming and ranching for 30 years. They dry farm cereal grains, irrigate corn, alfalfa and Sudan. They also have a cow/calf operation."*

*University of California Riverside, Chancellor's Advisory Council, 2010-2011

Additional information comes from Cindy Domenigoni's Pipi Profile:

Age, 57 years old
4th Generation California Rancher, 2500 acres, cattle and grains
Married, mother of 2 children
Equestrian
Family received the Boy Scouts of America Good Citizens Award
Organizes Domenigoni Charity Ride for Diabetes
Hobbies: Team Penning and Bowling

"Boy Scouts of America Good Citizens Award. Equestrian. Bowler. Mother of Two. Farmer/Rancher for 30 years. Organizers of a Charity Ride for Diabetes."

Does this woman sound like an enemy of the state to you? Is this the type of American that Abraham Lincoln envisioned, when he spoke about the "dangers amongst us." I think not. And yet our government attacked her, and her family. Read her gut-wrenching story carefully, and then re-read it. Is this the America our brave soldiers around the world think they are fighting for?

Here, in her own words, is the tragic story of the Domenigoni family, and the Nazi-like treatment they have received from the United States Fish & Wildlife Service, agents of the Government of the United States of America. Your government and my government.

Sworn Testimony of Cindy Domenigoni before Congress

Committee on Resources, United States Congress
Witness Testimony
Testimony of
CINDY DOMENIGONI
Before the Committee on Resources
May 20, 1996

Thank you, Mr. Chairman, for allowing me to appear before you today. I also want to thank you for allowing Mr. Rowe to accompany me to provide additional information for you. Our family owns a 2,500 acre cattle ranch and grain farm in Winchester, California. **Our son is the fifth generation to work the land that my** husband's ancestors settled over one hundred and twenty years ago.

I come before you today, with a rising amount of frustration, a good bit of indignation, and a healthy amount of anger. As I have testified on two previous occasions, our farm has been seriously impacted by the "endangered" listing of the Stephens' kangaroo rat. We have been stopped from farming parts of our land. We nearly lost our lives and all of our cattle in a devastating fire exacerbated by these prohibitions. And now, after simply standing up and telling our story, we have been unjustly attacked, impugned, and essentially called liars. What is most enraging to me is that, the Department of Interior has been using my tax dollars to spread misinformation about our story and to question our character.

Since I have provided testimony on the ESA before, I will briefly outline the impacts of the Endangered Species Act on our farm operation and our lives, and then speak to the government's added insults to our injury. I.

Impact of the Endangered Species Act on Our Farm

In 1990, without our knowledge or consent, over 1,600 acres of our ranch were placed in a reserve "study area" as part of a Habitat Conservation Plan for the Stephens' kangaroo rat, under section 10 (a) of the Endangered Species Act. We later discovered private biologists illegally trespassing on our ranch. These biologists then returned with a U.S. Fish and Wildlife Service biologist and an armed law enforcement officer. We were later informed that our planned preparation of over 800 acres of our farm for grain planting would constitute an illegal "take" of the kangaroo rats that they said were found inhabiting our fields. Because our property is in a reserve "study area" we are not allowed any incidental take. We would only be able to legally take kangaroo rats if we went through a very expensive and lengthy "Boundary Modification" process, asking for the removal of this designation from our property. The Riverside County Habitat Conservation Agency, California Department of Fish and Game, and the U.S. Fish and Wildlife Service would all have to sign off, allowing our property out of the study area, after we had paid for extensive surveys, a per acre "processing fee," and a flat fee for the privilege of requesting that our property have this designation that we never asked for, removed.

Our Boundary Modification application has been pending for over three years. **As a result of shutting down our ability to farm that property, we incurred over $75,000 in lost income for each of the three years that we were unable to grow grain there. We have also spent over $175,000 on legal fees, biological surveys, and other related costs. Our costs total over $400,000 in lost income and direct costs because of the impact of the Endangered Species Act. These costs do not include thousands of dollars in damages to our fences and equipment that occurred during the California Fire of October 1993.**

II. USFWS's Smear Campaign

After this disastrous fire of 1993, I was interviewed as part of the GAO investigation into the effects ESA prohibitions had on the damage caused by the fire. **We had hoped that the GAO would take a fair, objective look at the information we provided them. However, it later became apparent that the GAO was not interested in finding out the truth about what happened in Riverside county. Rather, the GAO was more interested in providing the defenders of the ESA status quo with a false "study" they could wave in front of the media and call it the definitive word on the fire whose publicity had so damaged the mythical image of the Endangered Species Act. As if this was not enough, we have since found that the GAO report is being used to attack our family personally, and to attempt to portray those who lost their homes in this tragedy as either misguided or untruthful.** Who are exaggerating the ESA's exacerbating effect on the damage caused by the fire.

Last year, I was shocked to learn that **I was targeted in a smear campaign waged by the U.S. Fish and Wildlife Service against individuals who have spoken up about injury they had suffered from implementation of the Act.** We received a document titled, "Facts about the Endangered Species Act." **One whole chapter in it is devoted to casting me and ESA victims who have had the courage to speak out in public as liars.** In the first portion of this document, the Service trumpets the "success stories" of species they claim owe their recovery to the Act. This portion of the "Fact" sheet proudly lists names and contact telephone numbers for Service personnel, and state wildlife agency personnel. It would have taken us one telephone call to get additional information about these "Endangered Species Act Success Stories." The "Fact" sheet attempts to unjustly cast as lies the stories of many of the people who have been seriously abused by this Act. They obfuscate and mislead the truth by creating several "strawmen" accusations. Under the heading of "The Allegation," they create outlandish charges that the ESA has done or caused things that no one has ever accused the Act of doing, the Service is then able to easily refute these untrue "allegations" that were never actually made. Yet, **also contained in this document were vicious attacks on numerous individual citizens who have had the courage to speak out publicly about the impacts they had suffered** These attacks were couched in the section titled, "The Endangered Species Act: The Rest of the Story." But in this section of the "Fact" sheet, the Service had no contact people, no telephone numbers, no authors or attribution anywhere. The Service obviously thought they would be able to publish this document, and no one would ever wonder where it came from. **Wasn't the Service worried that its distortions of fact, twists of real allegations, and construction of strawmen might cause those they maligned to fight back? Why didn't the Service stand behind this scandalous document? Why isn't it published on government letterhead? I believe the answers are obvious. The Service feared legal liability for printing blatantly false and hurtful accusations about the ESA's victims. I believe the Service also lacked the fortitude to stand up after launching this salvo.**

III. The Department of Interior Attempts to Hide From Scrutiny When we sought to find out the sources of the information used in the document, it took not only numerous unsuccessful phone calls, but also a formal Freedom of Information Act Request ("FOIA"). This FOIA request also required numerous telephone calls, and an additional FOIA Appeal in order to get any of the information that the Service relied on for the "allegations" and "responses" in the "Rest of the Story" section. We submitted our FOIA request in October 1995. **It was followed in December by a denial of our request. We filed anappeal on December 26th. That was answered with a partial reply that is still woefully incomplete. We still have not received all of the information we requested.**

In our official request for information, we asked eighteen specific questions, seeking the sources for the statements contained in the document. The first response by the Department of the Interior tried to absolve itself of any responsibility for the statements it made in the "Fact" sheet by stating that the Office of Public Affairs for the Service was, "not the office of record" for the documents they them

We appealed this determination by the Department, and their second answer came on February 14th, still largely incomplete and unresponsive. Of our eighteen questions, the Washington Office of Public Affairs, (the place where the document was published) referred us to the Regional Director's Office of the Fish and Wildlife Service in Portland Oregon, for nine of our questions. The Regional Director's Office still has not responded. The response then referred to a "pop up card" published by a group of labor interests for three of the questions, then cited the General Accounting Office report on the fire as the source for three more questions. A printing requisition form was the answer for one question, a National Wildlife Federation "document" for another, and, incredibly, they even cited my own Congressional testimony as one "source." We were shocked! Their response to our request for the persons responsible for developing and distributing the publication was a printing requisition sheet, and printing invoice, all referencing "Mark Newcastle, Printing Specialist."

First the Service nearly drives us out of business with its prohibitions stopping us from farming our own land. Then it nearly cost us our lives and our home and our cattle by forcing us to abandon safe fire prevention practices, then they attack us for simply telling what happened. Then, to top it all off, the Service uses my own testimony, and while knowing the true facts of the matter, blatantly and unrepentantly attempts to discredit and impugn my family and me. All the while using my tax dollars to accomplish this.

The most telling aspect of the response to our FOIA request is that the Service apparently has nothing to back up its "responses" that attempt to refute the stories. **The information we received in response to our FOIA Appeal indicates that the Service was aware of the true facts. However, it chose to ignore some and misrepresent others in the publication. They also try to create false impressions by glaring omission, such as not mentioning the prohibition placed on us lasted for three years.** We also found out that the document is regularly updated and widely distributed. One of the few documents actually disclosed to us is a printing requisition with instructions for distributing 2,500 copies of the May 1995 edition of the "Fact" sheet from the Washington office. We have since seen that there is a June/July 1995 edition circulating. I previously testified that the Service prohibited my family from farming

800 acres of land that we have farmed for over 100 years due to the presence of the Stephens' kangaroo rat ("SKR"). The publication attempts to cast doubt on the financial injury my family has suffered by calling it a mere "allegation." The Service has copies of my testimony, and no facts contradicting my testimony, but that didn't stop them from "responding" in the publication.

The Service's response falsely suggests that I inflated the acreage my family was prohibited from farming. It also fails to disclose that the Service's prohibition against our farming was in place for over three years. The three years we were prevented from farming our 800 acres was when the loss of crop income occurred in the amount of about $75,000 per year. Yet the Service, in a clear and calculated omission, first asserts that it is not "familiar" with 800 idled acres. They then follow with the statement that the property was allowed to be farmed again, totally omitting the fact that the land was idled for three years. The next statement in this document is very curious, yet also very revealing. The "Facts" document states that the property was allowed to be farmed again when, **"A Service biologist subsequently determined that the land in question was not k-rat habitat." There are several points I want to make about this statement. First, it is blatantly misleading to use the word "subsequently." This word implies a direct, responsive action, taken in some sort of timely manner, (which was obviously the impression the Service sought to leave with the reader.) However, "subsequently" is not an accurate word to use when it took over three years for the Service to "examine" our property when they found it not to be k-rat habitat. Second, in the intervening time, (after the Service personnel told us we could not farm the field in 1990) a Service biologist had examined our field, in June 1992. It was examined by a Service biologist after we had pleaded with the agency to allow us to disk a fire break in order to protect the safety of our neighbor, Mr. Rowe.** Mr. Rowe had sent us two letters asking us to remove the vegetation and brush that had built up over the previous five years (two years of fallowing preceded the three year ESA prohibition on the field) we were not farming the property next to his small farm and home. **He legitimately feared that, should a fire come, he would be in great danger of losing his home from the amount of fuel that had built up so close to his property.**

At that time, (and this is recorded in letters to us and Mr. Rowe from the Service) the biologist had found evidence of Stephens' kangaroo rats. That was the stated reason the Service was prohibiting us from disking the fire break. They told us not to disk the fire break, and they offered their own solution, that we mow a fire break. The Service biologist responded to our protests that the mowing machine would be a hazard itself in that area, (numerous fires are caused by mowers' hot exhausts or their blades striking rocks every year in California) and our position that the left over dead thatch would present an even more severe fire hazard, by telling us to hire a water truck (to wet the brush) and a hand crew to clean up the thatch. Obviously, this biologist had never tried to mow his lawn in the rain, let alone 800 acres. Third, after the fire in October 1993, my husband and I examined the land ourselves and found no evidence of k-rats on the area that had been cited as occupied habitat for the previous three years by the Service. **We then sought to have the Service reexamine the land to tell us if it would be all right for us to farm it again, since there were no k-rats left on the property. After his examination and his verbal go ahead to us, the Service biologist was attributed in our local paper with saying that it wasn't the fire that caused the destruction of the k-rats and their habitat. Rather, while we were under orders not to farm the land by the Service, the brush and weeds in the field had grown too thick for the krats' preference, and they had simply left the area, long before the fire occurred. This attribution was later denied by the Service, for obvious reasons. It shows that in their infinite wisdom, the agency charged with protecting this species had actually caused an area that had been used for farming and for habitat for over a hundred years, to be both unsuitable for the k-rats and unproductive for us.**

Obviously, it does not help the Service's reputation as wise stewards and benefactors of endangered species for this statement to stand. That is why they quickly distanced themselves from the statement after it appeared in the paper. Yet, in a typical about face, it appears that they have relied on it to smear us in a twisted manner in this document. This is evident in the Service response that the land was "subsequently" found not to be k-rat habitat. They are again relying on the examination after the fire in 1993. If their position was that the fire had been the cause of the k-rats' disappearance, they would have to state so in their response. Further evidence that the Service is reverting back to its position that the land was "not k-rat habitat" is found in the Department of Interior's response to our request under FOIA. In their response to our query about the source of the information for the statement that the Service biologist had found the area not to be habitat, the Department of Interior's FOIA response cites "conversations" with Service personnel in the Carlsbad field office, the Service's base for our area. Yet the "Facts" document never mentions the examination by the Service biologist in June of 1992, where he cited the presence of k-rats as the reason for the prohibition on disking fire breaks. Mention of this examination would reveal to the reader that the property had been inhabited by k-rats, and idled for at least eighteen months. This would not have kept with the impression they desired to leave by choosing to use the word "subsequently" in their response to the fact that they order farming stopped on the property.

Evidence proving the facts I have provided is contained in the paper titled, "Fire Protection, the Public and the Endangered Species Act." The report was compiled by the Golden State Resource Management Group, and contains the letters from the Service citing the presence of the k-rats in June of 1992, and the news article attributing the Service biologist with stating that the k-rats had left before the fire in 1993. I asked that this report be entered in the record of proceedings when I testified at a hearing of the Endangered Species Task force held in Riverside, California in April 1995.

The Service's publication also targets other property owners like me, who have testified before Congress and who were interviewed by the GAO.

IV. Top Fire Official Disagrees with GAO Findings
The Service selected statements from the GAO report that deflect criticism of its irresponsible prohibition against disking of fire breaks instituted as one of its Stephens' kangaroo rat protection measures.
As a result of the Service's prohibition on disking, and the fact that their alternative of mowing was in itself dangerous, likely to cause a fire, and also totally impractical. Brush in the fields where we were stopped from farming became overgrown and few fire breaks were accomplished at all in the habitat protection area. **The ones who had level land with few rocks to cause sparks from a fast moving mower blade, and chose to use the Service's alternative, were left with an incomplete and ineffective fire break.**

Riverside County Fire Chief Mike Harris also testified before the

Task Force in Riverside. There he stated that, **"Both California state law and Riverside County ordinances require the removal of flammable vegetation to <u>bare mineral soil around all homes and improvements.</u>** The intent of these laws is to break the unobstructed travel of fire from a wildland area into the structures or from the structures into the habitat. **These laws and ordinances have proven effective over the years at providing a reasonable and prudent level of public safety."** [emphasis added] Fire Chief Harris continued, discussing the Service's prohibition on disking fire breaks, stating: There were three major impacts from these actions:
1. The fire service lost a very valuable public protection tool.
2. The regulations caused confusion on the part of government officials and the public, leading in some cases to inaction.
3. The lack of proper hazard reduction contributed to the loss of homes and other improvements during the California fire." [emphasis added] Chief Harris continued,

"The General Accounting Office's report on the California fire concluded that the lack of hazard reduction activities had no impact on the losses caused by the California fire. I do not agree with their conclusions."

Later, during the question and answer period of the Task Force hearing, Chief Harris discussed another Riverside County fire that occurred in 1993, about one week after the California fire, under similar weather and wind conditions. However, Chief Harris noted that there were some significant differences between this fire, the Repplier fire and the California fire. First, there was a "much higher fuel loading" on the Repplier fire. Second, there were no (ESA) prohibitions on hazard reduction clearance, (disked fire breaks were allowed, and present). And third, there were only four homes lost in the Repplier fire, significantly fewer than were lost in the California fire were the disking prohibition was in place (even though many more homes were at risk in the path of the Repplier fire). For those homeowners who followed the Service's edict and mowed their fire breaks, Chief Harris provided a stark visual picture of the difference in the effectiveness of mowed fire breaks versus disked fire breaks "I can make a quick example here, if we assume this piece of paper is a structure and we provide a [disked] fire break so the direct flame impingement is out here somewhere, [Harris placed his hand several inches away from the paper you do not have to be a rocket scientist or the fire chief to figure out that that is [sic] less

potential for loss of this home than if you put that flame right here."
[Harris at this point placed his hand in contact with the paper he
was using to symbolize a home with a only mowed firebreak having direct contact with flames from a wildfire.] **The fire chief also
agreed with the other residents and us in that, had our 800 acres
been actively farmed at the time of the fire, the fire's intensity
would have been greatly reduced.**

Included with my testimony are two maps depicting the habitat
protection area, our property (including the areas we were not allowed to farm), Mike Rowe's residence, the origin of the fire, and
its direction of travel that first night. Also depicted on these maps
are representations of each of the 29 homes that were destroyed. We
were not able to show you where all of the 107 other destroyed
structures were located. I hope each of you will take a few moments
to examine these maps, and I request that these maps be entered in
the record. V. Maps and Photos Clearly Show Impact of Regulations
While examining these maps, keep in mind that the 800 acres that
were subject to the farming prohibition, would have been either
grazed off grain stubble, or completely denuded of any vegetation
at all. That area might have been disked completely at that time of
year, in preparation for the next year's crop planting. **Despite statements in the GAO report such as "the entire U.S. Army could not
have stopped this fire," with just a few yards of disked firebreaks,
and our normal agricultural practices, many of the homes could
have been saved. I must remind you that my husband and I were
out during the height of the fire, herding our cattle out of its path,
and into safer pastures. We were able to survive the fire burning
all around us, as we huddled with our horses and our cattle in a
tiny seven acre field that we had farmed that year. Had the entire
800 acres been farmed as well, others might have been more fortunate with their own homes and property. Bear in mind that in
the nearly one hundred and twenty years this area has been
farmed, we had never had as large or as damaging a fire as this
one.** The fires in the past had always been contained to minimal
acreage burned, and minimal damage due to the patchwork landscape effect from our agricultural practices.

**Because he was fortunate enough to have warning and a ready
tractor, Michael Rowe saved his house by cutting the fence between our properties and disking a fire break before the fire made
its way to his home. Yes, he was fortunate, his home stands today.**

His home is standing because of the action he took, not the "capriciousness" of the fire or the "shifting winds" in the GAO's version of events. I have also brought photographs of the area as it looked this past December 1995. Because of the fire and the Service's newly found flexibility that allows us to disk fire breaks, you will see good sized disked fire breaks in these photos of our property and Mr. Rowe's property. You can see that our field has only an inch or two of widely spaced grain stubble that has been grazed by our cattle. This is hardly enough fuel to keep a fire burning at all, much less the raging inferno that occurred in 1993.

Another photo shows our farmed property, and some vacant property owned by the Riverside County Habitat Conservation Agency, as part of the Stephens kangaroo rat reserve area, which also burned in the fire. As you can see, in just two short years the growth of brush and the amount of dead, flammable vegetation is already enormous. You can just imagine what the area that we are now able to farm was like after having more than five years growth of this brush on it.

VI. Congress Must Take Action

Clearly, the Service has attempted to capitalize on the GAO report's conclusions by absolving themselves of any wrongdoing, holding up this misleading red herring, all the while calling it the oracle from on high. They have used it to add repeated insult to injury to myself, my family, Mr. Rowe, and the rest of the victims of this terrible tragedy. Yet they continue to backstab and impugn honest citizens seeking redress of these government wrongs. Their lack of remorse is evident in their blatant disregard for the facts, even when the facts are in their possession as in this case. They make up lies and distortions, create favorable impressions for themselves through glaring omissions, and then thumb their nose at the people who try to find the source of their information through the processes set up by Congress for gaining access to information. The Service's publication is another indication that, despite its rhetoric, the Department of the Interior is not interested in working to implement the ESA in a manner that "avoids train wrecks" between species regulations and property owners. Quite the contrary, it appears the Department works very hard to deny the wreck ever happened. **Without Congressional remedy to the Endangered Species Act, the Service will continue to issue edicts, citing the Act as its authority, with no regard for the legitimate interests of safety, health, the privacy of individuals, and their Con-**

stitutionally guaranteed rights. It is incumbent upon Congress to investigate the abuses caused by the publication of this document, "Facts About the Endangered Species Act." Why isn't it attributed to the Department or the Service? Who wrote it? Why aren't there contact persons mentioned in the "Rest of the Story" section of the document? Why did the Service make up phony allegations in order to easily refute them, thus casting suspicion on the whole of the story? Why did the Service ignore the true facts when it had them in its possession? **How many other people are being abused by their government a second or third time by this document?**

This last point is the most important point to me. I sit before you today, just one of the people whose character has been assassinated by the mistruths published in this document. Michael Rowe, accompanying me, is another. Mrs. Rector, also testifying, is another. How many more people discussed in this document have been so seriously abused and mischaracterized? That is why it is imperative that you initiate an investigation into these issues surrounding this document today. Your action in doing so will be a first step in righting this egregious wrong by our government. I hope you will see to it that the light of day floods every dark corner that hides the truth about this. The document is nothing more than a thinly veiled effort to undermine the sensible reforms and redirection you are attempting to achieve in reauthorizing the Endangered Species Act for both the species it seeks to protect, and the people it affects every day. It is also an example of the one of the many ways that the U.S. Fish and Wildlife Service is abusing the broad authority given it under the Act. **We urge you to stay the course in reforming the Act to reign in the abuses and give strict guidance to the agencies responsible for enforcing this law. You must change the specter of fear landowners now have of both the federal agents and the presence of the species that cause landowners to have to deal with them. That is the only way the Endangered Species Act will ever change from a disaster and a failure, to a true success story.** Thank you."

Cindy Domenigoni, May 20, 1996

> "To take from one, because it is thought his own industry and that of his fathers has acquired too much, in order to spare to others, who, or whose fathers, have not exercised equal industry and skill, is to violate arbitrarily the first principle of association, the guarantee to everyone the free exercise of his industry and the fruits acquired by it."
> Thomas Jefferson

To the right is the intimidating letter sent from the U.S. Fish & Wildlife Service to Mr. Paul Smith, Fire Specialist Captain, for the Riverside County Fire Department, threatening Mr. Smith and his fellow county employees with "civil and criminal penalties."

It was Mr. Smith's job to protect the county residents, many of whom were his friends and neighbors, from the horrendous wildfires that plague southern California in periods of dry weather, which are quite common. Disking, rather than mowing, was the county law. The reason the law was passed, was because disking worked, mowing didn't.

So here is the choice the U.S. Fish & Wildlife Service gives this Fire Chief. If he disks, he protects human life and property, and risks going to prison. A few Kangaroo Rats might die. Or, he could order mowing only, and risk the lives and properties of those people he has sworn an oath to protect.

Please note that the U.S.F.W.S. "emphasizes" that the maps showing exactly where the Stephen's Kangaroo Rats are found aren't worth a damn. Instead, the Riverside County Fire Chief is warned not to allow disking anywhere "within the historical range and in potential habitat of this species puts the County and landowner at risk" of going to jail or being heavily fined.

This poor guy is a fire chief, not a biologist. How is he supposed to know what is potential habitat for this rat and what isn't? Consult his Ouija Board? All he wants to do is to keep homes from burning down. That seems to be a concept the United States Fish & Wildlife Service doesn't understand, or, more accurately, doesn't care about.

This is a ridiculous situation in which to put a civil servant.

United States Department of the Interior

FISH AND WILDLIFE SERVICE

FISH AND WILDLIFE ENHANCEMENT
SOUTHERN CALIFORNIA FIELD STATION
Laguna Niguel Office
Federal Building, 24000 Avila Road
Laguna Niguel, California 92656

July 5, 1990

Paul Smith
Fire Captain Specialist
Riverside County Fire Department
210 West San Jacinto Avenue
Perris, California 92370

Dear Mr. Smith:

As of June 21, 1990 the Fish and Wildlife Service (Service) has
not received the environmental assessment regarding Riverside
County Fire Department's weed abatement program. On June 20,
1990 during a drive-through of the Riverside County (County),
numerous parcels which had been recently disked (i.e. within 1
month of observation), were observed by Service personnel.

The Service would like to emphasize that the County could be
considered a responsible party if any Stephens' kangaroo rat
(Dipodomys stephensi) was taken subsequently to issuance of a
public weed abatement notice. We would also like to emphasize
that use of the maps generated by Michael O'Farrell and Curt
Uptain for the Department of Fish and Game (Distribution and
abundance of the Stephens' kangaroo rat) can be misleading.
Though they are very helpful in identifying where many population
concentrations occurred during the survey, they were unable to
survey the entire County. In many instances Stephens' kangaroo
rats have been found outside of the areas mapped by O'Farrell and
Uptain.

Therefore, disking within the historic range and in potential
habitat of this species puts the County and land owner at
risk of violating Section 9 of the Endangered Species Act (Act).
Section 9 prohibits the "taking" of a listed species without
necessary authorization. Civil and criminal penalties can be
levied against responsible parties.

The term "take" in the Endangered Species Act (Act) as defined
includes the terms "harm" and "harassment". "Harm" in the
definition of "take" in the Act means an act which actually kills
or injures wildlife. Such act may include significant habitat
modification or degradation where it actually kills or injures
wildlife by significantly impairing essential behavioral

Mr. Paul Smith   2

patterns, including breeding, feeding or sheltering (50 CFR 17.3).

"Harass" in the definition of "take" in the Act means an intentional or negligent act or omission which creates the likelihood of injury to wildlife by annoying it to such an extent as to significantly disrupt normal behavioral patterns which include, but are not limited to, breeding, feeding or sheltering (50 CFR 17.3).

Based on our knowledge of the biology of this species and the affects of disking on habitat which supports this species, it is likely that a "taking" would occur if occupied habitat were to be disked. Site specific information needs to be acquired prior to disking or another non invasive means of fire suppression need to be incorporated. These measures (e.g. mowing, grazing) need to be compatible with the continued existence of the Stephens' kangaroo rat.

The Service believes that the County needs to assume a more responsible role in regards to the impacts potentially incurred to the Stephens' kangaroo rat due to their weed abatement program. We look forward to assisting your agency in identifying areas where the Stephens' kangaroo rat occur. If you should have further questions contact Arthur Davenport at (714) 643-4270.

Sincerely,

FOR Brooks Harper
Office Supervisor

cc: CDFG/Long Beach, Attn. Bruce Eliason/Environmental Services)
USFWS Law Enforcement, Gardena, (ATTN: Special Agent Diane Petrula)
1-6-90-TA-533

To the right is a similarly intimidating letter sent from the U.S.F.W.S. to Mr. Michael Rowe, neighbor of the Domenigoni Ranch, who, due to the high fire risk that year, desperately wanted to disc a firebreak around his property.

He is clearly threatened with heavy fines and imprisonment by the United States Fish & Wildlife Service. **"Be advised that should you take endangered species or migratory birds you are liable for both State and Federal prosecution."** and they are forwarding the information to other law enforcement agencies. These are clear, unwarranted and illegal attempts at intimidation by government bureaucrats. This letter easily could have been written in the Germany of the 1930s. And, after all, what exactly was Mr. Rowe trying to do? Simply protect his home from wildfire.

Appendix V

United States Department of the Interior

FISH AND WILDLIFE SERVICE
FISH AND WILDLIFE ENHANCEMENT
SOUTHERN CALIFORNIA FIELD STATION
Carlsbad Office
2730 Loker Avenue West
Carlsbad, California 92008

June 5, 1992

Mr. Michael F. Rowe
P.O. Box 507
Winchester, California 92596

Dear Mr. Rowe:

The Fish and Wildlife Service (Service) would like to advise you of the potential presence of the federally listed endangered Stephens' kangaroo rat (*Dipodomys stephensi*) and also the potential presence of nesting birds protected under the Migratory Bird Treaty Act on the Domenigoni property in the vicinity of your proposed fire break.

It is my understanding that Mr. Davenport of my staff, and Special Agent Petrula of the Division of Law Enforcement, spoke with you regarding potential endangered species conflicts relating to your proposed fire break. I would further like to notify you that there could be an impact on nesting migratory birds. I am providing the following information on the Endangered Species Act and the Migratory Bird Treaty Act to provide you with clarification of these federal laws.

The Endangered Species Act states that ". . . it is unlawful for any person subject to the jurisdiction of the United States to . . . take any such species within the United States. . . "(16 USC 1538(a)(1)(B)).

"Person" is defined by the Endangered Species Act (Act) as an individual, corporation, partnership, trust, association or any private entity; or any officer, employee, agent, department or instrumentality of the Federal Government, of any state, municipality or political subdivision of a state; or any other entity subject to the jurisdiction of the United States. "Take" as defined by the Act means to harass, harm, pursue, hunt, shoot, wound, kill, trap, capture, or to attempt to engage in any such conduct. It should be noted that the Act provides for both civil and criminal penalties.

Furthermore, "take" in the Act as defined includes the terms "harm" and "harassment". "Harm" in the definition of "take" in the Act means an act which actually kills or injures wildlife. Such action may include significant habitat modification or degradation where it actually kills or injures wildlife by

·Mr. Michael F. Rowe   2

significantly impairing essential behavioral patterns, including
breeding, feeding or sheltering (50 CFR 17.3).

Additionally, "harass" in the definition of "take" in the Act
means an intentional or negligent act or omission which creates
the likelihood of injury to wildlife by annoying it to such an
extent as to significantly disrupt normal behavioral patterns
which include, but are not limited to, breeding, feeding or
sheltering (50 CFR 17.3).

The Migratory Bird Treaty Act states that ". . . it shall be
unlawful at any time, by any means or in any manner, to pursue,
hunt, take, capture, kill, attempt to take, capture, or kill. . .
any migratory bird, any part, nest, or egg of any such bird. . ."
(16 USC 703). "Take" means to pursue, hunt, shoot, wound, kill,
trap, capture or collect, or attempt to pursue hunt, shoot,
would, kill, trap, capture or collect. "Migratory bird" means
any bird, whatever its origin and whether or not raised in
captivity, which belongs to a species listed in 50 CFR 10.13, or
which is a mutation or a hybrid of any such species, including
any part, nest, or egg of any such bird. . . .

Be advised that should you take endangered species or migratory
birds you are liable for both State and Federal prosecution. The
Service is forwarding this information to other appropriate
agencies for their information and review.

It is my understanding that you have been unwilling to cooperate
with the Service in resolving this matter in a legal manner.
Potential methods exist to reduce fire hazards without taking
endangered species or nesting migratory birds. An example would
include moving the site and removing debris rather than disc-ing.
I would like to emphasize that the Service appreciates your
concern and we remain willing to work with you to resolve any
conflicts.

If you have any questions or would like additional information,
please contact Art Davenport of this office at (619) 431-9440.
Special Agent Petrula can be contacted at (310) 297-0062.

                              Sincerely,

                              Brooks Harper
                              Brooks Harper
                              Office Supervisor

cc: Diane Petrula, FWS Law Enforcement, Gardena Office

The United States Fish & Wildlife Service was insisting that home-owners risk their properties, by mowing firebreaks instead of disking them, as required by California law. The indisputable facts show that disking works, mowing does not. Please bear in mind, to the casual reader across the country, they may not have a lot of knowledge about fire suppression, disking, mowing, etc. In southern California, where the Santa Anna winds are infamous, they live and breathe this information. Clearly, the local U.S.F.W.S. people would know the extreme danger to which they were subjecting these citizens. The sad fact is, they didn't give a damn.

> ### Data from California Office of Emergency Services
>
> "Although the immediate causes of the losses were arson and accidental fire starts, we must look at the long-term need for fuels management to reduce California's fire losses. Our data clearly indicate the need to modify both structures and vegetation. **Between 1920 and 1989, California lost about 3,500 structures to wildfires. In the first 4 years of the 1990s we have now lost almost 4,500 structures. Loss of human lives has also increased dramatically.....** if flammable vegetation were cleared beyond 30 feet (9 meters), **structural survival rose from 15% to 90%"***

By disking, you increase the chance of saving your home to 90% or by a factor of 6X. But the Federal government, all too happy to tax that home, and the income you earned to build that home, says, in effect:

"No, you can't protect that home, your habitat. We, the unelected bureaucrats in the USFWS, don't really give a damn how hard you worked to earn the money that built that home. We don't care how much you sweat the mortgage payments. We don't care about the memories you have of your children playing in the backyard, or opening up Christmas presents under the tree. We don't care about the personal effects, the family photo albums, that reside in your home. We don't care about the cars parked in the garage. We don't care that your life and the life of your family may be threatened by wildfire. Rats come first."

Government Covering Government's Back
Ike Sugg is a Fellow in Wildlife and Land -Use Policy at the Competitivie Enterprise Institute. His scathing report entitled **Rats, Lies and**

*http://www.fire.uni-freiburg.de/iffn/country/us/us_5.htm

the GAO, A Critique of the General Accounting Office Report on the Role of the Endangered Species Act in the California Fires of 1993.* supports the testimony of Cindy Domengoni, the way her family was treated, and the lie after lie put forth by our government. The General Accounting Office, following the uproar over the California fires that destroyed 29 homes, investigated, and, basically, covered up, the role the U.S.Fish & Wildlife, had played in the destruction of these homes. Here are some of the highlights of Mr. Sugg's report:

Defenders of the ESA have taken the extreme and untenable position that there could be no correlation between preventing people from clearing firebreaks and the burning of their homes. The vigorous efforts of the environmentalists to discredit the fire victims and their voice in the property rights movement are inappropriate."

Twenty-nine American families lose their homes because the U.S. Fish & Wildlife forbade them from protecting their homes, because of rats. Then these same fire victims exercise their First Amendment right of free speech, denouncing the loss of their property, which is theoretically protected by the Fifth Amendment. And then, the environmental groups, instead of trying to help fellow Americans cope with a tragedy, denounce the victims as liars. This is monstrous, but typical of environmentalist groups disdain for humanity.

Here is what the National Wildlife Federation said: **"the GAO report "demonstrates conclusively" that the E.S.A. "had nothing whatever to do with" the tragedy, but instead shows that critics of the ESA "will go to almost any lengths of distortion, fabrication, and manipulation of he truth to gut America's most important conservation law."**

Mr. Sugg goes on to say:" Equally celebratory and no less vociferous were dozens of other environmental special interests, which rushed to announce that "without a doubt" the E.S.A. had been "completely vindicated". Any claim to the contrary was dubbed "a myth", part of a "selfish agenda" to "spread lies". This is evident, The Wilderness Society, tells us, because "the report is quite clear on the role the Stephen's Kangaroo rat and the prohibition on disking....played in the loss of 29 homes: **none**. According to The Wilderness Society, "this unequivocal conclusions was reached after the GAO interviewed state, county, and independent fire experts."

Mr. Sugg rightfully concludes that the GAO misrepresented what

*www.cei.org/pdf/4361.pdf."Rats, Lies, and the G.A.O. "

prevention of disking had nothing to do with the massive destruction is simply unsupported by any of the evidence.

In other words, one branch of the Federal Government, the General Accounting Office, covered up for another branch, The U.S. Fish & Wildlife Service.

In a letter to Senator Max Baucus and the Senate Committee on Environment and Public Works, Cindy Domenigoni concluded her letter with this statement:

> "During our interviews with the representatives of the GAO, these items and many other comments were made which have been distorted or not included in the report. This report creates a false sense of comfort with the true workings of the Endangered Species Act. The GAO as an investigative arm of Congress should not be driven by a political agenda which leads to financial and personal ruins of so many Americans. We urge you to amend the Endangered Species Act, as necessary, so that we achieve a true balance without victimizing people and eroding our property rights."
> Cindy Domenigoni

A Stephen's Kangaroo Rat.

Stephen's Kangaroo rats are cute, without question. As a species, I wish it no particular ill will. But why should its home, its habitat, its life, take precedence over Cindy Domenigoni's home, or her life or her property, or the 29 other families who lost their homes? Before the Endangered Species Act of 1973 came along, the Domenigoni family farm and the rats seemed to be adapting to each others' existence quite nicely. It was the United States Fish & Wildlife Service that created this problem, not the Domenigonis and the rats. The basis for our government, the United States Constitution, guarantees Americans that the government won't expropriate their property without "just compensation. Search that erstwhile document as I might, I see no such rights guaranteed to the Stephen's Kangaroo Rat.

Unfortunately, as you will see going forward, Cindy's pleas fell on deaf ears, and nothing happened to change the act. Nearly two decades of continued abuse of the Endangered Species Act of 1973 has helped bring the economy of the United States to the greatest depression since the 1930s, and has stomped all over the property rights of the American people.

> "I think myself that we have more machinery of government than is necessary, too many parasites living on the labor of the industrious."
> Thomas Jefferson

Chapter 2

Farmers vs. the Rats, Part Two

The Story of Immigrant Farmer Mr. Taung Ming-lin

> "The only power any government has is the power to crack down on criminals. Well, when there aren't enough criminals, one makes them. One declares so many things to be a crime that it becomes impossible for men to live without breaking laws."
> Ayn Rand

The American beacon of freedom has shone for over 200 years, and it shines in all directions, for thousands of miles. Dreams of liberty and the human spirit are inseparable. And so it was for Taiwanese immigrant Taung Ming-Lin, who gave up a successful import business to come to America, to work the land.

Ming-Lin had dreamed of owning a farm, having watched his grandfather for many years toil happily on eight acres of land in Taiwan. Taung was a savvy businessman, but farming presented a new challenge. Coming to America, he started a small bookbinding business in El Monte, California. "I have never farmed, but it's in my blood," Lin said. "My idea was to sell the bookbinding company one day and go back to the soil." His plan was to grow oriental vegetables, for the oriental market in nearby Los Angeles.

It takes a courageous man to come to a new country, with his wife and three children, to start a new life. Taung spoke very little English, but the language of freedom is universal. When you learn in grade school about the American Melting Pot, and the benefits of cultural diversity, it is people like Taung Ming-Lin your teachers are talking about. Taung Ming-Lin was absolutely no different than Angelo Domenigoni one hundred years earlier. Mankind's thirst for freedom is not endemic to a certain time period; no single generation can lay claim to its sovereignty. It is universal, it is unquenchable, and it is timeless.

> "It is the flag just as much of the man who was naturalized yesterday as of the men whose people have been here many generations. "
> Henry Cabot Lodge

Is there a more iconic picture of America than a farmer plowing his field? Whether it be a pioneer farmer behind a sodbuster plow and a

Farmers vs. Rats, Part Two

AMERICAN FARM SCENES.

team of mules, or the modern day farmer driving a huge John Deere, the image speaks of America: our taming of a wilderness continent, immigrant people coming from around the world to build a great nation, based on certain principles, inherent in the hearts of men, and enumerated by the framers of the U.S. constitution.

Our Founding Fathers, seeking to protect people's dreams, and the inalienable right of private property, crafted, as part of the Bill of Rights in the United States Constitution:

Fifth Amendment to the Constitution

No person shall be held to answer for a capital, or otherwise infamous crime, unless on a presentment or indictment of a Grand Jury, except in cases arising in the land or naval forces, or in the Militia, when in actual service in time of War or public danger; nor shall any person be subject for the same offense to be twice put in jeopardy of life or limb; nor shall be compelled in any criminal case to be a witness against himself, nor be deprived of life, liberty, or property, without due process of law; nor shall private property be taken for public use, without just compensation."

> "We on this continent should never forget that men first crossed the Atlantic not to find soil for their ploughs but to secure liberty for their souls."
> Robert J. McCracken

Unfortunately, for Taung Ming-Lin, bureaucrats at the United States Fish & Wildlife Service had set their sights on his land and his planned farming activities. The land was zoned for agriculture, and, in fact, the local Kern County Farm Bureau had assisted Mr. Lin with his irrigation system. (As a U.S. citizen, it is so comforting to know that our federal government, with The War on Drugs, Islamic jihad, trillion dollar federal deficits, record high unemployment, etc. notwithstanding, can focus on the truly important criminal activities of the country, such as farming.) Unbeknownst to Mr. Lin, the 770 acres of desert scrub, which he had purchased with his life's savings, turned out to be the home to the Tipton's Kangaroo Rat, a subspecies of the widespread Kangaroo Rat

And so, the day after Mr. Lin's fields are plowed, in swoops the U.S. Fish & Wildlife Service, using helicopters and 20 agents, many of them armed, scowering Mr. Lin's farm for plowed up Tipton's Kangaroo Rats. (Fortunately, Mr. Lin had forgotten to mount a Gatling gun to his Ford Tractor, and he and his farmhands had left their Uzis at home that day, so no gun battle ensued.) When informed by government officials he was facing three years in jail and a three hundred thousand dollar fine, the poor guy suffered a stroke. This is America, right? Reads more like something coming out of Germany in the 1930s.

According to the U.S. Fish & Wildlife Service, rats have more rights than tax paying, law abiding citizens, plowing a field to feed hungry people. Yes, to be certain, Mr. Lin hoped to make a profit, farming his fields. Since when, in an American society, based on capitalism, is that a crime? Answer: Ever since the Environmental Movement absconded with the well intentioned Endangered Species Act of 1973.

The agents scouring Mr. Lin's fields found parts of 3-5 dead Tipton's Kangaroo Rats. Not exactly a lot, when one looks at the 770 acres he plowed. (Picture 747.5 football fields.) This comes out, at the high end, to one dead rat, or part thereof, for every 150 football fields.

Predators of the Tipton's Kangaroo Rat, according to the University of

California, include "coyotes, San Joaquin kit foxes, long-tailed weasels, American badgers, owls, hawks, various species of snakes, and probably others. Except for small, isolated populations, predation is unlikely to threaten Tipton kangaroo rats." How many rats get eaten by all these predators in a single day, day after day, during the course of a year, is unknown. The human impact, of three to five rats taken, in the course of a once a year plowing, certainly seems minimal, in comparison.

Under the Endangered Species Act of 1973, humans get to pay a fine of $50,000 per rat, plus spend a year in prison. per rat. Coyotes, foxes, and snakes get off Scot free. Additional costs to the human community include the removal of 770 acres of farmland, which would feed thousands of humans per year, year after year, and would create jobs for many farm workers. Density of Tipton Kangaroo Rats varies a great deal, depending on drought and flood conditions. At the low end. Mr. Lin's property would have had 346 rats (.45 rats per acre) on the property, meaning his plowing might have killed about 1.4 percent of the rats. * On the high end, his property would have had 35.7 rats per acre, or a total of 21,166 rats, and his plowing would have taken .00023 of the rats on the property. Neither figure of annual harvest would significantly change the long term viability of Tipton's Kangaroo Rats.

> "Economic power is exercised by means of a positive, by offering men a reward, an incentive, a payment, a value; political power is exercised by means of a negative, by the threat of punishment, injury, imprisonment, destruction. The businessman's tool is values; the bureaucrat's tool is fear."
> Ayn Rand

*http://esrp.csustan.edu/publications/pubhtml.php?doc=sjvrp&file=chapter02J00.ht ml

"Federal Suit is Act 1 in Theater of the Absurd

By Tony Snow

July 14, 2000

Somebody call Stephen King!

The U.S. government has filed suit in a California federal district court against a tractor and a disc (an appliance used to break up chunks of soil). Uncle Sam has ordered the possessed implements to surrender on charges that they ground up animals that may appear on the government's endangered species list.

The case of "United States of America, Plaintiff, vs. One Ford Tractor, Mdl VC715V, Unit OH22B, Engine OH16A, its tools and appurtenances thereon, One Towner Offset Disc, Model A248, Serial Number 24C665, its tools and appurtenances thereon, Defendant(s)" marks one of the most bizarre episodes in modern environmentalism, challenged only by Washington's assault on the machinery's owner, Taung Ming-Lin.

Lin, an immigrant from Taiwan, arrived in the United States three years ago. He purchased 720 acres of desert land near Bakersfield, Calif., with plans to grow herbs and vegetables on the barren soil. He laid out his farm, hired some help and asked local officials if everything was OK. They told him: The land is zoned for agriculture. Grow what you want. Create jobs. Welcome to America!

Little did they know that federal agents had their eyes on Lin, who had no idea that his property was listed as natural habitat for the Tipton kangaroo rat, a member of the endangered species club. The feds keep such information secret and inform property owners of their legal liability only when they try to do something potentially criminal, like plowing a field.

On Feb. 20, a squadron of more than two dozen state and federal agents, accompanied by helicopters, descended upon the farm. They raced through fields taking pictures and looking for animal parts. They reportedly ordered a reluctant county fire department employee to haul away the scofflaw tractor and disc.

Five weeks later, the government told a court that Lin "did knowingly take and aid and abet the taking of an endangered species of wildlife, to wit, Tipton kangaroo rats." Last week, they threw in counts of harming San Joachin kit foxes and blunt-nosed leopard lizards.

The interesting thing is that the feds still do not know whether the animals they seized in February were Tipton kangaroo rats, which are virtually identical to some nonendangered rodents. The only thing that distinguishes them from the Herman's kangaroo rat, for instance, is that their rear feet are 1-100th of an inch longer — and they can be used as an excuse to seize private property.

Furthermore, Tipton kangaroo rats actually prefer plowed to uncultivated fields. Varmints all over the state have begun abandoning brush in favor of airier climes, and local farmers report that the vermin breed zestfully in churned up soil. No matter: Agents seized the murderous farm tools and threatened to fine Lin $300,000 — whereupon he had a mild stroke.

This sort of behavior is not unusual. The government has filed charges against Valley Communities Inc., also in Kern County, claiming that its operators have threatened Tipton kangaroo rats and blunt-nosed leopard lizards by plowing and irrigating fields. (A lawyer in the case says, "I know of no dead (animal) bodies.") If the Clinton administration wins the case, the city of Bakersfield may have to shut down part of its sewer system, since the water to treat the land comes from a city waste treatment plant.

Environmental officials also have asked the county to erect a $150,000 mesh fence outside a landfill, out of anxiety that Kangaroo rats might tumble in and injure themselves.

Such orders have turned the area into a hotbed of rebellion. A group called the Coalition to Protect and Preserve Private Property Rights organized a full-day festival, complete with a tractorcade/demonstration, property rights rally, barbecue fund-raiser and western dance/auction — in hopes of preserving a few endangered agrarians.

Meanwhile, the Kern County Board of Supervisors has endorsed a resolution that **"deplores the outrageous and abusive behavior of the U.S. Fish and Wildlife Service** toward Mr. Lin, Valley Com-

munities and other private property owners under cover of the Endangered Species Act, and <u>calls upon the president and the Congress to immediately investigate what appears to be a gross
misuse of authority and deprivation of due process by an unelected bureaucracy."</u>

"America is much more than a geographical fact. It is a political and moral fact - the first community in which men set out
in principle to institutionalize freedom, responsible government, and human equality."
Adlai Stevenson

The real cost in this tragedy is the loss of freedom in a theoretically
free country. And the freedoms that Americans assume are real are becoming more and more theoretical as time passes. Mr. Lin's story became a cause-celebre for many of the local California farmers, who came
to his assistance, holding rallies in his support, with parades of huge
tractors, and a call for the end to the "Bureau<u>rats</u>."

The U.S. Fish & Wildlife Service originally brought charges against
Taung Ming-Lin personally. His lawyer requested a jury trial. The
U.S.F.W.S.' lawyers, knowing they would get creamed in a jury trial,
dropped the charges. Lin and local farmers celebrated the victory. A
few weeks later, the U.S.F.W.S. brings a suit against Mr. Lin's corporation. Corporations are not guaranteed a jury trial. Fortunately, the
lawyer for Mr. Lin, Anthony Capozzi, sought and received a jury trial
for the corporation. The U.S.F.W.S. then decided to settle out of court,
and Mr. Lin agreed to make a $5000 donation to endangered species
protection. Government extortion, plain and simple.

"America is another name for opportunity. Our whole history appears like a last effort of divine providence on behalf
of the human race. "

U.S. Agrees to Drop Endangered-Species Case Against Farmer*

May 02, 1995 | MARK ARAX | Los Angeles Times STAFF WRITER
The federal government has agreed to drop its controversial case

*articles.latimes.com/1995../me-61449_1_u-s-endangered-species-act

Farmers vs. Rats, Part Two

against a bamboo farmer accused of plowing under critical habitat of three endangered species in Kern County and killing five kangaroo rats.

Attorneys for farmer Taung Ming-Lin declared a victory Monday in the yearlong case that has galvanized conservatives nationwide who argue that federal officials have gone overboard in enforcing the U.S. Endangered Species Act.

Lin admitted no wrongdoing in exchange for the federal government's agreement not to prosecute him or his company. In addition, the 52-year-old Taiwanese immigrant can still farm his land outside Bakersfield if he waits six months and obtains the proper state and federal permits.

Lin will donate $5,000 toward endangered species protection in Kern County as part of the agreement.

"There is no question that public sentiment had a lot to do with the resolution of this case," Lin attorney Anthony Capozzi said after the accord was signed by both sides in federal court in Fresno.
"The government didn't want a jury trial, because they knew we would win," he said.

Federal prosecutors would not comment publicly when asked if they were caving in to pressure from politicians and activists who have rallied around the Lin case as an example of all that they say is wrong with the Endangered Species Act.

But in private they maintain that Lin has become an unlikely poster boy for foes of the federal law, which has been targeted for overhaul this year by Republicans in Congress. They say the landowner's case took on a life of its own that had very little to do with the facts.

Lin, they point out, is no dirt-under-the-fingernails farmer but a millionaire businessman and investor who lives in South El Monte, far from the alfalfa and cotton fields of Kern County.

They say a quick glance should have told the savvy entrepreneur that the 723 acres he purchased from Tenneco in 1991 was just about the worst land for farming in these parts. Laden with salt and studded with desert scrub, it is home to the Tipton kangaroo rat, the blunt-nosed leopard lizard and the San Joaquin kit fox--three endangered species.

Lin was warned by the state Department of Fish and Game that the land was critical habitat, they say. He chose to ignore these warnings--delivered by registered mail--and instructed his farm manager to plow under the land, they add.

"I never received those letters telling me this was endangered species land," Lin told reporters Monday through his translator."

The above quote, about Mr. Lin not being a ""dirt-under-the-fingernails" farmer, but instead, a "millionaire businessman and savvy entrepeneur" give miles of insight into the thinking of bureaucrats within the Federal Government. Mr. Lin has a 770 acre farm, they don't. Mr. Lin has busted his butt all his life, and succeeded, they haven't.

> "Let me give you a tip on a clue to men's characters: the man who damns money has obtained it dishonorably; the man who respects it has earned it."
> Ayn Rand

> ""Mediocrity" doesn't mean average intelligence, it means an average intelligence that resents and envies its betters."
> Ayn Rand

Man: The Endangered Species*

Wednesday, May 2, 2001
By: Glenn Woiceshyn

Endangered Species Act Destroying Farmers' and Man's Rights

Imagine you are a farmer whose livelihood depends on water from a nearby reservoir. The government knows this but cuts off your regular supply to save some fish. You suffer crippling damages to

* Reprinted with permission from Glenn Woiceshyn of the Ayn Rand Institute in California. The highlighting is the author's.

crops and livestock--but are told that the fishes' "interests" supersede yours.

A tall fish tale? No, it actually happened on April 6, 2001, in the Klamath Basin to about 1,400 Oregon farmers who produce hay, potatoes and cattle on roughly 200,000 acres of land. Enforcing the Endangered Species Act (ESA), the Bureau of Reclamation cut off the water that these farmers normally receive--and desperately need--from the Klamath Irrigation Project (near the Oregon-California border) to protect "endangered" sucker fish and salmon.

According to state representative Bill Garrard, this single government action "sacrifices more than $65 million in farm income and risks more than $45 million in secondary income to the local community."

The endangered Oregon farmers had requested an injunction to restore irrigation flows; but on May 1 U.S. District Judge Ann Aiken effectively fed them to the fish: "Threats to the continued existence of endangered and threatened species constitute ultimate harm."

This vicious government assault on Oregon farmers is but one of countless examples of the ESA being used to block productive activities--i.e., activities beneficial to people--such as farming, mining, forestry and hydroelectric power. The northern spotted owl became famous when timber production was virtually halted in the Northwest to protect the species. Near Bakersfield, California, a farmer was arrested in 1994 by Fish and Wildlife officers for inadvertently killing five Tipton kangaroo rats while plowing his own field. His tractor and plow were seized as "murder weapons." Under the ESA, he faced heavy fines and three years in prison. Most recently, the ESA was used by environmentalists to block power generation in the Northwest, thereby contributing to the costly blackouts wreaking havoc on Californians.

What motivates environmentalists to protect "endangered" species, with so much zeal that they are oblivious to the harm inflicted on people?

Some environmentalists assert that "species diversity" is extremely beneficial to man. But environmentalists are the staunchest opponents of genetic engineering--which has vast potential for creating new species. Some environmentalists assert that an endangered species could possess medical secrets beneficial to man. But, in 1991, when taxol--processed from the Pacific yew tree--was discovered to be highly effective in treating certain forms of cancer, environmentalists blocked harvesting of the yew tree. Whenever man's needs conflict with the "interests of nature," environmentalists take the side of nature.

The real motive behind environmentalism is stated by David Graber (a biologist with the U.S. National Park Service): **"We are not interested in the utility of a particular species, or free-flowing river, or ecosystem to mankind. They have intrinsic value, more value--to me--than another human body, or a billion of them."**

This "intrinsic value" ethic means that man must value nature--not for any benefit to man, but because nature is somehow a value in and of itself. Hence, **nature must be kept pristine despite the harm this causes man. We must halt activities beneficial to us, such as farming, forestry and treatment of cancer, in order to safeguard fish, birds, trees and rats.**

Throughout history, people were told to sacrifice their lives to God, the community, the state or the Fuhrer--all with deadly consequences. Now we are being told to sacrifice our lives to nature. And current environmental legislation, such as the ESA, provides government with massive powers to enforce such sacrifices. What disasters could such power lead to?

Some environmentalists have expressed their wish. "Until such time as Homo sapiens should decide to rejoin nature," writes biologist Graber, "some of us can only hope for the right virus to come along." City University of New York philosophy professor Paul Taylor adds: **"[T]he ending of the human epoch on Earth would most likely be greeted with a hearty 'Good Riddance.'"**

While extreme, these anti-human sentiments are logically consistent with environmentalism's "intrinsic value" philosophy: Since man survives only by conquering nature, man is an inherent threat to the "intrinsic value" of nature and must therefore be eliminated. Environmentalism makes man the endangered species.

The only antidote to these haters of mankind and their anti-human philosophy is to uphold man's right to pursue his own life by means of his productive activities. Congress should begin the process of rescinding the ESA and any environmental legislation that allows government to sacrifice people to nature.

Meanwhile, Oregon farmers desperately need water to save their crops and cattle, and will stage a peaceful, "last hope" protest on May 7, in Klamath Falls, Oregon. The Bush Administration has the authority to grant exemptions to the ESA and should do so un-equivocally in the name of man's right to "life, liberty and the pursuit of happiness."

Critical Thinkers

The following is from a former environmentalist, known to me only as **"criticalthinker"**, posted on the web on September 18, 2009. I would like to personally thank him for speaking up, although I do not know his name. Simply an American, who cares.

"I am a native born Californian living in the heart of the San Joaquin Valley and also a RECOVERING ENVIRONMENTAL & POLITICAL ACTIVIST. I was in the environmental part of it for 4 years. Like most of us who left that environmental movement it was because what originally needed a nudge back to an equilibrium marched to a full blown over the top, over the edge outrageous attack against the good of man. So yes the Environmentalists have turned WHACKO. I got out when a farmer in the southern part of the valley had his farm confiscated because he ACCIDENTALLY ran over an endangered mouse with his tractor. Enough was enough for me."

Here are the thoughts of a few other great "critical thinkers."

"You and I have a rendezvous with destiny. We will preserve for our children (America), the last best hope of man on earth, or we will sentence them to take the first step into a thousand years of darkness. If we fail, at least let our children and our children's children say of us we justified our brief moment here. We did all that could be done."
Ronald Reagan

"Our lives begin to end the day we become silent about things that matter."
Dr. Martin Luther King

"The liberties of our country, the freedom of our civil Constitution, are worth defending at all hazards; and it is our duty to defend them against all attacks. We have received them as a fair inheritance from our worthy ancestors: they purchased them for us with toil and danger and expense of treasure and blood, and transmitted them to us with care and diligence. It will bring an everlasting mark of infamy on the present generation, enlightened as it is, if we should suffer them to be wrested from us by violence without a struggle, or to be cheated out of them by the artifices of false and designing men."
Samuel Adams, American Patriot

"Evil requires the sanction of the victim. "
Ayn Rand

"Men fight for liberty and win it with hard knocks. Their children, brought up easy, let it slip away again, poor fools. <u>And their grandchildren are once more slaves."</u>
D.H. Lawrence

My fervent hope is, that you, the reader, will learn from this book exactly how our freedoms in America are being slowly but surely, undermined, by an environmental movement that consistently obsfurcates their real goals. In many cases, citizens supporting the environmental or "green" movement think they are doing the right thing for America, when, clearly, just the opposite is true. I urge you to read this book carefully, and apply your own "critical thinking."

I am determined that my grandchildren will not be slaves.

Chapter 3

The Species Scam

"Contradictions do not exist. Whenever you think that you are
facing a contradiction, check your premises. You will find that
one of them is wrong."
Ayn Rand (Atlas Shrugged)

When Congress passed the Endangered Species Act of 1973, they
spoke about saving iconic species such as the Whooping Crane and
the Bald Eagle. They had no idea that the Environmental Movement
would immediately latch onto the law, and start using it to shut down
construction projects, farming, timbering, military preparedness, mining, and development across the nation. In 1978, construction of the
Tellico Dam in Tennessee, though 95% completed, was halted, due to
the finding of an "endangered" snail darter. Congress eventually cir-
cumvented the E.S.A., by attaching an amendment to an unrelated bill,
allowing the dam gates to be closed. Miraculously, other populations
of snail darter were later discovered in other rivers, and the species
did not become extinct after all.

As stated by Ayn Rand above, our problem exists because of an error
in the initial premise. The Endangered Species Act of 1973 defines
"species' to include "species, subspecies, and distinct population segments". Under this broad a definition of "species", the Environmental
Movement can pretty well list any group of animals, plants, or fishes
it pleases. When it can also list "habitat" and "potential habitat", there
is virtually nowhere in America it can't control. Wolves, for instance,
once roamed across North America. That makes Philadelphia, or
Cincinnati, or Chicago "potential" wolf habitat. Hence, "private property" ceases to exist. It now is under the control of the bureaucrats at
the United States Fish & Wildlife Service.

Here is the Merriam-Webster Dictionary definition of "Species'.

**"A category or biological classification, ranking immediately below
the genus or subgenus, comprising related organisms or populations
potentially capable of interbreeding, and being designated by a bi-
nomial that consists of the name of a genus followed by a Latin or
latinized uncapitalized noun or adjective agreeing grammatically
with the genus name."**

For example, human beings are the species "Homo sapiens." Visually,
humans have many different characteristics, and yet they are all a single species.

The Species Scam

Vast physical differences, but all the same species, Homo sapiens

Dogs are designated as Canis lupus familiarus."Canis lupis is the species, with "familiarus" as the subspecies designation. All the same species, but note the tremendous physical differences.

Dogs are, in fact, a subspecies of Canis Lupus, more commonly known as the wolf. For many years, scientists considered dogs a completely separate species, and named them Canis domisticus. However, recent DNA analysis shows them all to be the same species, Canis lupus, and dogs are now designated as Canis lupus familiarus. There are currently between 40,000 and 60,000 wolves in Alaska and northern Canada, about 30,000 in Russia, and about 20,000 in Europe. Populations are stable or growing, and hunting is an accepted method of maintaining stable wolf populations around the world. Listing the wolf as an endangered species in the United States is total nonsense, and really had more to do with eliminating cattle grazing on public lands.It had virtually nothing to do with recovery of an endangered species, which was never endangered in the first place.

As an iconic species, closely related to our family pet, and with adorable puppies, its listing was a great money maker for the Environmental Movement, which plays on the heartstrings of its contributors. To further confuse the issue, U.S.F.W.S. claims several subspecies of wolves, and has introduced them to the south (the Red Wolf), the southwest (the Mexican Wolf), and the upper Great Lakes (the Minnesota Wolf.) It's all the same wolf, Canis Lupis.

Photograph by Jeff Vanuga.

Wolves photographed in Yellowstone Park, Wyoming.

Stephen's Kangaroo Rat

Fresno Kangaroo Rat

San Bernardino Kangaroo Rat

Tipton's Kangaroo Rat

Morro Bay Kangaroo Rat

Heerman's Kangaroo Rat

Kangaroo Rats, all found in California, declared to be different "species" for purposes of the Endangered Species Act of 1973. Tiny, powerful tools of the Environmental Movement, encumbering much of California's rich farmland, "America's breadbasket." In some cases, scientists have to split their skulls to tell them apart. Some "species" have feet 1/100th of an inch longer than others. That's like saying my size twelves make me a different species from my son-in-law's size tens.

Lumpers and Splitters

Classifying species is not an exact science. Scientists which tend to group species more broadly are known as "lumpers"; more narrowly, as "splitters".

"Those who make many species are the 'splitters,' and those who make few are the "lumpers".
Charles Darwin in letter to J.D. Hooker in 1857

"King of the Splitters"

The Stephen's Kangaroo Rat is a species of Kangaroo Rat first listed as a separate species in 1894 by Clinton Hart Merriam, the first mammoligist with the United States Department of Agriculture. Here is what the Wikipedia Encyclopedia states in Merriam's biography(the emphasis is the authors):

"In 1886, he became the first chief of the Division of Economic Ornithology and Mammalogy of the United States Department of Agriculture, predecessor to the National Wildlife Research Center and the United States Fish and Wildlife Service. He was one of the original founders of the National Geographic Society in 1888. He developed the "life zones" concept to classify biomes found in North America. **In mammalogy, he is known as an excessive splitter,"**

The following is excerpted from a 2005 article by Joe Eaton in the Berkeley DailyPlanet:

"Taxonomists — biologists who name and classify organisms — come in two flavors: lumpers and splitters. Lumpers draw the boundaries of species and other units broadly, splitters narrowly. **C. Hart Merriam was the king of the splitters. Based on variations in teeth, claws, and pelt, he recognized 84 species of grizzly and brown bears in North America. That's full species, as in Homo sapiens.** Later authors boiled this down considerably, uniting all the big brown bears in Europe and America into Ursus arctos and relegating the grizzlies to the subspecies U. arctos horribilis."

Clinton Hart Merriam, the "King of the Splitters"

Most Americans don't have a great deal of knowledge about kangaroo rats. However, most Americans do have at least a cursory understanding of the grizzly bear: the first encounters of the species by the Lewis and Clark Expedition, the reverence given the bear by native American cultures, the more aggressive nature of the bear in comparison to black bears, etc. Clearly, if Clinton Hart Merriam's determined we had 84 species of grizzly bears in North America, he was, indeed, an" excessive splitter". This is a fact that is well known among all the trained biologists with which I have spoken.

The following article is courtesy of Mr. Don Corace:

Identifying the Stephen's Kangaroo Rat
from PRFA's Twelfth Annual National Conference on Private Property Rights
October 18, 2008
Fight the Good Fight for Private Property Rights
Don Corace
Real Estate Developer and Author, Naples, Florida

"One of the more interesting stories, when I was out in Southern California developing property, was about eighteen years ago, when I lived in Riverside County in Southern California. At that point, the U.S. Fish and Wildlife Service decided they wanted to list the Stephens' kangaroo rat as an endangered species. Of course, many of us developers and farmers were extremely interested in this issue, because most of the area to be developed in this certain valley in Riverside County were farm fields and that was where these little critters' habitat was (and in some cases also in the hills). So we went to a workshop sponsored by U.S. Fish and Wildlife.

A number of farmers and developers were listening to the biologists spew all these population figures and estimates as to how much habitat has been destroyed by development, how much future development is going to destroy habitat for the Stephens' kangaroo rat. And so we were filled with all these facts and figures. Then it came to the Q & A. One gentleman farmer stood up and said, "There's no g...damn way that there is Stephens' kangaroo rats, they're not extinct, they're not endangered, because they're all over our fields." So a lot of the people in the crowd just said, "Yes, yes, that's true, we see them all the time." The crowd was starting to get riled up.

Now the biologist that was providing all this information was someone with whom I'd had a recent run-in at a meeting. In fact, for those of you who know me, I sort of take these bureaucrats by the jugular and try to shake them a little bit, because in some cases that's the only way you're going to be able to get anything done. In a meeting with this bureaucrat, he was sitting right across the table from me and I called him a liar on some data. This gentleman was up in front of the group. I decided I was going to ask a question that I knew the answer to. And he knew I knew the answer, too, but I wanted to get the crowd riled up. So I said to him, **"These Stephens' kangaroo rats, aren't there a number of subspecies? In fact, aren't there twenty-two subspecies to kangaroo rats?" He said, "Yes, there are."**

So I said, "You haven't finished all your studies, you haven't furnished all your data. Is it possible that these kangaroo rats interbreed?" And he said, "Yes, we're trying to determine what type of kangaroo rat is in this particular area, in this valley."

And I said, **"Well, if not all the kangaroo rats were going to be put on the endangered species list, and let's say the Pacific kangaroo** rat, which is another subspecies which wasn't going to be put on, how do you tell the difference if they interbreed?"

So he kind of hemmed and hawed and kind of gave me a dirty look because he knew exactly what I was getting at. He said, "Well, we go on the ground. We go out and we identify the species and we look at their habitat and that sort of thing."

So he pointed to another person and he said, "Your question, sir?" And I said, "No, wait a minute, wait a minute. Everybody needs to understand how you identify a Stephens' kangaroo rat."

And finally he said, "We have to measure the thickness of their skulls." And I said, "OK, so you measure the thickness of their skulls. What do you have to do?" He said, "Well, we have to split open their skulls."

So I said, "Let me get this right" — and he's just fuming — "let me get this right. So you said you have to kill a potential endangered species to determine if it is an endangered species?" He said, "Yes."

"To argue with a man who has renounced his reason is like giving medicine to the dead."
Thomas Paine

The Environmental Movement, when it comes across a project that it doesn't want, either finds an endangered species, makes one up, illegally imports one, or declares the areas "potential habitat" for one. The following paragraph below is repeated from Henry Lamb's treatise.

"Stephen McCabe, chairman of a California NGO, opposed the expansion of Quail Hollow quarry. To block the company's expansion, he has proposed that the Mount Hermon June beetle be listed as an endangered species. He readily admits: "My goal is to protect the habitat...The best route at present is to try to get individual species listed and by doing that get protection for the habitat."

Mount Hermon June Beetle, just one of 350,000 identified beetle species*

If one reads the document entitled **"The Sandhills Conservation and Management Plan, A Strategy for Preserving Native Biodiversity in the Santa Cruz Sandhills"**, a document funded by the United States Fish & Wildlife Service (and dedicated to the above mentioned Stephen McCabe), you will see it is not just stone quarrying that the environmentalists in Santa Cruz wanted to stop. Specifically, they list as "stresses" to the various plant and wildlife species found there (including the infamous Zayante band-winged grasshopper), such human activities as horseback riding, hiking, and fire suppression. This is private property they are talking about, not public land. Heaven forbid a landowner rides a horse on his own property, or hike, or put out a fire to protect his home.

According to the March, 1998 National Geographic article entitled "Planet of the Beetles"*, there are 350,000 identified beetle species in the world, with the possibility of millions more species being identified. I am happy for the beetles of the world, but, as a member of the single species, Homo sapiens, I am most interested in the preservation of my own species. The concept of a "Planet of the Beetles" might make for a great "B" horror movie, but the concept may, in fact, become reality. If humans insist on continually interfering with nature's "survival of the fittest," man, himself, may not survive. Extinction of species, subspecies, and distinct population has been going on for billions of years. Artificial interferance by mankind, particularly government, has never proven to help much of anything, species included.

*"Planet of the Beetles, March, 1998, National Geographic Magazine, Page 101

Spotted Owls "Hybridizing" with Barred Owls

As most of America knows, the Northern Spotted Owl was used by the Environmental Movement to shut down millions of acres of timbering, both on public and private lands, in the northwestern United States. This has cost our country billions of dollars in lost jobs and revenues every year. In the meantime, it appears that Barred Owls, (a native species to much of North America, and not endangered,) have begun "hybridizing" (U.S.F.W.S. euphemism for "fornicating with") the Northern Spotted Owl. If Barred Owls can mate with, and produce fertile offspring with, Northern Spotted Owls, it creates a huge problem for the Environmental Movement. Somewhere, someday, some Right Wing, Constitution Waving, anti-Communist, Pro-American judge might decide that maybe this Spotted Owl designation as a separate species was not such a great idea after all. Mother Nature (i.e. the Owls) has already decided that there is a mutual sexual attraction between the two"species" Maybe the judge will even restore logging to its rightful place, as a worthwhile human activity, required to build homes and shelters for human habitat. Better yet, maybe Congress will wake up and eliminate the Endangered Species Act of 1973. That would not stop the Barred Owls from fornicating with the Spotted Owls, but it would stop the U.S.F.W.S. from fornicating the American people.

Barred Owl

Northern Spotted Owl

Gov't Announces New Way to Protect Spotted Owls: Kill Their Competition

Posted on July 1, 2011 at 9:18am by Jonathon M. Seidl

The northern spotted owl is a beautiful bird. It's also threatened under the Endangered Species Act. And now, the government is taking drastic measures to ensure it's survival by advocating the "removal" of the bird's major competition, while also seemingly targeting loggers.

"Removal" of the birds is really just another way to say shooting the barred owl, the spotted owl's rival. And it's part of a group of recommendations announced by the U.S. Fish and Wildlife Service to help revitalize the spotted owl population:

Management of the encroaching barred owl to reduce harm to spotted owls. Most of the recovery actions the U.S. Fish and Wildlife Service has carried out since finalizing the spotted owl's 2008 recovery plan deal with the barred owl threat. A major part of this is developing a proposal for experimental removal of barred owls in certain areas to see what effect that would have on spotted owls, and then to evaluate whether or not broad scale removal should be considered. This portion of the 2008 plan was not significantly revised.

The Seattle Weekly explains how "removal" has worked in the past:

Though the USFWS policy hasn't officially been released yet, The Oregonian reports that it's likely to include a strategy to kill off between 1,200 and 1,500 barred owls from northern California through Oregon and Washington.

Killing off invasive species is a common practice in wildlife management, but barred owls aren't invasive–they're native. And several environmental groups are arguing that killing them won't help the problem unless people are prepared to shoot the owls by the thousands every single year.

One biologist estimates the cost of such a plan to be $1 million annually.

Plus, by seemingly all accounts, the barred owl is simply a stronger

and better-adapted species. It eats a wider variety of food and nests in a wider variety of places than the spotted owl.
While the wisdom behind killing one species to save another is part of the debate, there's also controversy surrounding another aspect of the recommendations — protecting the spotted owl's habitat. But there's just one problem: that conflicts with local logging.

The Weekly reports that loggers are skeptical of the idea:

Under the new plan, both the elimination of barred owls and the preservation of forest land are used.

Jerry Bonagofsky, CEO of the Washington Contract Loggers Association, says that protecting spotted-owl habitat at this point is useless, and that the Obama plan will hurt the economy and kill jobs.

"Given that the barred owl is now part of the equation, it's not clear that protecting habitat will help at all," Bonagofsky tells us. "I think the Bush plan, given time, could have worked. In the present economy, locking up more timber land will have a huge effect on rural communities, jobs, and families."

All told, it would appear that environmentalists did get a bigger bone thrown to them under the new plan than the loggers did.

Another argument, it seems, is that environmentalists and anti-loggers can fight the industry under the guise of protecting the owls. For example, one environmentalist expressed his excitement that the plan opens the door to regulate private land.

"In some regards [the plan] takes important steps forward," Shawn Cantrell, executive director of the Seattle Audubon Society, told the Weekly. **"It talks about the need for non-federal land owners to do more and it points at gaps in the regulatory structure of non-federal lands.** It also recognizes the importance of protecting the remaining high-quality forest we still have. But on the downside, in some places, particularly on the east side of the Cascades, they seem to open the door to much more logging, saying **we have to cut down the forest in order to save the forest."** [

Is it ironic that in a story on owls, the proposals to protect them don't seem so wise?

What the above clearly shows, is what many Americans have known for years. The Environmental Movement, including the United States Fish & Wildlife Service, doesn't really give a damn about wildlife. If they did, why would they propose shooting Barred Owls, which aren't hurting anybody or anything? They are simply evolving and choosing habitat and suitable mates. What the U.S.F.W.S. is doing is akin to the Nazis in the 1930s, eliminating non-arians, so the Germanic race can remain pure. The Environmental Movement, and the USFWS, is all about controlling our lives, our private property, and eliminating our freedoms. Wildlife is the tool, not the finished product.

The Audubon Society talks about "gaps in the regulatory structure of non-federal lands." That, simply translated, means "holes in the ability of the Environmental Movement to control private land; your private land and my private land. Just as a reminder, here is the definition of "Private Property."

"Private property is the right of persons and firms to obtain, own, control, employ, dispose of, and bequeath land, capital, and other forms of property.[1] Private property is distinguishable from public property, which refers to assets owned by a state, community or government rather than by individuals or a business entity."*

The Washington Examiner
Ron Arnold: Federally funded, fundamentally flawed science behind Fish & Wildlife's Mousegate

By: Ron Arnold 03/10/11 8:05 PM
"Government science" is an oxymoron like "military intelligence," but the U.S. Fish & Wildlife Service is the exemplar.

The FWS is arguably the most powerful agency in the federal government because it enforces the Endangered Species Act, which in turn is arguably omnipotent because it can stop any personal or business activity dead in its tracks - not excluding military operations - if a bug or weed is harmed. It can even trump the Constitution, especially the due process and just compensation clauses.

Complying with the ESA is a nightmare, as it covers "endangered"

http://en.wikipedia.org/wiki/Private_property

species and their habitats, as well as "threatened" species and habitats. It even stretches to surreal dimensions by also covering subspecies and "distinct population segments" and their habitats. It's Big Green's biggest club.

Power lust constantly pushes FWS officials to list as many species, subspecies and populations as possible. The more they list, the more power they have to prevent people from using their property or resources. Don't expect compensation, either, as they just take your rights, not your property or resources themselves.

Matthew Cronin, a University of Alaska research professor of animal genetics, explains the problem: "It is well established that the subspecies category is subjective and the 'distinct population segment' is basically a judgment call. Federal biologists and environmental groups use these terms to inappropriately put local populations of an otherwise abundant species in the ESA list."

Cronin notes in Range magazine that he counts "70 percent of the ESA's listings of mammals in the United States are subspecies or populations."

And former Deputy Assistant Secretary of the Interior Julie Mac-Donald said "it was my observation that many ESA listing and habitat decisions by Fish & Wildlife were made first and supporting information was identified later, with all contrary information ignored. Many decisions were based purely on opinion, rather than data, and the ESA requires data. But courts may not second guess agency decisions, so we get legally binding 'specious species' that don't live up to the statute's data requirements."

Where does a regulatory agency run by political appointees find scientists willing to claim their subjective opinion is science? The FWS gets most of its science from U.S. Geological Survey biologists working in a closed loop: FWS gets science from USGS, USGS gets funded by FWS - which assures predetermined outcomes and no dissent. Interesting money trail, that, so where's Congress and the media?

The poster child for imaginary species is an innocent Rocky Mountain Meadow Jumping Mouse listed in 1998 by FWS as "threatened." It had the undeserved prefix of "Preble's" tacked on by subspecies mongers (naturalist Edward A. Preble found the mouse in Colorado in 1899). FWS estimates their Preble's listing costs public and private landowners about $18 million a year.

Then came Rob Roy Ramey II, curator of vertebrate zoology at the Denver Museum of Nature & Science, who did a thorough genetic study and found Preble's mouse was not a subspecies and should be delisted. Wrong answer. Ordinary Meadow Jumping mice give FWS no power.

FWS regional official Ralph Morgenweck hired USGS geneticist Tim King - who allegedly has near-supernatural powers to detect subspecies where others can't - to get the preferred answer. King and his all-USGS team produced an elegant scientific paper that saved the listing.

Ramey and his team then discovered the King team had not replicated his work as they claimed, but rather switched things during the proofing process to make it appear they did. I'm just a layman, but does that look like honest science to you? It's definitely a scientific no-no, and Ramey et al. said so in a response paper that FWS ignored.

The "Preble's" mouse was subsequently delisted in Wyoming (but not Colorado), and FWS continues to insist it is a "valid subspecies" but has not published any of Ramey's documents, so I will do it for them. Go here and take a look at Mousegate.

By the way, Ramey's respect for the truth cost him his job, but he's now an esteemed consultant and researcher with an impeccable reputation.

Examiner Columnist Ron Arnold is executive vice president of the Center for the Defense of Free Enterprise.

The Louisiana Black Bear
Sixteen Species of Black Bears, Are You Serious?

The United States Fish & Wildlife Service recognizes 16 subspecies of black bears, which is, of course, to say it gives each of them the same protection as a full species. The Louisiana Black Bear is listed as threatened. This is, to anyone with any sense of wildlife at all, ludicrous. Across North America, the current minimum total black bear population is thought to be about 600,000 animals, with the populations listed by the vast majority of states as either stable or increasing. When black bears were transplanted from Minnesota to Louisiana in the 1960s to help bolster the population, it was found to have zero effect on the genetic makeup of the Louisiana Black Bears.* Same genetic makeup, same species. Not coincidentally, the Louisiana Black Bear was originally designated a separate species by the "King of the Splitters", Clinton Hart Merriam, in 1893.

In doing my own research regarding the "Great Crashing Caribou Hoax" in the Northwest Territories, I found that going back to the original research was a critical component of analyzing certain issues. (as Ayn Rand says, "Check the Premise") In the case of the Louisiana Black Bear, I went back to the original papers, "The Yellow Bear of Louisiana", presented by C. Hart Merriam, M.D., to the Proceedings of the Biological Society of Washington, December 29, 1893.

Clearly, to anyone with much experience with black bears, the **"Yellow Bear Of Louisiana"** is simply a blonde phase of a black bear (which also comes in black, cinnamon, chocolate, blue (or glacier) and white (or kermode). Some black bears also come with a white blaze on their chests.)

The Louisiana Black Bear was originally described by Edward Griffith in 1821. Griffith came reluctantly to the same conclusion: ""Six years later, in the mammal part of his well-known edition of Cuvier's Animal Kingdom, Griffith reluctantly treats the species as "a variety of the American black bear...**we shall not venture to assert... that this bear forms a distinct species.**"*

In Merriam's own words, he states:

1. " it is desirable to issue a <u>preliminary</u> description of the species, **based on the meager material now in hand**." ....

2. **"Very little is known** of the geographic distribution of this bear further than the fact that it inhabits Louisiana." ..

3. ."If i were to hazard a guess, **in view of what little is known on the subject**, it would be to the effect that the normal color is black."

*Proceedings of the Biological Society of Washington, Volumes 6-9
 By Biological Society of Washington, Smithsonian Institution

4. "But this tooth is **subject to so much individual variation in bears** from the same locality that it would be **unsafe to place any reliance on the peculiarity here described.** unless it is found to held good in a larger number of individuals than are now available for comparison."

Clinton Hart Merriam, the King of the Splitters, is clearly very unsure about this species designation, basing it on just a few old bear skulls he had kicking around the Biological Society Museum in Washington, all from the same parrish in Louisiana.

The Louisiana Black Bear

All the bears pictured on the next page were harvested within 100 yards of the shoreline on Lake Isles-la-Crosse, in northern Saskatchewan, at my hunting camp. Note the blond, or "yellow" bear, very similar to the one described by Clinton Hart Merriam, only 2000 miles farther north, and over 100 years later. Genetically, these Saskatchewan bears are all the same, and are, undoubtedly, related to each other. It is not at all uncommon in this country to see a black sow, with a blond phase cub, a black cub, and a cinnamon phase cub, all in the same litter. Note the different skull shapes. Different skull shapes doesn't necessarily make it a different species. Look at the skull shapes of the father and son in the lower right hand photograph. Different shapes, same species, Homo sapiens. Compare the black bears with the photograph of the Louisiana black bear, pictured above. They are all the same species, and, most certainly, have no business being placed on the Endangered Species List, at least for scientific reasons.

Large, older bear, jet black. Similar to Louisiana Black Bear pictured. Note the wide skull.

Blond, or "yellow" black bear. Shot 2000 miles north of Louisiana.

Very large, old bear. Black in color. Note heavy, thick skull.

Large, older bear, cinnamon color phase. Note the flattened skull type.

Large cinnamon color phase black bear, heavy skull type

Note the difference is skull sizes in these two bears. Note also the skull size difference in the humans, who are father and son.

Governmental "Due Diligence"

Modern day scientists recognize two species of brown bear/grizzly bears, where C. Hart Merriam found <u>84</u>.! Government bureaucrats are, theoretically, working for us, the people. Right? One might think that the U.S. Fish & Wildlife Service would look pretty carefully into the history of the Stephen's Kangaroo Rat, or the Louisiana Black Bear, before it started using them as a tool to shut down people's farms, and take away their livelihoods. I believe in a court of law this might fall under the term "Due Diligenc"'. If I can find, in just a few minutes searching "Google", the information about Clinton Hart Merriam as an excessive splitter, shouldn't the "experts" at U.S. Fish & Wildlife be able to accomplish the same?

Merriams-Webster Dictionary Definition of <u>**"Due Diligence"**</u>

1. The care that a reasonable person exercises to avoid harm to another person or his property."

As American citizens, don't we have a right to expect this from our government, which we fund with our hard earned tax money?

Fortunately, our Founding Fathers mistrusted big government almost as much as they mistrusted the British. And so, as part of the U.S. Constitution, they gave us the Bill of Rights, and the Fifth Amendment. In the author's opinion, the government needs to get out their checkbook, and start writing Americans checks for the expropriation of their property. Clearly, telling a farmer he can't farm, or develop, his land, which he has paid taxes on for generations, is an expropriation of his property, for which the Constitution of the United States demands "just compensation."

If the government has to write enough checks, maybe the people, and our elected representatives, will finally start looking more carefully at this Endangered Species Act of 1973, what was its intent, what exactly is a definition of a "species", and has this law been corrupted over time?

Rats or People???

When the U.S. Fish & Wildlife tells the Domenigoni family (and thousands of other farmers across this country) they can't farm their land, what is the cost? The Domenigoni's say it cost them $75,000 a year in lost income (1993 dollars.) That is a lot of money for any family, but what about looking at this problem from a global human perspective.

How many people would the 800 acres that was closed down feed in a year's time?

Here is the question and answer from YAHOO! Answers:

Question: "How many people can live off of one acre of crops (eating nothing except things from that acre)?

Best Answer: 8 people per year per acre. *

In other words, the 800 acres that the U.S. Fish & Wildlife Service said the Domenigoni family could not farm, **would have <u>fed 6400 people for a year.</u>**

How many little children in Africa could we have saved? How many children in America go to bed every night, hungry? Now, as you will see later on in this book, multiply that number by the millions of acres of farmland being closed down by the Endangered Species Act. Ask yourself, and ask your Congressman. Ask your friends, family, and neighbors. Given the choice of feeding millions of hungry children, or preserving habitat for rats, which would they choose? Governing is about choices, with some choices harder than others. As American voters the choice should be ours, not some bureaucrat at the U.S. Fish & Wildlife Service, that wants to dictate our nation's morality. The Endangered Species Act of 1973 passed by a vote of 447 to 4. Clearly, for the Congressmen of that era, that choice was an easy one. No one believed at the time that this act would be used to hurt our nation.

Put the same vote to Congress today, with the correct set of facts before them, and the tally would be:

Feed Hungry Children: 451 votes
Save a Few Rats: 0 votes

Those, if any, that vote for the rats, should be advised against seeking re-election.

> "The care of <u>human</u> life and happiness, and not their destruction, is the first and only legitimate object of good government."
> Thomas Jefferson

*http://answers.yahoo.com/question/index?qid=20071028131143AAiPmqb

Chapter 4

A Nationwide System of Abuse by the United States Fish & Wildlife "Service"

Nationwide Abuse, Not Isolated Incidences

When I first started writing this book, it was my intention to write about the re-introduced wolves and burgeoning grizzly populations, and the destruction of wildlife populations here in my homestate of Montana, and the neighboring western states of Idaho and Wyoming. I knew from my own personal experiences, both here in the United States, and with my two Canadian companies, that government biologists and government officials lie to support the environmentalist agenda. That has been made abundantly clear to me, and it has cost me my businesses and my life's work. That is another story, for another day, as the case is currently being litigated, and I promised my attorney I would not argue the case preliminarily in the court of public opinion.

As my research into the Endangered Species Act of 1973 progressed, a nationwide pattern of abuse became clearer and clearer. I knew how much financial damage the U.S. Fish & Wildlife Service was causing locally. I had no clue as to the damages it was causing nationwide.

The following was written by former Idaho Congresswoman Helen Chenowith-Hage.

Mrs. Chenowith-Hage, as promised in her first Congressional campaign, limited herself to three terms in office. She was killed in an automobile accident in 2006.

[*]"Six years ago, I was elected to Congress on the promise that I would vigorously fight to reduce the excessive power of the federal government. As a resident of a Western state where the government owns most of the land, **I was especially determined to roll back the myriad regulations enforced by thousands of bureaucrats, ostensibly to protect the environment but which too often undermine Americans' constitutionally-protected property rights.**
To this end, I have fought to reform **environmental policies that have been systematically used by regulators to unfairly harass, intimidate or even deprive individuals of their hard-won property. These increasing incidences of regulatory abuse are the product of the unchecked growth in the size and power of government regulatory agencies over the past 30 years.** The staff of the Envi-

*www.bls.gov/web/laus/laumstrk.htm
**U.S. Fish & Wildlife website

ronmental Protection Agency, for instance, has nearly tripled from fewer than 6,000 employees in 1971 to more than 17,000 today while the number of pages in the Federal Register, which lists all federal regulations, skyrocketed from 2,000 in 1971 to more than 64,549 pages by 1997. It is estimated that the rapidly expanding list of environmental and risk regulations now cost more than $250 billion. But important as such statistics may be, this is not what the debate over regulation is about. **Regulatory abuse is not about agency budgets or the number of bureaucrats. It is not about cold statistics on risks and benefits.**

Regulatory abuse is about people - our friends and neighbors.

Most Americans don't know about these abuses. Unfortunately, before the abuses can be stopped the American people need to know there's a problem. They need to know about the very human cost of these regulations."

""Whenever the people are well informed, they can be trusted with their own government; that whenever things get so far wrong as to attract their notice, they may be relied on to set them to rights."
Thomas Jefferson Letter to Richard Price,

Stories from Across the Country

Here are stories, from around the country, of the damage being done to our nation by the Endangered Species Act of 1973. They represent just the tip of a huge iceberg, an iceberg of government regulation. Unfortunately, the U.S. Economy, like the Titanic, has already struck the iceberg. Companies across the country have already jumped ship, looking for safer, warmer business waters in other countries. Thousands of other companies, particularly small businesses, like the steerage class of the Titanic, are searching for the lifeboats in this country, the United States, which simply don't exist. They are doomed to a cold, heartless drowning, unless our U.S. Congress acts now._ Farming, Tourism, Real Estate, Manufacturing, Recreation, Housing, Energy, Timbering, Mining, even National Defense, are all sinking under the weight of this draconian law, and the enforcement of it by the U.S. Fish and Wildlife Service.

I shudder every time I have to type that word **"Service."** Whom exactly does this governmental bureaucracy think it is "servicing"? The preamble to the Constitution starts out "We the People". It doesn't start out "We, the Stephen's Kangaroo Rat, We the Delhi Sands Flower-Loving Fly, We the Puritan Tiger Beetle, We the Timber Wolf, We the Delta Smelt, We the Santa Anna Sucker. etc." We the People, means "we, the human beings, the Homo sapiens, the individual persons." It is people that have "inalienable rights', not plants, animals, and insects. That doesn't mean we shouldn't care about wildlife and plants, but there is a huge difference between caring about wild things, and giving them equal, or, in many cases, higher rights than human beings. All those brave men buried in Arlington National Cemetery, and in unmarked graves around the world, fought for human rights, not the rights of the Government Canyon Bat Cave Spider.

**New England
Cottontail Rabbit**

**Eastern Cottontail
Rabbit**

$1,000,000.00 for 15 Cottontail Rabbits

This story was sent to me by my 80 year old mother, regarding the preservation of the New England Cottontail Rabbit. Just to set the record straight, there are millions of cottontail rabbits found all across the United States. This "species", listed by Outram Bangs in 1895, can only be differentiated from Eastern Cottontail rabbits by examining the skulls and DNA evidence. This statement is from the Massachusetts Division of Fisheries and Wildlife website:

"Here in the Bay State, there are two species of cottontail rabbits, the New England cottontail (Sylvilagus transitionalis) and the Eastern cottontail (Sylvilagus floridanus). You can't tell these rabbits apart by looking at them in the field. **The differences can be determined with certainty only by skull characteristics and measurements and by DNA techniques."**

The crux of the newspaper article, entitled "Hope for State's Cottontail Rabbits", makes it sound like Cottontail Rabbits are in some sort of danger. Nothing could be further from the truth. Because hunters can't tell the difference between Eastern Cottontail Rabbits and New England Cottontail Rabbits, and they live in the same habitat, hunting for all rabbits has to be stopped, which of course, dovetails right into the Environmentalist Agenda. Here are excerpts from the article, which appeared in the Portland Morning Sentinel, September 5, 2011.

"Last summer the Portland International Jetport had to pay $1,000,000.00 in mitigation costs for taking rabbit habitat in a runway expansion project.....to relocate a colony of 15 rabbits during the runway expansion."

"Now a team of government agencies is making a major push-funded in part with about $400,000 in mostly public money-to reclaim disappearing habitat.. It is labor and resource intensive, says Sue Bickford, natural resouce specialist at the reserve....So far, the management effort appear to have worked. **Even though in ten years at the reserve, Bickford has yet to lay eyes on any of the rabbits, the latest studies show the resident population is thriving. Today, there are 20 rabbits, considered a large colony.** "

Are these people serious? $1,000,000 in "mitigation"(i.e. a bribe) to Environmental N.G.O.s not to hold up the airport runway expansion (needed to make humans safer.) In addition, hundreds of thousands of "mostly public money" has been spent, and the "specialist", in tens years, has yet to even see a single New England Cottontail Rabbit!

And America wonders why we have a government debt crisis? Does Congress ever actually look at any of these expenditures?

"We hold thes truths to be self-evident, that all <u>men</u> are created equal."*

No mention of Rats, Beetles, Spiders, Mussels, or Fungus. Why do you suppose that is?

*U.S. Declaration of Independence, July 4, 1776

The Tortoises "Home on the Range" *

"Howard Blair's family first arrived in the arid Mojave region of southern California in the late 1880s. Howard has spent all of his nearly 80 years on the family's Blair7IL Ranch. But the future of the ranch is now in jeopardy, because environmental groups want a court to oust the family in order to safeguard the Desert Tortoise, which is listed as federally-threatened under the Endangered Species Act. As of now, Howard Blair and his family are the last remaining ranchers in the once-thriving cattle community of Whiskey Basin.

On the 1,000-acre Blair7IL ranch, approximately 400 cows, 25 bulls and 300 calves are the only cattle still grazing within the boundaries of the Mojave National Preserve, which was created in 1994 by the California Desert Protection Act. Due to the regulations related to the protection of the Desert Tortoise, all of the other ranchers who once worked in the area have left during the past few years. Many of the properties have been purchased by environmental and non-profi t groups. While Blair still holds grazing rights on the land, all property within the MNP is technically owned by the Bureau of Land Management.

A 2001 court ruling dramatically reduced the ability of ranchers to graze on the federal land adjacent to the MNP. The Center for Biological Diversity, the Sierra Club and Public Employees for Environmental Responsibility filed the lawsuit bringing about the ruling, and these same groups are now seeking to file another lawsuit against the BLM to challenge grazing inside the Preserve. This would eliminate grazing by Blair's cattle. **Environmental groups, biologists and desert experts claim the tortoise's habitat is endangered by animals stomping on them and that grazing also eliminates native plant species**.

The Blairs contend that tortoises are not harmed by their activities because cattle avoid the tortoises because of their potent smell. While former neighbors have received between $3 and $4 million for their ranches, Rob Blair — Howard's son — contends, "This is our home and nobody wants to leave." Fortunately for the Blairs, they have a political ally in Senator Dianne Feinstein (D-CA). Although a sponsor of the CDPA, Feinstein visited the Blair7IL ranch in 1993 and says she plans to fight to protect the Blairs for "as long as I am breathing."

*Shattered Dreams, 100 Stories of Government Abuse, National Center for Public Policy Research

As you will note in the third paragraph, the lawsuit driving the Blairs and other ranchers off the land was brought, in part, by **Public Employees for Environmental Responsibility."** Last time I checked, public employees worked for the public, at least in theory. Federal grazing rights, on BLM, has been the law of the land for decades. I don't wish to step on anyone's First Amendment rights, but it is clear, these "public" employees are pushing forth their own agenda. Could it be possible this agenda is affecting their everyday work agenda as well? The Blair family, like the Domenigoni family discussed earlier, have ranched this land for over 120 years. The tortoises are still there, after 120 years, so the cattle can't be stomping them all to death, as the Environmentalists claimed. In fact, the U.S. Geological Survey , in the document entitled: **Threats to Desert Tortoise Populations: A Critical Review of the Literature,** says this:

"Grazing by livestock (cattle and sheep) is **hypothesized** to have direct and indirect effects on tortoise populations including: mortality from crushing of animals or their burrows, destruction of vegetation, alteration of soil, augmentation of forage (e.g., presence of livestock droppings, and stimulation of vegetative growth or nutritive value of forage plants), and competition for food.

"There are **very few data available** to determine if grazing has caused declines in tortoise populations..... . **No population trends in California** have been attributed with hard data to livestock grazing....Some observations of tortoises being crushed by livestock exist in the literature, but often with little or **no data** Berry (1978, p. 28) stated that "smaller tortoises can be crushed easily by cattle or sheep," but provided no data to support the statement......**No one has rigorously evaluated** whether livestock crush a significant proportion of tortoise burrows. Nicholson and Humphreys (1981) measured impacts of sheep grazing immediately after a band of 1000 sheep passed through their West Mojave study site for 12 days. Sheep trampled and partly collapsed a burrow with an adult female inside; apparently the tortoise was unharmed. Sheep completely destroyed the burrow of a juvenile tortoise while the animal was inside; the field workers extracted the unharmed tortoise."

Cattle, sheep, and horses do not deliberately step in holes, i.e. tortoise burrows. Animals, even dumb ones like cattle and sheep, tend to avoid activities that break their legs. Has an occasional tortoise been killed by a stampede of cattle? In all probability, yes. Turtles have been on the planet for approximately 230 million years.* That means they some-

*www.turtlepuddle.org/kidspage/questions.html

how managed to survive the huge Pleisticene Bison, which disappeared just 10,000 years ago, and were 25-50% larger than the bison of today.* My guess is that turtles are killed by cattle about as often as polar bears drown, Al Gore notwithstanding.

But what about the coyotes, kit foxes, feral dogs, bobcats, skunks, badgers, common ravens, and golden eagles, that, on a day to day basis, actually hunt turtles for food? Predators are always a serious threat. The fact is, by taking man off the landscape, which is a predator to coyotes, feral dogs and bobcats, the government has probably increased predation on the Desert Tortoise, not decreased it. This is to say nothing of the economic impact to the ranchers, and to America's food supply (for humans). Most wildlife species (with the notable exception of grizzly bears and wolves) get along just fine in the presence of humans, and many actually thrive because of the changes humans bring to an ecosystem.

Mice More Important than Horses
Unendangered Rodent Costs Colorado & Wyoming Millions**

CHUGWATER, Wyo. - Amy and Steve LeSatz want to be able to teach their clients the finer points of riding and roping without having to trailer their animals 25 miles to the nearest public indoor arena whenever the weather turns miserable. But the LeSatzes aren't able to build their own riding arena. **The only decent site on their property in southeastern Wyoming lies within 300 feet of Chugwater Creek, and building there is far too expensive because of Endangered Species Act restrictions intended to protect the Preble's meadow jumping mouse.**

"The mouse that doesn't exist," Amy LeSatz noted drily.

After six years of regulations and restrictions that have cost builders, local governments and landowners on the western fringe of the Great Plains as much as $100 million by some estimates, new research suggests the Preble's mouse in fact never existed. It instead seems to be genetically identical to one of its cousins, the Bear Lodge meadow jumping mouse, which is considered common enough that it does not need federal protection.

The new research could lead to loss of the Preble's "threatened" status and removal from Endangered Species Act protection. The U.S.

*https://www.dmr.nd.gov/ndfossil/education/pdf/bison.pdf
**http://www.citizenreviewonline.org/june2004/mouse.htm

Preble's Jumping Mouse

New Mexico Meadow
Jumping Mouse

Bear Lodge Meadow Jumping Mouse
Photo Courtesy of Tim Mullican

Fish and Wildlife Service plans to decide that question in December.

"We're trying to be deliberate in our work, trying to get the best science we can and review of the science we do have, in making this decision. Because we know it is very important and serious to a lot of people," said Ralph Morgenweck, regional director of the U.S. Fish and Wildlife Service in Denver. "But I would also say it is a lot more complicated than what it appears to be."

But far from closing the book on the Preble's mouse, the research by the Denver Museum of Nature and Science has opened a new volume of questions -- including what to do about landowners who have been affected, whether the Bear Lodge mouse also needs protection and whether the Endangered Species Act itself needs changes.

"If we've shown that the mouse doesn't exist, what happens to all that has been set aside? Because that's been a **huge economic bur-**

den," wondered Brian Garber, assistant director of governmental relations for the Colorado Contractors Association.

Meadow jumping mice live near streams, and nearly 31,000 acres along streams in Colorado and Wyoming have been designated critical mouse habitat. That includes large parts of the Colorado Front Range, which over the past several years has been rapidly developed with strip malls and housing subdivisions.

Front Range developers and local governments have had to set aside a lot of land to protect the mouse, though if protections are lifted, that does not mean all that land can be developed. Subdivisions, for example, have roads, sewers, water lines and other infrastructure designed for a certain number of homes. In many cases, adding more homes is not feasible.

But developers would like to see restrictions, which can be both expensive and annoying, ended for future development. **In one Colorado Springs, Colo., subdivision, for example, the restrictions include a requirement that cats be kept on leashes.**

In rural areas, protecting the mouse has meant telling ranchers they cannot clear weeds out of their irrigation canals -- reducing the amount of water that gets to their hay fields in the middle of summer. They are also restricted in how they can allow their animals to graze along streams -- another regulation the LeSatzes have to work around.

On top of that, the mouse also has blocked the construction of reservoirs amid a five-year drought in the Rocky Mountains.

"The bottom line is, it has been a wonderful tool for environmental groups to try to stop things," said Kent Holsinger, attorney for Coloradans for Water Conservation and Development, which has asked the Fish and Wildlife Service to remove the mouse from federal protection.

Indeed, **environmental groups are now calling for Endangered Species Act protection for the Bear Lodge mouse**. They say that subspecies -- which had been thought to be limited to the Black Hills of South Dakota and Wyoming but now appears to exist as far south as Colorado Springs -- suffers from the same habitat degradation.

Nationwide System of Abuse

The Preble's mouse was established as a distinct subspecies by a study 50 years ago that was cited in the 1998 decision to declare it threatened.

The man who did the 1954 study, Philip Krutzsch, now a professor emeritus with the University of Arizona, had examined the skulls of three mice and the skins of 11 others. It was an acceptable level of scrutiny at the time but "an extremely weak inference by today's standards," said Rob Roy Ramey II, curator at the Denver Museum of Nature and Science and project leader on the new DNA research that overturns Krutzsch's conclusion.

Ramey and his colleagues analyzed mitochondrial DNA, the cell's genetic code, from several of the 12 subspecies of meadow jumping mice, which range from the Pacific to Atlantic and as far south as Georgia.

They also repeated Krutzsch's skeleton measurements, using more specimens -- mainly from university and museum collections -- and more accurate tools. **They concluded that the Preble's mouse is actually a Bear Lodge meadow jumping mouse, not a separate subspecies.**

Despite being reversed, Krutzsch endorses the new research and its conclusion: "It's at the cutting edge of science today and it's very thorough and comprehensive. I think it clearly defines what is true biologically."

But, inadequate as it may have been, Krutzsch's old study was the best science that had been done up until the listing of the Preble's mouse. **The Endangered Species Act only requires that species protection be based on the best available science -- not the best possible science.**

Ramey's DNA study seems likely to usurp Krutzsch's as the best science to date. But **environmental groups are not willing to surrender.** They point out that Ramey's study has not been peer-reviewed. They also highlight criticism from Ramey's scientific peers that he did not compare the nuclear DNA, the molecular building blocks of entire organisms, of the mice subspecies -- something Ramey has begun examining at the Fish and Wildlife Service's request.

And Jeremy Nichols, spokesman for the Biodiversity Conservation Alliance in Laramie, Wyo., attacked Ramey's impartiality.

"Ramey has a clear anti-Endangered Species Act agenda," he said. "He's been testifying in Washington, D.C., in front of committees headed by members of Congress who would like nothing better than having the Endangered Species Act thrown away."
Ramey, who has studied endangered species more than 20 years, did testify in April before a House subcommittee that the Preble's mouse shows how the Endangered Species Act needs major changes. But he said his advocacy is for better science to bolster the legitimacy of endangered species status.

"I care about the act. I care about habitat. And that's why it's important to lay the issues out on the table," he said.

Ramey thinks the question of to-list or not-to-list should be based on the most up-to-date science and modern techniques. He also wants more science used in deciding the details of protecting species.

"You need to convince me that the hypothetical threats are real and observable and quantified, and set up a testable hypothesis," he said. "Otherwise it's opinion, and I don't trust opinion."

The LeSatzes, meanwhile, say the Preble's mouse has nearly caused them to throw in the towel several times. But they hope they will at last be able to build their riding arena -- by doing much of the design work and construction themselves -- if the regulations are lifted.

"A tiny little mouse comes in and changes your whole perspective," Amy LeSatz said. "I've had more of an education in endangered species than I've ever wanted."

"Only those afraid of the truth seek to silence debate, intimidate those with whom they disagree, or slander their ideological counterparts. Those who know they are right have no reason to stifle debate because they realize that all opposing arguments will ultimately be overcome by fact."
— Glenn Beck (Glenn Beck's Common Sense: The Case Against an Out-of-Control Government, Inspired by Thomas Paine

Kudos to Professor Philip Krutzsch, for acknowledging the work of Mr. Ramey, and the progress science has made over the past 60 years. This is what a true scientist does. But it didn't fit the Environmentalist Agenda, and so they discredited the work of Ramey, stating he has a "clear, anti-Endangered Species Act agenda."

"Ramey, reached in Baja, Mexico, where he is counting bighorn sheep for a conservation group, said his study had a "clear-cut" hypothesis and critical tests that allowed for "no wiggle room," while King's study "relied on interpretation."

He acknowledged having strong views about endangered species.

"You cannot make everything a top priority and expect to accomplish anything, in terms of preserving species," Ramey said. "If we focused on conservation of fewer genetically unique populations and pooled our resources, we might accomplish more for conservation."*

Clearly, Mr. Ramey "gets it". The Environmentalist movement is all about stopping development at any costs. They obviously have very little problem locating scientists willing to skew the data and drawing conclusions based on personal agendas, not good scientific method. All Americns want to accomplish more for conservation. That is a given. But, as stated previously, governing is about choices, and if Americans don't get the real facts, the chances of making the correct choices are greatly diminished.

Here is what the Environmentalists have to say: **

"Environmentalists say, for example, that what's good for a Preble's -- clean water to drink and open land on which to jump -- is good for other earthborn mortals too, including humans, and that having **the mouse on the threatened list has been a powerful lever** to safe-guard the regional environment in a rapidly developing corner of the West. If the mouse goes, they say, so too will those protections to the land. **The mouse's threatened status has compelled communities that are building new water projects to leave areas undisturbed for mouse habitat, park managers to keep hikers and bikers on trails, and ranchers to take extra care in maintaining drainage ditches where the mice can cluster.**
"Local and state governments have failed to protect environmental values in this region, and it's taken the Preble's to stop that,"

*Foxnews.com, January 30, 2006

**Excerpted from New York Times Article, June 27, 2004 "Debate Swirls Around Status of Protected Mouse" Kirk Johnson

said Jeremy Nichols, the endangered species program director at the Biodiversity Conservation Alliance, a conservation group in Laramie, Wyo. "We hope that people can look beyond that mouse, because if the habitat is lost, we stand to lose a lot more than a mouse.'"

Using the "endangered" mouse has become a **"powerful lever"** required, according to Mr. Nichols of the Biodiversity Conservation Alliance, necessary because **"Local and state governments have <u>failed to protect environmental values</u> in this region."** Whose environmental values is this bozo talking about? I lived in Wyoming for ten years. I will guarantee that the local and state governments are, in fact, representing the environmentalist values of the people of Wyoming, who, (as Amy and Steve LeSatz, of Chugwater stated)**"We consider ourselves good stewards of the land."** The people of Wyoming do not need, or want, some bureaucrat from Washington, D.C. to tell them what "is best". It may come as a surprise to these bureaucrats, but Americans do not, as a nation, place the "intrinsic value" of the Prebles Meadow Jumping Mouse, or the New Mexico Jumping Mouse, or the Silver Rice Rat, or the Stephen's Kangaroo Rat, or the San Bernardino Kangaroo Rat, or the Bear Lodge Meadow Jumping Mouse, or any rodent, for that matter, over and above the rights of the American people. These rights are guaranteed to us by the Constitution of the United States, and paid for, on a daily basis, with blood and treasure.

"At what point shall we expect the approach of danger? By what means shall we fortify against it? Shall we expect some transatlantic military giant, to step the Ocean, and crush us at a blow? Never! All the armies of Europe, Asia and Africa combined, with all the treasure of the earth (our own excepted) in their military chest; with a Buonaparte for a commander, could not by force, take a drink from the Ohio, or make a track on the Blue Ridge, in a trial of a thousand years. At what point, then, is the approach of danger to be expected? I answer, if it ever reach us it must spring up amongst us. It cannot come from abroad. If destruction be our lot, we must ourselves be its author and finisher. As a nation of freemen, we must live through all time, or die by suicide."
Abraham Lincoln. -- January 27, 1838 field, Illinois

It looks to me like the enemy has just taken a drink out of the Platte River in Wyoming, and is making tracks all over the Front Range of Colorado.

More mice could muddy waters in Preble's mouse fight

Posted: Friday, May 14, 2004 12:00 am

COLORADO SPRINGS, Colo. (AP) - Federal wildlife officials say there is no end in sight to the controversy surrounding a mouse blamed for costing Western developers millions of dollars because it is protected as a threatened species.

Ralph Morgenweck, regional director of the U.S. Fish and Wildlife Service, said Thursday a decision is expected next year on whether the Preble's meadow jumping mouse should be protected. The mouse's habitat includes Colorado's heavily populated Front Range and parts of Wyoming.

Morgenweck said he is concerned residents might think the "game is over" because a recent study by a Denver scientist found the mouse was not a genetically distinct subspecies - a key finding in giving the mouse protection.

If that work stands up, it would mean the Preble's mouse is the same as the Bear Lodge meadow jumping mouse found in Wyoming and South Dakota. Morgenweck said that finding could play a role in the agency's preliminary decision on protecting the Preble's mouse.

However, he said environmentalists might ask that the Bear Lodge mouse be listed as a threatened species - a request that would mean more studies and potentially more lawsuits. If the two mouse species are the same, any decision on the Bear Lodge mice might affect Preble's mouse habitat.

"We're looking really closely at the Bear Lodge and will almost certainly push to get it protected under the Endangered Species Act," said Jacob Smith, executive director of the Denver-based Center for Native Ecosystems. "The Bear Lodge is in trouble for a similar reason as the Preble's - their habitat is getting blasted."

The government has declared 57,000 acres of Colorado and Wyoming as critical habitat for the Preble's mouse. El Paso County, home to bustling Colorado Springs, has spent about $600,000 preparing a mouse management plan, while developers and landowners say they have spent millions more modifying projects or coming up with mitigation plans to protect the mouse.

The wildlife service has estimated **El Paso County would bear the greatest cost - as much as $103 million during the next decade - for protecting the mouse and restoring its habitat.**

Mr. Morgenweck, regional director of the U.S. Fish & Wildlife Service, refers to this whole battle of Colorado and Wyoming residents, fighting for their livelihoods and control of their own private property, as **"a game."** When you have a guaranteed weekly paycheck, and a fat government pension plan, and the Public Employees for Environmental Responsibility there to pay for your lawyers, maybe it does seem like "a game."

Last time I checked, "games" are supposed to be"fun." Ask the residents of El Paso County, Colorado, due to spend $103,000,000.00 over the next ten years, what they think of this "game." Ask them how much "fun" it is to write the Federal Government a check for income taxes, while at the same time, the Federal Government is destroying their economic opportunities, because of rodents. Ask Amy and Steve LeSatz, who can't even construct a lousy pole barn for training horses, how much they are enjoying this "game". Ask the folks across America, standing in the Unemployment Lines, how much they are enjoying this "game."

Right now, the rodents (species: *federalus bureau ratis*) are winning the game. But it's only halftime, and the American people can come back. Some might say we are in trouble, because Barack Obama is the quarterback. We can change quarterbacks, or Mr. Obama can read this book and bring his "A" game to the second half. That is up to him, and the American voter. I know this much. The vast majority of Congressmen are good people, and I don't believe, for a second, that they would willingly put rodents before American human beings. Democrats or Republicans, Liberal or Conservative, if they know the truth, they will act, and America will come back.It will right its economic ship, and freedom will endure.

The Endangered Species Act of 1973 passed Congress by a vote of 455-4. I would hope (and pray) that, after seeing and realizing what this act is doing to our nation, that it would be repealed unanimously. The Endangered Species Act of 1973 can be replaced by a law that works. America can't be replaced.

Beach Bummed in Favor of a Bird*

Oregon officials have proposed declaring an additional 48 miles to the existing 18 miles of state beaches that are already off-limits between the months of March and September over concerns that the presence of humans is harmful to the Pacific Coast population of the Western Snowy Plover, a bird protected by the Endangered Species Act since 1993. **In total, the bird's protection affects over 180 miles of Pacific coastline. This plover's protection as a threatened species already prevents people from walking dogs, flying kites, horseback riding and making campfires on as many as 24 public beaches in Oregon and several others in Washington and California during the restricted mating and nesting months**. Experts, however, are not confident the bird even should be listed as a threatened species.

Because the small bird lays its eggs in a small depression in dry sand, U.S. Fish and Wildlife Service (FWS) off cials argue, they can easily be destroyed, and therefore the FWS wants to extend restrictions to any beach site where the plover might possibly nest. Michelle Michaud, a biologist with the Oregon Parks and Recreational Department, says, "The plover's been here for a long time. It used to nest in 24 areas along the Oregon coast, and... this is an attempt to recover its habitat." Oregonians fear an economic backlash could result from beach closings. Doug Olsen of the Pacific City Chamber of Commerce worries, "People will go to Bend [along the western border in the center of the state] instead of the Oregon Coast. **Many businesses [on the coast] would lose out.**" FWS officials claim the recovery plan might create a profit for coastal businesses. Phil Carroll, spokesman for the FWS, argues that, "In 2001, 46 million birdwatchers generated $32 billion in retail sales." But this statistic is national in scope and in no way a predictor of future economic benefits specifically for Pacific coastline states.

Working on behalf of small business owners, avid beach users and other residents, in July of 2002, the Surf Ocean Beach Commission (SOBC) — a grassroots organization of people affected by the plover's listing — petitioned the FWS to remove the Pacific Coast population of the Western Snowy Plover from the federal list of threatened species. FWS officials are required by law to make a finding within 90 days to determine if the request is warranted. After prolonged inactivity on the petition — 18 months — the Pacific

*Shattered Dreams, 100 Stories of Government Abuse, National Center for Public Policy Research

Legal Foundation filed suit on behalf of the SOBC against the FWS in the U.S. District Court for the Eastern District of California in February of 2004, requesting that the plover bedelisted. **The PLF cited over 500 pages of scientific data, university studies, government documents and news articles to justify the plover's delisting and, as a result, for eliminating the restrictions on beach access and use. The PLF's Greg Broderick commented, "The government is still keeping people off of hundreds of miles of beaches based on junk science...** It just goes to show that the government puts people last when it comes to the Endangered Species Act." Officials from the FWS initially suggested a reexamination of the listing date in March of 2004, determining that the delisting of the Western Snowy Plover "may be warranted." However, in April, 2006. The FWS announced that these Pacific Coast plovers would continue to be listed under the ESA, so restrictions placed on human access to the beaches will continue.

The FWS responded to petitioners' arguments that the Pacific Coast populations of the Western Snowy Plover do not qualify as a distinct subspecies by arguing that "the Pacific Coast population of the Western Snowy Plover is markedly separate from other populations.

"It just goes to show that the government puts people last when it comes to the Endangered Species Act." — Greg Broderick,*
Pacific Legal Foundation

Beach Closed — Bird Warning*

Lora Brozovic and her husband traveled from Canton, Ohio to Hatteras Island, North Carolina to celebrate the 2004 Memorial Day weekend and engage in their hobby
of surf-fishing on the island's southern tip. But **when the couple arrived on the beach, they were approached by a National Parks Service (NPS) employee who told them to leave immediately.** No sharks had been spotted in nearby waters, nor was a tropical storm heading for the North Carolina coast. **No, four Piping Plover eggs were ready to hatch in a nearby nest.**

Brozovic described the NPS response to people venturing into this "bird nesting area" as being "like it was some kind of emergency."

*Shattered Dreams, 100 Stories of Government Abuse, National Center for Public Policy Research

The Piping Plover is threatened under the federal Endangered Species Act (ESA), and the nesting of the Piping Plover in 2004 prompted the closure of a half-mile stretch of Hatteras Island beach popular with visitors and locals. The NPS said the beach would remain closed for up to five weeks until the chicks were able to fly. This posed an unwelcome change of plans to unaware picnickers, off-road vehicle enthusiasts and fishermen such as the Brozovics, who vacation on the southern tip of Hatteras Island on a typical Memorial Day weekend and patronize local businesses that depend on their support. During the first busy weeks of the summer of 2004, the beach where plovers nested was off limits to all boat, pedestrian and four-wheel-drive traffic. "It's a great spot to go fishing," laments Lora Brozovic. "We're down to ten percent [of the beach] now for fishing, and the birds have 90 percent."

The affected beach is part of the Cape Hatteras National Seashore, a federal park stretching approximately 73 miles down North Carolina's Outer Banks. The ESA
requires that both the nesting habitat and the wintering habitat of the species be protected. **Between six and 20 Piping Plovers require a wintering habitat that stretches along 3,600 acres of beachfront. When permanent, temporary, seasonal and Piping Plover critical habitat area closures are combined, human beach access is reduced from over 38 miles to less than 16 miles. At one point, all 73 miles of beach had unrestricted access.**

Bob Eakes, owner of the Red Drum Tackle Shop in nearby Buxton, has two observations about the beach closure: **"One, it's an excessive amount of closure. Two, the biologists, they have no couth at all, running people off the beach like they were a pack of criminals."** Eakes asserts that, if beaches continue to be closed to vehicle and foot traffic, Hatteras Island will "no longer be a shining star in the state of North Carolina." An economic survey conducted in 2002 and 2003 indicates that tourism and spending by visitors would drop by 28 percent if beach access was banned or severely curtailed. "That would put all of us out here on welfare," explains David Goodwin of the Outer Banks Preservation Association, whose group commissioned the study. **The survey also concluded that, if all the economic and human damages of every hurricane to hit the area over the last 100 years were totaled, the figure would even not come close to the negative local economic effect of further beach restrictions.**

The Cape Hatteras Access Preservation Alliance, a subsidiary of the Outer Banks Preservation Association, joined by a coalition of other nearby affected groups, won a lawsuit filed in February 2003 to remove the Piping Plover critical habitat areas. In November 2004, a federal judge for the U.S. District Court for the District of Columbia lifted the U.S. Fish and Wildlife Service's critical habitat designation for the bird on more than 3,600 acres of the Outer Banks (but not elsewhere). The judge ruled that the FWS did not adequately account for the designation's economic effects and misapplied habitat protection law. "The [U.S Fish and Wildlife] Service may not statutorily cast a net over tracts of land with the mere hope that they will develop [the physical or biological features essential to the species' conservation] and be subject to designation," Judge Royce C. Lamberth wrote. In face of the ruling, the FWS dropped its appeal on the case in March 2005.

"America, America, from Sea to Shining Sea"*

Not any more. The beaches along the Atlantic and Pacific Oceans are habitat for Piping Plovers, and American citizens can no longer walk those beaches. And we call this "The Land of the Free"??

Omaha Beach, Anzio Beach, Utah Beach. It was okay for thousands of American soldiers to walk (and die) on those beaches, but now the United State Fish & Wildlife Service runs Americans off the very beaches at home for which those brave soldiers thought they were fighting. The children and grandchildren of those courageous men can't walk 24 public beaches, in Oregon and California, and thousands of acres in Cape Hatteras in North Carolina, and beaches in New York and New England, because of a shorebird, that many scientists argue isn't endangered at all. But the beaches remain closed.

Americans don't have to travel to the shores of France to find Nazi's to fight. They are right here, **"running people off the beach like they were a pack of criminals."** If I remember my history correctly, there were trials at Nuremberg that determined who were the real criminals. The "I was just following orders" excuse was ruled invalid.

It is time to repeal the Endangered Species Act of 1973, and create a law that makes sense for all Americans, including those that just want to take a walk on the beach.

*"America, the Beautful", lyrics by Kathy Lee Bates

Toads Halt Home Building*

Housing prospects may soon become more scarce and more expensive in San Diego, California. Federal regulators rejected a developer's plans to build a 280-home development because construction may have threatened an endangered toad. The decision inevitably will make it harder for lower-income families to find suitable housing, as a decrease in the amount of available housing tends to increase the price of homes. Rancho Viejo LLC, the developer, had planned to build 280 homes on 202 unincorporated acres in San Diego.

Not only would the development provide a rapidly growing community with additional needed housing, but it would increase San Diego's property tax base. The U.S. Fish and Wildlife Service (FWS) and the Army Corps of Engineers concluded that there was a possibility that building on parts of the proposed site could harm breeding areas used by the protected Arroyo Southwestern Toad, which has been classified as an endangered species since 1994. FWS officials sent a letter in May 2000 to Rancho Viejo informing it that a fence the company had built "has resulted in the illegal take [endangerment] and will result in the future illegal take of federally endangered" Arroyo Toads.

The FWS offered an alternative — and much more expensive — plan. The project would have been allowed to continue if soil was taken from a remote location. This alternative would have dramatically increased the construction costs and, therefore, would have likely made it impossible for the homes to be priced at standard market rates. Rancho Viejo rejected the alternative and filed a complaint against Secretary of Interior Gale Norton in U.S. District Court for the District of Columbia.

The case was dismissed on the grounds that regulating the site under the Endangered Species Act is constitutional, and that the development of the site would threaten the toad. The Federal Appeals Court upheld the ruling in April of 2003 and also denied Rancho Viejo's petition for a rehearing.

"As the Nation's principal conservation agency, the Department of the Interior has responsibility for most of our nationally owned

*Shattered Dreams, 100 Stories of Government Abuse, National Center for Public Policy Research

public lands and natural resources. This includes fostering the wisest use of our land and water resources, protecting our fish and wildlife, preserving the environmental and cultural values of our national parks and historical places, and providing for the enjoyment of life through outdoor recreation. The Department assesses our energy and mineral resources and works to assure that their development is in the best interests of all our people."

The above statement is the preamble to the U.S. Fish & Wildlife's Recovery Plan for the Southwestern Arroyo Toad. I must confess to the reader, that I have virtually no knowledge of toads, and specifically, the Southwestern Arroyo Toad. I do have some knowledge of San Diego county real estate values, and can estimate that the 280 houses that would have been built by Rancho Viejo would have have been worth in the hundreds of millions of dollars, all built on private land. The U.S.F.W.S. preamble above says it has "responsibility for most of our nationally owned public lands". **By stopping development on private land, the U.S.F.W.S. clearly takes on responsibility for all our lands, both public and private.**

The owners of Rancho Viejo had built a fence, which, according to the United States Fish and Wildlife Service, kept the toads from migrating to a local streambed. This was considered an illegal take, and a violation of the Endangered Species Act. Exactly how many toads are we talking about here? Well, Amphibiaweb puts the average density of Southwestern Arroyo Toads at 12 per hectare*, or about 4.85 toads per acre. On this 202 acres, that would mean there were 979 toads. Assuming they would all be killed by the project, (a highly unlikely assumption), and assuming the home values of the 280 homes was $1,000,000 each (cheap for San Diego) , then the **value of each Southwestern Arroyo Toad comes to $286,006.13. The same money, per toad, would feed 5,720 starving children in Africa for a full year.****

The $286,006.13 Southwestern Arroyo Toad

*http://amphibiaweb.org/cgi/amphib_query?where-genus=Bufo&where-species=californicus

**http://answers.yahoo.com/question/index?qid=20090709214029AAEeqIE

Shattered Dreams on the "Hunt of a Lifetime"

Dominick Demaria, a lifelong sportsman, dreamed of hunting in Alaska. A college professor in a small Connecticutt college, he built porches and decks in the summertime, to pay for his hunting trips. Dominick called my company, Shoshone Wilderness Adventures, and sought my advice as to what outfitter in Alaska he should hire. He wanted to hunt moose, and if possible, grizzly bear. I suggested Henry Tiffany, of Alaska Perimeter Expeditions, with whom I had sent many successful clients. Henry hunted in a remote part of northern Alaska, along the Salmon River. Henry guides the client personally, and, as an added bonus, films the hunter's adventure.

When Dominick returned from "hunt of a lifetime", he was ecstatic. Dominick had harvested a really large bull moose, an old boar grizzly bear, and, as a bonus, had also managed to harvest a black bear and a wolf. He gave Henry and his business high marks for his professionalism and hard work, and commented on what a great companion he had been in the wilderness.

A year later, at 8 o'clock in the evening, sitting at home in front of his fireplace, with his family, there came a loud knock on Dominick's door. It was the United States Fish & Wildlife Service, and Dominick was being charged with Lacey Act violations, transporting game illegally across state lines. The charge was this: After Dominick had harvested his moose, a "packer", hired by Alaska Perimeter Expeditions, had come in to pack out the moose he had harvested. It is the law in Alaska, as it is everywhere else, that game meat can't be wasted. It is a general outfitting practice that meat not flown home by the clients is served in camp, or given to guides and staff at the end of the season, to supplement their winter meat supply.

U.S. Fish & Wildlife claimed that the packer had left some neck meat on the carcass. What is "edible" meat, and what isn't, is always subject to some interpretation. Dominick, in this case, had shot the bull in the neck, and so much of the meat was bloodshot. The government claimed otherwise, and claimed that, since the moose carcass had meat on it, it was now "bait". Baiting game in Alaska with other game is illegal, and so the grizzly bear, the black bear, and the wolf were all taken illegally, even though they were shot quite a long distance from the actual moose carcass. The U.S.F.W.S. confiscated the shoulder mounted moose, along with the full body mounts of the grizzly bear, the black bear, and the wolf, as "evidence."

Dominick, naturally, contacted a lawyer to fight the charges. His lawyer told him he would need an Alaskan lawyer, and it would probably require a minimum of 3-4 trips to Alaska for legal proceedings. Meanwhile, Henry Tiffany, who had the entire hunt on videotape, was trying to get himself charged with a crime, instead of Dominick. The government refused to charge Henry, The lawyer estimated the legal fees would run upwards of $25,000. The U.S.F.W.S. was offering a "deal" for Dominick: plead guilty, pay a $5000 fine, forfeit the trophies, and lose his hunting privileges for five years. Dominick didn't have $25,000. He plead guilty to a crime he didn't commit, paid the $5000 fine, and hasn't seen his trophies since they were confiscated that night from his home.

The government never charged Henry Tiffany with any crime whatsoever. He had the money, and the evidence, and the will, to fight the government. Like the wolves, these bureaucrats tend to pick on the weak. They wanted nothing to do with Henry.

I have told this story many times, at campfires around the world. It sickens me, because I had recommended this hunt to this man. At the time, I assumed that this was an "isolated" incidence of the abuse of power by the U.S.F.W.S. This incidence happened back in the early 1990s, and I have since heard many similar stories from hunting clients all across the country. Sportsmen spend millions of dollars every year, through the Pittman-Roberstson Act, to support wildlife. The U.S.F.W.S. is supposed to be on the side of abundant wildlife. Instead, it is on the side of abundant power.

Dominick Demaria and the "Bait"

One Dead Garter Snake Halts Transit Rail Construction; Costs Taxpayers a Million Plus*

May 14, 2002
San Francisco Chronicle

Last year [2002] the discovery of a dead garter snake ground to a halt construction of a commuter rail line in San Francisco, costing taxpayers a whopping $1.07 million in delays, making the serpent the most costly snake in the world.

As NewsMax.com reported at the time, San Jose Mercury News reporter Aaron Davis said finding the snake, which is listed as a member of one of those precious endangered species without which mankind cannot survive, sparked an investigation to determine the cause of the snake's death by the sleuths at California's Department of Fish and Game.

"Nobody has ever been able to find out what happened to the snake and there was no evidence of foul play," BART spokesman Mike Healy told the Mercury News. "There was no evidence that the contractor or anyone was directly at fault."

The crushed body of that snake, an "endangered San Francisco garter snake," stopped construction of a BART (Bay Area Rapid Transit) rail extension dead in it tracks. And now another dead garter snake has shut down work on the project as sleuths nose about trying to learn who or what done the thing in.

State wildlife officials ordered work halted last Thursday after a worker found a dead snake at the entrance to a work site and turned it over to a biological monitor, according to the San Francisco Chronicle.

"We are working with BART to make sure they are sensitive to issues concerning the garter snake," Robert Floerke, regional manager for the state Department of Fish and Game, told the Chronicle. Officials told the Chronicle they did not anticipate a long delay.
The paper recalled that after the first snake was found dead, a 5 mph speed limit was posted in the area and workers were re-

*Shattered Dreams, 100 Stories of Government Abuse, National Center for Public Policy Research

quired to check under parked vehicles for the snakes.

The estimated $1.5 billion project to extend BART rail lines to **the San Francisco airport has already laid out an astonishing $6 million merely to comply with the state's wacky environmental laws and has relocated more than 75 snakes, the Chronicle revealed.**

An investigation into what killed the snake is being conducted by BART officials, biologists, and state and federal wildlife officials. We are not making this up.

Investigators are seeking to learn if the snake's death was due to natural causes or construction work, and to determine if BART and its contractors are doing everything in their power to protect the snakes.Even before construction began, the Chronicle recalls that "snake trappers caught as many as possible. Then special fences were erected to keep others from slithering into harm's way. And special biological monitors were hired to keep watch over the snake's territory."

After finding the first dead snake, workers were put through special snake training that taught them how to recognize the snake, Molly MacArthur, a spokeswoman for the extension project, told the Chronicle.

But representatives of BART and the state Department of Fish and Game said they didn't expect the work stoppage to last long this time.

That's providing, of course, that wildlife officials don't order an extended investigation to determine if Osama bin Laden had a hand in the dastardly deed, or declare a prolonged period of mourning for the late snake.

This story is ludicrous. The problem is, it is true. Even the San Francisco Chronicle reporter who wrote the story, felt obliged to tell the reader, midway through the article
                "We are not making this up."
I've been reading newspapers for over half a century. I have never seen a reporter say that, ever.

Federal Efforts to Protect Endangered Bird Leads to $10 Million Worth of Flooding*

In January 1993, the city of Temecula, California suffered over $10 million in flood-related damages because federal regulators, more concerned about protecting an endangered bird, refused to allow proper maintenance of the flood control system. A small bird called the Least Bell's Vireo lived just downstream from the Murrieta Creek flood control facility. Eager to expand its habitat, the United States Fish and Wildlife Service (USFWS) refused to allow the Riverside County Flood and Water Conservation District the right to remove vegetation and other debris from control channels. It seems the USFWS wanted to use the flood channel to make a home for the bird. Riverside County Commissioners and county engineers testified before Congress that their inability to remove the debris led to a clogging of the channel, which resulted in flooding that seriously, damaged businesses and homes. Ken Edwards, the chief engineer of the flood control agency, said "Ironically, after the flooding, federal authorities allowed the maintenance to take place."

Source: Field Hearing of the U.S. House of Representatives Committee on Natural Resources, April 26, 1995

Ho-hum. Just another 10 million dollars worth of flooding, brought to you courtesy of the United States Fish & Wildlife Service, and the Endangered Species Act of 1973. This 10,000,000.00 flood was just a blip on the radar screen, compared to the multi-billion dollar floods of 2011, caused by the Piping Plover in the Missouri River.

Ranch May Be Condemned by "Casual Visitor"*

John Hays found his cattle ranching business in jeopardy after United States Forest Service officials decided that parts of his rangeland contained habitat of the threatened Canada Lynx. **The Hays family has occupied and ranched the same land in Baker County, Oregon now roughly 15,000 acres — since 1850.** In 2001, USFS staffers informed Hays that he might be required to reduce or possibly even eliminate his herd of cattle entirely because parts of his

*Shattered Dreams, 100 Stories of Government Abuse, National Center for Public Policy Research

Canadian Lynx

property and additional federal land that he grazed his cattle on contained a suitable habitat for the lynx.

Hays was shocked to discover the lynx habitat even existed in his area. **No lynx has ever been spotted on the Hays property.** Furthermore, **there have been only 14 confirmed sightings of the Canada Lynx in the entire state of Oregon since 1897.** Larry Cooper, a staff biologist for the Oregon Department of Fish and Wildlife, commented that the **"lynx are a casual visitor to Oregon and no reproduction has ever been found... The documentation was presented under the ruse of science."**

At a meeting between USFS staff members and Hays and his attorney in May of 2001, an advisor to the USFS confirmed portions of Hays' property were determined to be lynx habitat. The official, however, did not believe that **"there were any lynx in the area, but that they are required to manage for lynx anyway."** While **no rancher, naturalist or member of the USFS witnessed or discovered any evidence of the Canada Lynx in the region, the USFS still recommended a drastic reduction in the number of cattle simply because the Hays property presented a suitable habitat for them.**

The severe economic strain on Hays and his family prompted Hays to sell over half of his cattle stock in 2002 in order to keep his ranch operational. Hays testified in 2003 before the U.S. House Rural Enterprises, Agriculture and Technology Subcommittee that the USFS would issue him a one-year grazing permit, not a 10-year permit Hays needed to present to his banker to obtain operational financing for his business. The financing is essential, as Hays contends, "My livelihood is dependent on the timely and continual issuance of the grazing permit."

The U.S. Forest Service also cancelled Hays' grazing permit in 2004. Facing financial difficulties, Hays sold part of his ranch in March of 2005. "I will probably have to end up selling my entire ranch and do something else as they have about broke me," says Hays. Hays is considering a lawsuit against the U.S. Forest Service for a Fifth Amendment takings violation without just compensation, along with other damages to his business. As Hays explains, he believes the canceling of his grazing permits was done unjustly: "I appear to have been singled out and not given any accommodations because the Forest Service officers had a desire to terminate my permit by all means available to them."

> "The marvel of all history is the patience with which men and women submit to burdens unnecessarily laid upon them by their governments. "
> George Washington

The problem is, as stated above by George Washington, Mr. Hays tried to cooperate with the government, unbelieving that the U.S.F.W.S. would actually do this to an American citizen. By the time he realized they were serious, he was too broke to fight the government. Its the wolfpack, circling the weak and wounded moose, finally destroying it. The wolfpack is the United State Fish & Wildlife Service. And American freeedom is the prey.

I don't like drawing that conclusion, any more than the reader likes reading it. Unfortunately, it is a conclusion supported by the facts. When I started writing the book, I started asking clients, from around the country, if they had ever had any issues with the Endangered Species Act. From a clergyman trying to get a church built (it cost the congregation hundreds of thousands of dollars more) to fishermen in Louisiana dealing with TEDs (that's aTurtle Escape Devices, to the uninitiated), It was amazing. And worst of all, what came through loud and clear from each conversation, was the Nazi-like attitude of the U.S. Fish and Wildlife Service personel. These people have lost sight of the fact that they work for us, the American people, not vice versa.

Over a Hundred Mine Workers Lose Jobs Because of Turtle*

In September 1996, the Mountain Pass mine in the Southern California desert, operated by the Molycorp Company, was the target of a **SWAT-style raid by federal agents over an alleged violation of the Endangered Species Act.** The mine's egregious offense: A few months before the raid, a waste water pipe burst during routine maintenance, spilling thousands of gallons of fresh water into the desert. **The Bureau of Land Management viewed this as a threat to the Desert Tortoise, a protected species. Susan Messler, an accountant at Molycorp, said that armed government agents - complete with badges, helmets and flak jackets - charged onto the mine's property to let them know that the fresh water they had accidentally spilled in the desert is considered a toxic waste.** That was only the beginning of the mine's troubles. After a dead tortoise was discovered on the property, **all 300 of Molycorp's employees had to attend a "Desert Tortoise worker education class"** even though it was never shown that any of the mine's employees were responsible for the tortoise's demise. To prevent harm to any other tortoises, employees were required to drive no faster than 15 miles per hour and stay at least 100 feet away from the tortoises. Heavy equipment could not be operated unless an authorized government biologist was present to make sure no tortoises were in the way. More serious, though, were the $6.2 million in fines the government assessed on Molycorp. Says Messler, "We probably didn't make that much money in a five-year period." As a result, the mine has had to lay off one-third of its employees with more cutbacks on the way.

Someone needs to explain to me why the United States Fish & Wildlife Service needs to make SWATS like raids using "guns, helmets and flak jackets". Was there some evidence that Osama Bin Laden was hiding out in this desert, along with the tortoises? Were the tortoises going to

*Shattered Dreams, 100 Stories of Government Abuse, National Center for Public Policy Research

use Delhi Sands Flower Loving Flies to fly into the walls of Dodger Stadium? Like the raid on Taung Ming-Lin's plowed fields, this reads more like a Gestapo raid than the U.S. Fish & Wildlife Service investigating the death of a single tortoise. 300 Mine employees (100 of which lost their job anyway) had to attend a "Desert tortoise worker education class." This sounds like a brainwashing session to me. What more did the mineworkers need to know about the Desert Tortoise, other than, "They are endangered, please don't drive over them. Class dismssed." A full time government biologist on hand whenever heavy equipment was being operated. Its a mine operating in 1996. Did the government think they would be using picks and shovels, or heavy equipment? A fine of $6,200,000.00 for the accidental death of one tortoise, which they never proved was caused by anyone, is an absurdity.

The U.S.F.W.S. suspected motor vehicles on the mine roads might have caused the accidental death of the single deceased tortoise , and the mine's employees were ordered to drive no faster than 15 m.p.h. In Machias, Texas, Darrel J. Minor was convicted in the accicental "death by Motor vehicle violation" in the death of David M. Prescott (a human being). He was fined $1000.

$1,000.00 for a dead human being, just 18 years old. in the prime of life. $6,200,000.00 for a dead tortoise , the age of which I couldn't care less. This is ridiculous. As I write this book, about every half hour, I feel like screaming "Are you fricking kidding me!!!!!" In fact, that is what I scream (more or less) every half hour. My wife thinks I may be going insane, but, as I explain to her, the real lunatic asylum is headquartered in Washington, D.C., with field offices scattered nationwide.

Under Seige: One Reason Our Military Readiness Is Down: We Won't Let Them Train*

By Sean Paige
October 31, 2001

As it prepares sailors, soldiers, and airmen to face enemies abroad, the U.S. military also finds itself under new pressure on the homefront. It's being told to close or curtail the use of training facilities the Pentagon says are vital to national security. From Puerto Rico to Farallon de Medinilla in the Pacific Ocean, and at numerous train-

*Competitive Enterprise Institute | 1899 L ST NW Floor 12, Washington, DC 20036 |

ing sites in between, **military men and women who should be practicing to go on the offensive are instead hunkered down, besieged by government regulators, national environmental organizations, and civilian citizen groups seeking to stop or severely restrict exercises they say are disturbing the peace, threatening endangered species, or polluting the air, land, and sea.** The agitation that is closing the Vieques Island bombing range is only the tip of a very large iceberg that could endanger thousands of American fighting men and women come the next shooting war.

Base commanders and Pentagon brass have suffered these mounting complaints and complications in relative silence, trying to disarm critics by being good neighbors and fostering a stewardship ethic. But as isolated criticisms have taken on the character of an all-out assault, and with no hope of a truce in sight, some officers are beginning to speak out about what they euphemistically call "encroachment" problems, and warning that military readiness will tumble unless the new obstacles to training are cleared away.

The first ever hearings on encroachment issues were held by the military readiness subcommittee of the Senate Armed Services Committee in March, and the House Armed Services Committee followed suit in May. Neither hearing generated the kind of media attention some experts believe the issue deserves. "Encroachment is often gradual and can go unnoticed, but its impact cumulatively erodes our ability to deploy combat-ready sailors and Marines," said Navy Vice Admiral James Amerault at the hearings. "Your Marines' success on the battlefield depends on having assured access to training ranges and installations on the land, sea, and in the air," added Marine Corps Major General Edward Hanlon, Jr., commander at Camp Pendleton. "However, our ability to train is being slowly eroded by encroachment on many fronts."

One aspect of the problem is the growing proximity of civilian communities to formerly remote military bases, and the growing intolerance of some citizens to noise, dust, and minor inconveniences that come with living near military activity. **A larger part of the equation, however, is clearly ideological antipathy by uncompromising environmental groups. Some of the critics are obviously buoyed by the idea that in defending the interests of endangered species on military bases they're also helping to monkey-wrench the machinery of war.**

Ground zero in the conflict is Vieques, a formerly obscure island off the eastern end of Puerto Rico that is the U.S. Atlantic Fleet's only live-fire training range. Vieques has been the subject of activist protests and national headlines since April 1999, when an errant bomb killed a civilian security guard working at the range. The death brought to a head years of simmering debate among Puerto Ricans about the island's status, and was seized on by headline-hunting politicians and environmentalists who claim the exercises are ruining the environment and threaten the health of the island's 9,000 inhabitants.

The Bush administration, in a move that shocked the Pentagon and raised the ire of some Republicans on Capitol Hill, suddenly surrendered to the protestors in June, announcing that the Navy will permanently halt training on the island in 2003. The Washington Post reported that politics played a part in the decision, as White House aides worried that the controversy threatened to undermine Hispanic support for the administration.

But the military is catching similar flak nearly everywhere it trains, and the result is dramatically altered military exercises not just on Vieques but at such storied institutions as **Camp Lejeune in North Carolina, Fort Hood in Texas, and Camp Pendleton in California. At Lejeune, access to base beaches is severely restricted each year during turtle nesting season, making realistic amphibious landing exercises impossible. Because of the presence of the red-cockaded woodpecker, a protected bird, inland maneuvers face similar restrictions.**

At Fort Hood, only 17 percent of the base's 185,000-acre training area remains unencumbered by one environmental restriction or another. Clean Water Act rules prohibit digging on nearly 70 percent of available training ground, meaning no breaking ground for foxholes or vehicle fighting positions. Clean Air Act rules prohibit the use of smoke, flares, chemical grenades, or any other pyrotechnic devices on about 25 percent of the available training area. From March through August, military vehicles are prohibited from straying from paved roads due to Endangered Species Act strictures. **Use of camouflage netting and bivouac is prohibited on 74,000 acres set aside as habitat for two birds, the golden cheeked warbler and black capped vireo.** Noise restrictions prohibit the firing of artillery or rocket launchers in some areas of the base.

At Pendleton, supposedly the U.S. Marine Corps' most complete amphibious training base, only about one mile of the facility's 17 miles of beach is available for exercises year round, due in part to endangered species restrictions. During one major exercise last March, the Thirteenth Marine Expeditionary Unit was limited to only 500 yards of beach because it was the breeding season of the endangered California least tern. Off-road maneuvering is also highly restricted, and digging is prohibited, severely limiting the ability of Marines to practice the construction of artillery and mortar firing positions.

The Army's Makua Military Reservation in Hawaii has been closed since 1998 because of environmental lawsuits concerning, among other things, the protection of a tree snail. Continued U.S. use of Farallon de Medinilla, a speck of coral near Guam that Seventh Fleet aviators use for bombing practice, is currently being challenged in court due to alleged violations of the International Migratory Bird Treaty Act. Submarine training at underwater sites near the Bahamas and off Hawaii faces limitations due to alleged conflicts with the Marine Mammal Protection Act. And Marine Corps training exercises at San Clemente Island, off the coast of California, are severely restricted due to the presence of the loggerhead shrike, an endangered bird, and a creature called the night lizard.

The presence of Sonoran pronghorn antelope on Arizona's Barry Goldwater Bombing Range has spurred protests, brought lawsuits, and could lead to closure of the facility. Protection for the Florida black bear and Florida scrub jay are two reasons why Green groups are opposing the Navy's continued use of the Pinecastle Bombing Range in Florida's Ocala National Forest. The beaches where Navy SEAL teams train at the Naval Amphibious Base, Coronado Island, California, shrink by 40 percent for seven months out of every year because of the presence of an endangered bird, the snowy plover. And opposition from environmentalists nearly derailed last year's $75 million expansion of the Army's National Training Center at Fort Irwin, in California's Mojave Desert, because it allegedly represented what one group called a "death warrant" for some desert tortoise.....

The military services have tried to counter the encroachment threat by becoming better stewards of the lands they manage and by becoming better neighbors to the communities at their gates. Few would argue that the U.S. military has always been a conscientious caretaker of the outdoors, but today it can claim to be a solid environmental citizen, particularly given the inherently destructive nature of its mission.

The Pentagon pumps tens of millions of dollars directly into its endangered species programs today, and probably spends billions of dollars annually on environmental education, monitoring, compliance, and clean-up activities. A large environmental bureaucracy has metastasized within the Department of Defense, demanding the attention of thousands of military personnel and government contractors. The DoD has spent millions of dollars developing lead-free "green" munitions that will be lethal to human targets but pose no health risks to battlefield bunny rabbits. Annual awards are given out by the department highlighting stewardship programs, innovative environmental technologies, and other successes. Officials in the Pentagon now even talk with a straight face about "environmental security" issues.

In 1991, the Navy built a turtle hatchery on Vieques, which incubates eggs collected on daily sweeps of the beach during training exercises. Since then the Navy has hatched more than 17,000 hawksbill and leatherback turtles from the facility and returned them to the wild, contributing to a growth in turtle populations that—in spite of the exercises there—reportedly exceeds any other shoreline in Puerto Rico. North Carolina's Camp Lejeune also has a hatchery for turtle eggs, which biologists remove daily from beaches during training times.

Officials at Camp Lejeune also take pride in the fact that nesting clusters of red-cockaded woodpeckers on the base today number 53, up from 35 just three years ago—"an increase unmatched by any other land manager in eastern North Carolina," Hanlon recently boasted in his testimony. The birds have enjoyed a similar resurgence at the U.S. Army's Fort Jackson, South Carolina which also won a Department of Defense   Environmental Security Award last year for its erosion-control projects and tree-planting activities.
The military has taken a leading role in efforts to eradicate the brown tree snake in Guam, an invasive species that has wiped out almost all the native birds on the island. Officials at Fort Carson, Colorado have been working since 1981 with the U.S. Fish and

Wildlife Service to improve habitat for the greenback cutthroat trout in the Arkansas River, and even had a broodstock pond constructed for rearing the young fish. **On San Clemente Island, California the Navy spends $2.5 million annually for the protection of 42 endangered loggerhead shrike, and keeps 64 of the birds in a captive breeding population.** And the population of snowy plovers is growing so rapidly at the SEAL training areas at Coronado Island that officials there reportedly worry that their "success" will lead to even more of the beach being closed to training during nesting season.

The Navy has spent $18 million to study whether active sonar and underwater charges are bothering marine mammals, and has created artificial reefs off Oahu, Hawaii for fish. After a mother and calf West Indian manatee were killed in a collision, the Navy's submarine base at Kings Bay, Georgia outfitted tug boats and other vessels with special propeller guards, and has established no-entry zones in areas the animals are known to frequent. And the Navy has allowed marine biologists to use its once top secret Sound Surveillance System, a string of underwater receivers used during the Cold War to track Soviet subs, to conduct whale research.

The military sometimes goes to what might seem extreme lengths to be seen as good stewards. **At Arizona's Barry Goldwater range, exhaustive research has been conducted into the habits of the flat-tailed horned lizard, including when during the day the creatures prefer to lie out on paved roadways, so traffic can be stopped during those times.** Military personnel are also present on the range during bombing sorties to wave off planes if pronghorn antelope stray into the vicinity.

Before launching training flights over one Gulf of Mexico bombing range, officials at Florida's Eglin Air Force Base first consult with the U.S. Fish and Wildlife Service to ensure that gulf sturgeon tagged for research purposes aren't swimming in the range's vicinity. At Marine Corps Air Station Miramar, the service has spent more than $1 million to construct and monitor dozens of shallow mud puddles — scientists call them "vernal pools" — that are habitat for the fairy shrimp, a tiny, supposedly endangered creature that has tied development in knots all across Southern California.

Self-interest and self-preservation have as much to do with such actions as ecological altruism, of course. The Marine Corps and other services accept that aiding endangered species issues is essential — even if it means turning part of a base into a de facto nature sanctuary — lest lawsuits or government regulators shut down an entire facility and bring training there to a grinding halt. **Camp Pendleton, which since 1994 has seen its number of on-base endangered species rise from ten to 17, was not long ago in peril of losing use of well over half of its 125,000 acres to "critical habitat" designations for endangered species. That's because the Endangered Species Act not only requires the protection of threatened animals, but also preservation of their favorite sites.** But the Corps worked cooperatively with the Fish and Wildlife Service to develop a natural resource management plan for the base, thereby avoiding the critical-habitat designation. Environmentalists at the Natural Resources Defense Council consider the compromise a cave-in, and have sued the government to force the effective closure of approximately 70,000 acres of the base. **At nearby Air Station Miramar, host to ten endangered species, "critical habitat" designations by Fish and Wildlife also threatened to close nearly two-thirds of the facility, with a potentially devastating impact on operations. The base dodged a bullet when USFW determined the designation was not justified, but that decision has also been challenged in court by the NRDC.**

The possibility that the Barry Goldwater range in Arizona might be designated as critical habitat for Sonoran pronghorn antelope could "seriously limit" Air Force use of the range, Major General Buchanan told the Senate. The Navy's representative at the hearing, Vice Admiral Amerault, expressed concern not only over the permanent closure of Vieques, but about the serious impact on readiness if environmentalists also succeed in curtailing the military's use of San Clemente Island and Farallon de Medinilla.

"The [three] ranges are the only U.S.-owned locations on the East and West Coast where both naval surface fire support and air-to-ground training operations can be conducted using live ordnance," Amerault reminded senators. Without use of Farallon de Medinilla, the air wing of the U.S. Seventh Fleet would degrade to "unready" combat status within just six months, according to Amerault. And if the suit filed last December succeeds in blocking use of the atoll, the admiral expressed fear that environmental groups will bring similar suits against every other naval training facility where migratory birds are found.

At the same hearing, Army Major General Van Antwerp warned that **"while we have been successful at managing endangered species, some of these actions have come at the expense of training capabilities."** He expressed "great concern" **that the forced closure by the EPA of firing ranges at the Massachusetts Military Reservation set a precedent that could severely affect military readiness if followed elsewhere. "The potential impact of further administrative cease-fire orders cannot be measured," said Van Antwerp, who suggested that the EPA shut down the facility without a basis in sound science.**

For his part, Major General Hanlon of the Marines told senators that the service "cannot be expected to shoulder a disproportionate share of environmental protection and still meet our readiness requirements." **As a result of environmental restrictions that lessen the realism of military exercises, "we are training a generation of Marines who will have less experience in the intricacies of combat operations,"** he added. "Many of today's junior leaders may initially face the full challenges of combat not during training, but during conflict," the Camp Pendleton commander warned.

Hanlon asked that members of Congress "consider the unique nature of military activities when developing or reauthorizing these [environmental] laws." One top congressional staffer involved in the issue suggests that "the key thing we need is genuine balance and some legal middle ground, where you build in enough flexibility to allow the military to do the things it needs to do to do its job." **This will require reform of the Endangered Species Act and other environmental laws.** But unless some kind of détente can be struck between military bases and encroaching civilian communities, the alternative is an endless series of legal battles and public relations skirmishes, and an ever-constricting horizon within which U.S. troops can train for their critical and dangerous service to the nation.

The above article was written just 50 days after the 9/11/2001 tragedy at the Twin Towers of New York, the Pentagon in Washington, and a farm field in rural Pennsyvania. Maybe, just maybe, if the U.S. military had spent the millions of dollars it is blowing every year on protection of endangered species, the jihadists of 9/11 might have been foiled ahead of time. Is it the very best use of military personel, and our military budget, to play crossing guard for the flat tailed horned lizard? Is the annual expenditure by the Navy of $2,500,000.00 to protect 42 San Clemente Loggerhead Shrike the best possible use of our limited military funds?

U.S. Troops Short on New Body Armor
NewsMax.com Wires
Tuesday, Oct. 14, 2003
WASHINGTON -- Nearly one-quarter of the 130,000 U.S. troops in Iraq still have not been issued a new type of ceramic body armor strong enough to stop bullets fired from assault rifles. Delays in funding, production and shipping mean it will be December before all troops in Iraq will have the vests, which were introduced four years ago, military officials say.

$59,528 **per** San Clemente Loggerhead Shrike, but not enough funding for body armor for American soldiers. How would that make you feel if your son or daughter had been wounded or killed in Iraq? I can't even imagine, and our Congress should be held responsible. Where has good governance and common sense gone in this country?

Forty Dead Fish Cost Taxpayers $200 Million*
Motorists who commute across the Carquinez Straight near Benicia, California experience some of the most aggravating traffic in San Francisco's East Bay area. To ease
congestion, the Metropolitan Transportation Committee (MTC) and the California Department of Transportation (CALTRANS) planned to build a new bridge that would
nearly double the number of highway lanes. Unfortunately, bureaucratic and environmental problems have held up the project for years and added more than $600
million to the original cost. **In one case, approximately 40 dead fish cost taxpayers more than $200 million.**

Construction of the bridge requires that 8 1/2 feet wide steel tubes

*Competitive Enterprise Institute | 1899 L ST NW Floor 12, Washington, DC 20036 |

be driven deep into the ground with a large hydraulic hammer — a technique referred to as pile driving. The tubes, called pilings, are then drilled out and fi lled with concrete and steel to create the base of the bridge. Soon after pile driving began in November of 2002, construction officials noticed approximately 40 dead fi sh near the work site. CALTRANS officials immediately halted bridge construction while they consulted with National Marine Fisheries Service officials. It was determined that the process of pile driving sent sound waves through the water that burst the bladders of nearby fish. The dead fish were a common species, Striped Bass, which was introduced to the San Francisco Bay from the mid-Atlantic as a sport fish in the late 1800s. **No endangered species were harmed. Regardless, NMFS offi cials ordered the pile driving halted because they feared the project could possibly harm two fish, the Delta Smelt and SacramentoSplittail, both of which are listed as federally-protected threatened species.**
The splittail has subsequently been delisted by order of the U.S. District Court for the Eastern District of California. For three months, construction was stalled. Rod McMillan, a senior engineer for the project, estimated that delays cost between $100,000 and $200,000 per day. MTC submitted a plan that was approved by NMFS officials in February of 2003.

The plan would allow pile driving to continue during slack tide and would use a method in which air bubbles are continuously pumped around the piling to absorb much of the
sound waves. CALTRANS officials have said the process could add $200 million or more to the cost of the bridge. The project was first estimated to cost $286 million and be completed in 2000. Current estimates put the cost at $1.057 billion, with an estimated completion date of October 2007.
The 40 dead fish found at the construction site cost taxpayers $5 million per each dead fish.

Only $5,000,000.00 per fish, and they aren't even endangered! Is it any wonder our nation is running trillion dollar deficits? When anaylzing the cost of the Endangered Species Act of 1973, one can't just look at the annual budget of the U.S.Fish & Wildlife Service. You have to look at the billions of dollars they add on to the cost of building roads, home construction, hospitals, military preparedness, energy, dams, levees, etc.

Clean Energy a "No Go" Thanks to Environmental Concerns*

While communities in West Virginia, Pennsylvania and New York are trying to take advantage of wind power as a clean source of alternative energy, the U.S. Fish and
Wildlife Service is hindering their efforts. Why? Concerns that windmills might harm endangered birds and bats. It's a controversy pitting environmentalists against environmentalists with local residents the ultimate losers, thanks due to delays based on mere assumptions.

A study conducted by Fish and Wildlife Service biologists found that at least 400 bats died during their 2003 fall migration after collisions with the blades of 44 existing wind turbines on Backbone Mountain, West Virginia. Although the bat carcasses recovered were of mostly common species such as Red Bats, Eastern Pipstrelles and Hoary bats, FWS officials and environmental activists fear bat species protected by the Endangered Species Act — especially the endangered Indiana Bat — risk a similar fate. FWS biologist Albert Manville told Windpower Monthly, **"What's scary is that we may be finding only a small percentage of what's been killed."**

FWS officials are now demanding pre-construction wildlife studies for all future wind energy projects. The participation of energy companies in such studies remains voluntary in cases where the FWS can't prove endangered species may be at risk, but future wind projects are nonetheless affected because FWS biologists insist the studies must be conducted over a two-year period.

This means many planned wind energy projects in the region are significantly delayed. The developers of wind projects already under construction or even recently completed — such as FPL Energy, which built a 20-turbine project in Meyersdale, Pennsylvania — are also threatened with lawsuits because of claims that the previously conducted pre-construction studies were not thorough enough. Environmental groups contend the Meyersdale project's placement in the Indiana Bat's "migratory flight path" is enough to justify further study while industry experts dispute the claims. Michael R. Gannon, a bat biologist hired by FPL Energy to assess the environmental groups' complaints, concluded that, while the

*Shattered Dreams, 100 Stories of Government Abuse, National Center for Public Policy Research

majority of industry biologists do not believe the turbines pose a risk, the burden of proof still lies with the developers.

"Unless and until these data [resulting from a two-year study] are available," Gannon
wrote, "it should be assumed that this site is a flight path of the Indiana Bats and that
Indiana Bats will be killed." This is not an isolated case. Similar concerns are stalling the construction of wind turbines in New York. There, it's the prospect of birds, not bats, colliding with windmills that bog down wind energy developments. After New York state officials announced $100 million in private investment in wind power in 2002, ten towers in Wethersfield constructed in 2000 remain the only operational turbines in the western part of the state. As in West Virginia, the FWS is calling for a two-year study before a 34-turbine wind project spearheaded by Jasper Energy can proceed. The birds at issue in New York are threatened Bald Eagles and other birds of prey, which, environmental groups claim, use turbine airspace when migrating.

Jasper Energy maintains the potential harm to birds is "biologically insignificant,"pointing to a study it previously commissioned that placed the mortality risk for birdspassing through the area occupied by the wind turbines at one in 10,000.
Sources: Windpower Monthly (February 2, 2001), The Buffalo News (July 8, 2004),

The Indiana Bat

What is "scary" is not the number of bats being killed. What is scary, is that these environmentalists are even trying to stop "green" energy projects. Exactly what kind of energy do these people expect Americans to utilize?

ESA blamed for firefighter deaths

Written By: James M. Taylor
Published In: Environment & Climate News > October 2001
Publisher: The Heartland Institute

An investigation into the July 10 "30-mile fire" in central Washington state has uncovered that the Endangered Species Act (ESA) played a central role in the deaths of four young firefighters combating the blaze.

The U.S. Forest Service initially denied that environmental concerns had anything to do with the July 10 events, but then changed its story after evidence showed a largely contained fire had flared up to an uncontrolled emergency after **firefighters were denied necessary water due to concerns over endangered fish living in a local river.**

After the fire flared up, the four firefighters were cornered by flames in a narrow canyon and were killed by the flames before permission was finally granted to scoop water from the local river.

Salmon, trout delay water delivery

An elite firefighting crew had initially brought the fire under control and was awaiting the arrival of a promised water delivery helicopter to put a final conclusion to the flames. At 9:00 a.m., the specialists yielded the scene to a green "mop-up" crew of approximately 20 young firefighters. With the fire under control and the final water delivery due within the hour, the situation was deemed safe for the relatively inexperienced crew.

However, the helicopter was delayed several hours while Forest Service officials debated the environmental ramifications of scooping water from the nearby Chewuch River. The Chewuch River contains endangered salmon and trout, and Forest Service

officials feared scooping river water might accidentally scoop
some fish from the river as well. Forest Service officials debated
using Chewuch River water until 2:00 p.m., when final approval
was given.

While Forest Service officials delayed the promised water delivery
as they debated the environmental impact of using Chewuch
River water, the fire gained new life. The first delivery of water arrived at 3:00 p.m., too late to quench the rejuvenated fire. By 5:25
p.m. firefighters Tom Craven, 30, Devin Weaver, 21, Jessica Johnson, 19, and Karen Fitzpatrick, 18, had all died after flames cornered and then engulfed them in a narrow canyon.

Was deference to ESA required?

Forest Service Fire Chief Dale Bosworth attempted to absolve the
ESA of any responsibility for the firefighters' deaths. Bosworth
claimed that under standard procedure, firefighters are not con-
strained by the ESA when facing an emergency.

Jordan St. John, public affairs officer for the National Oceanic Atmospheric Association, agreed firefighters are not required to take
ESA considerations into account when human life is at risk. St.
John suggested the ESA was not to blame, but rather Forest Service dispatchers had misinterpreted Forest Service procedures.

What remains unclear, however, is whether the Forest Service's
standard ESA procedures required deference to ESA factors in a
situation like the 30-mile fire, where the blaze had been deemed
relatively safe and largely contained. **Evidence shows it was deference to the ESA during the relatively safe mop-up phase that
allowed the fire to regain its deadly form.**

At the time the Forest Service was debating the impact of taking
water from the Chewuch River, "there was no threat to life or
property, it was a mop up," concluded Jan Flatten, the environmental officer for the Okanogan and Wenatchee Natural forests.
"It was not until the fire blew up [that] it became a threat to life
and property."

**U.S. Representative Scott McInnis (R-Colorado) criticized defer-
ence to the ESA before the House subcommittee on Forests and**

Forest Health. "If we're dealing with human life at risk, I don't give a damn what the Endangered Species Act says," McInnis told reporters before addressing the subcommittee.

Democrats on the committee in turn blasted what they deemed a "politicization" of the tragedy.

"My best friend"

Ken Weaver, father of fallen firefighter Devin Weaver, said officials have told him privately there is no reason why his son should have died in the fire.

"He was my best friend," stated Weaver. He recalled how he and his son had recently watched the movie The Patriot, in which a father loses a son. "I turned to him and said 'I could never do that. I could never lose you.'"

"He trusted them and they weren't very careful with his life, and that makes me very angry and sad," stated Devin's mother, Barbara.

Earthjustice Legal Defense Fund staff attorney Todd True dismissed any role played by the ESA in the firefighters' deaths. "I don't think you can blame the Endangered Species Act for what a wildfire does," True stated.

Fox News reported the story slightly differently.

Endangered Fish Policy May Have Cost Firefighters' Lives

Firefighters struggling to contain a blaze in central Washington State that ultimately killed four of their own were hampered in their efforts by a federal policy to protect endangered fish, Fox News has learned.

Firefighters were unable to douse the deadly fire in Okanogan National Forest in Winthrop, Wash., in July because of delays in granting permission for fire-fighting helicopters to use water from nearby streams and rivers protected by the Endangered Species Act, according to sources close to the fire.

Firefighters Tom L. Craven, 30, Karen L. Fitzpatrick, 18, Devin A Weaver, 21, and Jessica L. Johnson, 19, burned to death while cowering under protective tents near the Chewuch River, home to protected species salmon and trout. Seventeen other firefighters survived the ordeal.

Forest Service policy in the Northwest requires that special permission be obtained before fire helicopters can dip into certain restricted rivers, lakes and streams. The fear is that the dippers could accidentally scoop up protected species of fish.

A 17-member team from the Forest Service and other federal agencies is now investigating whether the four firefighters died as a result of the policy.

Rep. Scott McInnis, R-Colo., chairman of the House Subcommittee on Forests & Forest Health, said the committee is also looking into allegations that environmental policy and bureaucracy were factors in the deaths.

AP
July 13, 2001: The Thirty Mile Fire burns in the Okanogan-Wenatchee National Forest.
Testifying before the committee Tuesday, USFS Fire Chief Dale Bosworth said that under standard procedure, firefighters would have used the Chewuch water to fight the fire and addressed any environmental violations or restrictions after the fire was extinguished. He said he was investigating why dispatch waited for approval before sending the helicopters.

"We get the water where we can get it and ask questions later," Bosworth said.

Forest Service District Commander John Newcom told Fox News last week that the Chewuch River's population of salmon, steelhead trout and bull trout are all considered when fighting fires, but insisted helicopter permission was never delayed or denied because of the policy.
But the USFS reversed that position Tuesday with the release of

a timeline of events that depicts the harrowing plight of a band of very young, inexperienced firefighters waiting desperately for helicopter relief that never came.

According to the timeline, the first team of firefighters, an elite crew called "Hot Shots," had contained what came to be known as the "30-mile fire" by the very early morning and requested a helicopter water drop at 5:30 a.m. However, they were told one would not be available until 10 a.m.

At 9 a.m., the Hot Shots were replaced with a young "mop-up" crew expecting helicopter relief to arrive within the hour. When the mop-up crew inquired about the missing helicopter just after noon, the dispatch office told the crew field boss that helicopters could not be used in the area because the Chewuch River contained endangered fish.

AP

July 12, 2001: A team investigates the deaths of four firefighters in the Thirty Mile Fire. Final permission to use Chewuch water wasn't granted until 2 p.m.

Jan Flatten, the environmental officer for the Okanogan and Wenatchee Natural forests, confirmed that environmental concerns caused crucial delays in dispatching the helicopter.

"At 12:08, the dispatch office ordered the helicopter," Flatten told Fox News. "However, because there are endangered species in the Chewuch River, they wanted to get permission from the district in order to dip into the river."

However, the dispatch office could not reach anyone at the district with the authority to approve the helicopter drop. Flatten said those authorities — Newcom, Fire Manager Peter Sodoquist and the Methow Valley biologist — were actually meeting during that time to approve an exemption to the policy.

"That time lag of about two hours was when they were trying to locate someone with the authority to tell them they could go ahead and take water out of the Chewuch River," Flatten said.

The USFS did not explain why the intra-agency team required to approve an exemption did not convene until 12 p.m., two hours after firefighters had been told the helicopter would be available.

Two former USFS firefighters familiar with the Thirty Mile Fire said getting permission to dip into the Chewuch caused the delays that led to the death of their colleagues.

"(The crew) were told that (the Chewuch River) was a protected water source and they needed to go through channels to use this water source," one of the former firefighters told Fox News.

The first load of helicopter water was dumped on the fire around 3 p.m., but the fire was by then out of control. An hour later, air tankers had to be turned back and the ground crew fled on foot to the river where they deployed their survival tents. **The crew was completely surrounded by the flames with no avenue for escape.**

Fox News' William LaJeunnesse and Robin Wallace contributed to this report.

Four young firefighters are dead for a reason.

Earthjustice Legal Defense Fund staff attorney Todd True **"dismissed any role played by the ESA in the firefighters' deaths.** "I don't think you can blame the Endangered Species Act for what a wildfire does," True stated. "

Facts are facts. Water was withheld from firefighters because of Bull Trout, Steelhead Trout, and Chinook Salmon, all living in the Chewuch River. None of these species are actually endangered. The Bull Trout, is, in fact, a Dolly Varden, which is plentiful. There are millions of Steelhead and Chinook salmon swimming all over the Pacific Ocean and rivers of the Northwest.

These four young people died because of a bad law. The attorney from Earthjustice doesn't give a damn, because he needs the Endangered Species Act of 1973 to win his legal cases against farmers, ranchers, construction projects, and other American economic activity that he sees destroying our planet.

This is an American tragedy.

"To the living we owe respect, but to the dead we owe only the truth."
Voltaire (1694-1778)

Financially-Vulnerable Ranchers Get Hurt First Under Environmentalist Group's Legal Strategy*

Jimmy Goss and his wife, Frances, may be forced to close their century-old cattle ranching operation because of a lawsuit filed by environmentalists. In June of 2002, a federal judge determined that the Gosses' cattle had chewed a significant amount of the vegetation in parts of the Sacramento Mountains, allegedly threatening the habitat of the Mexican Spotted Owl, a violation of the Endangered Species Act. As a result, the Gosses were forced to decrease their cattle herd from 553 to 330 and to move their herd to a neighbor's field at substantial cost. The elderly couple from Weed, New Mexico, is now paying about $2,000 more per month to graze their cattle.

The Forest Guardians, a group based out of Santa Fe, New Mexico that claims America's public lands have been 'grazed to the bone' by livestock, filed the complaint against the Gosses. The Guardians are represented by the Earthjustice Legal Defense Fund (formerly the Sierra Club Legal Defense Fund), which regularly files lawsuits opposing the use of federal lands for ranching. Earthjustice lawsuits often claim that 'excessive' grazing damages plant and animal habitats. When Earthjustice and the Guardians triumph in court, it means that ranchers who raise cattle on federal land can be forced to reduce the number of cattle they raise or move their business elsewhere.

A 2002 article by Jim Carlton in the Wall Street Journal described the Guardians' legal strategy this way:

Hardline environmentalists, the Guardians are leaders of the zero-grazing movement, which aims to clear every head of cattle off the 265 million acres of wildlands the U.S. government owns in 11

*Shattered Dreams, 100 Stories of Government Abuse, National Center for Public Policy Research

Western states. The Guardians use an unusual legal approach. First, they track down ranchers who have permits to feed their livestock on federal land for just pennies a head. The next step is to sue under the U.S. Endangered Species Act or other laws, accusing the government of mismanaging the land where the ranchers' cows graze. If the Guardians win in court, or if the government settles, the number of cows a rancher is allowed to graze with his permit is cut. That hands the Guardians a double victory: Not only does the land get a breather, but the rancher has to pay much more to feed his displaced cows on private land. Indeed, the Guardians' most controversial tactic is to single out the financially vulnerable — ranchers who have used their permits as collateral for bank loans, a common form of financing for small ranching operations.

"We want to put the squeeze on ranchers to get off the land," says John Horning, the coordinator of the Guardians' antigrazing campaign. "If some ranchers go out of business along the way, so be it." Facing Forest Guardian pressure, Jimmy Goss is worried about the future of his ranching business. Over a century ago, his grandfather came to the Lincoln National Forest and began the cattle-grazing operation, which became a family legacy. "My granddaddy worked to give us this [settlement]," he explains, "and I'm busting my behind so my grandkids can have it too." The prospect of losing the family business is a real concern. The amount of beef the Gosses sold in 2002 was 100,000 pounds less than in the previous year.

The harm to family businesses is apparently not a concern of the Forest Guardians.
The group proudly claims to have cleared 5,000 head of cattle from two million acres of federal land. The Guardians have won 18 lawsuits so far concerning federal grazingpermits and have many other suits pending.
Sources: Wall Street Journal (November 1, 2002), Mountain Monthly (May 2000), Albuquerque Journal (November 22, 2002), Jimmy and Frances Goss

And the average American wonders why the price of beef is skyrocketing in this country? You have the environmental movement to thank, led by American ranching hating communists like the Forest Guardians. "Cattle Free in '93" was the slogan of these environmentalists trying to get ranchers off of Federal land. They didn't quite get it done, but they are making great progress. For the record, the Forest Guardians claim that public lands are "grazed to the bones" is an absolute lie. Just walk around the mountains here in western Montana, where I live, and often hunt, and the grass is up to my waste, and cattle grazing are an everyday sight, even miles from a road. The idiots at the Forest Guardians claim cattle grazing is affecting the Mexican Spotted Owl. Here, from the Defenders of Wildlife website is a description of the owl's habitat.

"Mexican spotted owls inhabit forested mountains and canyons with mature trees that create high, closed canopies, which are good for nesting. They prefer old-growth forests, and the distribution of spotted owls correlates with the distribution of forest land that has been protected from destruction and logging. Spotted owls remain in one place unless harsh winters and heavy snows force them to move downslope in mountainous regions. In milder areas, winter ranges may expand to increase prey availability. They are described as "perch and pounce" predators, typically locating their prey from an elevated perch by sight or sound, then pouncing on the prey and capturing it with their talons."

The last time I checked, cows still ate grass. I have not seen in any scientific literature to date where the pesky cattle have started munching on "mature trees that create high, closed canopies, which are good for nesting." In fact, "high, closed canopies" means less growth of grass, and less feed for cattle, and so, they graze elsewhere.

I believe that Congress should repeal The Endangered Species Act of 1973. If anti-American organizations like the Forest Guardians, Defenders of Wildlife, and the Earthjustice Legal Defense Fund **"go out of business along the way, so be it."**

_Man Harassed for Protecting Wife, Children from Wolf*

A secret government operation. An innocent victim. A cover-up and conspiracy. It may sound like the plot of a suspense novel, but **it's a real-life tragedy** that plagues Richard Humphrey to this day. In March of 1998, the U.S. Fish and Wildlife Service began releasing endangered Mexican Wolves that were bred in captivity into designated areas of Arizona and New Mexico. Their intent was to re-

*Shattered Dreams, 100 Stories of Government Abuse, National Center for Public Policy Research

store natural ecosystems to public lands. Citing the dangers wolves pose to cattle, livestock and humans, the New Mexico Cattle Growers Association and other livestock organizations sued the FWS, hoping to stop the release.

Environmental groups, however, threatened to sue if the wolves were not released. **This prompted the Department of the Interior to release the wolves in secret**, allegedly to avoid criticism for giving in to environmentalists' demands while the livestock organizations' lawsuit was pending. Because the wolf release program was a clandestine operation, Richard Humphrey and his family didn't know that the wolves were released in the Gila National Forest in southwestern New Mexico. Had they known, they would not have been camping there on April 28, 1998.

A knowledgeable camper and outdoorsman, **Humphrey emerged from his tent to find several wolves with radio collars mauling his dog, Buck**. Humphrey began shouting in an attempt to scare the wolves away without harming them. One of the wolves became frightened and ran off, but another charged toward his wife and two daughters. Fearing for the lives of his family, Humphrey shot and killed the wolf. Though Buck needed immediate medical attention, Humphrey still followed all of the mandated procedures after harming an endangered species: he quickly alerted the proper authorities and recounted his story to both state and federal wildlife agents.

Over the next six weeks, Humphrey was repeatedly questioned and interrogated, both over the telephone and in person. Finding nothing illegal about the situation, FWS offi cials did not charge Humphrey with any crime. This decision prompted a firestorm of harassment directed at Humphrey by environmental groups and the media. Bobbie Holaday of Preserve America's Wolves demanded in the Arizona Republic, **"We've got to make an example of this guy."** The Wildlife Damage Group printed and distributed bumper stickers that read, **"Real men don't kill wolves."** Before any of the facts of the case were made public, the Center for Biological Diversity put intense pressure on DOI officials to indict Humphrey. Inflammatory remarks were repeatedly quoted and reported as fact by the Tucson Citizen, a prominent area newspaper. While Humphrey was never indicted or prosecuted for defending his family, his name still appears on environmental websites as an enemy of their cause.

With wolves threatening both humans and cattle, communities in New Mexico and Arizona have lobbied the federal government to end the wolf release program to no avail. Environmental groups are continuously threatening litigation, while DOI officials have not stopped the release program. Wolf attacks on livestock, pets and humans have become increasingly common since the release program began in 1995.

> "Each man must for himself alone decide what is right and what is wrong, which course is patriotic and which isn't. You cannot shirk this and be a man. To decide against your conviction is to be an unqualified and unexcusable traitor, both to yourself and to your country, let men label you as they may."
> Mark Twain

U.S. Fish & Wildlife acted properly in not charging Mr. Humphrey with a crime. It is a case, in front of a jury, that they had zero chance of winning. The crime was their illegal introduction of the wolves in the first place. As shown elsewhere, Mexican Grey wolves are exactly the same as wolves found anywhere else in the world, Canis Lupis. Wolves are not currently endangered, nor have they ever been. The introduction of wolves into New Mexico and Arizona is all about forcing ranchers off of Federal Land: it has nothing to do with the recovery of a "species."

The Catron County Commission on Thursday issued a "24 Hour Notice of Intent to Remove Mexican wolf Durango AF924" to U.S. Fish and Wildlife Service.*

By Mountain Mail staff
SOCORRO, New Mexico (STPNS) —

"This family and the County have tried to get FWS to remove that wolf for two months," said Ed Wehrheim, chairman of the Catron County Commission.

*http://www.stpns.net/view_article.html?articleId=42749779728634998

The female wolf, AF924, has been stalking the ranch house of Mark and Debbie Miller in a remote area of the Gila National Forest since its release into the wild in late April. Catron County manager Bill Aymar said federal wolf biologists have documented two cattle kills by AF924. A third incident would require the agency to remove the wolf.

"Why would this group of people not be interested in removing her if she's in proximity to this ranch, to calves and cows?" Aymar said. **"Their own rules say three strikes and you're out. This program isn't even fair to the wolf. If she gets that third strike, we don't even have to argue whether she's hanging out. According to their rules, she's done."**

The county has issued two letters of demand for removal of the wolf. **The first cited the wolf's past history of depredation and a report that the wolf had bitten a human.** The second letter cited six incidents involving problem behavior over six weeks, **all of which were reported to, investigated and confirmed by the agency,** Aymar said.

"They're not following their own rules about these habituated wolves hanging around homes and presenting a danger," Aymar said.

The Mexican wolf recovery program guidelines provide for the removal of nuisance or problem Mexican wolves when hazing and other methods prove inadequate. In the county's 24 Hour Notice, Aymar wrote that no action has been taken by any agency to "respond to the demand for removal, nor has any adequate action been taken by your agency or any other agency to reduce the risk to humans from AF924."

When the family and the ranch owner each finally appealed in writing to the Catron County Commission to provide the protection they needed from the wolves, the County Commission sent the 24 Hour Notice to FWS and all the agencies involved in the wolf program.

The agency's only response was to send law enforcement officers to observe the County's Wolf Interaction Investigator Jess Carey, who is attempting to protect the family from any more incidents with this problem wolf.

"The Endangered Species Act supercedes county ordinances," Fish and Wildlife spokeswoman Victoria Fox said. **"Any action violating the law would result in prosecution."**

She said law enforcement personnel are on the scene to make sure there's no violation of federal law.

"We continue to work with the county, and the presence of a field team is to insure that the wolves are deterred from any other interaction with livestock," Fox said. "We are there to take measures to move them away from human interaction or livestock. We're trying to achieve that balance in Catron County."

Fox also said the agency has offered a variety of tools to ranchers, including radio receivers, flag fences and radio activated guard boxes.

"All those options have been offered," Fox said. "We're doing everything we can and keep open communication."

Aymar said the agency isn't doing enough to protect ranchers and their livestock or to protect the wolves.

"They're not being responsive to the needs of the citizens by any means," Aymar said. "They're just waiting to see what the county will do."

Carey has set up camp outside the family's house and intends to trap the wolf and turn it over to the agency. Aymar said the **law enforcement officers are waiting for a court injunction for the County and the County's investigator to cease and desist the trapping.**

"Something semi-unique to this situation is that this family lives in a little cabin with an outhouse," Aymar said. "If you have to walk between the house and the outhouse in the middle of the night with a wolf hanging around, it's not a good thing. It's easy for some in Santa Fe who walks down the hall to the bathroom to be critical." Aymar said he doesn't expect Fish and Wildlife personnel to respond to the demand letter.

"If the Fish and Wildlife Service was to go out there and snatch up 924 and take her away, that would be tantamount to the feds saying that the Catron County ordinance is a valid legal issue," he said. "I don't think they're going to do that."

Just another poor family, in a poor region of the country, being bullied by the United States Fish & Wildlife Service. The Endangered Species Act of 1973 supercedes the local law of Catron County, New Mexico. But there is such a thing as natural law, where a man has the "inalienable right to seek "Life, Liberty, and the Pursuit of Happiness." That is the very foundation of our nation.

"We all declare for liberty; but in using the same word we do not all mean the same thing. With some the word liberty may mean for each man to do as he pleases with himself, and the product of his labor; while with others, the same word may mean for some men to do as they please with other men, and the product of other men's labor. Here are two, not only different, but incompatible things, called by the same name - liberty. And it follows that each of the things is, by the respective parties, called by two different and incompatible names - liberty and tyranny."
Abraham Lincoln, April 18, 1864 -

Tree Farm May be Sold to Developer to Protect Nonexistent Salmon*

Endangered species restrictions ostensibly to protect salmon are keeping tree farmers Greg and Sue Pattillo from being able to use so much of their land that they **are considering selling it to developers,** a move that will harm all of the plant and animal species that thrive on their property. **As for salmon: They've never lived on the property and never will, government regulations not withstanding.**

There are two designated creeks on the Pattillos' 700-acre tree farm in Raymond, Washington. Although considered creeks, they are lit-

*Shattered Dreams, 100 Stories of Government Abuse, National Center for Public Policy Research

tle more than strips of mud that are devoid of fish of any kind. Because they are designated "creek," however, under the Forest and Fish Law of 1999, the Pattillos are prohibited from harvesting timber up to 200 feet from them. Government officials, environmental activists, timber industry representatives and Indian tribal leaders negotiated these restrictions under Washington State's Forest and Fish Law in an attempt to protect salmon populations. While the agreement places buffer zones around streams based on factors such as width, slope and flow, it does not take the actual presence and viability of salmon — or lack of same — into consideration. In 2003, the Pattillos estimated that the buffer zones had effectively locked-up 40 percent of their tree farm. An accurate assessment of their losses requires a professional (and expensive) survey conducted by a forester, a financial impossibility for them at this point.

The Pattillos run what they consider to be an environmentally-sensitive tree farm on private land. They cut down less than two percent of their timber each year and claim to have more trees on their land today now than they did in 1988. **Their land is home to many bears, cougars, elk, deer and birds.** But this may change, as the Pattillos' business has been hurt to the degree that they may sell their land to developers. "We know the environment's important, but this is going to have the wrong effect," says Greg. "The sad part is that people are getting discouraged and want to sell their land." In an effort to save their tree farm, in April 2005 the Pattillos agreed to a new "alternative plan" to the Forest and Fish Law. The plan exempts small timberland owners who harvest less than two million board feet of timber per year. Under the plan, the Pattillos are allowed commercial thinning of trees closer to streams than otherwise would be permitted under the Forest and Fish Law agreement. However, further harvesting on the exempted land is curtailed after thinning down to 100 trees per acre.

The exemption increased the land available for Pattillos' harvesting business, but Pattillo does not see it as advantageous for his business in the long term. **Because the couple will not be allowed full management on much of their own property, the Pattillos say the alternative plan will not necessarily save their tree farm. It may only provide a "stay of execution."**
Sources: Alliance for America, Greg Pattillo, Sue Pattillo, Tidepool.org news service (September 2, 2003)

"Executing" businesses, all across America, is exactly what the Endangered Species Act of 1973 accomplishes best. The Patillo's tree farm is home to all kinds of wildlife. Isn't that what the Endangered Species Act was about, wildlife? Clearly, that is what Congress and the American public thought. Perhaps, in the beginning. Now, most certainly, it is no longer about wildlife, but about governmental control of Americans and private property. In effect, it turns all private land into public land, without compensation.

As far as the Patillo's hope that they might sell their 700 acre farm for developing? With habitat for non-existing salmon, a builder will have to go through the E.S.A. "s "incidental take" process, in order to secure the proper building permits. As you will learn in Chapter 7, that is a paperwork nightmare, not to mention hundreds of thousands of dollars and years of heartache. In fact, the government has rendered the Patillo's farm virtually worthless.

But to paraphrase the environmentalist at Forest Guardians in New Mexico: "If a few tree farmers go out of business, so be it."

ESA Protection Measures Go Too Far, Home Builders Charge*

WASHINGTON, July 22 /PRNewswire/ -- The National Association of Home Builders (NAHB) has joined in a lawsuit that calls into question the U.S. Fish and Wildlife Service's protection of a California fly that, by the government's own admission, is doomed to extinction.

The lawsuit is in response to the government's protection measures for the Delhi Sands Flower-Loving Fly, which have included forcing San Bernardino County to move a proposed hospital 250 feet and fence in eight acres of fly preserve thus adding more than $3.5 million to the price of the hospital; preventing the County from making improvements to an emergency road leading to the hospital; and attempting to either close a major commuter highway during fly mating season, or drop the speed limit for that highway to 15 mph.

According to papers filed by NAHB with the United States District Court, in the case of the Delhi Sands Flower-Loving Fly, **the federal**

*http://www.thefreelibrary.com

government is making species protection a higher priority than emergency road access to a hospital.

"This is another example of the Endangered Species Act gone haywire," said NAHB President Randy Smith, a home builder from Walnut Creek, Calif. "We should be protecting species that truly need protection, and we should be doing it in ways that make sense."

In the lawsuit, filed in federal court in March along with the California Building Industry Association, the Building Industry Legal Defense Foundation, the California cities of Fontana and Colton, and San Bernardino County, NAHB asks the court to prevent the Department of Interior and the Fish and Wildlife Service (FWS) from enforcing the provisions of the ESA that prevent home builders and other citizens from using their private property. Under the ESA, certain activities which affect species' habitat, such as construction, are considered species "takings," and are illegal.

The fly, whose only known habitats are in San Bernardino and Riverside counties, was added to the endangered species list by FWS in September of 1993. Since then, the federal government has placed prohibitions on local landowners and on local governments. Despite noting that the fly will probably be extinct by the turn of the century, the federal government has taken some extraordinary steps to protect it.

One of these steps was forcing San Bernardino County to move the building "footprint" for a proposed hospital so that fly habitat for an estimated 6-8 flies would not be disturbed. The medical center was also required to fence in "fly preserve" areas. And, **the federal government did not allow the County to improve emergency access to the hospital, despite local officials' concerns that without the improvements, ambulances would be hindered in their efforts to get patients to the hospital in a speedy manner.**

The federal government also attempted to shut down Interstate 10, one of California's busiest highways, so that the fly's mating habits would not be disturbed. Another option, the federal government told local authorities, was dropping the road's speed limit during August and September to 15 mph. Eventually, the federal government rescinded these demands.

Local landowners have also felt the impact of these protection measures and have not been compensated for loss of development rights, NAHB says in the lawsuit.

"San Bernardino County's battle over the fly illustrates the problems the Endangered Species Act causes local governments and home builders. Preventing a local government from enhancing public safety so that fly habitat is not disturbed is senseless," Smith said.

His sentiments were echoed by Frank Williams, executive officer of the Building Industry Association of Southern California's Baldy View Region in Rancho Cucamonga, who said, "The federal government's position in this case is outrageous and their **lack of concern for the health and safety of our citizens, and obsession with the fly, is immoral."**

The federal government has argued that NAHB's request should be denied. "The balance of hardships and the public interest dictate ... that the injunction be denied," and that FWS fly protection measures continue. A decision in the case is expected during the summer.

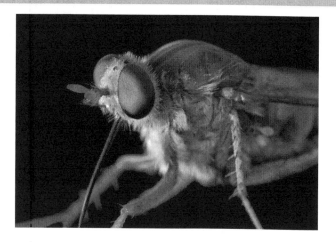

The Delhi Sands Flower Loving Fly. It took 4 months for photographer Joel Sartore to get a permit to take this photo. Several Federal agents stood by, and a federally permitted fly handler caught the fly unharmed, gassed it with CO_2, then let it wake up.

"The Delhi Sands Flower- Loving Fly, which is protected by the federal Endangered Species Act, has stalled or altogether blocked dozens of projects that would have brought jobs, revenue and much needed residential development to the region. The U. S. Fish and Wildlife Service listed the Delhi Sands Fly as an endangered species in 1993. Just how many of the flies exist is impossible to know or even estimate because they only emerge from their underground burrows once a year to mate, sip nectar and then quickly die. The entire life-span of a Delhi Sands Fly is only two days. The fly's habitat — the sand dues of the Inland Empire — is fragmented over approximately 40 square miles. The actual usable habitat may be as small as 1,200 acres."*

Any rational human being, reading the above article says to themselves "Please tell me you are kidding me." 6-8 flies, and we have to move an entire hospital? Are you serious. Suppose the flies decide to fly to 250 feet over to where you've just moved the hospital. Suppose a Delta Sands Flower Loving Fly starts flying around the operating room, in the middle of open heart surgery. Does the U.S. Fish & Wildlife want the doctors to get an "incidental take" permit, before the head nurse crushes the fly into Delta Sands Flower Loving Fly heaven?

Hospitals have what they call "Emergency Rooms," where ambulances come speeding in with people who are deathly ill or have suffered a terrible accident. Saving human lives is what hospitals are designed to accomplish. Picture yourself in the back of the ambulance with your deathly ill little girl. The ambulance driver tells you he has to slow down to 15 mph, because it is fornicating season for the Delhi Flower Sands Loving Fly.

This is a family friendly book, and so I won't speculate what the distraught father says to the ambulance driver. I know this. If it was my little girl, the distinct population *Homo sapiens ambulancia driverus* might have to be added to the Endangered Species list.

Species Flys In Face of Continued Development*

Ever since the Delhi Sands flower-loving fly was listed as an endangered species in 1993, it has been a poster child for opponents of the federal Endangered Species Act. Now, the fly is the latest endangered species to take center stage in the continually urbanizing

* California Planning & Development Report: http://www.cp-dr.com/node/1443

Inland Empire.

Other controversial endangered species, such as the Quino Check-erspot Butterfly and the gnatcatcher, can at least win support for aesthetic reasons.

But a fly? Few people are easily convinced of the redeeming value or beauty of flies.

Environmentalists and the U.S. Fish & Wildlife Service argue, how-ever, that there is more than meets the eye in this argument. For one thing, it's an unusual insect, a 1.25-inch creature with green eyes that hovers like a hummingbird during its brief life span. Saving the fly also saves the Delhi Sands, a habitat with unique plant life. "It's not just the fly, it's the ecosystems on which it depends," said Fish & Wildlife Biologist Mary Beth Woulfe. Preserve land for the fly, and other animals of the ecosystem, such as the Jerusalem cricket, the meadowmark butterfly, and the legless lizard, are also pre-served.

In recent months, the fly has become an issue in development proj-ects in the cities of Rialto, Colton, Ontario and Fontana, and in un-incorporated San Bernardino County. In adjacent Riverside County, the Endangered Habitats League is litigating over development in possible fly habitat. Local government officials contend they do not clearly know what they are supposed to do and are upset the fly is stalling development projects.

The flap over the Delhi Sands flower-loving fly might have been avoided if either Riverside or San Bernardino County had adopted a regional multi-species habitat conservation plan. These plans are designed to set aside land for endangered species while providing developers certainty as to where they can build. The Clinton ad-ministration has supported such planning as a way to avoid fights over a single species. Both counties have such plans underway but are years from completing the documents.

Riverside County's plan could take two to five years to finish. San Bernardino County's multi-species plan received funding authori-zation in January, and is could be done in three years, according to Randy Scott, the county's planning manager for the species plan. In the interim, there have been court battles and heated rhetoric.

Some cities in the San Bernardino area hired a lobbyist in Washington D.C. to exert influence on the matter there, Scott said.

The planning official said the fly has a "chilling effect" on development in the county. "In a lot of instances, people are looking elsewhere," he said. But some government officials are saying, "Here it is, we've got to deal with it.

So get on with it."

That is happening in meetings between local governments and Fish & Wildlife Service officials, where an interim habitat conservation plan for the fly is being crafted. San Bernardino Congressman George Brown, who died recently, brought the parties together for a first meeting in April. Since then, the local governments in San Bernardino County have offered various sites totaling about 400 acres throughout the county for fly habitat. The Fish & Wildlife Service is expected to announce whether it will agree to the plan by the end of August.

"We're not really optimistic that they'll agree," Scott said.

But some kind of agreement is eventually expected.

"I'm hopeful we can come to terms with the cities," said Woulfe, of the Fish & Wildlife Service. The fly's habitat once covered 40 square miles, but the fly is now located in only a few areas. Woulfe said there is not a good population estimate, although few scientists think there are more than a few hundred of the flies. The largest population is thought to be in the city of Colton.

Listing the fly as an endangered species led to additional costs of building San Bernardino County's medical center, when fly habitat was discovered on the site. But in a suit brought by the county, Fontana, Colton and building groups, a federal court upheld the Fish & Wildlife Service restrictions on building the hospital in fly habitat, and the U.S. Supreme Court refused to consider the matter on appeal. The fly is now again affecting the hospital, Scott said, because projects for both traffic and flood control mitigation there could disturb fly habitat.

In recent months, the city of Fontana has been a focal point of fly-related activity as it tries to expand its manufacturing base. (See

CP&DR, July 1999.) Two property owners have stopped paying taxes on about 400 acres at the Empire Center while a study determines whether the land is home to the fly. Because of the delinquent tax payments, about $46 million in municipal bonds could go into default, affecting about 9,000 bondholders.

Also in Fontana, the Fish & Wildlife Service sued Angeles Block Co. in May over construction on part of a 90-acre parcel. The lawsuit was settled with an agreement to set aside about 15 acres for fly habitat. A related lawsuit over the site by the Endangered Habitats League is also expected to be settled.
"It certainly has caused delays," said Rialto City Attorney Robert A. Owens. "I'm hopeful the federal government can do something which will enable local jurisdictions to apply rational rules to provide for orderly development, while also protecting endangered species such as the fly. It's frustrating from a public agency perspective not having a clear set of rules."

Dan Silver, EHL executive director, said the group has also sued Riverside County, which approved a negative declaration for a 50-acre warehouse project. Consultants hired by the developer determined the land was not occupied by the fly, he said. Silver said that while it could not be proven that the land is Delhi Sands habitat, the area is a recovery area for the fly.

The fly is also an issue in ongoing EHL litigation against the city of Ontario over its plans to annex an agricultural preserve, he said.

Noting that several thousand acres are slated for development in just one of the county's enterprise zones, Silver said saving the fly will not "make much of a dent in development. ... It's a problem that's imminently solvable."

Is it any wonder the California economy is a train wreck? Just read this article carefully: "the chilling effect on development".... "additional costs of building"...."The city of Fontana has been a focal point of fly-related activity as it tries to expand its manufacturing base"...."Both counties have such plans underway but are years from completing the documents"..... "In a lot of instances, people are looking elsewhere," ....."Two property owners have stopped paying taxes on about 400 acres at the Empire Center while a study determines whether the land is home to the fly. Because of the delinquent tax payments, about $46 million in municipal bonds could go into default, affecting about 9,000 bondholders."

If America goes into default, you can place the blame directly on the Endangered Species Act of 1973, and the people with the authority to change the act, the United States Congress.

More Secure Border is for the Birds*

As part of the "Illegal Immigration and Immigrant Responsibility Act of 1996," Congress mandated better fortifications along a 14-mile stretch of the U.S.-Mexico border south of San Diego. Construction was completed on nine miles of the new triple fence border, but the remainder of the project has been blocked by the California Coastal Commission, a state agency that manages conservation and development along the coast. **It issued a report in February of 2004 stating that a series of more secure border fences would threaten an "environmentally sensitive habitat" of two endangered birds: the Least Bell's Vireo, Southwestern Willow Flycatcher and the threatened Coastal California Gnatcatcher.**

The Bureau of Customs and Border Protection (CBP), now a division of the Department of Homeland Security, was charged by Congress with constructing the second and third line of fences in an effort to curb the stream of illegal aliens crossing into the U.S. south of San Diego. The San Diego border sector stretches from the Pacific Ocean to the base of the San Ysidro Mountains. The project, called "Operation Gatekeeper," is also meant to safeguard area military facilities — especially the San Diego Naval Station — from terrorists. Lights, sensors and surveillance technology have been installed, and a 130-foot wide patrol road between two of the fences ensures that border agents can safely make U-turns at high speeds.

Mike Nicley, chief patrol agent for the San Diego sector, told the Washington Times that the San Diego border sector has historically been violated by illegal aliens more than any other border area. Since Operation Gatekeeper was enacted, border arrests are "down to a trickle." Completion of the project, however, is being stalled by the California Coastal Commission. In justifying its February 2004 rejection of the final portion of the CBP's fence construction, the Commission concluded it "does not properly balance border patrol

*Shattered Dreams, 100 Stories of Government Abuse, National Center for Public Policy Research

and resource protection needs." **A biological study claims the project would harm <u>one pair</u> of Least Bell's Vireos and another pair of Southwestern Willow Flycatchers by removing 2.57 acres of brush they feed and nest in from their overall habitat.** <u>Three</u> **Coastal California Gnatcatchers would also be harmed** by the removal of nearly 45 acres of coastal sage scrub in its habitat. The Commission also objects to the use of fill in the "Smuggler's Gulch" area to construct a safe patrol road. **Three Border Patrol agents have been killed in accidents along the area's steep terrain in recent years.**

"From our office's perspective, we think homeland security is a top concern," said Gary Winuk, deputy director of the California Office of Homeland Security. But the California Coastal Commission argues that border protection "must be balanced against habitat protection."

Once again, environmentalists put bird life (in this case, one pair of Least Bell's Vireos and three Coastal California Gnatcatchers, before America's homeland security. Three border patrol officers have already lost their lives in this area, which the California Office of Homeland Security is trying, desperately, to make more secure. Just a personal opinion here, but I would be happy to trade 1000 American enviro-Nazis for a single, hard working, legal, Mexican family man. A program like that, over the next 20 years, would do wonders for turning around the American economy. Unfortunately, it would create even more pressure on immigration, as the Mexican economy would be in the toilet.

School Board Pays $400,000 to Protect Area that May or May Not Contain Endangered Species*

With each new school year more students are brought into the already overcrowded West Chester Area School District in West Chester, Pennsylvania. Administrators hoped that building Bayard Rustin High School would reduce class sizes, shorten commutes and create a better learning environment for West Chester students. But government officials were forced to add $400,000 to the construction costs of the proposed school to protect a federally threatened turtle that might not even be in the area.

*<u>Shattered Dreams, 100 Stories of Government Abuse</u>, National Center for Public Policy Research

The Bog Turtle

Heavy rains in the spring of 2003 expanded existing wetlands near the proposed school, engulfing new terrain that included the proposed location of some of the school's sewage pipes. While regulators from the Pennsylvania Department of Environmental Protection did not complain about the intrusion of the pipes onto the wetlands, they did have a problem with how the pipes may affect the habitat of the threatened Bog Turtle. Yet no one knew if the turtle was actually there.

To determine if Bog Turtles lived in the wetlands abutting the school's property, the school district first conducted tests that concluded that the area was conducive to the turtles' habitat. Another experiment was necessary actually to find out if the reptiles are there. This test, however, can only be conducted in May when it has not rained for 48 hours and the soil and water temperatures are both above 55 degrees. To the dismay of school officials, no day in May 2003 met these stringent requirements. Without a complete "turtle analysis," school administrators cannot build the school as originally planned. Officials had two options: either wait until May 2004 (hoping weather conditions allow the test to be conducted) or reroute the sewage lines around the potential turtle habitat.

Re-routing would cost approximately $400,000. Delaying construction any further would be even more expensive, and the modifications had already pushed back the opening of the school from 2005 to 2006. Because the other two high schools in the area cannot accommodate more students, additional delays were infeasible. **So the decision was made to spend the $400,000, so the school could open in 2006.** Some of the $400,000 will come from contingency funds for the new high school, but these reserve monies cannot accommodate the entire expense. **Instead, money is being diverted from other places — perhaps from the budget for books or computers — to protect turtles that may never be proven to exist.**

The school board had to move forward, despite the expenditure of $400,000 in taxpayer money. Under the circumstances, do you blame them? A full blown "incidental take" permit could cost years of delay and hundreds of thousands of dollars. The kids needed to go to school. Imagine that, putting the kids before the bog turtles.

Both my wife and my step mother went to West Chester University, and I grew up not far from there. Turtles are a common sight, sunning themselves on rocks along swamps and creek beds. I have no doubt that they would have utilized the sewer pipe going across "their" swamp the same as they do rocks. Sit on one when they need warmth, and use it for shade when they need to cool off (reptiles are ectotherms.)

These are just "isolated" incidences, right? Just the odd story, here and there, where the well meaning government screwed up, right? Googling up "Bog Turtle", I came across the website of Amy S. Greene, an environmental consultant in nearby New Jersey. Her website describes her company as follows:

"AMY S. GREENE ENVIRONMENTAL CONSULTANTS, INC. is certified as a Small, Woman Owned, Disadvantaged Business and Emerging Small Business (DBE, WBE, SBE, ESBE) with agencies in multiple states:"

This "Small, Woman Owned, Disadvantaged" has done, according to her website:

"Amy S. Greene Environmental Consultants, Inc. has completed over 3,400 projects within 11 states. ASGECI has provided environmental services to public clients at the federal, state, and local level and to private sector clients."

Her employees include "U.S. Fish and Wildlife Service Recognized Bog Turtle Surveyors."

The U.S. Department of Labor, in 2008, says there are 85,900 Environmental Scientists and Specialists in the United States labor force, 44% of whom work for the government. If a "small, woman owned, disadvantaged" Environmental Consulting Firm has done 3400 of these projects, and there are tens of thousands of these Environmental Scientists across the country, how many projects are we talking about, and what is the cost to the American taxpayer and our economy?

Here is what the U.S. Government Department of Labor says:

Job Outlook*

"Job prospects. In addition to job openings due to growth, there will be additional demand for new environmental scientists to replace those who retire, advance to management positions, or change careers. **Job prospects for environmental scientists will be good, particularly for jobs in State and local government.**

During periods of economic recession, layoffs of environmental scientists and specialists may occur in consulting firms, particularly when there is a slowdown in new construction; layoffs are much less likely in government."

Follow the Money

The more endangered species we have, the more work for the environmental scientists. This includes both governmental and non-governmental scientists. It is a closed loop, which can't be broken. I fear for my country when our government is borrowing forty cents of every dollar it spends, but can afford somebody in the government that can certify somebody else, in the private sector, as a "United States Fish and Wildlife Recognized Bog Turtle Surveyor."

"While politicians come and go, bureaucrats are forever."
Rob Rivett, Pacific Legal Foundation

*United State Bureau of Labor Statistics, http://www.bls.gov/oco/ocos311.htm

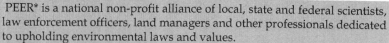

PEER* is a national non-profit alliance of local, state and federal scientists, law enforcement officers, land managers and other professionals dedicated to upholding environmental laws and values.

Public employees are a unique force working for environmental enforcement. In the ever-changing tide of political leadership, these front-line employees stand as defenders of the public interest within their agencies and as the first line of defense against the exploitation and pollution of our environment. Their unmatched technical knowledge, long-term service and proven experiences make these professionals a credible voice for meaningful reform.

PEER works nation-wide with government scientists, land managers, environmental law enforcement agents, field specialists and other resource professionals committed to responsible management of America's public resources. Resource employees in government agencies have unique responsibilities as stewards of the environment. PEER supports those who are courageous and idealistic enough to seek a higher standard of environmental ethics and scientific integrity within their agency. Our constituency represents one of the most crucial and viable untapped resources in the conservation movement.

Objectives of PEER

Organize a broad base of support among employees within local, state and federal resource management agencies.
Monitor natural resource management agencies by serving as a "watch dog" for the public interest.
Inform the administration, Congress, state officials, media and the public about substantive environmental issues of concern to PEER members.
Defend and strengthen the legal rights of public employees who speak out about issues concerning natural resource management and environmental protection. Provide free legal assistance if and when necessary.

The above is from the Public Employees for Environmental Responsibility website. It demonstrates the closed loop which includes the scientists, the bureaucrats, the enforcement agents, and the land managers, all pushing the environmentalist agenda. You see, they know what is best for us. When unelected bureaucrats are given this much power, America is doomed, unless we change things.

*http://www.peer.org/about/index.php

Regulations Deny Elderly Handicapped Woman Access to Home**

John Taylor, an 80-year-old resident of Mount Vernon, Virginia, can not build a small modular home on his lot to accommodate his wheelchair-bound wife because the U.S. Fish and Wildlife Service (FWS) says it harms a bald eagle nest located 90 feet away.

The FWS says it would allow Taylor to construct the home but only if he agrees to several onerous conditions:

1) Contribute money to a salmon restoration plan because eagles like to eat salmon;

2) Build two eagle platforms;

3) Contribute money to a bald eagle exhibit. In addition, Taylor would not be permitted to mow his lawn or allow children to play on his lot between the months of November and July.

"There are a dozen houses around that nest," said Taylor. "I don't know why my government singled me out - especially since I have done everything I can to protect that nest."

The FWS's demands are also questionable since the agency recently announced that the bald eagle is no longer endangered.

In March 1999, Taylor filed a lawsuit against the agency seeking just compensation for the loss of his property under the U.S. Constitution's Fifth Amendment.

An elderly man wants to build a modular home for his ailing wife, which is okayed by the U.S. Fish & Wildlife, but only if he pays a "bribe" to a salmon restoration plan. (There have never been any salmon in the nearby Potomac River to restore.) He has to build two bald eagle platforms, but it doesn't say where. He already has one bald eagle nest, why does he need two more? He also has to contribute money (another bribe) to a bald eagle exhibit, that his wife is too crippled to go see. On top of that, his grandchildren and great grandchildren can't play in the yard from November to July. That is probably best, because he is not allowed to mow his yard, so the little ones might get lost in the high grass. The unmowed grass really endears Mr. Tay-

**Source: Defenders of Property Rights

lor to the neighbors there in Mt. Vernon, as it helps keep the real estate market depressed.

As the former head real estate guy in Mt. Vernon once said:

> "Government is not reason, it is not eloquence, it is force; like fire, a troublesome servant and a fearful master. Never for a moment should it be left to irresponsible action. "
> George Washington

It would appear that we have ignored Mr. Washington's sage advice, having left the United States Fish & Wildlife Service to "irresponsible action", not "for a moment", but for the past 38 years, since the passage of the Endangered Species Act of 1973,

Government Bureaucrats May Put Small Town Out of Business to Protect Rare Bird*

The East End of Long Island, New York is a popular vacation spot but it is also a popular breeding area for a bird called the Atlantic Coast piping plover - a "tourist" that many Long Islanders wish would go away.

The plover has been listed as an endangered species by the U.S. Fish and Wildlife Service (FWS) since 1986. Every year between late March and early September, plovers migrate to Long Island to breed. This happens to coincide with the busy tourist season. **To accommodate the bird, local officials are forced to adhere to an onerous and expensive set of regulations.**

Gary Veglianti, the mayor of West Hampton Dunes, says that in one case a plover had made a nest 10 feet from a road and the FWS recommended that the road be closed to everyone except essential people. **"What do I do," asked Veglianti, "get some Nazi traffic cop to stand there and decide who's essential and who isn't?"** What's worse is that the plovers' migration occurs during peak beach season and the road is the only way in or out of the village. There's no way the road could be shut down.

"Some of these recommendations are too much," observed Veg-

*Shattered Dreams, 100 Stories of Government Abuse, National Center for Public Policy Research

lianti. But the FWS has told Veglianti that if he doesn't follow their recommendations they might put him in jail for violating the Endangered Species Act.

West Hampton Dunes has had to spend $7 million over three years for plover protection.

For an endangered species, these pesky Piping Plovers sure do show up in a lot of places. They've shut down hundreds of miles of beaches from New York, North Carolina, Oregon, Washington and California, and caused billions of dollars of flooding all throughout the midwest. Maybe the U.S.F.W.S. will hire a "Nazi traffic cop" for Mayor Veglianti. They seem to have some expertise in that area.

$7,000,000.00 for just three years of Piping Plover protection is a lot of money, even for an expensive area of the country like Long Island. I am absolutely certain that there were other, more pressing, uses that could have been found for 7 million bucks worth of taxpayer dollars.

Playing Cupid for Love-Starved Turtles*

Efforts to ease traffic congestion in the growing community of Hampstead, Maryland have been thwarted by federal regulations protecting the endangered bog turtle.

Hampstead officials desperately want to build a five-mile bypass road to ease traffic congestion on its main street. During the weekday mornings and evenings, the street is jammed with commuters and without a bypass, according to one businessman, the traffic will be "backed up two miles below Hampstead."

Helen Utz, director of the Carroll County Chamber of Commerce, says it is critical that the bypass get built so prospective businesses will not be deterred by the traffic from locating in the county's industrial park.

But researchers have discovered 18 bog turtles in a wetland that lies in the path of the proposed bypass. The four-inch turtle was listed as a threatened species by the U.S. Fish and Wildlife Service (FWS) in 1997. The bypass project is now on hold because Dr. James

*Shattered Dreams, 100 Stories of Government Abuse, National Center for Public Policy Research

Howard, a university biologist who has studied the turtles at the request of the state of Maryland, has recommended that engineers build a bridge across a small stream instead of filling it so that turtles could use the stream to travel from one bog to another. Howard also wants to extend his investigation for at least one more year to determine if there are other turtles dwelling in wetlands along the proposed bypass route.

If there are other turtles, they too may be given special protection. Howard says the turtles need protected "corridors" so that they can breed with turtles from other bogs. If the turtles can't mate with other populations, he argues, they will become in-bred.

Frustrated at having to delay the much-needed bypass so a biologist can play cupid for a bunch of turtles, local officials are understandably exasperated.

Says Julia Gouge, president of the Board of County Commissioners, **"It's becoming one of the most ridiculous situations we have seen."**
Source: Washington Times

The government biologist wants to spend another year, looking for more turtles of different species. This is called a "make-work program", with the beneficiary in charge of the program. What, exactly, would the "discovery" of more turtle species do to change his recommendation? Would he build a four lane bridge for the turtles, instead of a one-lane bridge? Because of all the turtle traffic, would the bridge have to be re-engineeered to support all the weight of the turtles (the bog turtle is 4 inches long.) Maybe they need to hire "some Nazi traffic cop" to keep the lovesick turtles from crushing each other in a mad rush of fornication fever. Without question, they would need at least one U.S.F.W.S. Recognized Bog Turtle Surveyor. As a nation, when we build new bridges so bog turtles can screw, while bridges built for humans are collapsing, it is Americans getting screwed, not the turtles.

75-Year-Old Woman's Plan for Quiet Retirement Dashed by Endangered Species Act

For nearly ten years, Lani Odenthal and her husband Bob worked hard to develop their 80-acre golf course in Okanogan County, Washington into a beautiful, prosperous resort. After Bob passed

*Shattered Dreams, 100 Stories of Government Abuse, National Center for Public Policy Research

away in 1998, 75-year-old Lani had no desire to run the Sunny Meadows resort anymore and decided to sell it and live the rest of her life in quiet retirement.

In the spring of 1999, that plan was shattered when the National Marine Fisheries Service (NMFS) ordered the local irrigation company, Skyline Ditch, which served Sunny Meadows and its neighbors, to stop releasing water. **Lani's once-lushly-green oasis is now virtually useless as it is now marred by dying brown grass, receding ponds and weedy flower beds.**

Citing new Endangered Species Act regulations adopted in early 1999, NMFS alleges that the irrigation provided by Pacific Northwest water companies, such as Skyline Ditch, harm salmon because it diverts water from streams and rivers vital to salmon survival. NMFS adopted these strict regulations despite serious scientific concerns over whether such regulation of the salmon's freshwater habitat will significantly improve their survivability rates. **What is certain, however, is that the denial of vitally-needed water to farmers and other small businesses, such as Lani's golf resort, is having catastrophic consequences.**

Soon after Lani decided to sell Sunny Meadows in November 1998, a woman living in the area who frequented Sunny Meadows offered her $1.3 million for the resort - certainly enough for a comfortable retirement. But after the irrigation company cut off the water supply on NMFS's orders, the prospective buyer informed Lani that she couldn't invest when water rights were in doubt.
Stuck with a property she couldn't sell, Lani had to shut down Sunny Meadows as she can no longer offer the golfing, fishing and hiking that once made the resort so popular. To make ends meet, she sold her motor home and other personal belongings. Still, Lani doesn't know if she can pay the rent for her apartment.

Lani says that although her late husband was the kind of man who could find the bright spot in any situation, "I'm just glad he isn't

The United States Fish and Wildlife Service thinks nothing of destroying people's lives, by shutting off irrigation water to farmers, ranchers, golf courses, orchards, wineries, you name it. Human beings need water to exist. That is not a newsflash. They need irrigation to turn parched lands into productive lands. Irrigated farmlands are what feeds millions of people around the world.

The United States is a nation of laws. Occasionally, humans, being humans, pass a really lousy law, even with the best of intentions. Prohibition (although technically a Constitutional Amendment) comes to mind right away. The fix here is easy enough. Simply repeal the Endangered Species Act of 1973. The question is, will Congress have the political courage to do the right thing, or will they bend to the special interest Environmental Lobby? The Environmentalists will counter that this is some kind of Right Wing conspiracy, and that those favoring repeal are themselves a Special Interest Group.

I agree with that. Farmers, ranchers, developers, loggers, home builders, miners, tourists, hikers, bikers, road builders, dam builders, savvy entrepeneurs, campers. retired people, golfers, doctors, equestrians, , school children, Marines, etc. should be considered a special interest group. And the name of that special interest group is the American People.

Left Wing? Right Wing? Moderate? Who cares? Let's just put America back to work, and restore our hard earned freedoms.

A Quick Word Here on Salmon Stocks

Overfishing, particularly by the Japanese, is a huge problem that must be addressed by nations around the world. Shutting off an American farmer's irrigation supply simply exacerbates the worldwide shortage of food, and does very little to help the salmon. As with most wildlife, it is predation (in this case, by humans) that has caused most of the wildlife problems around the world, fish included. Years ago, with much less efficient fishing methods than utilized today, the cod fishery of New England was virtually destroyed. So it can happen with our salmon, and it needs to be addressed immediately. Nothing in this book is meant to denigrate worthwhile conservation efforts, as envisioned by Theodore Roosevelt and many others.

Wildlife is being used as a tool by people who want to control other people's lives. Time and time again, the environmental movement has shown its true stripes, making virtually all its decisions based on money and power, and not based on what is best for wildlife.

> "There is nothing wrong with America that can't be fixed by what is right with America."
> Bill Clinton

New Jersey Man Loses Land So Owl Might Keep Options Open

For 17 years, Jeffrey Dautel has been paying taxes on a lot he owns in a picturesque lakeside neighborhood in Sparta, New Jersey. The lot is 1.27 acres in size, and Dautel wanted to build his own house on a small part of the land. Because the lot is near a lake, he needed a wetlands permit to build there. However, a small part of his land that fell under the wetlands designation was deemed wetlands of an "exceptional resource value" by the New Jersey Department of Environmental Protection (DEP). This is because Dautel's property is allegedly vital to the northern barred owl, an endangered species in New Jersey. **It's debatable that the barred owl should even be considered an endangered species given that there are a lot of them. Indeed, there are so many in the Pacific Northwest that they are becoming a menace to the spotted owl, a federally-protected species. (The U.S.F.W.S. in fact, is shooting barred owls to keep them from fornicating with Spotted Owls, thus creating hybrids.)**

In reality, there are no barred owls living on Dautel's property. Even the DEP concedes that. **Nevertheless, the DEP reasons that Dautel cannot build his house because some day the barred owl might stop in for a quick snack. Although Dautel cannot build a house on his lot, the town still expects him to pay taxes.** Dautel's situation could be remedied with a strong dose of the Fifth Amendment, which prohibits the government from taking a person's property without just compensation. But Dautel does not want to sue because he is fearful of angering the bureaucrats who will decide the outcome of his case. He is still working with the DEP in hopes of reversing their earlier decision.

Unfortunately, out-of-control environmental bureacrats are not found just in the U.S.Fish & Wildlife Service; they can often be found in many state agencies as well. Taking away a man's property, without compensation, is protected, by the Fourteenth Amendment, which is basically the Fifth Amendment, applied to the states. 1.27 acres of "potential" Barred Owl habitat., and they expropriate this guy's property, while elsewhere, the government has a million dollar program shooting Barred Owls. That's ridiculous.

Casualties of the Northern Spotted Owl*

In 1979, Barbara and Dick Mossman mortgaged their farm to buy a

*Shattered Dreams, 100 Stories of Government Abuse, National Center for Public Policy Research

new International log truck to start their own logging business in the Pacific Northwest. Initially, the Mossmans experienced hard times, losing virtually everything except their truck and a few other goods during the 1980-1981 recession. In 1986, however, they landed a good job hauling logs in Forks, Washington - at the time the logging capital of the world. Things gradually improved for the Mossmans. **They got rid of their debt, restored a good credit rating, started a modest savings account and bought a four-acre farm.**

Then in June 1990, the United States Fish and Wildlife Service (USFWS) declared the Northern Spotted Owl an endangered species. **Since the owl was found virtually anywhere there was logging, the timber industry collapsed.** The Mossmans' business was no exception. In 1990 alone, their revenue dropped by 33%. **By October of 1991, less than 18 months after the USFWS ruling, the Mossmans went out of business.** Because they were self-employed, they could not apply for unemployment benefits. As a result, the Mossmans had to sell their boat, trailer, welder, tools and motorcycles to get the cash they needed just to make ends meet. That was not enough, though. **In the spring of 1992, they received a foreclosure notice on their farm.** The electricity was turned off, leaving the couple without heat, lights and water. The Mossmans were unable to respond to collection notices and deputies began knocking on the door with lawsuits in hand. **However, Barbara says the most degrading thing of all "was being forced to walk into a public assistance agency, after 13 years as independent truckers, and ask for a voucher for food, because we were hungry."**

Barbara has since become a spokeswoman for the thousands of other families whose lives were ruined by this reckless application of the Endangered Species Act. "I am not interested in pointing a finger of blame," says Barbara. "What I am interested in is a commitment from the Members of Congress that they will change this cruel and vicious law, so that no other families, no other community will have to endure the pain we in the timber community have been forced to endure."

My wife, Anita and I, have endured much the same as Barbara and Dick Mossman, albeit in Canada. My family and I have "walked a mile in their moccasins." Still in court, that is about all I am currently permitted to say. There will someday be a book on the subject, entitled

*Shattered Dreams, 100 Stories of Government Abuse, National Center for Public Policy Research

"Rogue Biologists, The Great Crashing Caribou Hoax." The Environmental Movement is not just an American movement. Like Communism before it, it is a worldwide ideology, seeking governmental control of private property everywhere, and using our beloved wildlife as its primary tool.

Couple Loses Timber So Government Can Play Cupid*

The state of Oregon's Board of Forestry has forced Alvin and Marsha Seiber to set aside 37 acres of commercially-harvestable forestland to protect the northern spotted owl. The state is not offering any compensation. The Seibers have been prevented from harvesting for more than a year now.

The Seibers filed suit against the state alleging that their property rights had been violated. In defending its actions, **the state argued that the Seibers had to accept the restrictions on the use of their property because they made the decision to harvest timber and are thus obligated to accept any restrictions the state may choose to impose on private timber operations.** The state also argued that since the state may one day decide to lift the restrictions on timber harvesting, the Seibers can not claim that they suffered a permanent taking of their property that would justify compensation. Additionally, the state argued that since the Seibers could still use the other 163 acres of their 200-acre plot, they didn't deserve compensation for the regulatory taking of nearly 20 percent of their land.

But it seems the state and environmentalists involved in the case weren't just satisfied with making the argument that government has the right to compel private property owners to protect wildlife at the owners' expense. **Oregon officials and the Audubon Society argued in their legal brief that the Seibers should be prevented from harvesting timber because they do "not have the right to prevent the reproduction of a species that is in danger of extinction."**

The Seibers' lawyers argued in court that the state of Oregon's claim that the Seibers and other private landowners have an affirmative duty to set aside their property for wildlife preservation whenever the government says they should without compensation blatantly violates the U.S. Constitution's Fifth Amendment protection of private property.

*Source: Pacific Legal Foundation

The lawyers observed that a perverse consequence of the state's dangerously broad interpretation of its power to protect wildlife would be to encourage property owners to destroy forests that could conceivably serve as habitat for the northern spotted owl.

The Spotted Owl debacle has been well documented, and is probably the most well known and the most destructive application of the Endangered Species Act of 1973. It has cost our country thousands of jobs and billions of dollars. Perhaps more importantly, it emboldened the Environmental Movement to move forward with its anti-development, anti American agenda. For the people at the U.S. Fish & Wildlife Department, they got a taste of the incredible power this law gives their department, and they have been wielding that power like a scythe through the American economy every since.

Federally-Protected Bird Costs Elderly Woman Her Retirement Investment*

In 1973, Margaret Rector bought 15 acres of land on a busy highway west of Austin, Texas as a retirement investment. In 1990, the Golden-Cheeked Warbler was listed as endangered, and the United States Fish and Wildlife Service (USFWS) classified Rector's property as suitable habitat. Her land, located in the fastest-growing part of the county, is now unusable. Its assessed value fell from $831,000 in 1991 to $30,000 in 1992. USFWS says she might be able to get a permit to develop the property, but this would require her to finance extensive studies and to mitigate any impact on the Warbler. However, Rector views this as an option available only to large corporations engaging in multi-million-dollar developments.

The value of Margaret Rector's land dropped by over 96% in one year, despite a booming Texas real estate market. U.S. Fish & Wildlife Service simply shrugs off her loss, saying she can get "an incidental take" permit. As Mrs. Rector rightfully surmises, the time, money, and delays for such a permit are simply too onerous for a single person to tackle. Mrs. Rector has to pay taxes for years on a property, and the government renders it worthless, virtually overnight.

Note that the property was simply judged to be "suitable habitat", and

*Shattered Dreams, 100 Stories of Government Abuse, National Center for Public Policy Research

some unelected government bureaucrat makes that call. It is an incredible extension of the E.S.A, because "suitable habitat" is so subjective. Fighting the call falls squarely on the shoulders of the citizen, who supports his adversary with his tax money. As discussed elsewhere, humans have a natural propensity to love and support wildlife. However, when economic losses as catastrophic as this one are experienced, it is bad for all wildlife. People will simply destroy the wildlife, and destroy the wildlife habitat. That is exactly counter to what the Endangered Species Act of 1973 intended.

> "To compel a man to subsidize with his taxes the propagation of ideas which he disbelieves and abhors is sinful and tyrannical."
> Thomas Jefferson

What the hunting industry has proven throughout the world, is that, by creating economic value for wildlife, it becomes important to the local people , who then strive to preserve it, as opposed to poaching it. Americans don't need to poach wildlife to eat (yet), but if you asked the lady above, would she destroy, or move, a Golden Cheek Warbler nest if she found one (knowing what the consequences would be), what do you think she would do? Golden Cheek Warblers are beautiful little creatures, but $801,000.00 nice? Hearing her story, what do you think the neighbors did? I guarantee this government action did nothing but threaten further the chances of the Golden Cheek Warbler surviving as a species. Some people describe the phenomenon as "Shoot, Shovel, and Shut-up." In a nation based on laws, that is anarchy. Better to change a bad law, than to develop a nation peopled by citizens deciding unilaterally which laws are "good", and which ones are to be disobeyed.

Couple's Home Imperiled by Beetle Protection*

Mr. and Mrs. Richard Bannister wanted to take steps to prevent erosion that placed their beach home in jeopardy. Unfortunately, foot-dragging by the Maryland Department of Natural Resources (DNR) delayed the project, resulting in the loss of a 15-foot section of the Bannisters' property. The reason for the DNR delay? Concern for the welfare of the Puritan Tiger Beetle.

*Shattered Dreams, 100 Stories of Government Abuse, National Center for Public Policy Research

The Bannisters merely wanted to construct a stone revetment, or face, at the base of a 60-foot cliff in their backyard. They intended to grade the top to a more moderate slope and plant grass. They were told by the DNR, however, that any action they took should "not entail destroying [Puritan] Tiger Beetles."

While the Bannisters wasted time and money wrestling with bureaucrats, their home was put at greater risk when a 15-foot section of their property crumbled into the beach.

Puritan Tiger Beetle

Jeopardizing the residence of a human family, to protect 15 feet of **potential** residence for a "family" of a Puritan Tiger Beetles is the height of absurdity. If a subspecies is so close to extinction, that a piece of land the width of your own bedroom is so critical, then man stepping in to protect it is simply an artificial interference with the four billion year old ecological process of natural selection and species extinction. There are 350,000 species of beetles identified on planet Earth, with perhaps millions of unidentifed species.** The loss of one is not the end of the world. It is the way ecosystems work and evolve.

Beetles have been around for about 265,000,000 years. Man has been around, at the most, 200,000 years. That means beetles have been on earth 1,325 times as long as mankind, and they have 350,000 times (at least) as many species. Would someone please explain to me why we are worried about beetle species, instead of human species?

*National Geographic Magazine, May 1998, "Planet of the Beetles."

Montana Man Fined For Shooting Attacking Grizzly in Backyard**

In September 1989, Montana sheepherder John Shuler discovered four Grizzly Bears on his property. He went outside and fired warning shots that scared off three of the animals. Returning to his house, he found another one blocking his path. The huge beast reared on its hind legs in an obviously menacing manner. In self-defense, Shuler shot and killed the animal. However, officials with the Department of the Interior fined Shuler $5,000, arguing that he couldn't claim self-defense because he purposely entered a "zone of imminent danger." That zone was his backyard. For more than eight years, Shuler fought this outrageous fine. Finally, on March 17, 1998 a federal judge found the Interior Department's fine to be unjustified since Shuler's life was clearly endangered by the Grizzly.

This bear was shot by an Inuit guide, as it charged a client.

A man shoots a grizzly bear in self defense, and he spends eight years and thousands of dollars in legal fees defending the action. Hasn't our government got more serious crimes to pursue than this? My best friend and accountant, Jerry Bodar, was involved in a similar grizzly incident, while bowhunting for elk in northwestern Wyoming. Jerry and his neighbor, Curtis McStay, had taken horses into the wilderness northwest of their home in Dubois, Wyoming. Both men are highly experienced outdoorsman. Curtis' fiance, Heidi Gustafson, accompa-

*Shattered Dreams, 100 Stories of Government Abuse, National Center for Public Policy Research

nied them, but stayed in camp, while the men hunted. Having harvested an elk, Curtis took the horses and was packing his elk meat back to camp. They soon discovered that a big male grizzly bear was tracking them. When Curtis arrived at camp, he retrieved his .44 Magnum from the tent, and emptied a full cylinder at the feet of the grizzly bear, trying to scare it off, to no avail. Reloading, when the bear got to within 15 feet of the couple, and fearing for his fiance, Curtis shot the bear. The bear ran off, ambling right by Jerry, who was coming down the trail with an elk of his own.

Using a satellite phone, the trio immediately contacted the United State Fish & Wildlife Service. Packing up camp, and riding out to the trailhead, they were met by agents from U.S.F.W.S. They were immediately separated, and told this incident would be treated "exactly like a murder investigation." They were questioned separately for several hours, including a return to the "scene of the crime." Jerry, who stands an athletic 6'4" and 220 pounds, is not a person easily intimidated. He told me the questioning experience was something right out of Nazi Germany.

What saved Curtis from a similar experience to what sheepherder John Shuler experienced, was that the grizzly bear was never found. Without a dead body, prosecuting "a murder" is much more difficult. The environmentalists would probably say "Real men don't shoot grizzly bears." They don't eat quiche either, but they do protect their loved ones from a serious mauling or worse. That is what the Founding Fathers would have called "an inalienable right."

_Man Threatened with $15,000 Fine for Endangering Protected Species Not on His Property*

The United States Fish and Wildlife Service (USFWS) has threatened to fine a Utah man $15,000 for farming his land and allegedly posing a risk to the Utah Prairie Dog, a protected species. The only problem is that there are no Utah Prairie Dogs on his property. Originally, the USFWS told the man that he should hire an outside expert to determine if any Utah Prairie Dogs were present. The expert prepared a report which indicated that there were no Utah Prairie Dogs, so the farmer proceeded to work his land. But the USFWS told him that they will fine him anyway. The USFWS reasons that

*Shattered Dreams, 100 Stories of Government Abuse, National Center for Public Policy Research

since it is theoretically possible for Utah Prairie Dogs in the surrounding area to migrate onto the property, they have the right to issue a fine for harming a potential habitat.

S

The United States Government, back in the 1950s and 1960s, spent millions of dollars poisoning prairie dog towns all across the west, including the subspecies, the Utah Prairie Dog. In those days, our government was actually "partnering" with ranchers and farmers, helping them make their land more productive. There are still millions of prairie dogs all across the west; the Utah Prairie dog is just a subpopulation that environmentalists got listed to slow down Utah's surging development.

The above example shows the problems with the concept of "potential habitat" designation. That tool, for the U.S. Fish & Wildlife Service, can be used to interpret (and they are the interpreters) virtually any piece of ground in the United States. For instance, virtually all the farmland from the Ohio Valley west to the Rocky Mountains, was once habitat for the buffalo, or American Bison. Now, much of it is farmland and ranchland. It remains "potential habitat", and, without question, is in the sights of the Environmental Movement.

Lake Who-Can-Use-It*

Lake Koocanusa is a large reservoir in northwestern Montana that straddles the U.S.-Canadian border. **When it was built in the 1970s, the Army Corps of Engineers promised the residents of Libby, Montana and the Canadians that they could use it for fishing and tourism. Eventually, salmon and other fish species thrived in the lake. As it gradually became a tourist attraction, the lake started generating significant income for Libby - which it desperately needed due to the collapse of the mining and timber industry.** The demise of these industries was largely due to Endangered Species and Clean Water regulations. However, in 1992, just as things started to look good, the salmon was listed as a protected species. **The United States Fish and Wildlife Service and the National Marine Fisheries Service decided to conduct a 50-year experiment where they would increase the volume of water on the Columbia**

*Shattered Dreams, 100 Stories of Government Abuse, National Center for Public Policy Research

River by releasing large amounts of water upstream. They wanted to know if the increased water volume would help the salmon. These water releases included Libby and Lake Koocanusa 800 miles away from the Columbia. Now, every summer - during the height of the tourist season - so much water is released from Lake Koocanusa that the shoreline recedes to 300 feet from the docks. Much of the lake is a mudflat that, ironically, leaves the spawning grounds of the salmon and other fish exposed. **Not surprisingly, the tourism industry has taken a dive since no one wants to fish in a mudflat.** In another ironic twist, it seems that the federal government's efforts to save the salmon are threatening the White Sturgeon, another protected species, which dwells below Lake Koocanusa. The White Sturgeon needs low water in summer and high water in spring to thrive. But the government holds back water in the spring to release it in the summer - the exact opposite of what the sturgeon requires. Libby resident Bruce Vincent says there is a lot of "teeth-gnashing" going on among the federal regulators. Vincent says this tragedy is an all-too-typical result of federal environmental policy. **"They suffer from a serious tunnel vision in which they take one species at a time. What they fail to realize is that species don't exist in a vacuum. What you do to help one species will invariably impact another." Vincent says that since nobody, human or fish, can use the lake anymore, the bumper sticker around town now refers to it as "Lake Who-Can-Use-It."**

Source: Bruce Vincent

Libby, Montana, is just a few hours drive from my home. Lake Kookanusa should be a mecca for sportsmen all across North America. The setting, in the beautiful Cabinet Mountains, is without peer. Every spring, my son-in-law and I spend a long weekend, in a cabin located just two miles below the dam. We go there for the black bear hunting, but we would love to be able to fish the lake during the day As stated above, you can't get anywhere near the actual water, the docks are so far away. I assumed the lake was deliberately emptied, getting ready to control the annual springtime snowmelt, I had no idea it was virtually closed to human usage to protect the White Sturgeon.

The above article talks about a 50 year experiment, to see if releasing more water into the Columbia would increase salmon stocks. Once a lake impoundment is full, you can release all the water coming into the lake, and the lake stays full. There is no "extra" water created by

A Nationwide System of Abuse

keeping lake levels low. Additionally, a scientific experiment has to have a single variable to draw a proper conclusion. If the Japanese are allowed to continuing slaughtering salmon, you can have all the water you want in the Columbia River, and it won't make a damn bit of difference, the salmon will decline. There are too many variables to make this 50 year experiment valid. Its like claiming the Endangered Species Act of 1973 saved the bald eagle. It was the banning of DDT in 1972, not the Endangered Species Act of 1973, that saved the bald eagle.

This "experiment" is about controlling American lives, stopping farming along the Columbia River watershed, and recreation in Montana.

"I accuse the present Administration of being the greatest spending Administration in peacetime in all American history - one which piled bureau on bureau, commission on commission, and has failed to anticipate the dire needs or reduced earning power of the people. Bureaus and bureaucrats have been retained at the expense of the taxpayer. We are spending altogether too much money for government services which are neither practical nor necessary. In addition to this, we are attempting too many functions and we need a simplification of what the Federal government is giving the people."
Franklin D. Roosevelt

In New Mexico, Support for the Endangered Species Act is Drying Up*

"What will we do when there is not enough water for our kids?" Albuquerque Mayor Martin Chavez wonders. "What will we say when they ask why we let our homes, our industries, and our cities take a back seat to a well-meaning but outdated federal statute?"

For years, Endangered Species Act (ESA) enforcement has killed jobs in New Mexico. Now environmentalist lawsuits filed under the ESA to protect the Rio Grande silvery minnow may cut the amount of water available to New Mexico's metropolitan areas as well as to its farmers.

Local residents say this would be a disaster for local residents. If so,

*Shattered Dreams, 100 Stories of Government Abuse, National Center for Public Policy Research

Rio Grande Silvery Minnow

it would be just one more endangered species-related blow to this hard-hit state.

Albuquerque's Mayor Chavez isn't the only prominent New Mexican who believes the ESA is making life harder.

As the Albuquerque Journal reports, **Sante Fe Mayor Larry Delgado worries that lawsuits by environmentalists over the Mexican spotted owl could hinder a forest thinning project designed to reduce fire and flood in his part of the state.**

Danny Fryar, county manager in New Mexico's Catron County, located 200 miles southwest of Albuquerque, told the Journal, **"They started closing down logging in the national forest in 1989 and by 1992 it was all over. Environmental lawsuits just about destroyed us and they haven't quit yet."**

Alex Thal, a professor at Western New Mexico University, says of the situation in Reserve, Catron County's county seat: **"When the sawmill in Reserve closed in 1992, it reduced the economy in that area by about $8.6 million a year, counting direct, indirect and induced income.**

Because of financial pressures, Reserve's population has declined a whopping 25 per cent. Businesses have gone under. As the public school has been de-populated, public school classes have been cut back to just four days a week.

"There's a whole host of things that go wrong in a community when this happens. You read about divorces, substance abuse, truancy, suicide: indicators of a social system breaking down." Howard Hutchison, a local resident and executive director of the Coalition of Arizona/new Mexico Counties, told the Journal:" We've had increases in every one of those areas. If what happened here with the unemployment situation were to happen in Albuquerque, 100,000 people would be out of a job."
Northern New Mexico is likewise affected. Alberto Baros, an assistant county planner in Rio Arriba County, north of Santa Fe, believes some environmental activists are abusing the ESA. **The Act brings people to a point that they won't recover. They'll be out of business soon. And for some of those people it's a loss of custom and culture."**

"Basically, we're in a straitjacket, Antonio "Ike" DeVargas of La Madera, a town in Rio Arriba County, has told the paper: **"(Environmentalists) don't want us to have cows, they don't want us to cut wood, they don't want us to mine. They just want us to set everything aside so nobody can use it."**

Environmentalist have filed at least 134 lawsuits in New Mexico since 1995 seeking greater enforcement of endangered species regulations.

In the minnow case, a federal court has ruled that the law gives minnows the greatest right to the water. Following a joint appeal by the city of Albuqueque and the state of New Mexico, in October 2002, implementation of this order was delayed pending a full appeal of the order in January, 2003.

In September, 2002, Albuquerque Journal poll, two-thirds of New Mexico's registered voters said they believe the ESA goes too far. Should the city and state lose their appeal in the water case, this number is likely to go much higher.

This article is pretty self explanatory. Cutting off water for humans to protect the Rio Grande Silvery Minnow is abominable. Because of the way the Endangered Species Act of 1973 is written, many judges don't have an alternative but to rule in favor of the environmentists. In many cases, they disagree with the action, but, in a nation of laws, they are stuck enforcing the laws that are on the books. The judges get labeled as "activist" judges, but the law is there, and they have a job to perform. Two hundred years ago, when John Adams' administration passed the "Alien and Sedition Acts" (basically doing away with free speech), the judges were forced to uphold the hated acts. Fortunately, bad laws do eventually get repealed, or declared unconstituional.

In this case, the job of repealing a bad law belongs to Congress.

Klamath Basin Area Struggles on One Year After Federal Government Shut Off Water*

In the spring of 2001, federal authorities shut off water to 1,500 farmers and over 200,000 acres of Upper Klamath Lake region of Oregon and northern California in order to save two endangered species: the sucker fish and the coho salmon. The federal agencies took this step in response to lawsuits filed by environmental groups that claimed the government had not adequately protected these endangered species since a 1991 drought.

With no water for irrigation, farmers lost their crops. Businesses lost revenue, as farmers had no money to spend. Other wildlife that depended on plentiful waters, such as waterfowl, suffered, but were deemed less important than the endangered fish.

Residents complained to the federal government, and the case received national attention, but the irrigation canals remained dry.

In early 2002, the National Research Council released an interim report on scientific issues relating to the water shutoff. According to the report, there is "no clear connection between water levels in Upper Klamath Lake and conditions that are adverse to suckers. In fact, the highest recorded increase in the number of adult suckers occurred in a year when water levels were low." Because of this report, the Department of Interior released water for irrigating in 2002.

Many area farmers, however, did not make it through the dry sum-

*Shattered Dreams, 100 Stories of Government Abuse, National Center for Public Policy Research

mer of 2001, and had to sell equipment, livestock, and, in some cases, the farms themselves.

Steve Kandra, whose family has farmed in the basin for nearly a century, said, "We are on our last run and 2002 will make or break 92 years of farming for my family." Kandra typically had been able to produce about 140 bushels of wheat per acre on irrigated land. Last year, on un-irrigated land, his yield was only six bushels per acre.

Farmers are not the only victims of the federal decision to keep water in Klamath Lake for endangered fish. Wetlands were also cut off. Wildlife that depended on the water in Klamath wetlands-such as bald eagles and ducks-disappeared.

Local businesses that depend on farmers as customers also were hurt. Bob Gasser, who runs Basin Fertilizer in Merrill, Oregon, said, "People who have paid me for 27 years have been unable to settle their bills. Do I tell them no this year? I can't.

Land in the region that was valued at $2500 per acre is now $50 per acre. Even at this bargain price, there are few willing buyers. No one will buy farmland where the future availability of water is un-certain.

Farming is an essential form of human behavior. America prospers because of American farmers' productiviity. If you have been to the grocery store lately, it is easy to see the nationwide economic damage that the Environmental Movement is doing to **each and every American**, not just the farmers directly affected. As shown elsewhere, it is not just the Klamath Basin being affected. The Delta Smelt has closed down much of the Central Valley of California, often called the "Breadbasket" of America. Millions of acres of farmland were ruined this spring (2011) , because of flooding in the midwest, due to Piping Plover and Least Tern Protections. Cattle ranchers all across the country are being run off the land, to protect everything from tortoises to wolves.

America needs to send a clear and simple message to Congress:

"Americans want to feed their families, and that basic need trumps the "intrinsic value" that the unelected bureaucrats at the U.S. Fish & Wildlife Service ascribe to such creatures as the the New Mexico

Silvery Minnow, the Delta Smelt, and the Appalacian Monkeyface Pearly Mussel. "

Food first. It 's not a difficult concept to grasp, even for Congress.

The Death of Lake Lowell*

CANYON COUNTY — About a thousand people gathered Saturday to make their point loud and clear: don't prohibit recreation on Lake Lowell.

"The Death of Recreation Parade" attracted boat owners, horseback riders, fishermen, hunters and many others who recreate at Lake Lowell.

The fear is that if the Deer Flat National Wildlife Refuge enforces a proposal to shut down some of the lake to activities such as boating and water sports, Canyon County's economy will suffer.

Because Lake Lowell is part of a national refuge, the U.S. Fish and Wildlife Service is responsible, due to congressional mandates, to protect wildlife, specifically migratory birds.
That's why they're creating a new plan for the lake this summer which, among other changes, could potentially limit wake-causing activities to the western pool near the Lower Dam Recreation Area and only allow them between noon and sunset.

The proposed plan would also limit no-wake boating, swimming, bicycling and hunting, and ban dog-walking and horseback riding.

Fishing areas would be extended, however.

"They're trying to take away recreation, and not just the recreation part but the income of the county," boater Lance Miller said. "I mean, think of all the hot dogs, hamburgers, gas, everything that people buy to go out to Lake Lowell to picnic. And if you take that away, it's got to effect our economy locally, and we've got enough problems with the economy as it is. We don't need more."

Canyon County Commissioner David Ferdinand pointed out the

* 2011 Idaho Press-Tribune July 10, 2011

hundreds of boats that participated in the parade.

"Look at all this value that you have," he said. "All of this would go away."

One of the parade's initiators, General Manager Justin Harrison of Idaho Water Sports, said the refuge's potential plan for Lake Lowell could mean the end of the company.

"We're down 80 percent from the economy, the recession, already," Harrison said. "So if we lose this recreation — this diamond in our Canyon County — we're out of business, realistically."

And if the 4,700 registered boat owners in Canyon County do choose to boat at places other than Lake Lowell, "it's going to put pressure on already congested lakes," Harrison said.

Beyond the economic impact, many families oppose the potential changes to Lake Lowell because recreating at the lake is a long-standing tradition for them.

"It's important for family," said Darla Braun, who has lived in Idaho for 27 years and takes her three boys to the lake each summer. Kids need a place to go for good fun and clean activities, she said.

Some parade attendees wanted to know why the lake's rules need to change in the first place.

"There's no reason to change things from the status quo," Brandon Christoffersen of Boise said. "I hunt, I wakeboard, and don't get me wrong, I want as many ducks out there as possible. But there's no proof that at Lake Lowell the boating or the horseback riding or the dog walking is hurting any of the wildlife."

The refuge's Visitor Services Manager Susan Kain has strongly encouraged the public to voice their opinions about the plan. And that's a big reason why the Save Lake Lowell parade, hosted in part by Tea Party Boise, was created.

"It's just about getting the word out about what's going on at this reservoir," Harrison said. "There's so many people that just don't know what's happening."

Parade participants met at 9 a.m. Saturday in the Karcher Mall parking lot and made their way to Lake Lowell to comment at the refuge's open house.

Crapo Warns Of Choppy Waters For Lake Lowell Users
May 27, 2011 Idaho Senior Senator Mike Crapo issued a press release Friday warning users of Lake Lowell within the Deer Flat Wildlife Refuge of potential boating restrictions in the near future.

Not wanting to make waves among boaters, fishermen, and wildlife managers, Crapo points to a 100 year record of co-existance among the groups AND the waterfowl frequenting the refuge.

"I am disappointed with today's announcement because it appears this may be a case of the U.S. Fish and Wildlife Service proposing a solution that is in search of a problem. My feeling can be generally categorized as 'if it isn't broken, don't fix it.' Based on this preliminary recommendation, it appears that the agency may simply be satisfying a bureaucratic requirement that ignores the facts on the ground," said the senior Senator.

A Crapo spokesman noted the refuge and lake wouldn't exist without the water and the water is ALL owned by the irrigators. The source of the water is from the Boise River which fills Lake Lowell via the New York Canal, irrigating crops and residential land along the way from Lucky Peak Reservoir east of Boise. See the Deer Flat USFWS proposals HERE.

CRAPO ON LAKE LOWELL: IF IT ISN'T BROKEN, DON'T FIX IT
Reminds USFWS to note century of success on the ground at the lake

Washington, D.C. – The U.S. Fish and Wildlife Service today issued preliminary recommendations for changes at southwest Idaho's Lake Lowell and Deer Flat National Wildlife Refuge. Under the agency review process, a public comment period will now open regarding the agency's preferred alternative plan for the lake, which is to restrict public access and boating. Idaho Senator Mike Crapo issued the following statement following an initial review of the agency's recommendations:

"Lake Lowell has a one-hundred year track record of outstanding performance when it comes to wildlife protection, and use by recreationalists, sportsmen, irrigators and a host of multiple user groups. While I will review this latest proposal from the agency in depth, I encourage the public to again weigh in and I pledge that I will continue to work with citizens, local leaders and my Delegation partners and the agency to help craft a permanent solution.

"I am disappointed with today's announcement because it appears this may be a case of the U.S. Fish and Wildlife Service proposing a solution that is in search of a problem. My feeling can be generally categorized as 'if it isn't broken, don't fix it.' Based on this preliminary recommendation, it appears that the agency may simply be satisfying a bureaucratic requirement that ignores the facts on the ground."

Senator Crapo is the duly elected United States Senator from the State of Idaho. What he is going to find out, is that the unelected bureaucrats at the U.S. Fish & Wildlife Service will "thumb their nose" at his pleas of "If it isn't broke, don't fix it." You see, Mr. Crapo, these people "have the power." They know what is best. Your job, as Senator, is irrevelant. That is the attitude of the people in this runaway governmental department.

The stories in this book come from all across the country, by reporters at dozens of different news bureaus. There is no consistent thread of Right Wing, Left Wing, Republican, Democrat, Liberal, Conservative. These reporters are just telling a local story, about the local abuse of the U.S. Fish & Wildlife Service. It is not until you read the stories in their totality, that one realizes the scope of the problem, and the damage being done to our nation.

As we have seen, it is not a problem that can be addressed locally, because it is a federal law that is being enforced. Only Congress can address the problem, and only Congress can fix the problem.

Take just a minute, and ask yourself, what would the Founding Fathers say about a United States Government that: prohibits plowing your own field, building your own home, protecting your home from wildfire, protecting your livestock from predators, eschews military preparedness, outlaws walking on a beach, forces you to destroy your own crops, makes you abandon your home to beetles, refuses to secure our national borders, threatens you with fines for killing flies, refuses to let trees be harvested on one's own private property, allows brave young firemen to die to save a small minnow, or refers to farmers as "irrelevant".

"And what country can preserve its liberties, if its rulers are not warned from time to time, that this people preserve the spirit of resistance? Let them take arms. The remedy is to set them right as to the facts, pardon them, and pacify them. What signify a few lives lost in a century or two? The tree of liberty must be refreshed from time to time, with the blood of patriots and tyrants."

Regina, the Pig, sold 15 times as Neighbors Help a Neighbor Fight the United States Fish & Wildlife Service

The following is excerpted from my local newspaper, The Missoulian, September 18, 2011

Bonners Ferry, Idaho. To understand the deep rift over federal regulation of endangered species, one only has to sit in the stands of the annual 4-H auction at the Boundary County Fairgrounds in Bonners Ferry, Idaho, last month, when 14-year-old Jasmine Hill's handsome pig, Regina, went up for sale.

First, it's important to know the background story: Jasmine's father, Jeremy, had been charged by the U.S. Justice Department a few weeks earlier with shooting a grizzly bear-a federally designated threatened species-40 yards from the back door of the family home at the base of the Selkirk Mountains.

Hill, his neighbors said, was protecting his home and his family. He was doing what any of them might have done. And now a man trying to raise six children out in the woods on a backhoe operator's earnings was facing up to a year in prison and a $50,000 fine.

So when Jasmine started shyly prodding her prized pig aound the arena, Sam Godge, the owner of a wood-chip mill, quickly bought it at $4.50 a pound, or $1143. Then Fodge said "Give it back, sell it again." The pig sold next to North Idaho Energy Logs, then Pluid Logging, then Three Mile Cafe. In all, Regina was sold 15 times, raising a total of $19,588.00 for Hill's legal defense. Jasmine hung her head, dumbfounded, in the arena. Jeremy and his wife, Rachel, were in tears.

"Some pig, some community" Bonners Ferry News Publisher Mike Weland wrote the next day. After that, Jeremy Hill won support from Republican Governor C.I. "butch" Otter, the state's congressional delegation, the Boundary County Board of Commissioners and even county prosecutor Jack Douglas, who in an extraordinary public statement said that seasoned state wildlife investigators looked into the case and did not ask him to file charges.

Grizzly Bears are unpredictable, dangerous predators, Douglas said. "In my mind, there's no question that the Hill family was likely in danger or that Jeremy, did what he did in defense of his family and his property.

Federal Officials, however, said Hill violated the Endangered Species Act, which allows landowners to shoot one of the region's struggling population of grizzlies only if its directly threatening a human life. U.S. Attorney Wendy Olsen said in explaining the filing of federal criminal charges: We have an obligation in all cases to make decisions based on the evidence that is presented in the course of the investigation and based on the law as it stands."

The conflict between state and federal views of wildlife management has played out like a stage drama across Western states over the past few decades, with constant disputes over logging, mining, and grazing. Such battles have a uniquely emotional pitch when it comes to efforts to boost populations of violent predators, such as wolves and grizzlies.

Local residents insist the issue is not the bears, but the law.

"One of the flaws of the ESA is the premium it places on protecting species at the expense of everything else" Otter wrote in protesting the charges against Hill.

To Hill's neighbors at the auction that day, **shouting out a bid on a pig was a way of drawing a line in the sand.** "I told Jeremy from the very beginning, this could happen to any of us. We are in this together. We do have your back. And we will support you any way we can, said logger Robert Pluid.

Perhaps nowhere has the reach of federal law been more acutely felt than in boundary County, which over the years has seen its big timber mills close because of a poor timber market and tightening federal forest restrictions. In Bonners Ferry, a town of 2,540 people and an unemployment rate of 14.5 percent, many residents say economic recovery is impossilbe in an area where the federal government owns 75 percent of the land.

Two enormous grizzly recovery areas, made up largely of federally owned land, surround Bonners Ferry, and townspeople say the protected bears increasingly are wandering out of the mountains killing elk and causing fear.

Hill said he was getting out of the shower on Mother's Day in May when his wife spotted a female grizzly and a pair of two year old juveniles nosing around the pigpen 40 yards outside. The two began shouting for their children, who had last been seen playing basketball on the opposite side of the house, but got no answer.

While Rachel went to look for the children, Hill picked up his gun and went onto the back deck. He leveled his weapon at one of the young bears, which was climbing into the pigpen, and fired. The other juvenile bear and the sow rushed into the woods in fright, while the young bear Hill had shot limped off, and then turned and moved back toward the house.

Hill fired two more shots, deciding it was better to finish the bear off than have a wounded animal around the property. He immediately notified state fish and game officials.

Last week, the U.S. attorney's office in Boise, **faced with outrage bordering on insurrection** in Northern Idaho, dropped the charges in favor of a citation that will require Hill to pay a $1,000.00 civil fine.

The apparent compromise may do little to quiet the wider controversy over the Endangered Species Act. "People think they have to come in here and save us from ourselves" That we're not smart enough to manage this kind of area. For crying out loud, we've lived here all our lives; we know what's best for our land." resident Guy Patchen said in an interview before the dismissal of the criminal charges.

This article brought me to tears as I copied it into this book from this morning's Sunday newspaper. Only an hour before, I was outside, playing basketball with my two little granddaughters. Large predators here in the west are out of control. Just last month, the next door neighbor shot a mountain lion, eating a rabbit on her front porch. In the same Sunday Missoulian newspaper, right below the above quoted story, it says this:

Hunter tries to save friend from bear
"A 39-year old hunter killed by a wounded grizzly bear he yelled out to draw the 400-pound male bear toward him in an effort to keep it from attacking his young hunting partner... Steve yelled at it to try and distract it, and it swung around and took him down. Its what my son would have done automatically for anybody."

As explained elsewhere, grizzly bears in northwestern Montana, Wyoming, northern Idaho, and southern British Columbia are flourishing, not struggling. In British Columbia, where the logging industry is still active, the bears are hunted and still flourishing. But in the United States, the federal government shuts down logging, under the auspices of protecting bears. Protect them from what? Logging doesn't kill grizzly bears. The bears simply move away, temporarily from logging activity, and then move back when the loggers leave. Environmenalist aren't shutting down logging, grazing, and mining to save grizzly bears; the bears are just a convenient tool to shut down America.

"Outrage, bordering on insurrection" is what Americans are feeling about the Endangered Species Act of 1973. And shouting out a bid on a pig, to help a fellow American fight it's own tyrannical government, was the folks of Bonner's Ferry, Idaho's way of "drawing a line in the sand."

In March of 1836, near the end of the siege of the Alamo, commander William Barrett Travis, drawing his sword, **"drew a line in the sand"**, asking those who wished to stay and die for freedom, to cross that line in the Texas sand. All but one crossed, including former Congressman Davy Crockett, and the critically injured Jim Bowie, who had to be carried across the line on a stretcher. Certain death awaited these men.

How many of today's Congressmen are going to summon up the courage to cross **"the line in the sand"**, and repeal the Endangered Species Act of 1973?

Tapley Holland* was the first to cross the line, accepting his certain death, in order to buy time and freedom for his fellow Texans. Just one example of thousands of men who have perished throughout our nation's history, fighting for the rights of Americans. These brave men did not go to their grave with the idea that some bureaucrat would someday give equal rights to the Chihuahuan Mud Turtles or the Cascade Cavern Salamanders.

*http://hollandhistory.blogspot.com/2009/08/tapley-holland-in-painting-in-alamo.html

Chapter 5

The Delta Smelt, Stopping American Farmers

> "If a drought strikes them, animals perish--man builds irrigation canals; if a flood strikes them, animals perish--man builds dams; if a carnivorous pack attacks them, animals perish--man writes the Constitution of the United States."
> Ayn Rand

In 2004, in a speech made to the American Farm Bureau Federation, Secretary Gale Norton, head of the United States Interior Department described the Endangered Species Act as follows:

"It is a law designed for confrontation."

Since when is a law, any law, let alone one that passed the United States Congress by a vote of 447-4, "**designed for confrontation**"? Confrontation with too much government is the very reason for the Declaration of Independence. The United States Constitution was specifically designed to protect the American peope from too much government confrontation.

"Law" is defined by Wikipedia as "**Law is a system of rules and guidelines, usually enforced through a set of institutions.**

The institution which enforces the Endangered Species Act of 1973, is the United States Fish & Wildlife Service, which falls under Mr. Norton's Department of the Interior. Laws are passed as part of a system of rules and guidelines for the people of the United States of America to follow, theoretically, to enhance and improve the quality of our lives. **Exactly when did the United States government start to pass laws "<u>designed for confrontation</u>" with the people it is governing?**

> "Occupants of public offices love power and are prone to abuse it."
> George Washington

And abuse it they have. Interior Secretary Norton's statement clearly demonstates how perverse some Washington bureaucrats have become in their thinking. The object of government, as envisioned by the framers of the Constitution, was to help Americans in their search for "life, liberty, and the pursuit of happiness." I can assure you, from personal experience, that confrontation with government is the last thing any free person wishes to experience.

When government oversteps its boundaries, boundaries clearly established in the constitution but eroded over time, we have a right, and a duty, as American citizens, to fight them. That fight may come through the court system, or through the ballot box.

As a human being, I like to eat. I make zero apologies for that fact. I do not feel guilty about it. I do not feel guilty when I cook a hamburger on the family barbeque, nor do I mourn for the dead cow that provided that hamburger. When I put lettuce and tomato on that hamburger, I do not, in the least bit, feel sorry for the Kangaroo rat that may have been displaced, so that a California farmer could grow that lettuce and tomato. I do not hold religious services, praying for the lost souls of the Delta Smelt, that may have been killed in the irrigation pumps, that allow the California farmers to grow my food, in an efficient manner, so that I can afford it. Instead, my family and I often say a prayer at dinnertime, thanking God for our American farmers, who work so hard.

I am thankful for the pioneers, who traveled to California in the late 1800s, often at great personal risk, and, through their government, built dams, and irrigations canals, and water systems, turning a desert wasteland, into productive farmland, so that human beings, myself included, might have food for our table. If in that process, rats, or spiders, or beetles, or bats, were dispossesed, I am sorry. Governing is about choices. It is the author's opinion that any government which chooses rats, and spiders, and beetles, and bats, over human beings, will eventually, as suggested by Thomas Jefferson, be "refreshed."

The following article appeared in the Wall Street Journal, September 2, 2009

California's Man-Made Drought
The Green War Against San Joaquin Valley Farmers

California has a new endangered species on its hands in the San Joaquin Valley—farmers. Thanks to environmental regulations designed to protect the likes of the three-inch long delta smelt, one of America's premier agricultural regions is suffering in a drought made worse by federal regulations.

The state's water emergency is unfolding thanks to the latest mishandling of the Endangered Species Act. Last December, the U.S. Fish and Wildlife Service issued what is known as a "biological opinion" imposing water reductions on the San Joaquin Valley and environs to safeguard the federally protected hypomesus transpacificus, a.k.a., the delta smelt. As a result, tens of billions of gallons of water from mountains east and north of Sacramento have been channelled away from farmers and into the ocean, leaving hundreds of thousands of acres of arable land fallow or scorched.

For this, Californians can thank the usual environmental suspects, er, lawyers. Last year's government ruling was the result of a 2006 lawsuit filed by the Natural Resources Defense Council and other outfits objecting to increased water pumping in the smelt vicinity. In June, things got even dustier when the National Marine Fisheries Service concluded that local salmon and steelhead also needed to be defended from the valley's water pumps. Those additional restrictions will begin to effect pumping operations next year.

The result has already been devastating for the state's farm economy. In the inland areas affected by the court-ordered water restrictions, the jobless rate has hit 14.3%, with some farming towns like Mendota seeing unemployment numbers near 40%. Statewide, the rate reached 11.6% in July, higher than it has been in 30 years. In August, 50 mayors from the San Joaquin Valley signed a letter asking President Obama to observe the impact of the draconian water rules firsthand.

Governor Arnold Schwarzenegger has said that he "doesn't have the authority to turn on the pumps" that would supply the delta with water, or "otherwise, they would be on." He did, however, have the ability to request intervention from the Department of Interior. Under a provision added to the Endangered Species Act in 1978 after the snail darter fiasco, a panel of seven cabinet officials known as a "God Squad" is able to intercede in economic emergencies, such as the one now parching California farmers. Despite a petition with more than 12,000 signers, Mr. Schwarzenegger has refused that remedy.

The issue now turns to the Obama Administration and the courts, though the farmers have so far found scant hope for relief from the White House. In June, the Administration denied the governor's request to designate California a federal disaster area as a result of the drought conditions, which U.S. Drought Monitor currently lists as a "severe drought" in 43% of the state. Doing so would force the Administration to acknowledge awkward questions about the role its own environmental policies have played in scorching the Earth.

As the crisis has deepened, the political stakes have risen as well. In late August, Agriculture Secretary Tom Vilsack came to the devastated valley to meet with farmers and community leaders. Democratic Senator Dianne Feinstein has pledged to press the issue with Interior Secretary Ken Salazar. "There are 30 lawsuits on the biological opinions and two separate opinions, one for the smelt and one for the salmon," Ms. Feinstein said, "The rules need to be reconsidered."

The Pacific Legal Foundation has filed a lawsuit on behalf of three farmers in the valley, calling the federal regulations "immoral and unconstitutional." Because the delta smelt is only found in California, the Foundation says, it does not fall under the regulatory powers provided by the Constitution's Commerce Clause. On a statutory basis, the Fish and Wildlife Service also neglected to appropriately consider the economic devastation the pumping restrictions would bring.

Things in California may have to get so bad that they endanger Democratic Congressional incumbents before Washington wakes up, but it doesn't have to be that way. Mr. Salazar has said that convening the God Squad would be "admitting failure" in the effort to save the smelt under the Endangered Species Act. Maybe so, but the livelihoods of tens of thousands of humans are also at stake. If the Obama Administration wants to help, it can take up Governor Schwarzenegger's request that it revisit the two biological opinions

Hypomesus Transpacificus-the Delta Smelt

The following article appeared in the Washington Times, August 20, 2009

Farmers Vs. Fish for California Water

Supporters of California agriculture called on the Obama administration and California Gov. Arnold Schwarzenegger on Wednesday to lift water restrictions that were imposed to protect the endangered delta smelt, saying the fish is putting farmers out of business.

The Pacific Legal Foundation presented a "Save Our Water" petition with 12,000 signatures at a Sacramento news conference, calling on Mr. Schwarzenegger, a Republican, to request that the Obama administration convene the federal Endangered Species Committee, also known as the "God Squad," to remove the water curbs.

"California should be known for the Rose Bowl, not a dust bowl. But there's a danger of a dust bowl being created in the Central Valley by extreme [Endangered Species Act] regulations," said foundation President Rob Rivett. "Instead of stimulating jobs, federal environmental officials are turning recession into depression and stimulating economic hardship for businesses, farms and families."

State Rep. George Radanovich, a Republican from the hard-hit San Joaquin Valley, said that"when it comes to water policy, humans come before fish."

The God Squad is a rarely invoked but potentially powerful provision within the Endangered Species Act that lets the committee override species protections in cases of economic emergency.

During a trip to the Central Valley in June, Interior Secretary Ken Salazar appeared to reject the idea.

Convening the committee, Mr. Salazar said, "would be to admit failure, it would defeat ecosystem restoration efforts. It has been rarely invoked and usually leads to litigation," according to Aquafornia.com, a Web site on the state's water issues.

As a result, proponents of emergency action are urging Mr. Schwarzenegger to throw his clout behind the idea and make the request to the Interior Department on behalf of the state.

Lester Snow, director of the California Department of Water Resources, said the governor had sent requests for reconsultation on the smelt and chinook salmon to the Interior and Commerce departments.

"The governor would look at the God Squad as indication that the federal government isn't responding. It's an action of last resort," Mr. Snow said. "It rarely works the way anyone wants it to. What the governor wants is a strong federal partner."

Nobody doubts the economic devastation to the Central Valley. The unemployment rate in agriculture communities ranges from 20 percent to 40 percent, while 250,000 acres of farmland are lying fallow or dying. The region's agricultural output is expected to decline by between $1 billion and $3 billion this year over last, according to estimates by agricultural and business groups.

Whether the delta smelt is to blame lies at the heart of the debate. While some blame the fish for the severe reductions in pumping from the Sacramento-San Joaquin Delta, others argue that the region's three-year drought is primarily to blame.

Some environmentalists say the agriculture industry needs to adapt to the reduced water supply and live within its means.

"Big Ag must now learn to do more with less," campaigner Brian Smith wrote on Earthjustice.org. "The days of copious taxpayer-subsidized water exports from the Delta are coming to an end. And the idea of killing off numerous native fish species, decimating Northern California fishing communities and turning the Delta into a fetid swamp is simply not allowed under federal law."

The situation for farmers is likely to get worse before it gets better. Federal regulators are poised to enact more water restrictions to protect the chinook salmon, the steelhead and other fish. Estimates are that the cutbacks could result in the removal of 500,000 acre-feet of water.

Scaling back the Central Valley agriculture industry, also known as America's fruit basket, would have an economic impact that stretches beyond California. Americans undoubtedly would find themselves buying more fruits, vegetables and nuts from foreign sources, Mr. Rivett said.

"It's certainly going to impact our food security. We know our farmers here produce a product that's safe and healthy; we don't know what will happen if we're importing those products," he said.

Others supporting the "Save Our Water" petition include the California Chamber of Commerce, which urged state and federal officials to protect agricultural water supplies "from measures that will inflict serious economic and social harm on millions of Californians."

In May, the foundation filed a lawsuit against the Fish and Wildlife Service on behalf of several Central Valley farmers challenging the agency's authority to issue regulations on behalf of the delta smelt.

Before Pumps Turned Off   **After Pumps Turned Off**

"Big Ag must now learn to do more with less,"

wrote campaigner Brian Smith wrote on Earthjustice.org. "Big Ag" is what feeds America, and much of the world. "Big Ag" is more efficient than "Little Ag" , which is why Americans enjoy the least expensive food supply in the world. Ask the starving people of Zimbabwe, once known as "Africa's breadbasket" what happened when Mugabe's government broke up the "Big Ag" farms and gave it back to the subsistent farmer ("Little Ag"). Ask them what it's like to see their children go to bed, not just hungry, but dying. Ask them how they like tyrannical government.

If "Big Ag" must learn to do with less, as suggested by Earthjustice, than so must the American people that eat the food "Big Ag" grows. The Environmental Movement says: "More to the Delta Smelt, more to the Santa Anna Sucker, more to the Tipton Kangaroo Rats. Less to the children of America and the world."

I reject that concept, and I believe the vast majority of Americans reject that concept.

> "Man cannot survive except through his mind. He comes on earth unarmed. His brain is his only weapon. Animals obtain food by force. man had no claws, no fangs, no horns, no great strength of muscle. He must plant his food or hunt it. To plant, he needs a process of thought. To hunt, he needs weapons, and to make weapons - a process of thought. From this simplest necessity to the highest religious abstraction, from the wheel to the skyscraper, everything we are and we have comes from a single attribute of man -the function of his reasoning mind."
> Ayn Rand (The Fountainhead)

A "reasoning mind" does not give rights to fungus, spiders, flies, bats, wolves, salamanders, mussels, smelt, and scorpions. That is the reason there is no mention of these issues in the Declaration of Independence or the United States Constitution. The "reasoning minds" of Thomas Jefferson, George Washington, Thomas Paine, Benjamin Franklin, et. al. never fathomed that such an idiotic concept could ever come to pass. And these creatures have, not just equal rights to Americans, but superior rights.

Americans, (and its habitat, America), should be the next species listed on The Endangered Species List.

The following article appeared in the Capital Press, October 21, 2010

Critical habitat reaching critical mass

Consider for a moment the bull trout. Once called the Dolly Varden, the fish is closely related to the char that proliferates in Alaska and Canada.

Like the gray wolf, the bull trout is a close relative of a species that is plentiful to the point of brimming in one part of the continent yet considered to be endangered or threatened in another.

That's how the federal Endangered Species Act works.

Thousands of gray wolves live in Canada and Alaska, yet they are protected in the Lower 48, even as they spread across the U.S.'s northern tier.

As a part of the process of protecting animals that may or may not need it, the U.S. Fish and Wildlife Service designates "critical habitat" areas. Critical habitat means some activities that might in some way affect that species are banned or curbed.

Especially on federally owned land, the impact can be huge. Consider the fact that the federal government owns most of the West. For example, it owns 84.5 percent of Nevada, 53.1 percent of Oregon, 50.2 percent of Idaho, 45.3 percent of California and 30.3 percent of Washington state.

Many ranchers who graze cattle on federal allotments feel the crush of critical habitat designations, as do logging companies that bid on timber sales in national forests.

According to the U.S. Fish and Wildlife Service, critical habitats have been designated for 220 endangered or threatened animal species, many in the West. Though such a designation does not automatically stop all human activity, it does affect any that require a federal permit. That includes ranching and logging, among others.

What you ultimately have is layer after layer of "critical habitats" superimposed on one another, each with a set of restrictions.

This fact came up recently when the critical habitat area for the bull trout was quadrupled. Instead of a critical habitat of 4,800 miles of river and lake shorelines, now about 19,700 miles of shorelines are included. Bull trout don't even exist in some of those areas, yet they are protected. About 800 miles of those rivers and 16,700 acres of lakes haven't seen a bull trout in who-knows-how-long.

But here's the kicker -- 97 percent of that critical habitat for the bull trout is also critical habitat for one or several other species, according to a Fish and Wildlife Service spokeswoman.

Which brings up this question: How many layers of protection are required in those areas? One? Three? A dozen?

This is a case of Uncle Sam wearing a belt and suspenders at the same time to protect the species.

The Pacific Legal Foundation works to protect another endangered "species" -- resource industries in the West. Over regulation by the federal government and harassment from environmental groups have decimated the ranks of companies that rely on natural resources.

"At some point you're going to reach a tipping point," said Damien Schiff, a PLF lawyer. "You're going to cause economic harm as a result of excessive regulation."

For example, he said, one critical habitat designation might restrict one activity; another might restrict another. Still another might restrict a third. Pretty soon, no one can do anything.

If you were to compile a map showing the critical habitat of all of the endangered, threatened and otherwise noteworthy animal species currently under consideration for listing under the Endangered Species Act, what would it look like?

Nearly every river, lake and stream has some sort of sucker fish, bull trout, steelhead, salmon, smelt or other fish. Nearly every old-growth forest in the Northwest is home to the northern spotted owl, which is deemed threatened. Throw in much of the West, where the sage grouse is being studied for protection, and the Palouse, where the wily giant Palouse earthworm roams and that environmentalists want to protect.

And don't forget about the gray wolf. Some environmentalists want it returned to its historical range -- most of the continental U.S.

For good measure, there are endangered shrews and kangaroo rats to add to the mix.Combined, all of the species being considered for protection and the critical habitat they would add cover a lot of territory.

We suspect that, eventually, it would include nearly all of the continental U.S.

The following article appeared in the Capital Press, October 14, 2010

Beware of politics hijacking 'science'

We are told that we must look to the "best science" when deciding questions of public policy. That's the only way, the reasoning goes, that the needs of the many, the greater good, can overcome political or economic considerations that favor the narrow interests of a few.

We find no fault in the logic that science should play a role when we consider solutions to the problems facing society. There's no substitute for hard facts. But what happens when the science is wrong, or its results are fashioned to favor a political agenda?

In 2006, the California Legislature passed the Global Warming Solutions Act. It was a sweeping measure designed to reduce carbon emissions to 1990 levels by 2020. Towards that goal, the state's Air Quality Board adopted tough new regulations in 2007 on off-road diesel emissions. To meet the standards, thousands of construction and other businesses will have to buy new equipment or perform costly retrofits on their existing equipment.

Last week the San Francisco Chronicle reported that in making its case to justify its harsh regulations, the Air Quality Board overestimated emissions from off-road diesel engines by 340 percent. The board has yet to explain the miscalculation.

Critics have suggested, however, that the board's "best science" was influenced by the political agenda of the environmental movement. Accurate estimates would prove inconvenient to those who desired sweeping regulations. Fudging the numbers by a factor of nearly three and a half provided a problem tailor-made for a radical solution.

Of course, mistakes happen. It appears no one knows that better than the staff of the Air Quality Board. The Chronicle also reported that board scientists last year said that 18,000 Californians die prematurely each year because of diesel emissions. The board later said that number was a bit high -- double, in fact, the number of deaths that could actually be attributed to the emissions.

Mary Nichols, chairwoman of the board, told the paper that these

revelations don't cause her to question other calculations made by board scientists.
We should think not. Science, after all, evolves. Today's scientific fact is tomorrow's discredited theory.

Australian biologists at the University of Queensland studied 180 species that had been declared extinct by other scientists. Their findings, released last month, found that a third of the species were still alive and unaware that scientific study had rendered them unequivocally dead.

When making important decisions, elected officials, bureaucrats and the public should use the "best science" available. It's important, however, that we understand its limitations. At its best, science is only as good as the data used to reach a conclusion. It is a snapshot of what is now known, subject to change as new data is discovered.

When the data is conjured to reach a preconceived conclusion, it really isn't science. And of that we should all be wary.

Photographs from USA-wethepeople.com
Dead Orchards and the San Joaquin Valley Dustbowl

Congress created the dustbowl, Congress can fix the dustbowl. All it has to do is repeal the Endangered Species Act of 1973. Pander to Americans for a change, instead of an Environmental Movement gone berserk.

The following is from the U.S. Department of the Interior, Bureau of Reclamation website: http://www.usbr.gov/mp/cvp/about.html

About the Central Valley Project (CVP)

The CVP Today

The CVP serves farms, homes, and industry in California's Central Valley as well as the major urban centers in the San Francisco Bay Area; it is also the primary source of water for much of California's wetlands.

In addition to delivering water for farms, homes, factories, and the environment, the CVP produces electric power and provides flood protection, navigation, recreation, and water quality benefits. While the facilities are spread out over hundreds of miles, the project is financially and operationally integrated as a single large water project.

The C.V.P. reaches from the Cascade Mountains near Redding in the north some 500 miles to the Tehachapi Mountains near Bakersfield in the south.

Is comprised of 20 dams and reservoirs, 11 powerplants, and 500 miles of major canal as well as conduits, tunnels, and related facilities.

Annually delivers about 7 million acre-feet for agriculture, urban, and wildlife use.

Provides about 5 million acre-feet for farms -- **enough to irrigate about 3 million acres or approximately one-third of the agricultural land in California.**
Furnishes about 600,000 acre-feet for municipal and industrial use, enough to supply close to **1 million households with their water needs each year.**

Dedicates 800,000 acre-feet per year to fish and wildlife and their habitat and 410,00 acre-feet to State and Federal wildlife refuges and wetlands pursuant to the Central Valley Project Improvement Act (CVPIA).
During an average water year, generates about 4.8 billion kilowatt hours of **electricity to meet the needs of some 2 million people.**

As noted earlier, it takes approximately 1/8 of an acre of farmland in California to feed one human being for a year. Multiply the three million acres the Central Valley Project irrigates times 8, and you get 24,000,000 people a year, every year, year after year, that this region is feeding. In addition to that, the system provides electricity for two million people, along with water for wildlife refuges, wetlands, and fish and wildlife habitat. Additionally, it provides water for 1 million households per year, or about 3 million people.

Food, Electricity, Water, Jobs, Wildlife Habitat, Wetlands. It is pretty easy to see why the Environmental Movement wants to shut down the water pumps. People were living, working, and prospering in California. We certainly can't have that sort of thing happening in America, can we?

The following article appeared January 9, 2009, at SFGate.com

Shutting off the water pumps to save delta smelt unwarranted

January 08, 2009 | By Craig Manson and Brandon Middleton

There's great cause for concern over the biological opinion issued by the U.S. Fish and Wildlife Service in the form of a new rules to protect the delta smelt, a fish species that is listed as threatened under the federal Endangered Species Act.

That's because millions of Californians depend upon the continued operation of two large irrigation projects for a reliable supply of water. And the scientific reasons for shutting them down to protect the smelt are dubious at best.

The two water operations in question, the Central Valley Project and the State Water Project, depend on pumps located at the southern end of the Sacramento-San Joaquin Delta, to move water flowing into the delta from Northern California to water users through Southern California and the Central Valley. Recent court decisions have identified the operations' pumps as a major cause of the smelt's decline, and the Fish and Wildlife Service's decision will force a dramatic reduction in pumping.

Obviously, protecting the delta smelt and other delta fish species is important. But unfortunately, the numerous farmers who will be severely affected by the water restrictions cannot take solace in knowing that their pain will be ameliorated by the delta smelt's gain.

There is little science to support the notion that pumping restrictions will solve the problem of the smelt's decline.
Myriad factors negatively affect the well-being of the delta smelt. These include, but are not limited to, a low food supply, presence of predatory fish and a toxic water habitat for the smelt. The pumps play a role through entrainment, meaning that smelt can sometimes get sucked into the pumps.

But the significance of this and how it affects the species is unknown. No one knows how many smelt are in the delta.

Moreover, no study has shown a definitive link between the pumps and smelt viability. As a federal judge overseeing litigation concerning the delta smelt has noted, there is no one cause for the smelt's decline. And yet, as a 2008 CALFED report indicates, the pumps are "blamed for many of the delta's ills," despite their being "no conclusive evidence that export pumping has caused population declines" of delta fish species.

Man Is the Endangered Species*
By David Ross

Half of the endangered species in the U.S. are west of the Mississippi. Half of those are in California. Half of those are in Southern California. Half of those are in San Diego County. **Which goes a long way towards explaining why it is the most environmentally terrorized community in the United States, with regulators scheming to put half of the developable private land into permanent open space.**

With 2.6 million people, San Diego County has over 200 plants and animals that are endangered or nearly so. That's more than most U.S. states. Camp Pendleton, the Marine Corps' pristine reservation of 125,000 acres, has 18 endangered species, which prompted a recent ban on the Marines using most of their 17 miles of beachfront for exercises. The situation is also pretty bleak for property-owners. **You may think to yourself, "Well, that's too bad for San Diego, but it'll never happen here." Think again. The Interior Department regards San Diego's solution to endangered species as the way the whole country should approach it.**

The region, one of the most desirable areas in the U.S., has also been targeted by Big Environmentalism, which wants to shut down as much private property as possible. Tangential strategies include adamant opposition to expansion of the region's freeways and harassing lawsuits by green groups such as one called Save Our Forests and Ranchlands (SOFAR), which for several years created an effective building permit moratorium in all of the county's agricultural lands.

The presence of coastlands, wetlands, grasslands, land near seasonal streams, any kind of land except concrete covered land, provides an excuse to put restrictions on its use and to require "mitigations." **Owning and selling "mitigation" land at a big profit has become something of a cottage industry in San Diego.**

So has acquiring land by the tactic of making it almost worthless as an economic asset. Then "selfless" land conservancies can swoop down and offer to buy the now worthless land for cheap. It's a ruse as old as the Old West range wars.

Representatives of these same conservancies and green groups often speak at planning commission and other land use hearings, lobbying to downzone properties whose owners they will later approach to buy.

Hence it is nearly impossible for a landowner to build without giving some property to the government for an open space or biological opens space easement.

A prominent land use attorney, William Schwartz, while participating in hearings for the upcoming revision of the County's General Plan, an eruptive property-taking of Krakatoan proportions, was heard to grumble that a 70 percent set aside of his client's land for open space for "the public good" ought to be sufficient. The county's land planners were proposing 90 percent.

Bill Horn, a conservative county supervisor, pointed out ten years ago that government in its federal, state and county incarnations already owned more than 58 percent of the land.

"When you consider that 75.8 percent of the acreage in our county is already classed as open space, and more than 58 percent of all acreage is government owned, the question comes to mind, **when is enough, enough?**", he wrote, and was quoted again elsewhere as saying, "It's really not an endangered species issue, it's a land control issue."

Ten years ago San Diego County pioneered something quite revolutionary called the Multiple Species Conservation Program. It set aside 172,000 acres of prime developable land (including 55,200 acres in San Diego City and the rest in the unincorporated part of the County) and made it off-limits to development. That was the stick. The carrot was that MSCP supposedly eliminated much of the environmental red tape for building on what private land was left.

Some of the best criticism against MSCP came early on when some scientists objected that it was based on intuition and not science. Those pushing MSCP conceded that point, but argued it was more important to acquire the habitat before it was developed because no one knew which lands were important and which weren't. Eventually it became clear that all undeveloped land is considered potentially important.

When the MSCP was introduced, **County government promised that it would be voted on by the people, that funding must be approved by the people and that if public funding was not found within three years the program would end.** Supervisors who were reluctant to approve it were warned that enviros would stall every development pending until it was adopted. **None of those promises were kept** and the program is still in place.

Today there are MSCPs all over California and in several Western states, but San Diego's is still the most ambitious. The biggest victims of ambitious endangered species plans in San Diego are farmers. Often the only people who have consistently cared for the land, farmers are under increasing attack from city-based critics, such as the earlier mentioned SOFAR.

The greens want to be able to jump into their Prius or hop onto their Segway and ride into the back country and not see houses or other habitation. Farmers, who often want to sell off parcels when water prices rise too high, are their natural enemies.

Ranchers, who for generations have raised cattle, often find that without being told, their land has had a sensitive habitat overlay put on it that effectively prevents them from doing something so simple as plowing without a permit. For them it may seem as though

The following article appeared in The Daily Caller, on May 27, 2011.

Crazifornia: Delta Smelt Refuses to Die in Pumps

In Tracy, California, where the massive California Water Project pumps stand ready to move up to 15,450 cubic feet of Sacramento-San Joaquin Delta water southward every single second, it's been a busy spring.

The pumps have been a mere shadow of their old selves ever since U.S. District Court Judge Oliver Wanger began ratcheting them down in 2007 in response to environmentalist lawsuits brought under the auspices of the Delta smelt. The environmentalists blamed the pumping for the precipitous drop in the smelt population, ignoring any number of other Delta ills that could be decimating the little fish, including ammonia from Sacramento's sewage plant, farm chemical runoff and hungry non-native bass prized by the very sports fishermen who joined the environmentalists in blaming the pumps.

But the 2010-2011 storm season has been a wet one, with about twice the average rainfall and snowfall. That, and his growing skepticism of the adequacy of the science justifying restrictions on pumping, has loosened Judge Wanger's grip on Southern California's spigot, and the pumps have been running at up to 80 percent of their capacity. As the water rushes out of the Delta and toward the pumps, it's channeled through an ingenious series of sieve-lines designed to keep the smelt away. In a nearby building, traps catch any that do get through, and whenever the pumps are running, state employees stand ready to count any dead smelt — and if even a few are found, the pumps can be stopped or slowed down.

So what have they found? With all those pumps spinning away and all that water hurtling south, smelt corpses should be piling up as fast as debt in D.C. Any other result would cast the scientific theories of the smelt's champions as not much better than alchemy and astrology, right?

Right. According to Tom Philp, executive strategist for the Metropolitan Water District of Southern California (the user of most of that water), the sum total smelt body count since they switched on the California Water Project pumps is zero.

Philp says turbidity — muddy water — saved the smelt. Since big fish like to eat little fish, smelt like to hide in turbid water, and Delta turbidity this year has been far from the pumps. The muddy conditions in the Delta caused by this year's high runoff levels from the mountains couldn't come at a better time, because Judge Wanger recently gave the slow-moving biolocrats (or is it burologists?) at the U.S. Fish & Wildlife Service two more years to clean up their science or give up trying to justify continued pumping restrictions.

If it can be shown that pumping levels should be controlled by the proximity of turbid water to the pumps instead of fish counts in non-turbid water or, for that matter, where we happen to be in the smelt's reproductive cycle, much more water will be able to move south than can now. The volume of data supporting the turbidity theory as a viable alternative to the "the pump ate my fish" theory favored by the environmentalists is growing, but no one expects Gaea's Army to meekly retreat.

Instead, we fully expect new environmentalist legal motions and "scientific" studies to be falling as thick as last winter's snow in the Sierras. This is California, after all.

Laer Pearce, a veteran of three decades of California public affairs, is currently working on a book that shows how everything wrong with America comes from California.

Unfortunately, it is not just California. The Endangered Species Act of 1973 is being used all across the country. Farming, Manufacturing, Mining, Housing, Transportation, Recreation, Energy, Tourism, Military Preparedness, are all under attack. In short, all the activities associated with being American, and being human.

Here is what Stanley D. Shift, head of the U.S. Delegation to the U.N.

Stopping American Farmers

Habitat Conference, participated in the Forum, and in the U.N. Habitat Conference. The Conference report begins:

"Private land ownership is a principal instrument of accumulating wealth and therefore contributes to social injustice. Public control of land is therefore indispensable."

The Conference recommended:
"Public ownership of land is justified in favor of the common good, rather than to protect the interests of the already privileged."

The "already privileged", like the guy in New Jersey, that couldn't build a house on his 1.27 acre country estate?

The U.N. Habitat Conference says accumulating wealth contributes to social injustice. That reads like something right out of the teachings of Karl Marx. I hope Americans will remember, when the alarm clock goes off tomorrow morning at 5:00 A.M. so they can go to work, that they are contributing to "social injustice". I hope they will remember when they seek the "American Dream" of home ownership and a few bucks in the bank ("accumulating wealth"), that they are contributing to "social injustice." For those Americans that own a piece of land, I hope they will remember they are considered "the already privileged."

And I hope they will remember to vote.

"We are fast approaching the stage of the ultimate inversion: the stage where the government is free to do anything it pleases, while the citizens may act only by permission; which is the stage of the darkest periods of human history, the stage of rule by brute force."
Ayn Rand

Chapter 6

Grizzlies in my Garden
The ESA Compliance
Nightmare

The Grizzly Bear, UrsusArctos Horriblus

"No Charges Will Be Filed in Griz Shooting"

Page 1, Section B, **The Missoulian**, May 24, 2011

"No charges will be filed against a Ronan-area landowner who shot and killed a female grizzly bear that had killed his chickens on May 14. It was one of two grizzlies killed in Montana that weekend. ....The bear had been on the man's property earlier in the day and was shot when it returned." The shooting took place near Ronan, Montana, on the Confederated Salish and Kootenai Reservation. "Tribal officials are encouraging landowners who have, or could have, similar problems with bears to attend a free electric fencing clinic next month. **"A properly constructed electric fence is safe for people and pets,"** said tribal bear biologist Tracy Courville, " and has proven to be effective in deterring bears"......electric fencing can help deter bears from apiaries (beehives), fruit trees, gardens, live-stock pens, rabbit hutches, garbage containers, dog kennels, chicken coops, compost piles, storage sheds, and more... The death of the grizzly three miles east of Ronan was the fourth grizzly lost from the Flathead Reservation in the past ten months...An adult female and two cubs that had developed a taste for chickens were captured and removed to the Louisville (Ky.) Zoo in August....The same weekend the grizzly was shot in Ronan, an antler hunter shot and killed a sow grizzly in the Blackfoot-Crow Wildlife Management Area.....Montana Fish, Wildlife, and Parks officials determined that, too, was a justifiable self defense, and no-charges were filed."

The fact is, humans and grizzly bears are not very compatible. Grizzly bears, particularly sows with cubs, can be very aggressive. These conflicts have gone on time immemorial, from pre-historic times, to Lewis & Clark, Hugh Glass, and present day inhabitants of the northern Rocky Mountains. Several humans every year are killed or mauled by these bruins. Despite what the Environmental Movement wants you to think, their numbers are increasing, not decreasing. Less than 50 miles north of Whitefish, Montana, about a days walk for a grizzly, in British Columbia, there are 25,000 grizzly bears, and about 300 are legally harvested by sportsmen every year. The bears are flourishing. In our own state of Alaska, bears have become so numerous, that some Game Management Units have no closed season. The areas around Yellowstone and Glacier National Park have become increasingly dangerous, as the bear populations grow, seeking more and more space. Without limited hunting to control the burgeoning bear populations, the rate of conflicts will rise, and people will die.

Bear, chicken conflicts on the rise; landowners advised to protect their poultry

By TRISTAN SCOTT of the Missoulian

WHITEFISH - More grizzly bears are keying in on unprotected chicken coops in western Montana, with increasingly deadly consequences - both for the bears and the pilfered poultry.

The rise in bear-related chicken raids is ruffling the feathers of state and federal wildlife managers who are forced to move or kill bears that receive a food reward, be it from a trash can, a fruit orchard or a bird pen. The conflicts are entirely avoidable, managers say, but it's the responsibility of landowners to buck the disturbing trend.

"Chickens have become a real pain," said Chris Servheen, Montana's grizzly bear recovery coordinator for the U.S. Fish and Wildlife Service. "We're seeing a lot of people who are just being irresponsible. They want to have chickens in bear country, and then when they get bears they want Fish and Game to come fix a problem they created. The only way to fix the problem is by preventing it from happening in the first place, before the bear gets the food reward. It's really a sad state of affairs when the bear managers are picking up the pieces."

Servheen and other managers are encouraging landowners to build electric fences around chicken coops and other attractants, like sweet corn, vegetable gardens, fruit orchards and beehives. The fences are cheap and when constructed properly will deter even the craftiest bears.
"We have found that when people put up a good fence around orchards, gardens, beehives, chicken coops, it is a very good deterrent," said Tim Manley, bear management specialist with Montana Fish, Wildlife and Parks. "Bears respect the electric fence, and if you get a good hot fence bears will stay away."

Late last month, Manley trapped and relocated two grizzly bears that killed about 100 chickens at a residence near Lake Five, several miles from West Glacier. An adult female grizzly and yearling male killed the chickens - mostly chicks - over a period of two nights, Manley said.

With help from FWP, the landowners installed an electric fence around their chicken pen and a nearby rabbit pen, a step Manley said will dramatically reduce the chance of another encounter.

"The bears just don't come near the fences," he said.
In Missoula, chickens and hobby farms have grown in popularity since a December 2007 city ordinance made it OK to keep chickens. With passage of the ordinance came added potential for bear-human conflicts.

"I sometimes get calls daily on chickens, whereas I used to never hear about it," said Jamie Jonkel, FWP's bear management specialist in Missoula. "Chickens are the new garbage. There are so many chickens on the landscape that it's like having garbage cans with wings just tempting the bears."

Jonkel is confident that bears and humans can co-exist in Montana, and he doesn't see any reason why chickens can't be in the mix, too. But it requires added vigilance and responsibility on the part of the landowner.

"Usually what I see is someone buys a box of chicks, they don't have any setup, and the next thing you know they've got a shabby coop and 40 chickens running around," Jonkel said. "They're throwing the slop in the backyard and gathering eggs, and pretty soon they've got game trails coming off the ridge and leading into their backyard."

Bear managers hold out little hope for a bear that's received a food reward from a human setting, and the problem is only compounded when cubs are involved.

"We can't fix bears that have gotten a food reward. We can move them, but they're going to come back," Servheen said. "And if it's a family group, the cubs are learning future behaviors. If the mother teaches them how to key in on a chicken coop, they will continue to do that. And if they are orphaned, then that becomes the only food source they know. It's like if you're growing up as a kid and your mom only takes you to McDonald's. You don't know there are other restaurants out there. That really creates a long-term problem."

In the Mission Valley, east of St. Ignatius, an adult female and her two yearlings have been targeting the same unprotected chicken coops for the last two seasons. Recently, the mother mysteriously disappeared.

"I don't have a lot of hope for those bears, and I'm suspicious of what happened to the mother," said Stacy Courville, a bear biologist with the Confederated Salish and Kootenai Tribes. "Now we've got two yearlings running around getting into trouble at the same residence, all because people won't secure their attractants."

Courville said too many grizzly bears are meeting their fate because of residents' ignorance about chickens and other attractants, like sweet corn, which has become another problem.

This spring, tribal officials trapped and relocated a chicken-eating grizzly on the Flathead Indian Reservation and released it in the North Fork of the Flathead. The bear continued to get in trouble, however, coming out of the mountains to feed on chickens and goats in the Trego area. Montana Fish, Wildlife and Parks labeled it a nuisance bear and killed it.

Grizzlies in My Garden

In May, a Ronan-area landowner shot and killed a 2-year-old grizzly after the bear killed his chickens.

Last summer, a sow and two cubs on the reservation who found chicken dinners both tasty and easily accessible were trapped and sent to the Louisville Zoo.

In total, about a half-dozen grizzlies were lost from the Flathead Reservation in less than a year to poultry-related incidents, Courville said.

"We are talking at least five grizzly bears dead because of poultry in the last two seasons on the reservation alone," he said. "And I couldn't even begin to tell you how many black bears we've had to destroy.

"This problem should be nonexistent," he continued. "We shouldn't be destroying grizzly bears because people are refusing to protect their chickens, especially when there's a cheap solution. An energizer is a hundred bucks and the wires are even less. We are destroying grizzly bears because people won't protect their attractants. That's the bad part and the sad part."

Electric fencing is such a proven and effective solution that Defenders of Wildlife, a nonprofit wildlife preservation organization, has launched an electric fence incentive program.

Erin Edge, the Bear Aware coordinator for Defenders of Wildlife in Missoula, said the group will contribute $100 to the cost of installing an electric fence around livestock, chicken coops or beehives.

"The chicken thing has really increased in the last five years and hobby farms are starting to pop up all over the place," Edge said. "There's a push for local food and sustainable agriculture, which is great, but bears are learning about these new attractants. When you live in this wildlife-urban interface you have to be responsible."

Manley said an electric fence for an average-size chicken coop will cost about $200, including the energizer, posts and wires. To be effective, the fence must be at least four feet high and have seven strands of electric wires, and an energizer with a joule rating of at least .5.

He said to test a fence's effectiveness one wildlife manager put an electrified perimeter around a horse carcass in bear habitat, and installed remote-sensor cameras to monitor the area. Although bears were present, they stayed away from the carcass.

"A horse carcass is pretty tempting," Manley said.

Brochures on installing electric fencing are available at FWP headquarters and on the agency's website at fwp.mt.gov.

In Missoula, Jonkel said one woman inherited chickens from a friend and built a chicken coop he described as "a fortress." It was both aesthetically pleasing and effective, he said.

"It's bulletproof," Jonkel said.

A poor and late berry crop in the high country is keeping bears down in the valley looking for food, and Courville said he expects conflicts between bears and humans to increase this fall unless more people get the message.

"I'm worried about the next two months," he said.

Courville has been putting literature about electric fences in the mailboxes of landowners with unprotected coops, and displaying brochures next to the chicken scratch at feed stores.

"It's starting to work, but we are playing catch-up and there are still a lot of unfenced coops," he said. "We're getting through to some people, but not all of them. If people are going to have chickens in bear country, they're going to have to take extra precautions."

"We're seeing a lot of people who are just being irresponsible. They want to have chickens in bear country, and then when they get bears they want Fish and Game to come fix a problem they created."

Can you imagine the nerve of these humans, growing sweet corn, taking out their trash, planting vegetable gardens, and raising chickens? As described in the newspaper article, many of the bear problems are taking place on the Flathead and Blackfoot Indian Reservations, where unemployment often exceeds 70%. Did it perhaps occur to anyone at the U.S. Fish & Wildlife Service that these poor people might actually need these gardens and these chickens to feed themselves and their families? Is that being "just irresponsible". (Let's not mention that it was government that forced these people onto the reservations in the first place. Now we don't even let them raise chickens!)

These bears come into the valley, near humans, because they are hungry, and because their range is expanding, because there are too many bears and wolves in the backcountry. The reason they are hungry, is because much of the game, particularly the moose and elk, have been devastated by the unhunted wolf populations. Large predators, like all wildlife around the world, need to be managed. Despite what environmentalists want you to think, wildlife is not self regulating. It is the U.S. Fish & Wildlife Service that is acting irresponsibly here, not the local citizenry, trying to grow food for their families.

I have 10,000 volt fences around my hunting camps in the Northwest Territories, to keep the grizzly bears away from the sleeping clients. They are effective some of the time, not all of the time. Bears are intelligent and persistent, and they will return many times to the scent of food, even if they don't actually get a "food reward." In the Northwest Territories, we shoot the bears whenever they come near camp, with rubber bullets loaded in 12 gauge shotguns. This is not only legal in the N.W.T., but mandated by the government, as part of my Tourism License and Bear Abatement Program. The rubber bullets sting the bears, and help instill a fear of human beings, which they seldom encounter. In the United States, where grizzly bears can't be hunted, (or shot with rubber bullets,) no such fear of humans exists, since it has been generations (of bears) since they were hunted here. The death and mauling of many human beings every year, can be directly attributed to the Endangered Species Act of 1973.

Franklin Delano Roosevelt stated: *"The winds that blow through the wide sky in these mounts, the winds that sweep from Canada to Mexico, from the Pacific to the Atlantic - have always blown on free men."*

Now the United States government wants Americans to put up bear fences around their **"apiaries (beehives), fruit trees, gardens, livestock pens, rabbit hutches, garbage containers, dog kennels, chicken coops, compost piles, storage sheds, and more."** "Life, Liberty, and the Pursuit of Happiness" is not living inside 10,000 volt electrical fence enclosures. That lifestyle is meant for bank robbers, rapists, murderers, and certain politicians, and I find it outrageous for any government bureaucrat to recommend such a thing. It is virtually impossible to keep a hungry grizzly bear from coming and investigating food smells. That is what bears do. They are highly intelligent animals, and can be effectively deterred, and taught, to avoid human beings. By keeping the bear populations in check through carefully controlled hunting, and by authorizing the use of more force when bears do come around humans, this problem can be minimized.

Dealing with any Endangered Species, as the act is currently administered, is extremely time consuming, complicated, and expensive. For instance, the government recommendation to install electric fences, all 10,000 volts of them, is probably a violation of the act itself. By design, the fence would "harass" a grizzly bear, should one contact said electric fence. (Having seen bears touch electric fences many times, it rolls them pretty good. The damper the ground, the harder it rolls them.) By law, you need an "Incidental Take Permit" to "harass" an endangered species. The fence, by itself, could be considered altering the bears habitat to prevent it from feeding, also requiring an Incidental Take Permit. In order to acquire such a permit, you need a "Habitat Conservation Plan. The chart on the following page, courtesy of the U.S. Fish & Wildlife Service website, gives a map of the "typical" application process.

Incidental Take Permit*

An "incidental take permit"* is a permit issued under Section 10 of the Federal Endangered Species Act (ESA) to private, non-federal entities undertaking otherwise lawful projects that might result in the take of an endangered or threatened species. Application for an incidental take permit is subject to certain requirements, including preparation by the permit applicant of a conservation plan.[1]

"Take" is defined by the ESA as **harass, harm,** pursue, hunt, shoot, wound, kill, trap, capture, or collect any threatened or endangered species. Harm may include significant habitat modification where it actually kills or injures a listed species through impairment of essential behavior (e.g., nesting or reproduction).[2] In the 1982 ESA amendments, Congress authorized the United States Fish and Wildlife Service (through the Secretary of the Interior) to issue per-

*http://www.nmfs.noaa.gov/pr/pdfs/laws/hcp_handbook.pdf

mits for the "incidental take" of endangered and threatened wildlife species (Section 10a(1)B of the ESA). Thus, permit holders can proceed with an activity, such as construction or other economic development, that may result in the "incidental" taking of a listed species.

The 1982 amendment requires that permit applicants design, implement, and secure funding for a Habitat Conservation Plan or "HCP" that minimizes and mitigates harm to the impacted species during the proposed project. The HCP is a legally binding agreement between the Secretary of the Interior and the permit holder."

Figure 2: Typical Processing Steps for Section 10(a)(1)(B) Incidental Take Permit Applications Requiring an EA

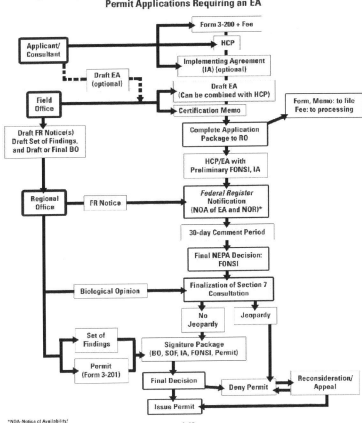

*NOA-Notice of Availability/
NOR-Notice of Receipt of Permit Application

1-12

The Endangered Species Act of 1973 applies to everyone, rich or poor, black or white, left or right, young or old. No exceptions, period. So, if you want to plant a garden in Montana grizzly bear country, or build a home in Texas, where the Tooth Cave pseudoscorpion lives (underground), or irrigate a field with Stephen's Kangaroo Rats, or shore up a crumbling bank where Puritan Tiger Beetles live, you had best pay attention to the following, because it affects you directly. Take a good look at the chart on Page 253, and then the 16 page application for an "Incidental Take Permit." Remember, there are no exemptions from this act. No garden is too small. No taking too minor to ignore. Swatting a Delhi Sands Flower Loving Fly comes with exactly the same, draconian penalties as shooting a grizzly bear.

In my opinion, every member of Congress should be forced to fill out the following application for an Incidental Take Permit. That way, if, one Halloween night, an Indiana Bat flies into their bedroom, they already have the proper permit in place, and they can, in good conscience, and over and above the screams of their wife, deprive it of "Life, Liberty, and the Pursuit of Happiness." And they won't have to worry about a knock on the door, from the United States Fish and Wildlife "Service."

I apologize to the reader for including this application, all 16 pages of it, in its entirety, but I have done so for good reason. Read the application carefully. Look at the multitude of steps and requirements. Then picture a small businessman, perhaps wanting to build a small development, or some storage units, or just a homeowner, perhaps down on his luck, needing to build a chicken coop, in grizzly bear country, to feed his children.

This is what tyranny in America looks like: American citizens having to beg some unelected bureaucrat in the United States Fish and Wildlife Service for permission to use their own land.

Department of the Interior
U.S. Fish and Wildlife Service

Federal Fish and Wildlife Permit Application Form

OMB Control No. 1018-0094
Expires 12/31/2013

click here for return address

Return to: U.S. Fish and Wildlife Service (USFWS)

Type of Activity: Native Endangered and Threatened Species –

Incidental Take Permits Associated with a Habitat Conservation Plan (HCP)

Complete Sections A or B, and C, D, and E of this application. U.S. address may be required in Section C, see instructions for details.
See attached instruction pages for information on how to make your application complete and help avoid unnecessary delays.

A.	Complete if applying as an individual			
1.a. Last name		1.b. First name	1.c. Middle name or initial	1.d. Suffix
2. Date of birth (mm/dd/yyyy)	3. Social Security No.	4. Occupation	5. Affiliation/ Doing business as (see instructions)	
6.a. Telephone number	6.b. Alternate telephone number	6.c. Fax number	6.d. E-mail address	

B.	Complete if applying on behalf of a business, corporation, public agency, tribe, or institution			
1.a. Name of business, agency, tribe, or institution		1.b. Doing business as (dba)		
2. Tax identification no.	3. Description of business, agency, tribe, or institution			
4.a. Principal officer Last name	4.b. Principal officer First name	4.c. Principal officer Middle name/ initial	4.d. Suffix	
5. Principal officer title		6. Primary contact		
7.a. Business telephone number	7.b. Alternate telephone number	7.c. Business fax number	7.d. Business e-mail address	

C.	All applicants complete address information				
1.a. Physical address (Street address, Apartment #, Suite #, or Room #; no P.O. Boxes)					
1.b. City	1.c. State	1.d. Zip code/Postal code:	1.e. County/Province	1.f. Country	
2.a. Mailing Address (include if different than physical address, include name of contact person if applicable)					
2.b. City	2.c. State	2.d. Zip code/Postal code:	2.e. County/Province	2.f. Country	

D.	All applicants MUST complete
1.	Attach check or money order payable to the U.S. FISH AND WILDLIFE SERVICE in the amount indicated on pages 2-3. Federal, tribal, State, and local government agencies, and those acting on behalf of such agencies, are exempt from the processing fee – attach documentation of fee exempt status as outlined in instructions. (50 CFR 13.11(d))
2.	Do you currently have or have you ever had any Federal Fish and Wildlife permits? Yes ☐ If yes, list the number of the most current permit you have held or that you are applying to renew/re-issue: _____ No ☐
3.	Certification: I hereby certify that I have read and am familiar with the regulations contained in Title 50, Part 13 of the Code of Federal Regulations and the other applicable parts in subchapter B of Chapter I of Title 50, and I certify that the information submitted in this application for a permit is complete and accurate to the best of my knowledge and belief. I understand that any false statement herein may subject me to the criminal penalties of 18 U.S.C. 1001.

Signature (in blue ink) of applicant/person responsible for permit (No photocopied or stamped signatures)   Date of signature (mm/dd/yyyy)

Please continue to next page

** See page 15 for additional instructions on completing the above form. See page 16 for information on the Paperwork Reduction Act, Privacy Act, and Freedom of Information Act aspects of this application form.

Section E. ALL APPLICANTS COMPLETE SECTION E. Provide the information outlined in Section E on the following pages. Be as complete and descriptive as possible. Please do not send pages that are over 8.5" x 11", videotapes, or DVDs.

INCIDENTAL TAKE PERMITS ASSOCIATED WITH A
HABITAT CONSERVATION PLAN (HCP)

Have you obtained all required Federal, tribal, State, county, municipal or foreign government approval to conduct the activity you propose? Please be aware that there may be other requirements necessary to conduct this activity such as an import permit, collection permit, permission to work on Federal or tribal lands, Federal bird banding permit, Corps of Engineers permits, Environmental Protection Agency NPDES permits, tribal, State, county or municipal permits, etc.

      ☐ Yes. Provide a copy of the approval(s). List the Federal agency, tribe, State, county, municipality or foreign countries involved and type of document required. Include a copy of these documents with the application.

      ☐ I have applied. List the Federal agency, tribe, State, county, municipality or foreign countries involved and type of documents required. Provide the reasons why the permits have not been issued

_____

      ☐ Not required. The proposed activity is not regulated.

Application Processing Fees

You may update your name, address, telephone number, fax number, or e-mail address in your current application package on file at any time. These changes are considered an administrative change, and no application processing fee is required. If you wish to make an administrative change, please fill out page 1 and indicate the information that you are updating. Then check the box below, provide your permit number, and send the completed pages 1-2 to the appropriate Regional Office (see attached list).

      ☐ Administrative change for permit number: _____

If you wish to make changes other than an administrative change, then an application processing fee is required as described below.

The application processing fee for a new Incidental Take permit, or to renew/substantively amend an existing valid permit *(with major changes)* is $100. If permit amendment *(with minor changes)* is required at a time other than renewal, the processing fee is $50. For additional information on the application processing fee and the requirements to qualify for a fee exemption, please see the instructions for section D. on page 15.

If the information in your current application package on file has changed in a manner that triggers a substantive amendment or a change not otherwise specified in the permit, then you **must** apply for a substantive amendment to your valid permit. For example, such major changes may include changes in location, activity, amount or type of take, or species to be covered by the permit. Please contact our Ecological Services Field Office located closest to your proposed activity for technical assistance in making this determination. The contact information for our Ecological Services Field Offices can be found on the U.S. Fish & Wildlife Service's (Service) office directory web page at http://www.fws.gov/offices/directory/listofficemap.html

Check the appropriate box below and enclose check or money order payable to the *U.S. Fish and Wildlife Service* in the amount of:

      ○ $100 [or ○ fee exempt (attach justification if required)] for a new permit. Use Option I. below to provide the required information.

            OR

      ○ $100 [or ○ fee exempt (attach justification if required)] to renew or substantively amend my existing valid permit *(with major changes)* using my current application package on file. Use Options I. and II. below to provide the required information. Please indicate the information that you are changing.

            OR

○ $100 [or ○ fee exempt (attach justification if required)] to renew/re-issue my existing valid permit (*without changes*) using my current application package on file. Use Option III. below to provide the requested information.

OR

○ $50 [or ○ fee exempt (attach justification if required)] to amend my existing valid permit (*with minor changes*) at a time other than permit renewal. Use Options I. and II. below to provide the required information. Please indicate the information that you are changing.

Please check the type of amendment you are requesting –

☐ add species (specify) _____

☐ add new activity with previously permitted species (specify) _____

☐ add a geographic area   ☐ change in personnel

☐ other (specify) _____

If this application includes transfer or succession of a valid Incidental Take permit, please check the box below:

☐ Transfer or succession of a valid Incidental Take permit associated with a HCP using the current application package on file. No application fee is required.

Application Processing

To expedite a final decision on your application, you are urged to coordinate with us as soon as possible for guidance in assembling a complete application package. If you are renewing or amending a valid permit, your complete application package must be received at least 30 days prior to the expiration of the valid permit. The following estimates of application processing time begin with our acceptance of a complete permit application package and do not include any time required for requesting clarification or additional information about your application.

The time required to process an application for an Incidental Take permit will vary depending on the size, complexity, and impacts of the HCP involved. Procedurally, the most variable factor in application processing is the level of analysis required for the proposed HCP under the National Environmental Policy Act (e.g., whether an application requires preparation of an Environmental Impact Statement, Environmental Assessment, or whether a categorical exclusion applies), although other factors such as public controversy can also affect application processing times. The target processing timeline from when we accept a complete application package to our final decision on a permit application is: up to 3 months for low-effect HCPs (with a 30 day public comment period), 4 to 6 months for HCPs with an Environmental Assessment (with a 60 day public comment period), and up to 12 months for HCPs with a 90-day comment period and/or an Environmental Impact Statement – assuming that the applicant is responsive to the Service's request for information and/or clarification, and the application adequately addresses permit issuance criteria. Although not mandated by law or regulation, these targets are adopted as U.S. Fish & Wildlife Service and National Marine Fisheries Service (NMFS/NOAA Fisheries) policy and all offices are expected to streamline their Incidental Take permit programs, and to meet these targets to the maximum extent practicable.

The information provided in your permit application will be used to evaluate your application for compliance with the Endangered Species Act, its implementing regulations (which may require a 30, 60, or 90 day public comment period), and with U.S. Fish and Wildlife Service policy. Receipt and possession of a permit under the Endangered Species Act should be regarded as a privilege, as we must balance permit issuance with our duties to protect and recover listed species.

Up-to-date annual reports and any other required reports under your valid permit(s) must be on file before a permit will be considered for renewal, re-issuance or amendment.

If your activities may affect species under the authority of the National Marine Fisheries Service (NMFS/NOAA Fisheries), then you may need to obtain a separate permit from that agency. In addition we share jurisdiction with NMFS/NOAA Fisheries for sea turtles (e.g., we evaluate applications for permits to conduct activities impacting sea turtles on land, and NMFS/NOAA Fisheries evaluates applications for permits to conduct activities impacting sea turtles in the marine environment). To apply for a permit to conduct activities with sea turtles in the marine environment or other species under NMFS/NOAA Fisheries jurisdiction, please contact them via their permit web page at http://www.nmfs.noaa.gov/pr/permits/

We cannot issue an Incidental Take permit under Section 10(a)(2)(A) of the Endangered Species Act unless you submit a conservation plan that specifies: (i) the impacts that are likely to result from the incidental take associated with your activity; (ii) what steps the applicant will take to minimize and mitigate such impacts, and the funding that will be available to implement such steps; (iii) what alternative actions to such taking the applicant considered and the reasons why such alternatives are not being utilized; and (iv) such other measures that the Secretary may require as being necessary or appropriate for purposes of the plan.

Our general permit regulations at 50 CFR 13.12(a)(9) allow us to collect such other information as we determine that is relevant to the processing of a permit application. Before you submit an application for an Incidental Take permit, we may require that you conduct biological surveys to determine which species and/or habitat would be impacted by the activities sought to be covered under the permit. Biological surveys provide information necessary to develop an adequate HCP, and to assess the biological impacts of the proposed activities. In addition, the information provided in a biological survey can reduce the applicant's risk of take under Section 9 of the Endangered Species Act by ensuring that affected species and/or habitat are identified and appropriately covered under the permit.

You are required to obtain a Scientific Purposes, Enhancement of Propagation or Survival permit (commonly called a Recovery permit) from us before engaging in any biological survey activities that would take listed species. Contact our Ecological Services Field Office closest to the location of your activity to obtain technical assistance in determining the need for both a biological survey and a Recovery permit for your survey activity. The contact information for our Ecological Services Field Offices can be found on the U.S. Fish & Wildlife Service's office directory web page at http://www.fws.gov/offices/directory/listofficemap.html.

If a biological survey is required, you will need to send us your complete Recovery permit application package and have it accepted at least 3 months prior to commencement of survey activities to facilitate processing of your Recovery permit application. The Recovery permit application is designated as U.S. Fish & Wildlife Service form # 3-200-55 and can be found on our Endangered Species permit web page at http://www.fws.gov/forms/3-200-55.pdf

We maintain a list of Recovery permittees (such as biological consultants) who have authorized the release of their contact information to third parties for conducting biological surveys on a contract basis. This list is provided to the public at the discretion of each U.S. Fish and Wildlife Service Regional Office as time and workload allow. Please be aware that this list does not represent an endorsement by us of any particular permittee.

****

If you are not applying as an individual but as a business, corporation, tribe, institution, or non-Federal public agency (block B. on page 1 of the application), the person to whom the permit will be issued (e.g., the landowner, president, director, executive director, or executive officer) is legally responsible for implementing the permit. Although other people under the direct control of the permittee (e.g., employees, contractors, consultants) receive third party take authorization in their capacity as designees of the permittee, the individual named as the permittee ultimately is legally responsible for the permit and any activities carried out under the permit except as otherwise limited in the case of permits issued to State or local government entities under 50 CFR 13.25(e).

****

If you wish to coordinate the processing of this permit application through an authorized agent, and to have that agent represent you as the primary contact with us, check the box below. Sign (in blue ink) and date the authorization statement, and provide contact information for your authorized agent.

    ☐ I hereby authorize the following person to act as an authorized agent on my behalf in the processing of this permit application and to furnish, upon request, supplemental information in support of this permit application.

_____   _____

signature (in blue ink)   date

_____

please print name legibly

Your Authorized Agent's Contact Information (please print legibly)

City: _____ State: _____ Zip Code: _____

Telephone: _____

Fax: _____

E-Mail: _____

INCIDENTAL TAKE PERMIT APPLICATION INSTRUCTIONS

You have 4 options for providing the required information for an Incidental Take permit application.

Incidental Take Permit Application: Option I. New Incidental Take Permit & Supplementary Information for Renewal or Amendment of an Existing Valid Permit (*With Changes*).

General permit regulations for the U.S. Fish & Wildlife Service can be found at 50 CFR 13. Regulations for an Incidental Take permit under the Endangered Species Act can be found at 50 CFR 17.22(b)(1) for endangered wildlife species and 50 CFR 17.32(b)(1) for threatened wildlife species.

Each landowner who wishes to be covered under a new or amended Incidental Take permit associated with an HCP must sign (in blue ink) and date the Incidental Take Permit Application Certification Notice at the end of this application, unless the landowner will be covered under this U.S. Fish & Wildlife Service Incidental Take permit via another vehicle, such as a certificate of inclusion (50 CFR 13.25(d)). Any change in the language of the Certification Notice must be reviewed by the Department of the Interior, Office of the Solicitor and approved by the U.S. Fish & Wildlife Service. The same person who signs in box D. on page 1 of the application must sign the certification.

If the information in items A. - D. below is already provided in your final HCP (or Implementing Agreement, if applicable), then you do not have to provide it here. Instead, check the box below and use the spaces provided in items A. - D. to indicate the page numbers in your HCP or Implementing Agreement that provide the requested information.

☐　　I am not providing the following information for items A. - D. as part of my Incidental Take permit application, because it is already provided in my final HCP or Implementing Agreement (copy attached or already submitted).

If the requested information in items A. - D. is not provided in your final HCP or final Implementing Agreement, or you are using Option II. to renew or amend your existing valid Incidental Take permit, then attach separate pages for the missing information. In order to assist us in processing your request, please provide the item number (A. 1 a., etc.) of the required information before each of your responses. Thank you.

Please ensure that your final HCP and Implementing Agreement (if applicable) are attached if it has not been previously submitted.

If you have previously submitted a final draft HCP or Implementing Agreement, please indicate the document's date.

　　　　　　Date of final draft HCP _____

　　　　　　Date of final draft Implementing Agreement _____

Applications for an Incidental Take permit associated with an HCP must provide the following specific information (relevant to the activity) under items A.- D. below in addition to the general information on pages 1-5 of this application.

A.　　Identify species and activity:

　　　1.　　For a new Incidental Take permit:

　　　　　　a.　　Provide the common and scientific names of the species requested for coverage in the permit and their status (endangered (E), threatened (T), proposed endangered (PE), proposed threatened (PT), candidate for listing (C), or species likely to become a candidate (LC)).

　　　　　　b.　　Provide the number, age, and sex of such species to the extent known.

　　　　　　c.　　Quantify the anticipated effects to their habitat.

　　　　　　d.　　Describe each activity associated with your project that would result in the incidental take of each species.

　　　2.　　For an amended Incidental Take permit:

a.   Identify the activities and/or species to be added to your valid permit (provide both the scientific, to the most specific taxonomic level, and common names), as well as the species status (see 1.a.. above).

b.   Provide the number, age and sex of such species to the extent known.

c.   If any activities requested in this application differ from those in your valid permit, then for each species state the current activity, the requested new activity, and how the new activity will impact each species.

d.   Describe each activity associated with your project that would result in the incidental take of each species.

e.   Quantify any anticipated effects to the habitat of each added species.

f.   Identify activities and/or species to be deleted from your valid permit and the reason(s) for the deletion.

Page(s) & source document: _____

B.   Identify location of the proposed activity:

1.   Provide the name of the State, county, tribal land, and the specific location of the proposed activity site(s). Include a formal legal description, section/township/range information, county tax parcel number, local address, or any other identifying property designation that will precisely place the location of the proposed activity site(s). Attach a location map and plat of the project site clearly depicting the project boundaries and the footprint and location of all portions of the property that would be affected by your proposed activities.

2.   Provide the total number of acres covered by the HCP _____

        Is this the total acreage of the parcel? (check one) ◯ yes   ◯ no

3.   Provide the approximate number of acres to be impacted _____

4.   Provide the approximate number of acres to be protected _____

5.   Provide a complete description, including timeframes, for implementation of proposed voluntary management activities to enhance, restore, or maintain habitat benefiting federally listed, proposed or candidate species, or other species likely to become candidates. Include schedules for implementing these activities.

Page(s) & source document: _____

C.   Describe the proposed activities in the conservation plan:
You must submit a Habitat Conservation Plan. We strongly encourage you to ensure that your HCP is consistent with the Habitat Conservation Planning Handbook, subsequent Handbook addendums, and current policies in order to minimize delays in evaluating your application. The Handbook and other HCP information is available on the U.S. Fish & Wildlife Service's Endangered Species web page at http://www.fws.gov/endangered/what-we-do/hcp-overview.html.

Provide a complete description of activity(ies) or reference the applicable HCP or Implementing Agreement page numbers identifying the subject information.

The HCP must specify:

1.   The impact that will likely result from the incidental taking. A discussion of the impact that will likely result from the incidental take must include quantification of any anticipated effects to the habitat of the species sought to be covered by the permit.

2.   The steps that will be taken to minimize and mitigate such impacts, the funding that will be available to implement such steps, and the procedures to deal with unforeseen circumstances.

3.   The steps that will be taken to monitor and report on such impacts, including a copy of the monitoring plan. We are

authorized to require reports of activities conducted under a permit per the U.S. Fish & Wildlife Service's general permit regulations at 50 CFR 13.45.

4. Alternative actions to such incidental taking that have been considered and the reasons why these alternatives are not proposed for use.

5. The biological goals(s) and objectives for the HCP.

6. The duration requested for the proposed permit.

Page(s) & source document : _____

D. Implementing Agreement

An Implementing Agreement

is   is not   (FWS *Regional Office* to circle one)

a part of the permit application for a Habitat Conservation Plan.

This Implementing Agreement must be signed at finalization of the HCP. Are you willing to commit to an Implementing Agreement at finalization of the HCP?

◯Yes, I am willing to commit to an Implementing Agreement. Please submit any unsigned, draft Implementing Agreement that you have prepared with our Field Office.

◯No. I am not willing to commit to an Implementing Agreement.

n: Option II. Renewal or Amendment of an Existing Valid Incidental Take Permi

her required reports under your valid permit(s) must be on file before a permit will be co

re proposing to renew or amend an existing valid Incidental Take permit, including make
nclude changes in location, activity, amount or type of take, or species to be covered by t

ge 1 of the application must also sign (in blue ink) the following statement. This certific:
.3.22(a).

and information submitted in support of my original application for a U.S. Fish and Wil
mit # _____ are still current and correct, except for the changes listed in O
please check either ⃝renewal or ⃝ amendment) of that permit.

_____   _____
ink)   date

_____
legibly

inges to your valid permit (answer the appropriate questions for these changes requested
Option I. above). Please submit completed pages 1 - 9 of this application form (along wi
on I. above) to our Regional Office (see attached list) covering the location of your prop

Incidental Take Permit Application: Option III. Renewal/Re-issue of an Existing Valid Incidental Take Permit (*Without Changes*) Using My Current Application Package On File.

Up-to-date annual reports and any other required reports under your valid permit(s) must be on file before a permit will be considered for renewal or re-issue.

Sign the following statement if you are applying to renew or re-issue an existing valid Incidental Take permit without changes. If you are proposing changes to your Incidental Take permit, you must use Options I and II above.

The individual signing box D on page 1 of the application must also sign (in blue ink) the following statement. This certification language is required under 50 CFR 13.22(a).

> I certify that the statements and information submitted in support of my original application for a U.S. Fish and Wildlife Service Incidental Take permit # _____ are still current and correct and hereby request (please check either ○ renewal or ○ re-issuance) of that permit without changes.

_____   _____

signature (in blue ink)   date

_____

please print name legibly

* Please note: If you have signed the above statement, then your renewal/re-issue request is complete. Please submit this page and completed pages 1- 5 of this application to our Regional Office (see attached list) covering the location of your proposed activity. Requests for renewals/re-issuance must be complete and accepted by the Service no later than 30 days prior to permit expiration to ensure that your current permit remains in effect while we process your request.

Incidental Take Permit Application: Option IV, Permit Transfer or Succession of a Permit

Complete the following if you are applying for transfer of an existing valid Incidental Take permit to you or obtaining rights of succession of an existing valid Incidental Take permit. In addition, you and the current permit holder may also need to sign an Assumption Agreement. Please contact our Ecological Services Field Office nearest your activity to determine whether you and the current permit holder need to execute an Assumption Agreement. The contact information for our Ecological Services Field Offices can be found on the U.S. Fish & Wildlife Service's office directory web page at
http://www.fws.gov/offices/directory/listofficemap.html

Please indicate the name of the HCP to be transferred or succeeded, and indicate the document's date.

Name of HCP _____

Date of HCP _____

An Assumption Agreement

is   is not   (FWS *Ecological Services Field Office* to circle one)

required as part of the transfer or succession permit application for the HCP.

Incidental Take Permit Application

Certification Notice

The same person who signs in box D, on page 1 of the application must sign (in blue ink) the following certification.

By submitting this application and receiving an Incidental Take permit pursuant to Section 10(a)(1)(B) of the Endangered Species Act, I

_____ (print name(s)) attest that I/we own the lands indicated in this application, or have sufficient authority or rights over these lands to implement the measures of the Habitat Conservation Plan (and Implementing Agreement if applicable) covered by the Incidental Take permit. Further, upon receipt of the Incidental Take permit, I/we agree to conduct the activities as specified in the Habitat Conservation Plan (and Implementing Agreement if applicable) according to the terms and conditions of the Incidental Take permit and its supporting documents.

_____   _____
signature (in blue ink)   date

_____
please print name legibly

_____   _____
signature (in blue ink)   date

_____
please print name legibly

<u>USFWS Regional Contacts for Native Endangered & Threatened Species Permits</u>

Pacific Region (Region 1): HI, ID, OR, WA, American Samoa, Commonwealth of the Northern Mariana Islands, Guam, and the Pacific Trust Territories

U.S. Fish and Wildlife Service
Endangered Species Permit Office
911 NE 11th Avenue
Portland, Oregon 97232-4181

Web: http://www.fws.gov/pacific/ecoservices/endangered/index.html
Phone: (503) 231-2071
email: permitsR1ES@fws.gov
Fax: (503) 231-6243

Southwest Region (Region 2): AZ, NM, OK, and TX

U.S. Fish and Wildlife Service
Endangered Species Permit Office
500 Gold Avenue S.W. (street address)
P.O. Box 1306 (mailing address)
Albuquerque, New Mexico 87103-1306

Web: http://www.fws.gov/southwest/es/EndangeredSpecies/
Phone: (505) 248-6649
email: permitsR2ES@fws.gov
Fax: (505) 248-6788

Midwest Region (Region 3): IA, IL, IN, MI, MN, MO, OH, and WI

U.S. Fish and Wildlife Service
Endangered Species Permit Office
5600 American Blvd. West
Suite 990
Bloomington, Minnesota 55437-1458

Web: http://www.fws.gov/midwest/Endangered/
Phone: (612) 713-5343
email: permitsR3ES@fws.gov
Fax: (612) 713-5292

Southeast Region (Region 4): AL, AR, FL, GA, KY, LA, MS, NC, PR, SC, TN, and U.S. Virgin Islands

U.S. Fish and Wildlife Service
Endangered Species Permit Office
1875 Century Blvd., Suite 200
Atlanta, Georgia 30345

Web: http://www.fws.gov/southeast/es/#
Phone: (404) 679-7313 (HCP coordinator) or (404) 679-7140 (R4 Endangered Species main office)
email: permitsR4ES@fws.gov
Fax: (404) 679-7081

Hadley, MA 01035-9589

Web: http://www.fws.gov/northeast/endangered/
Phone: (413) 253-8628
email: permitsR5ES@fws.gov
Fax: (413) 253-8482

Mountain-Prairie Region (Region 6): CO, KS, MT, NE, ND, SD, UT, and WY

U.S. Fish and Wildlife Service
Endangered Species Permit Office
Denver Federal Center
P.O. Box 25486
Denver, Colorado 80225-0489

Web: http://www.fws.gov/mountain%2Dprairie/endspp/
Phone: (303) 236-4256
email: permitsR6ES@fws.gov
Fax: (303) 236-0027

Alaska Region (Region 7): AK

U.S. Fish and Wildlife Service
Endangered Species Permit Office
1011 E. Tudor Road
Anchorage, Alaska 99503-6199

Web: http://alaska.fws.gov/fisheries/endangered/index.htm
Phone: (907) 786-3323
email: permitsR7ES@fws.gov
Fax: (907) 786-3350

Pacific Southwest Region (Region 8): CA and NV

U.S. Fish and Wildlife Service
Endangered Species Permit Office
2800 Cottage Way, Suite W-2606
Sacramento, California 95825

Web: http://www.fws.gov/cno/es/
Phone: (916) 414-6464
email: permitsCNES@fws.gov
Fax: (916) 414-6486

PERMIT APPLICATION FORM INSTRUCTIONS

The following instructions pertain to an application for a U.S. Fish and Wildlife Service or CITES permit. The General Permit Procedures in 50 CFR 13 address the permitting process. For simplicity, all licenses, permits, registrations, and certificates are referred to as a permit.

GENERAL INSTRUCTIONS:
- Complete all blocks/lines/questions in Sections A or B, and in C, D, and E.
- An incomplete application may cause delays in processing or may be returned to the applicant. Be sure you are filling in the appropriate application form for the proposed activity.
- Print clearly or type in the information. Illegible applications may cause delays.
- Sign the application in blue ink. Faxes or copies of the original signature will not be accepted.
- Mail the original application to the address at the top of page one of the application or if applicable on the attached address list.
- Keep a copy of your completed application.
- Please plan ahead. Allow at least 60 days for your application to be processed. Some applications may take longer than 90 days to process. (50 CFR 13.11)
- Applications are processed in the order they are received.
- Additional forms and instructions are available from http://www.fws.gov/permits/.

COMPLETE EITHER SECTION A OR SECTION B:

Section A. Complete if applying as an individual:
- Enter the complete name of the responsible individual who will be the permittee if a permit is issued. Enter personal information that identifies the applicant. Fax and e-mail are not required if not available.
- If you are applying on behalf of a client, the personal information must pertain to the client, and a document evidencing power of attorney must be included with the application.
- Affiliation/Doing business as (dba): business, agency, organizational, or institutional affiliation directly related to the activity requested in the application (e.g., a taxidermist is an individual whose business can directly relate to the requested activity). The Division of Management Authority (DMA) will not accept doing business as affiliations for individuals.

Section B. Complete if applying as a business, corporation, public agency, tribe, or institution:
- Enter the complete name of the business, agency, tribe, or institution that will be the permittee if a permit is issued. Give a brief description of the type of business the applicant is engaged in. Provide contact phone number(s) of the business.
- Principal Officer is the person in charge of the listed business, corporation, public agency, tribe, or institution. The principal officer is the person responsible for the application and any permitted activities. Often the principal officer is a Director or President. Primary Contact is the person at the business, corporation, public agency, tribe, or institution who will be available to answer questions about the application or permitted activities. Often this is the preparer of the application.

ALL APPLICANTS COMPLETE SECTION C:
- For all applications submitted to the Division of Management Authority (DMA) a physical U.S. address is required. Province and Country blocks are provided for those USFWS programs which use foreign addresses and are not required by DMA.
- Mailing address is address where communications from USFWS should be mailed if different than applicant's physical address.

ALL APPLICANTS COMPLETE SECTION D:
Section D.1 Application processing fee:
- An application processing fee is required at the time of application; unless exempted under 50 CFR13.11(d)(3). The application processing fee is assessed to partially cover the cost of processing a request. The fee does not guarantee the issuance of a permit. Fees will not be refunded for applications that are approved, abandoned, or denied. We may return fees for withdrawn applications prior to any significant processing occurring.
- Documentation of fee exempt status is not required for Federal, tribal, State, or local government agencies; but must be supplied by those applicants acting on behalf of such agencies. Those applicants acting on behalf of such agencies must submit a letter on agency letterhead and signed by the head of the unit of government for which the applicant is acting on behalf, confirming that the applicant will be carrying out the permitted activity for the agency.

Section D.2 Federal Fish and Wildlife permits:
- List the number(s) of your most current FWS or CITES permit or the number of the most recent permit if none are currently valid. If applying for re-issuance of a CITES permit, the original permit must be returned with this application.

Section D.3 CERTIFICATION:
- The individual identified in Section A, the principal officer named in Section B, or person with a valid power of attorney (documentation must be included in the application) must sign and date the application in blue ink. This signature binds the applicant to the statement of certification. This means that you certify that you have read and understand the regulations that apply to the permit. You also certify that everything included in the application is true to the best of your knowledge. Be sure to read the statement and re-read the application and your answers before signing.

ALL APPLICANTS COMPLETE SECTION E.

Please continue to next page

APPLICATION FOR A FEDERAL FISH AND WILDLIFE PERMIT
Paperwork Reduction Act, Privacy Act, and Freedom of Information Act – Notices

In accordance with the Paperwork Reduction Act of 1995 (44 U.S.C. 3501, *et seq.*) and the Privacy Act of 1974 (5 U.S.C. 552a), please be advised:

1. The gathering of information on fish and wildlife is authorized by:
   (Authorizing statutes can be found at: http://www.gpoaccess.gov/cfr/index.html and http://www.fws.gov/permits/ltr/ltr.html)

   a. Bald and Golden Eagle Protection Act (16 U.S.C. 668), 50 CFR 22;
   b. Endangered Species Act of 1973 (16 U.S.C. 1531-1544), 50CFR 17;
   c. Migratory Bird Treaty Act (16 U.S.C. 703-712), 50 CFR 21;
   d. Marine Mammal Protection Act of 1972 (16 U.S.C. 1361, *et seq.*), 50 CFR 18;
   e. Wild Bird Conservation Act (16 U.S.C. 4901-4916), 50 CFR 15;
   f. Lacey Act: Injurious Wildlife (18 U.S.C. 42), 50 CFR 16;
   g. Convention on International Trade in Endangered Species of Wild Fauna and Flora (TIAS 8249), http://www.cites.org/ 50 CFR 23;
   h. General Provisions, 50 CFR 10;
   i. General Permit Procedures, 50 CFR 13; and
   j. Wildlife Provisions (Import/export/transport), 50 CFR 14.

2. Information requested in this form is purely voluntary. However, submission of requested information is required in order to process applications for permits authorized under the above laws. Failure to provide all requested information may be sufficient cause for the U.S. Fish and Wildlife Service to deny the request. We may not conduct or sponsor and you are not required to respond to a collection of information unless it displays a currently valid OMB control number.

3. Certain applications for permits authorized under the Endangered Species Act of 1973 (16 U.S.C. 1539) and the Marine Mammal Protection Act of 1972 (16 U.S.C. 1374) will be published in the Federal Register as required by the two laws.

4. Disclosures outside the Department of the Interior may be made without the consent of an individual under the routine uses listed below, if the disclosure is compatible with the purposes for which the record was collected. (Ref. 68 FR 52611, September 4, 2003)

   a. Routine disclosure to subject matter experts, and Federal, tribal, State, local, and foreign agencies, for the purpose of obtaining advice relevant to making a decision on an application for a permit or when necessary to accomplish a FWS function related to this system of records.
   b. Routine disclosure to the public as a result of publishing Federal Register notices announcing the receipt of permit applications for public comment or notice of the decision on a permit application.
   c. Routine disclosure to Federal, tribal, State, local, or foreign wildlife and plant agencies for the exchange of information on permits granted or denied to assure compliance with all applicable permitting requirements.
   d. Routine disclosure to Captive-bred Wildlife registrants under the Endangered Species Act for the exchange of authorized species, and to share information on the captive breeding of these species.
   e. Routine disclosure to Federal, tribal, State, and local authorities who need to know who is permitted to receive and rehabilitate sick, orphaned, and injured birds under the Migratory Bird Treaty Act and the Bald and Golden Eagle Protection Act, federally permitted rehabilitators; individuals seeking a permitted rehabilitator with whom to place a bird in need of care, and licensed veterinarians who receive, treat, or diagnose sick, orphaned, and injured birds.
   f. Routine disclosure to the Department of Justice, or a court, adjudicative, or other administrative body or to a party in litigation before a court or adjudicative or administrative body, under certain circumstances.
   g. Routine disclosure to the appropriate Federal, tribal, State, local, or foreign governmental agency responsible for investigating, prosecuting, enforcing, or implementing statutes, rules, or licenses, when we become aware of a violation or potential violation of such statutes, rules, or licenses, or when we need to monitor activities associated with a permit or regulated use.
   h. Routine disclosure to a congressional office in response to an inquiry to the office by the individual to whom the record pertains.
   i. Routine disclosure to the General Accounting Office or Congress when the information is required for the evaluation of the permit programs.
   j. Routine disclosure to provide addresses obtained from the Internal Revenue Service to debt collection agencies for purposes of locating a debtor to collect or compromise a Federal claim against the debtor or to consumer reporting agencies to prepare a commercial credit report for use by the FWS.

5. For individuals, personal information such as home address and telephone number, financial data, and personal identifiers (social security number, birth date, etc.) will be removed prior to any release of the application.

6. The public reporting burden on the applicant for information collection varies depending on the activity for which a permit is requested. The relevant burden for an **Incidental Take** permit application is **3 hours**. This burden estimate includes time for reviewing instructions, gathering and maintaining data and completing and reviewing the form. You may direct comments regarding the burden estimate or any other aspect of the form to the Service Information Clearance Officer, U.S. Fish and Wildlife Service, Mail Stop 222, Arlington Square, U.S. Department of the Interior, 1849 C Street, NW, Washington D.C. 20240.

Freedom of Information Act – Notice

For organizations, businesses, or individuals operating as a business (i.e., permittees not covered by the Privacy Act), we request that you identify any information that should be considered privileged and confidential business information to allow the Service to meet its responsibilities under FOIA. Confidential business information must be clearly marked "Business Confidential" at the top of the letter or page and each succeeding page and must be accompanied by a non-confidential summary of the confidential information. The non-confidential summary and remaining documents may be made available to the public under FOIA [43 CFR 2.13(c)(4), 43 CFR 2.15(d)(1)(i)].

The following is from the U.S. Fish and Wildlife Service website. The sections framed in gray are from the website. The author's comments are in the black boxes.

U.S. Fish & Wildlife Service
Habitat Conservation Plans
Section 10 of the Endangered Species Act
Introduction

Why should we save endangered species? Congress answered this question in the introduction to the Endangered Species Act of 1973(Act), recognizing that endangered
and threatened species of wildlife and plants "are of esthetic, ecological, educational, historical, recreational, and scientific value to the Nation and its people." After this finding, Congress said that the purposes of the Act are ". to provide a means whereby the ecosystems upon which endangered species and threatened species depend may be conserved [and] to provide a program for the conservation of such . . . species. . . ." Habitat Conservation Plans (HCPs) under section 10(a)(1)(B) of the Act provide for partnerships with non-Federal parties to conserve the ecosystems upon which listed species depend, ultimately contributing to their recovery.

What are HCPs?

HCPs are planning documents required as part of an application for an incidental take permit. They describe the anticipated effects of the proposed taking; how those impacts will be minimized, or mitigated; and how the HCP is to be funded. HCPs can apply to both listed and nonlisted species, including those that are candidates or have been proposed for listing. Conserving species before they are in danger of extinction or are likely to become so can also provide early benefits and prevent the need for listing.

Who needs an incidental take permit? Anyone whose otherwise-lawful activities will result in the "incidental take" of a listed wildlife species needs a permit. The U.S. Fish and Wildlife Service (FWS) can help determine whether a proposed project or action is likely to result in "take" and whether an HCP is needed. FWS staff can also provide technical assistance to help design a project to avoid take. For example, the project could be designed with seasonal restrictions on construction to minimize disturbance to a species.

What is the benefit of an incidental take permit and habitat conservation plan to a private landowner? The permit allows the permit-
holder to legally proceed with an activity that would otherwise
result in the unlawful take of a listed species.
The permitholder also has assurances from the FWS through the
"No Surprises" regulation.

Benefit? Benefit to whom? Are these people serious? All I want to
do is plant a vegetable garden to feed my family. Now you tell me
I have to beg the government for permission to use my own land,
and you say this is somehow beneficial to me? My land is going
to sit unused for years, as that is how long these processes typically take. Obviously, I will need to hire attorneys and biologists
familiar with Habitat Conservation Plans. Not coincidentally, the
USFWS has a list of recommended biologists. The only people
benefitting from this are personnel at the U.S. Fish & Wildlife
Service, whose power over our country grows on a daily basis.

Most small businessmen, looking at the process of acquiring an
Incidental Take Permit, are simply going to throw up their hands
and say: "Are you out of your flipping mind?" And they either
won't invest at all, or they will take their investment elsewhere,
where human jobs and productivity are deemed more important
than rats, spiders, bats, and scorpions.

"Government "help" to business is just as disastrous as government persecution... the only way a government can be of
service to national prosperity is by keeping its hands off."
Ayn Rand

What is "take"?
The Act defines "take" as ". . . to harass, harm, pursue, hunt, shoot,
wound, kill, trap, capture, or collect, or to attempt to engage in any
such conduct."
Section 9 of the Act prohibits the take of endangered and threatened
species. The purpose of the incidental take permit is to exempt non-

Federal permit-holders—such as States and private landowners—
from the prohibitions of section 9, not to authorize the activities that result in take. **Harm may include significant habitat modification
where it actually kills or injures a listed species through impairment
of essential behavior , such as breeding, feeding or sheltering.**

Not only is my electric fence around my garden going to "harass"
the incoming grizzlies by jolting them with 10,000 volts of electricity, but the fence is going to create "significant habitat modification." This "habitat modification" would harm the grizzly
bear, through "impairment of essential behavior, such as feeding." What about my human "essential behavior", i.e. eating???

Can't happen, right? Well, a federal judge, Donald Molloy,
stopped 100 acres of helicopter logging, because he deemed it "essential habitat" for the Cabinet-Yaak subpopulation of grizzly
bears in the Kootenay National Forest. For the record, the Kootenay National Forest is 2.2 million acres. There are 40-50 bears in
the Cabinet-Yaak subpopulation of grizzly bears. That makes the
odds of a bear being actually being on the 100 acres of timber sale
at 1 in 440. If a bear was there, it would take him about ten sec-
onds to leave the 100 acres, which he would do when the logging
helicopter approached. I have observed this on numerous occasions. After leaving the 100 acres, he would still have 2,199,900
acres of bear habitat to live on, not including the millions of acres
adjacent to the Kootenai National Forest. It works out to about
43,998 acres per bear. After the logging helicopters leave (a week,
at most) he could return to the 100 acres, if he so wished.

Judge Halts Helicopter Logging in grizzly habitat

By Katie Oyan, Associated Press, 08-01-08
HELENA – A federal judge has halted a small portion of a northwestern Montana logging project, saying its effect on grizzly bears
hasn't been adequately addressed.

U.S. District Judge Donald Molloy in Missoula said the U.S. Forest Service and the Fish and Wildlife Service failed to sufficiently
consider the effects of helicopter logging on "core" grizzly habitat
in the Kootenai National Forest.

The July 30 ruling stops the helicopter logging on about 100 acres pending an "adequate assessment."

Molloy said other logging included in the nearly 1,800-acre project, northeast of Troy, can move forward.

The Alliance for the Wild Rockies filed its challenge to the Northeast Yaak timber sale in December 2007.

It cited documentation for two timber sales in Idaho in which the Fish and Wildlife Service determined helicopter logging was likely to harm grizzly bears.

Molloy ruled the Forest Service and the Fish and Wildlife Service failed to distinguish the helicopter logging in the proposed Northeast Yaak timber sale from the Idaho sales to arrive at the conclusion that it wouldn't harm bears.

The judge noted estimates show there are only 30 to 40 grizzlies in the Cabinet-Yaak grizzly bear recovery zone, where the timber sale is located.

"The Fish and Wildlife Service determined that the Cabinet-Yaak grizzly population was low enough to warrant reclassification from threatened to endangered in 1993 and reaffirmed its finding in 1999," Molloy wrote.

Since then, agency scientists have determined there is 91.4 percent probability that the population is declining.

Michael Garrity, executive director of the Alliance for the Wild Rockies, praised Molloy's ruling.

"We are very pleased that the court stopped the helicop er logging in grizzly bear habitat," Garrity said Friday. **"The Forest Service keeps logging more and more grizzly bear habitat, even though the scientific evidence shows that logging grizzly bear habitat is driving grizzlies in the Cabinet-Yaak grizzly bear recovery zone towards extinction."**

The last statement is an absolute lie. Logging does nothing to harm grizzly bears. What do these environmentalists think happens when a helicopter approaches? Do they think the bear just falls over dead? Nonsense. They simply leave the area, and return (when the loggers are finished) to feed on grubs found in the stumpage, and prey on the game that browse on the leftover slash piles, and the new plant growth which comes with increased sunlight. In the spring, these clearcuts are the first place grizzlies head to, as they feed on grass to get their digestive systems restarted after a long winter of hibernation.

What do habitat conservation plans do?

In developing habitat conservation plans, people applying for incidental take permits describe measures designed to minimize and mitigate the effects of their actions — to ensure that species will be conserved and to contribute to their recovery. Habitat conservation plans are required to meet the permit issuance criteria of section (a)(2)(B) of the Act:

- (i) taking will be incidental;
- (ii) the applicant will, to the maximum extent practicable, minimize and mitigate the impacts of the taking;
- (iii) the applicant will ensure that adequate funding for the plan will be provided;
- (iv) taking will not appreciably reduce the likelihood of the survival and recovery of the species in the wild; and
- (v) other measures, as required by the Secretary, will be met.

Synonyms for the term "incidental" include "accidental", "fluke", "irregular", and "random". Putting up a bear fence with 10,000 volts running through it plans on the bear touching the fence, so that it is heavily jolted, frightened (harmed or harrassed) , and thus, leaves. There is absolutely nothing accidental, irregular, or random about it

"The applicant will ensure that adequate funding for the plan will be provided." This Habitat Conservation Plan is not a one-time, slam-bam-thank you ma'am, arrangement. For as long as this plan is in place, oftentimes "in perpetuity", you are responsible with funding it. This includes all future governmental monitoring of the project. This is, of course, in addition to any taxes that you already pay on the property in question. This funding must be set aside and guaranteed.

What needs to be in HCPs?

Section 10 of the Act and its implementing regulations define the contents of HCPs. They include:
• an assessment of impacts likely to result from the proposed taking of one or more federally listed species.
• measures that the permit applicant will undertake to monitor, minimize, and mitigate for such impacts, the funding available to implement such measures, and the procedures to deal with unforeseen or extraordinary circumstances.
• alternative actions to the taking that the applicant analyzed, and the reasons why the applicant did not adopt such alternatives.
• additional measures that the Fish and Wildlife Service may require.

In the proposed HCP, we need "the procedures to deal with unforeseen or extraordinary circumstances." This is a real beauty. By definition, an "unforeseen circumstance" is an occurrence which is wholly unanticipated, and therefore, can't be planned for. For example, the framers of the U.S. Constitution (many of whom risked their lives in the Revolution) never foresaw that the U.S. Government would one day want to give rights to the Government Canyon Bat Cave Spider, and the Appalacian Monkeyface Pearly Mussel. Hence, there is no mention of them in the Constitution. They did, however, foresee the power of the government growing too strong. Hence, the Fifth Amendment of the Constitution.

*We must all hang together, gentlemen...else, we shall most assuredly hang separately"
Benjamin Franklin

Americans have a tendency to take for granted the sacrifices made by our forefathers, all in the name of freedom. Benjamin Franklin was the leading printer in the colonies. George Washington and Thomas Jefferson owned huge tracts of land in Virginia. John Adams was a leading Boston attorney. These men and thousands of nameless patriots risked not just their personal fortunes, but their lives, to create a free nation. They succeeded. Will this generation squander the liberties we've been bequeathed?

HCPs are also required to comply with the Five Points Policy by including:

1. biological goals and objectives, which define the expected biological outcome for each species covered by the HCP;
2. adaptive management, which includes methods for addressing uncertainty and also monitoring and feedback to biological goals and objectives;
3. monitoring for compliance, effectiveness, and effects;
4. permit duration which is determined by the time-span of the project and designed to provide the time needed to achieve biological goals and address biological uncertainty;
5. public participation according to the National Environmental Policy Act.

These five points are the equivalent of a Welfare Program for Unemployed Biologists, and ensures the U.S. Fish & Wildlife Service almost complete power over the scientific community. I just want to grow food for my family. That is my "biological goal and objective." #3. "Monitoring for compliance, effectiveness, and effects" means I have to hire someone (undoubtedly one of the recommended biologists mentioned in the Incidental Take Permit Application.) for the entire length of my Habitat Conservation Plan. Suppose I am a young farmer, just starting out in life. I live in Tennessee, and a small stream runs through the property. As luck would have it, the stream is potential habitat for the Appalacian Monkeyface Pearly Mussel. This means I have to have the U.S. Government monitoring my farm, at my expense, for the next 50 years! We folks in Tenneseee thought the Revenuers were bad, but this is ridiculous! But suppose, just suppose, I get tired of this Bovine Excrement (to be politically correct), and want to sell my farm. The neighboring farm, also for sale, doesn't have any potential habitat for Appalacian Monkeyface Pearly Mussels on it. Which one do you think will sell? The fact is, the farm with endangered species on it has been made virtually worthless.

What are "No Surprises" assurances?

The FWS provides "No Surprises" assurances to non-Federal landowners through the section 0(a)(1)(B) process. Essentially, State and private landowners are assured that if "unforeseen circumstances" arise, the FWS will not require the commitment of additional land, water, or financial compensation or additional restrictions on the use of land, water, or other natural resources beyond the level otherwise agreed to in the HCP without the consent of the permitholder. The government will honor these assurances as long as permitholders are implementing the terms and conditions of the HCPs, permits, and other associated documents in good faith. In effect, the government and permit-holders pledge to honor their conservation commitments.

I am shocked to see this "No Surprises" Assurance still on the U.S. Fish and Wildlife website. This is a sales pitch for the use of Habitat Conservation Plans, which has, basically, been thrown out by they courts.

'No Surprises' Ruling Throws Habitat Plans Into Limbo

1 August 2004 - 12:00am
Environment Watch John Krist Vol. 19 No. 08 Aug 2004
Habitat conservation plans have become popular tools for balancing development with protection of imperiled plant and animal species. Since Congress authorized them in 1982, nearly 500 habitat conservation plans (HCPs) have been adopted nationwide.

The plans were not always so popular. Only 20 HCPs won approval during the program's first 12 years. Their use accelerated in 1995, when the Clinton administration began promoting them in the hope of blunting congressional efforts to rewrite the Endangered Species Act (ESA). And they really took off in 1998 with adoption of the controversial "no surprises" policy, which made HCPs more attractive to landowners by promising them relief from future regulatory meddling.

The no surprises policy was immediately attacked by environmental organizations, which recently won a court ruling overturning it. Although not quite the decisive victory the plaintiffs sought, the ruling nevertheless resulted in the suspension of the federal government's HCP program and has cast doubt on its long-term future.

As originally adopted in 1973, the ESA made it a crime to "take" a species listed as threatened or endangered, "take" being defined as any activity that kills or harms listed species or destroys their habitat. In 1982, Congress amended the ESA to allow federal agencies to issue permits for the "incidental take" of listed species during the course of otherwise lawful activity. Any application for an incidental take permit must be accompanied by an HCP that spells out how the effect of the permitted activity on a listed species will be minimized, monitored and mitigated.

Landowners initially were unenthusiastic, mainly because of a requirement that HCPs include a clause allowing their terms to be changed whenever federal agencies deemed it necessary. Why go to the trouble and expense of developing a habitat plan, landowners reasoned, if the government could rewrite the permit at any time?

The "no surprises" policy, originally announced in August 1994, was adopted to cure that perceived shortcoming. The policy required that federal agencies approving HCPs provide "assurances" to landowners that once an incidental take permit was approved, the government would not later change the permit's terms in a way that increases the landowner's costs or further restricts the use of natural resources. Under "no surprises," no additional conservation or mitigation measures could be imposed even if changed circumstances rendered the HCP inadequate to protect a listed species.

Biologists and environmentalists decried the policy, charging that it opened a gigantic loophole in the ESA and ignored the uncertainty inherent in the science of conservation biology and ecosystem management. In 1996, several groups filed a lawsuit alleging that the policy had been adopted in violation of the Administrative Procedures ,ich requires public notice and an opportunity for public comment before such reguae adopted.
The federal government settled that suit by agreeing to delay final adoption until the government had solicited public comment. About 800 comments subsequently were received, 755 of them opposing the policy. Many comments came from conservation biol-

ogists who warned that without a mechanism to respond to such "surprises" as drought, disease, fire, storms and floods, the HCP program would guarantee the loss of species and habitats.

But the federal agencies adopted the original policy virtually unchanged. In 1998, six environmental groups sued again, arguing that the government still had failed to comply with administrative law and that the policy violated the ESA.

While that suit was pending, the federal government adopted yet another policy making it more difficult to revoke incidental take permits. The plaintiffs, including the Spirit of the Sage Council and the Humane Society of the United States, amended their suit to allege that the revocation policy also violated the ESA and the Administrative Procedures Act.

Intervening as defendants in the litigation were the city and county of San Diego — where large-scale HCPs are a particularly popular conservation tool (see CP&DR Environment Watch, February 2003) — Orange County, Irvine Ranch Water District and a coalition that includes the National Association of Home Builders, the Building Industry Legal Defense Foundation, the Kern Water Bank Authority, and the American Forest and Paper Association.

In December 2003, Judge Emmet Sullivan of the federal district court in Washington, D.C., ruled that the federal government had, indeed, violated the Administrative Procedures Act by adopting both the "no surprises" and permit revocation policies without prior public notice and without providing a meaningful opportunity for public comment. He suspended both policies and ordered officials to start over.

"The ruling is a huge victory for imperiled animals and plants, as well as the public's basic right to have a say in how public resources are managed," said Leeona Klipstein, executive director of Spirit of the Sage Council.

The defendants were less enthusiastic.

"The inability to give 'no surprises' assurances to landowners would not only be a breach of faith with those landowners, it would also be a serious impediment to our ability to conserve and enhance habitat for imperiled wildlife," said Craig Manson, assistant secretary of the Interior.

Duane Desiderio, vice president of the National Association of Home Builders, was more blunt. "Now, a permit isn't worth the paper it's written on," he told the Associated Press.

The legal saga did not end there. Following the judge's ruling, USFWS Director Steven Williams issued a memo directing his regional managers to continue approving HCPs containing the no surprises clause, as long as they also included legal language noting that the remaining stipulations in each HCP would remain in effect if the no surprises policy were subsequently invalidated.

The plaintiffs went back to court, and on June 10, Judge Sullivan ordered the agencies to stop issuing HCPs containing the no surprises clause. He also gave the agencies until December 10 to complete the process of developing new permit rules. Williams then issued another memo directing his agency to stop approving incidental take permits altogether, but not before the USFWS on June 22 approved an HCP and incidental take permits covering 1 million acres and 146 species in rapidly growing western Riverside County. The Riverside County plan, perhaps the most ambitious HCP to date, does not contain the no surprises guarantee, although federal officials could add it later.

Significantly, Judge Sullivan did not rule on the substantive claim in the lawsuit: that the no surprises policy violates the ESA. Absent such a ruling — and given the popularity of no surprises HCPs — it is likely the federal agencies will simply readopt the polices after the legally prescribed public comment process has been completed. If that happens, another round of litigation is likely.

Are incidental take permits needed for listed plants?

There are no Federal prohibitions under the Act for the take of listed plants on non-Federal lands, unless taking those plants is in violation of State law. However, the FWS analyzes the effects of the permit on listed plant species because section 7 of the Act requires that issuing an incidental take permit may not jeopardize any listed species, including plants. In general, it is a good idea to include conservation measures for listed plant species in developing an HCP.

In other words, plants in the Habitat Conservation Plan must be addressed as well, which simply drives up the cost of this process, and the control the government has over you and your property, even more.

What is the process for getting an incidental take permit?

The applicant decides whether to seek an incidental take permit.
While FWS staff members provide detailed guidance and technical assistance throughout the process, the applicant develops an HCP and applies for a permit. The components of a
completed permit application are a standard application form, an HCP, an Implementation Agreement (if applicable), the application fee, and a draft National Environmental Policy Act (NEPA) analysis. A NEPA analysis may result in a categorical exclusion, an environmental assessment, or an environmental impact statement. While processing the permit application, the FWS prepares the incidental take permit and a biological opinion under section 7 of the Act and finalizes the NEPA analysis documents. Consequently, incidental take permits have a number of associated documents. How do we know if we have listed species on our project site? For assistance, check with the appropriate State fish and wildlife agency, the nearest FWS field office, or the National Marine Fisheries Service (NMFS), for anadromous fish such as salmon.

"Payment to an established conservation fund or bank". In the America I grew up believing in, this was called a "BRIBE"!!!! In my hypothetical home garden, surrounded by a grizzly bear fence, how, exactly, is a payment to a fund going to "mitigate" the 10,000 volts these grizzlies are going to get jolted with? Read the article below. I am not the only person that sees these Habitat Conservation Plan fund payments as a bribe, plain and simple.

"Groups Trade Gas Pipeline Approval for $20 Million Conservation Fund"*

By Bea Gordon, 7-26-10

"Habitat conservation because of a natural gas pipeline? Two environmental organizations are promising just that, thanks to an unlikely partnership with a natural gas company.

The Western Watersheds Project (WWP) and the Oregon Natural Desert Association (ONDA) reached a $20 million conservation agreement with the Houston-based El Paso Corp. over its proposed installation of the Ruby Pipeline, a 675-mile transmission line that would stretch from the Opal Hub in southwestern Wyoming to Malin, Oregon.

In the deal, El Paso plans to establish a $15 million conservation fund for the Idaho-based Western Watersheds Project and a $5 million fund for the Oregon Natural Desert Association over a period of ten years.

In turn, WWP's Executive Director Jon Marvel tells the Elko Daily Free Press, both groups have "agreed not to try to delay or litigate Ruby Pipeline."

If completed, the pipeline will cross four Western states: Wyoming, Utah, Nevada, and Oregon. In its initial design capacity it could stand to transport 1.5 billion cubic feet per day. The company estimates that its installation will cost about $3 billion, according to an official project summary. The project is currently awaiting Federal Energy Regulatory Commission and approval from state historical preservation offices.

El Paso Western Pipeline Group President Jim Cleary tells Adella Harding of the Elko Daily Free Press that the agreement reflects "El Paso Corp.'s industry-leading commitment to environmental stewardship and to this end represents a significant component of the unprecedented voluntary mitigation efforts being applied to Ruby's construction and operation."

Both organizations already have big plans for their respective

http://www.newwest.net/topic/article/groups_trade_gas_pipeline_approval_for_20_million_conservation_fund/C35/L35/

funds (which will not go directly to the organizations, instead to separate funds that will be be overseen by three-member boards.)

The Oregon group's executive director Brent Fenty, said in the same article, "Protecting the area around Hart Mountain and Sheldon Refuges is critical to ensuring the survival of high desert species like sage grouse and pronghorn antelope." The Hart-Sheldon conservation Fund could create restoration and conservation initiatives for 5 million acres of habitat.

The Western Watersheds Project, on the other hand, plans to focus almost exclusively on using the money to retire grazing permits by buying them from willing ranchers. The organization is first working on Congressional approval to allow federal agencies to retire these permits, however.

Marvel, a longtime opponent of grazing on public lands, argues that ending grazing along the pipeline would be better for wildlife, water quality, recreation and the environment. "It's time to end public lands grazing," he said.

Marvel tells the Green River Star, "These funds will be used to protect sage grouse habitat and the mule deer population in Wyoming."

The deal is precedent setting and it hasn't gone unnoticed by the region's ranching community, which has historically relied on public lands grazing.

David Sparks, a commentator for AgInfo.Net, lambasted the agreement, saying, "So let me get this straight. Marvel and WWP are on a legal crusade to stop the devastion of our public lands by cattlemen (who incidentally have been stewards of the land for over a century) but it's OK to deal with oil and gas companies and let them have at the land. Gulf oil spill and the like...no big deal with $20 million in your hypocritical pocket."

Here's the comment from David Sparks;

"Ah...saving the earth and wilderness. The great earth watcher from Sun Valley, Jon Marvel, who has filed a billion lawsuits to prevent beef producers from grazing on public land has reached

an intriguing agreement with the El Paso Corporation. Advocates for agriculture printed an article saying El Paso Corp. has
reached a precedent-setting, $20 million arrangement for habi-
tat protection with two environmental organizations that
protested the company's planned Ruby Pipeline that will extend from Wyoming to Oregon.

The company will set up conservation funds with the Western
Watersheds Project and the Oregon Natural Desert Association,
and the organizations in turn are dropping objections to the natural gas pipeline. So let me get this straight. Marvel and WWP
are on a legal crusade to stop the devastion of our public lands
by cattlemen (who incidentally have been stewards of the land
for over a century) but it's OK to deal with oil and gas companies and let them have at the land. Gulf oil spill and the
like...no big deal with $20 million in your hypocritical pocket.
Beef producers...just a thought...want your new best friends to
be Marvel and WWP? Line his pockets with big bucks."

"Every government interference in the economy consists of
giving an unearned benefit, extorted by force, to some men at
the expense of others. "
Ayn Rand

What is the legal commitment of a HCP?

Incidental take permits make binding the elements of HCPs. While
incidental take permits have expiration dates, the identified mitigation may be in perpetuity. Violating the terms of an incidental
take permit may institute unlawful take under section 9 of the Act.

This is the government threatening the holder of an Incidental
Take Permit, with heavy fines and prison, should he somehow violate the terms of the Incidental Take Permit. The fines are up to
$50,000 and one year in prison, per take. In other words, Mickey
Mouse, when he swatted "seven flies with one blow", if they had
been Delhi Sands Flower Loving Flies, would have been looking
at seven years in prison, and a $350,000 fine. An additional civil
penalty of $25,000 per take can also be assessed.

Who approves an HCP?

The FWS Regional Director decides whether to issue an incidental take permit, based on whether the HCP meets the criteria mentioned above. If the HCP addresses all of the requirements listed above, as well as those of other applicable laws, the FWS issues the permit. What other laws besides the Endangered Species Act are involved? In issuing incidental take permits, the FWS complies with the requirements of NEPA and all other statutes and regulations, including State and local environmental/planning laws. Who is responsible for NEPA compliance during the HCP process? The FWS is responsible for ensuring NEPA compliance during the HCP process. However, if the Service does not have sufficient staff resources, an applicant may, within certain limitations, prepare the draft NEPA analysis. Doing so can benefit the applicant and the government by expediting the application process and permit issuance. In cases like this, the FWS provides guidance, reviews the document, and takes responsibility for its scope, adequacy, and content.

This is simply placing control over your property, and, perhaps, your life's work and savings, in the hands of an unelected bureaucrat, the Regional Director of the U.S. Fish & Wildlife Service. If he doesn't like you personally, or doesn't like the project you have in mind, or is your ex-wife's second cousin, or whatever, you are screwed. The bureaucrat has the power of the government behind him: unlimited time, unlimited money, unlimited attorneys, unlimited access to the press. What do you, plain old Joe Bagodonuts Citizen, have?

Does the public get to comment on our HCP? How do public comments affect our HCP?

The Act requires a 30-day period for public comments on applications for incidental take permits. In addition, because NEPA requires public comment on certain documents, the FWS operates the two comment periods concurrently. Generally, the comment period is 30 days for a Low Effect HCP, 60 days for an HCP that requires an environmental assessment, and 90 days for an HCP that requires an environmental impact statement. The FWS considers public comments in permit decisions.

The government considers public comment about a decision it is going to make about your private property, the property you own and pay taxes on? What business of this of the public. If the public wants to have a say, it should pass a tax levy, and buy your property. Than it can do with it whatever it wishes. This is what the Fifth Amendment of the Constitution anticipated, protecting private landowners from public greed.

"Individual rights are not subject to a public vote. A majority has no right to vote away the rights of a minority. The political function of rights is precisely to protect minorities from oppression by majorities, and the smallest minority on earth is the individual."
Ayn Rand

What kind of monitoring is required for a HCP, and who performs it?

Three types of monitoring may be required: compliance, effectiveness, and effects. In general, **the permit-holder is responsible for ensuring that all the required monitoring occurs.** The FWS reviews the monitoring reports and coordinates with the permit-holder if any action is needed. Does the Fish and Wildlife Service try to accommodate the needs of HCP participants who are not professionally involved in the issues? Because applicants develop HCPs, the actions are considered private and, therefore, not subject to public participation or review until the FWS receives an official application. The FWS is committed to working with people applying for permits and providing technical assistance throughout the process to accommodate their needs. **However, the FWS does encourage applicants to involve a range of parties, a practice that is especially valuable for complex and controversial projects.**

Applicants for most large-scale, regional HCPs choose to provide extensive opportunities for public involvement during the planning process. Issuing permits is, however, a Federal action that is subject to public review and comment. There is time for such review during the period when the FWS reviews the information. In addition, the FWS solicits public involvement and review, as well as requests for additional information during the scoping process when an EIS is required.

The permit-holder, should he eventually acquire one, is responsible for all the required monitoring. The Endangered Species Act is theoretically for some greater good and the intrinsic value of Kangaroo rats, but it is the individual landowner who gets to foot all the costs and responsibilities. "The FWS does encourage applicants to involve a range of parties", many of whom the FWS recommends. This increases the power of the bureaucracy in the local community.

"Today, when a concerted effort is made to obliterate this point, it cannot be repeated too often that the Constitution is a limitation on the government, not on private individuals -- that it does not prescribe the conduct of private individuals, only the conduct of the government -- that it is not a charter _for_ government power, but a charter of the citizen's protection _against_ the government."
Ayn Rand

Are independent scientists involved in developing an HCP?

The views of independent scientists are important in developing mitigation and minimization measures in nearly all HCPs. In many cases, applicants contact experts who are directly involved in discussions on the adequacy of possible mitigation and minimization measures. In other cases, the FWS incorporates the views of independent scientists indirectly through their participation in listing documents, recovery plans, and conservation agreements that applicants reference in developing their HCPs. How does the FWS ensure that species are adequately protected in HCPs? The FWS has strengthened the HCP process by incorporating adaptive management when there are species for which additional scientific information may be useful during the implementation of the HCP. These provisions allow FWS and NMFS to work with landowners to reach agreement on changes in mitigation strategies within the HCP area, if new information about the species indicates this is needed. During the development of HCPs, the FWS and NMFS discuss any changes in strategy with landowners, so that they are aware of any uncertainty in management strategies and have concurred with the adaptive approaches outlined.

Absent the government, the economic prospects for "indepen-dent scientists" that are experts in such species as the Chiracahua Leopard Frog, the American Burying Beetle, and the White Warty-back Mussel, are somewhat limited. Therefore, wanting to please the only future employer out there, how "independent" are these independent scientists? My personal experience, albeit in the N.W.T. and not in the U.S., is that scientists will lie and manipu-late data to please their employer.

"Few men have ther virtue to withstand the highest bidder."
George Washington

What will the FWS do in the event of unforeseen circumstances that may jeopardize the species?
The FWS will use its authority to manage any unforeseen circum-stances that may arise to ensure that species are not jeopardized as a result of approved HCPs. In the rare event that jeopardy to the species cannot be avoided, the FWS may be required to revoke the permit.

"The FWS will use its authority". There's a comforting thought. The government controls the "independent scientists", and so, creating a situation where "jeopardy to a species cannot be avoided" is actually very simple to create, simply by controlling and manipulating the data. The continual threat of permit revo-cation, translates into continual fear of governmental action. Note the FWS doesn't say anything about compensation for the said revocation of your permit.

How can I obtain information on numbers and types of HCPs?
Our national HCP database displaying basic statistics on HCPs is available online from our Habitat Conservation
U. S. Fish and Wildlife Service
Endangered Species Program
4401 N. Fairfax Drive, Room 420
Arlington, VA 22203
703-358-2171
http://www.fws.gov/endangered/whatwe-do/hcp-overview.html

The Same Story, Two Different Versions

Looking at the U.S. Fish & Wildlife website, one gets the impression that these Habitat Conservation Plans are the creation of some kind of teamwork between a governmental agency and private landowners. In fact, nothing could be further from the truth. They are simply the product of a governmental agency out of control, using force, fear, and coercion, to push its environmentalist agenda.

Following is the story of the Washington County, Utah Habitat Conservation Plan, and how the local citizens felt, and the government's completely different view of the plan, four years later. This Habitat Conservation Plan is to protect the Desert Tortoise, which lives in the Mojave and Sonoran Deserts, a combined area of 92,800,000 acres. The Washington County Habitat Conservation Plan, designed by environmentalists to stop rapid growth in southern Utah, set aside 4,320 acres or roughly .000046 of the total potential habitat. Not coincidentally, the land set aside was "worth some $36,000,000.00", which (at $8,333.33/acre) is a helluva a lot more than most of the Mojave Desert is worth. Assuming roughly similar tortoise densities across the area, it comes to an initial cost of $223,602.48 per tortoise, plus the annual cost of the four full time government employees to monitor the tract (despite virtually no human activity being allowed there.) It also requires part time government employees when it comes time to actually count the turtles. The good news is, the plan calls for acquiring another 12,000 acres, worth $100,000,000.00.

The United States Government (also sometimes referred to "We, The People") has multi-trillion dollar debts, but U.S. Fish & Wildlife says we need to acquire $136,000,000.00 worth of desert, for the Desert Tortoise.

Congress, Please Wake Up!!!

The $36,000,000 Washington County Habitat Conservation Area

The Desert Tortoise

MOST AT HEARING DISLIKE PLAN TO PROTECT TORTOISE

Published: Saturday, Oct. 16, 1993 12:00 a.m. MDT By Brent Israelsen, Staff Writer

The desert tortoise is probably unaware of the controversy that surrounds him and the pains that governments and individuals are taking to protect him.

And he's likely oblivious to the wrath that such protection is creating in people who own and use the land on which the hard-shelled creature crawls.But had the tortoise wandered into a recent round of federal hearings, which ended Thursday in St. George, he might have wished he were back in the Mojave Desert, burrowed comfortably beneath some rock.

REJECTION OF TORTOISE PLAN LEADS TO DISMAY – March 28, 1993
It's not that people don't like the animal per se, they simply don't like the U.S. Fish and Wildlife Service's plan to designate 6.6 million acres of land as "critical habitat" for the slow-moving reptile.

Critical habitat offers additional federal protection to the tortoise, which has enjoyed a high degree of protection since it was listed as an endangered species in 1990.

In Utah, the FWS proposes to designate 137,200 acres of federal, state, private and Indian land as critical habitat. About 63,000 acres are north of St. George, a prime area targeted for real-estate and other development.

During Thursday's hearing, most of the three dozen speakers opposed the plan, saying it is unnecessary, an infringement of private property owners' rights and a breach of contract on the part of the federal government.

"We feel we are being oppressed by a federal government and bureaucracy that is taking away what we've had for generations," said Jerry Spillsbury, Las Vegas, who is part owner of 520 acres northwest of Hurricane, Washington County.

Spillsbury's land, which was settled by his great-great-grandfather, is being considered for inclusion in a national conservation area, which would require Spillsbury and his relatives to exchange their land for federal lands that are not critical habitat.

That proposed exchange and the national conservation area are part of the Habitat Conservation Plan proposed by a Washington County committee of local developers, politicians and environmentalists.

The HCP, which has been in the works for several years, would allow the county to develop some areas of critical habitat, thereby destroying tortoises, in exchange for measures elsewhere that would help the tortoise to recover from its endangered status.

As part of the national conservation area, which would be managed with strict federal protection, the HCP proposes that the federal government exchange Bureau of Land Management lands for much of the 28,000 acres of state school trust lands that fall within the critical habitat.

"We feel we are being oppressed by a federal government and bureaucracy that is taking away what we've had for generations,"

The reason Mr. Spillsbury feels oppressed by a federal government and bureaucracy is because he is being oppressed by a federal government and bureaucracy. But the United States Fish & Wildlife doesn't care about any of that. You see, they themselves as the deliverer of a moral ethic for out nation.

"The duty of a patriot is to protect his country from its government."
Thomas Paine

Now folks, put on your rose colored glasses. This article is how the government views the Washington County Habitat Conservation Plan, and the "work" being done there.

Washington County's HCP: Four Years Later

Desert tortoise habitat covered by the Washington County HCP also benefits other sensitive species in the area.

By Ted Owens

In the May/June 1996 Endangered Species Bulletin, biologist Marilet Zablan outlined the difficult process of developing a Habitat Conservation Plan (HCP) for Washington County, Utah. The plan was designed to protect important desert tortoise habitat while allowing development to proceed in many less sensitive areas. So how is it working?

Washington County, located in the southwestern corner of Utah, is one of the fastest developing parts of the United States. This area also contains vital habitat for the threatened Mojave population of the desert tortoise (Gopherus agassizii). In 1996, to resolve conflicts between development pressures and the well-being of the tortoise, the Fish and Wildlife Service issued the Washington County Commission a 20-year, county-wide permit for incidental take of the tortoise in accordance with the county's approved Habitat Conservation Plan.

Administratively, the plan is functioning well. The Washington County Habitat Conservation Advisory Committee (HCAC) meets monthly about important issues concerning the tortoise reserve, such as proposals for the installation and maintenance of utility lines, minor boundary changes, administrative budgets, and quarterly reports prepared by the county.

When the HCAC needs biological input on proposals (e.g., construction of a utility line), it assigns the technical committee the task of reviewing the matter and providing advice on any biological impacts. The technical committee is composed of biologists and land managers from various agencies. The HCAC then uses this advice in making its determinations, which must receive approval from the Service. Utility development is discouraged within the reserve, and must follow strict guidelines if no other practical alternative is available.

Since issuance of the permit, about 1,500 acres (600 hectares) of habitat have been legally cleared of tortoises and are in various stages of residential and commercial development. A total of 161 tortoises have been legally "taken." **Since permit issuance, the tortoise issue has largely fallen by the wayside for most Washington County residents.**

Biologically, much has been accomplished on the ground to benefit the desert tortoise.

First and foremost, a contiguous reserve has been established. The Dixie (Utah) Field Office of the Bureau of Land Management (BLM) has moved quickly to carry out land exchanges and acquisitions. **To date, 4,320 acres (1,750 ha) worth some $36 million have been acquired for the reserve by the BLM or state of Utah.** Most of this acquisition has been through exchanges, although some parcels were bought with funds from the Service and the Land and Water Conservation Fund, and other parcels were donated. If more extensive development had continued within what is now the reserve, tortoise populations would be more fragmented today and they would most likely eventually succumb to extirpation.

In addition to land acquisition, a list of accomplishments completed in the past 5 years is nothing less than amazing. Because cattle compete with tortoises for forage, some 99 percent of grazing permits within the reserve's tortoise habitat have been retired by Washington County. The county also has funded a full-time BLM law enforcement officer whose sole responsibility is protection of the reserve. The BLM also has prohibited off-road vehicle (ORV) use except on a few select designated roads and trails. Consequently, formerly degraded habitat has become noticeably healthier. Further, the BLM has withdrawn the entire reserve from new mining claims. On its part, Washington County employs a full-time WCHCP administrator, biologist, and technician who coordinate and carry out the day-to-day activities vital to accomplishing conservation measures on the ground. The county also annually funds seasonal technicians with the Utah Division of Wildlife Resources (UDWR) to monitor tortoise populations within the reserve. Over 30 miles (48 kilometers) of fencing have been built by various entities to exclude desert tortoises from roads or other hazards and to control illegal dumping, vandalism, and ORV use.

Development of a nature education center focusing on sensitive

reserve species is forthcoming. In the meantime, Washington County has provided information on tortoises and other wildlife to thousands of its residents, thereby increasing public support for the reserve. The county has also helped fund a multi-species plan for other wildlife in the reserve, which summarizes current knowledge and contains strategies for monitoring various sensitive species throughout the county, including six other listed species and dozens of species of concern. A translocation experiment is providing valuable information about which habitats tortoises prefer, how far they will travel, and whether or not successful translocation is even possible.

Although the HCP's implementation generally is going well, there are several areas of concern. Many local residents feel that the reserve should be open to unlimited recreational use. The Service, UDWR, and BLM are concerned that unrestrained recreation could have harmful impacts on the tortoises and their habitat. A public use plan has been developed to address these issues. Another ongoing area of concern is the cost of acquiring the remaining 12,000 or so acres (4,850 ha) of property within the reserve. The BLM has done an outstanding job in acquiring reserve property as quickly as administratively possible, but it has a limited budget and has been unable to acquire some needed acreage quickly enough to avert the threat of development. Properties within the reserve still to be acquired are **currently worth about $100 million.**

Despite some areas of contention, the Washington County HCP is promoting tortoise and other species conservation while accommodating the demand for development.

Ted Owens is a Fish and Wildlife Biologist with the Service's Salt Lake City, Utah, Office.

"Accomplishments completed in the past 5 years is nothing less than amazing"
What is amazing is the amount of money being spent on 4,320 acres or tortoise habitat, which is valued at $36,000,000.00 of taxpayer money, with only $100,000,000.00 more to spend! How much good for human beings can be done for $136,000,000.00?

"A full time BLM law-enforcement officer, whose sole responsibil-

ity is protection of the reserve. " Are you serious? The area is roughly 2.5 x 2.75 miles in size, and has 30 miles of fencing around it, to keep turtles in and people out. What could this guy possibly do all day long, besides drink coffee?

In addition to the full-time policeman, we have a full time **Washington County Habitat Conservation Plan Administrator, a full-time biologist, and a full time technician.** Thank goodness, when it comes to counting the tortoises, they are able to bring in temporary help, to assist with the workload.

"Because cattle compete with tortoises for forage, some 99 percent of grazing permits within the reserve's tortoise habitat have been retired by Washington County." I am so pleased we got rid of food for humans, so the turtles can eat. You know how those pesky, profit seeking ranchers are, wanting their cows to eat all the turtle food.

"The BLM also has prohibited off-road vehicle (ORV) use except on a few select designated roads and trails. Over 30 miles (48 kilometers) of fencing have been built by various entities to exclude desert tortoises from roads or other hazards and to control illegal dumping, vandalism, and ORV use."
So the government acquires $36,000,000 of land, for a public purpose, and then tells the public to "KEEP OFF". That's just beautiful. Additionally, we get 30 miles of fence to make sure the people stay out, just in case the full time BLM law enforcement officer is overwhelmed with keeping the tortoises from committing whatever crimes it is tortoises commit.

"The BLM has withdrawn the entire reserve from new mining claims."
This Habitat Conservation Plan reads like the Defenders for Wildlife Manifesto: No mining, no ranching, no housing, no roads, no recreation, no liberty.

"Since permit issuance, the tortoise issue has largely fallen by the wayside for most Washington County residents."

This is the saddest statement on the whole website. It means the people gave up, overrun by the United States Fish & Wildlife Service, their own "oppressive" government.

"When wrongs are pressed because it is believed they will be borne, resistance becomes morality."
Thomas Jefferson

The following is from the Congressional Record, March 13, 2001.

"H.R. Bill 880 is a voluntary legislative taking of 1550 acres of land in Washington County, Utah.........The owner has been unable to sell, trade, or develop this property for years because of the actions of Fish &Wildlife Service......This disagreement goes back to 1983......Following years of negotiation, in 1996 a Habitat Conservation Plan for the desert tortoise was reached.....For the past ten years, ELT (the property owner) has paid taxes and interest on its property without ability to sell or develop that land, or even set foot on it."

"The Right of property is the guardian of every other Right, and to deprive the people of this, is in fact to deprive them of their Liberty"
Arthur Lee

Is this what Congress intended, when it passed the Endangered Species Act of 1973 by a vote of 455-4? Was there months of debate about American's rights to private property? No, there was not. Since the law has now evolved into a tool for taking American's private property rights, Congress has a duty to the people to reopen that debate, and look more carefully at where this law has taken our nation.

Congress won't have to look very far. Just check the unemployment rates, the price of groceries, the flooding in the Midwest, the plunging price of real estate, and the feeling of American hopelessness and helplessness.

Chapter 7

Wolf Reintroduction: The Greatest Wildlife Tragedy Since the Buffalo Were Slaughtered

Wolf killed after attacking dogs on edge of Hamilton

By PERRY BACKUS Ravalli Republic missoulian.com | Posted: Tuesday, May 24, 2011 6:30 am

HAMILTON - Jason and Sarah Ekin's 5-year-old son loves to roam around their yard catching butterflies.

In her oversized white sunglasses, their 3-year-old daughter often makes a beeline from the front door to the backyard where the couple's three hunting dogs lounge.

But the Ekins say they will think twice before letting their kids wander around their home on the edge of Hamilton after last Saturday morning.

The couple was abruptly awakened shortly after 5 a.m. that day when their dogs let out a terrified bark.

"The sound just exploded from our backyard," Sarah said. "It sounded like they thought their lives were going to come to an end."

Jason Ekin and son examining their wounded pet.

A moment later, they heard one of the dogs begin to yelp.
"I could tell that one of them was being hurt," Jason said. "I didn't
know what was going on."

They peered out a large window and spotted the shape of a large
black dog standing a few yards away from one of the dog houses.

"I told my wife that I thought it was a wolf," Jason said. "I told her
to go get the gun. When I lifted the shade, he started to leave."
Jason went out onto the second-story deck with his rifle. At first, he
thought the wolf had left, but minutes later it reappeared and
walked to within 12 feet of the dog's house and stared inside at the
70-pound Walker hound.

"That wolf had to know that I was there, but he just didn't seem to
care," Jason said. "It looked to me that he had come back to finish the
job."

When the wolf turned broadside to him, Jason shot it.

The wolf flipped over once before falling dead on a patch of grass
now stained reddish-brown. It died 34 yards from the couple's deck.

Montana Fish, Wildlife and Parks Warden Lou Royce said the
shooting was justified.

"Under state and federal law, he's covered," Royce said. "He was defending his dog's life."

One dog was bitten during the wolf attack.

"I definitely could see a bite mark on the side of the dog," Royce said. "It was pretty stove up. It was obviously hurting a bit."

The wolf weighed 86 pounds. Royce said it was probably less than 2 years old.

FWP wolf biologist Liz Bradley said the wolf may have been a disperser from another pack.

"This kind of thing can happen any time of year," Bradley said. "Wolves see dogs as competitors. They are very territorial."

Royce and Bradley agreed that it is unusual for a wolf to show up in such a residential area so close to town.

The Ekins live on North Canyon Drive, which is just west of Hamilton and less than a mile from the city limits.

"I was surprised at how many houses there were right around their house," Royce said. "I thought maybe they lived in the trees when I got the call. Their dogs were all chained and near their house. I've never handled one exactly like this before."

On Monday, Sarah was scheduled to baby-sit thee other young children at her home.

"I terrified about that actually," she said. "Do I even dare to let them go outside? I think we'll live in fear for a while before we get comfortable again. It's just not something that we would expect to have happen here."

Since Saturday, the couple has received a number of phone calls from neighbors who said they had seen the wolf near their own homes. Some called to report they had lost dogs or cats over the past couple of weeks. Others just wanted to thank Jason for killing the animal.

"I didn't do this because it was something I wanted to do," he said. "I did it because I had to do it to protect my dogs."

The above story happened in my hometown of Hamilton, Montana, in a subdivision, just outside of town. Jason Ekin, the man who shot the wolf, protecting his dogs, is a neighbor, and former employee. Fortunately, for his dog, Jason is a hunter, and he was able to dispatch that wolf in time. Instead of the pet dog, that wolf could have just as easily attacked a small child, playing in the backyard. Suppose the grandmother was babysitting that day, and wasn't quick enough to the rescue? Wolf sightings now are common here in western Montana. My wife saw one the other day, on the way to our office, about 20 yards from where the local school bus picks up children every morning. The wolves are here, right in civilization, because they have destroyed or displaced their food source, the ungulate populations of elk, deer, and moose, in the adjoining Bitterroot National Forest and Selway Bitterroot Wilderness areas. They are here because they have been mismanaged by the U.S. Fish & Wildlife Service.

2 days later, the following headlines appeared:

Pack of wolves kills horse near Darby

By PERRY BACKUS for the Missoulian missoulian.com | Posted: Saturday, May 28, 2011 10:00 am |
Paul Shirley and his horse, Jack, are shown together in this family photo. Jack was chased into a fence and killed Thursday night by a pack of wolves near Darby.

DARBY - Montana Fish, Wildlife and Parks officials have authorized the killing of up to nine wolves south of Darby after recent attacks on a horse and a calf.

The horse was killed within 200 yards of the Two Feathers Ranch manager's home Thursday night. The ranch is about 1 1/2 miles south of Darby.

"Our favorite horse was killed by a wolf last night," said ranch owner Paul Shirley. "He was always the one who would come up

The Shirley's favorite horse, "Jack"

for treats and we could give kids rides on him without any worry."

The quarter horse was named Jack.

"The wolves ran him through a fence and then tore his guts out," Shirley said. "It was terrible. ... These wolves are on our property most nights, and I'm terrified for my animals. I'm not sure what I'm supposed to do with my livestock."

Rancher manager Jeff Rennaker spent Friday morning alongside a federal government trapper who looked over the kill site and then set four traps around the property.

"We are going to be pretty proactive the next couple of days," Rennaker said. "We're going to have to wait to see what the night brings. I've got 13 horses out there and 160 cattle. I'll be out there most of the night."

FWP wolf biologist Liz Bradley suspects wolves in the Trapper Peak Pack were responsible.

"They were in trouble last year on a different ranch," Bradley said. "We authorized the removal of the pack at that time."

Some of the wolves were killed, but not all.

"It's pretty likely that pack," Bradley said. "We know that they cycle through that area."

Five kill permits were issued to the landowner.

"We're hoping to get it wrapped up as quickly as possible so we don't have any more problems," she said.

The Trapper Peak Pack has frequented the ranch in the past, but Rennaker said they haven't had any losses of livestock up until now.

Rennaker said he's seen wolves in his front yard on a several occasions.

Just across the highway, CB Ranch cattle manager Jeff Snavely said that operation lost a calf about a week ago. The attack also marked the first time that ranching operation had a confirmed wolf kill.

"We've had them on the ranch for a long time," Snavely said. "They have killed elk and deer before, but we've never had any kills on livestock."

Officials authorized the removal of four wolves from the Divide Creek Pack as a result of the depredation.

Last week, a Hamilton man shot a wolf just outside of town after it attacked one of his dogs.

With the amount of snow remaining in the high country, Bradley said wolves and other wildlife are at lower elevations this spring. As the snow begins to melt and wolf pups get bigger, <u>she expects them to start pulling up into higher elevations.</u>

The elk and deer here have changed their habits, and they no longer make long treks from the lower elevations in the winter to the high country for the summer and fall. You see, predation is the number one mover of wildlife. Not food, not habitat. Predators. Wolves move in, ungulates move out. It is that simple, and I have personally seen it happen dozens of times, all across Alaska, Yukon, the Northwest Territories, British Columbia, Alberta, Saskatchewan, Montana, Idaho, and Wyoming. Wolves, are perhaps the smartest of all predators, and they fear human beings, their only predator. The elk, deer, and moose hang closer to civilization, because the wolves are afraid to come into civilization. Unfortunately, hungry wolves will eventually take chances, forced to come into populated areas or risk starvation. As you can see from the story below, dated August 28, the wolves are in the valleys, slaughtering sheep. The wolves no longer move into the high country, following the game, because the game is either gone, or stays low in the valleys, seeking the protection of man.

Wolves kill 120 sheep at ranch near Dillon

HELENA - August 28, 2009. While the debate about how many wolves are enough to ensure a healthy population will again come to a head in a federal courtroom Monday, a Dillon-area ranch is picking up the pieces from the largest known wolf depredation in recent history.

In a highly unusual move for wolves, they killed about 120 adult male sheep in one incident on the Rebish/Konen Livestock Ranch south of Dillon last week.

That compares with a total of 111 sheep killed by wolves in Montana in 2008, according to Carolyn Sime, the statewide wolf coordinator for Montana Fish, Wildlife and Parks.

"This is one of the most significant losses that I've seen," Sime said. "That situation is really unfortunate."

Suzanne Stone with Defenders of Wildlife added that in the 20 years she's been working toward ensuring healthy wolf populations, this is the first time she's heard of such a mass killing.

"I've heard of bears or mountain lions doing that, but what usually happens is the sheep panic and jump on top of one another or fall into a ditch and suffocate," Stone said. "I've never heard of any situation where wolves killed so much livestock in such a short period of time.

"... This is the most extreme case I've ever heard about."

The ranch has suffered confirmed wolf depredations twice in three weeks. In late July, three wolves - two blacks and a gray - killed at least 26 rams. The gray wolf was lethally shot by a federal wildlife manager, and one of the blacks was injured. They thought that would scare off the rest of the pack.

Last week, wolves struck again. This time, they took out 120 pure-bred Rambouillet bucks that ranged in size from about 150 to 200 pounds, and were the result of more than 80 years of breeding.

"We went up to the pasture on Thursday (Aug. 20) - we go up there every two or three days - and everything was fine," rancher Jon Konen said. "The bucks were in the pasture; I had about 100 heifers with them on 600 acres."

He had some business to attend to in Billings, so Konen told his son to be sure to check on the livestock while he was gone.

"He called me, and said it was a mess up there. He said there were dead bucks all up and down the creek. We went up there the next day and tried to count them, but there were too many to count," Konen recalled.

"I had tears in my eyes, not only for myself but for what my stock had to go through," he added. "They were running, getting chewed on, bit and piled into a corner. They were bit on the neck, on the back, on the back of the hind leg.

"They'd cripple them, then rip their sides open."

Montana Fish, Wildlife and Parks has taken the lead in wolf man-agement from the U.S. Department of the Interior's Fish and Wildlife Service, and the state agency has a "memorandum of un-derstanding" with the federal Department of Agriculture's Wildlife Services to provide damage management services when livestock are killed by wolves.

After the dead sheep were found, Graeme McDougal with Wildlife Services flew in a small plane over the sheep pasture, looking for the one or two remaining black wolves to complete the control work requested by Montana FWP. Within a half-mile of the sheep pas-ture, he spotted the Centennial pack of three adult gray wolves and five pups.

McDougal shot and killed the one uncollared adult wolf, but wasn't authorized to remove any more wolves.

This was the first known depredation incident for the Centennial pack in 2009.

Konen doesn't want to wade into the debate over the reintroduction of wolves in the Rockies, but said that in his opinion, it's time to stop managing wolves and start controlling them.

"My bucks were on private ground, in a pasture where we've been pasturing them for 50 years. The wolves were intruders that were in the wrong place," he said.

Wolves were recently taken off the list of animals protected under the Endangered Species Act, and both Montana and Idaho have instituted hunting seasons for them this year. Idaho will allow 265 wolves to be taken by hunters, in a season that starts Tuesday. Montana will allow 75 wolves to be taken, with the season starting Sept. 15.

Montana is home to an estimated 500 wolves, while Idaho has at least 850. Wyoming also has wolves, but they remain under Endangered Species Act protection.

In Stone's opinion, hunting wolves could create even more problems for ranchers.

"If the adults are shot, then the young ones are dispersed too early," Stone said. "Young pups on their own might turn to livestock to survive, and that's not a good situation for anybody."

Her organization has put out a book to educate ranchers on proactive steps they can take to prevent livestock loss, like hiring range riders, hanging "fladry" - closely spaced cloth - on fences, and minimizing attractants such as dead carcasses.

Defenders of Wildlife has spent more than $895,000 since 1998 to help pay for installation of nonlethal methods to prevent conflicts.

Since 1987, they've also made 885 payments totaling $1.35 million to ranchers to compensate for livestock killed by wolves.

In Montana, the Legislature has earmarked $150,000 to compensate ranchers for livestock lost to wolves, and U.S. Sen. Jon Tester, D-Mont., co-sponsored a bill that includes $5 million in federal funding over five years for depredation losses.

George Edwards, state livestock loss mitigation coordinator, said the Rebish/Konen Ranch probably will receive $350 per dead sheep.

But he added that the loss is more than just monetary to ranchers.

"The compensation still doesn't make up for the loss by any means," Edwards said. "The rancher still needs to make up his breeding stock, and people in town may not realize the attachment livestock folk get to their animals. The emotional toll it takes is just indescribable."

Stevensville landowners say wolves driving herd onto properties

By PERRY BACKUS Ravalli Republic missoulian.com | Posted: Thursday, January 20, 2011 10:17 pm

Montana Fish, Wildlife and Parks officials met Thursday night with landowners from northeast of Stevensville to provide information about an elk herd that has taken up residence there. STEVENSVILLE - Farmers and ranchers packed a meeting house on Burnt Fork Road on Thursday night to voice their frustration over a growing number of elk that are living in their pastures and hay fields.

And many weren't happy either with the wolves they believe are driving the elk from their traditional winter ranges higher up on the surrounding mountainsides.

Montana Fish, Wildlife and Parks officials called the meeting to offer advice on keeping elk out of haystacks and to talk about the potential for future joint projects to build wildlife-friendly fences.

Landowners living on the edge of the Sapphire Mountains northeast of Stevensville have been dealing with a herd of nearly 170 elk this winter that ventured down into areas where they had not been seen before.

Several farmers in the crowd of about 60 who attended the meeting said they have been dealing with growing elk numbers for several years.

Some said the elk were putting a huge dent in their farming business, and profit margins are already thin.

Dave Golay said he can spend up to $60,000 in seed and fertilizer to prepare his annual hay crop.

"And then the elk come and eat me off," Golay said. "I'm feeding 150 elk and maybe deer. ... How much do we have to give? It seems like we're already giving a lot more than we should."

Golay said he's been dealing with this issue for three or four years now.

George Bettas said he and his neighbor first saw seven or eight elk show up on their place at the end of Burnt Fork in 2009. This spring, there were close to 40 and by September there were 100 staying an irrigated circle.

The elk are staying most of the year now, including calving season. Up higher on the mountainside, Bettas said it's not unusual to find wolf tracks.

"They are having their calves here now where they're not bothered by predators," Bettas said. "People want to have elk around, but we need to find a way to manage them, too."

Keith Marchuk sounded angry when he spoke up.

"You won't even admit wolves are the problem," he told FWP offi-

Elk, living near man, for protection from wolves.

cials. "You could drive those elk back up into the hills with five helicopters, but they wouldn't stay there. They'd double back and come right back down here.

"Wolves are why the elk aren't going back up there," he said. "Your problem isn't elk. It's the damned wolves."

Rod Knutson didn't disagree that wolves were a problem, but he said some landowners are creating their own set of problems when it comes to elk.

Some landowners - especially those who don't live here full time - have tolerance for large numbers of elk on their properties, Knutson said. While that would be fine if the elk would stay put, he said that's not what happens.

"The elk end up going onto their neighbor's lush crops, who are trying their best to make a living off their land," Knutson said.

FWP's Bitterroot biologist Craig Jourdonnais said the state wants to work toward finding some kind of middle ground that keeps farmers and ranchers solvent while maintaining wildlife populations.

In populated areas, like the Bitterroot Valley, that can be a challenge.

"My job is to look after elk while also understanding how important private landowners are to wildlife in Montana," Jourdonnais said.

FWP regional wildlife manager Mike Thompson said the department will focus on finding ways to make the elk uncomfortable in hopes they will eventually move back into higher country.

To make that happen, Thompson said FWP and local landowners will need to work together.

I resent having to worry about my grandchildren playing in their own back yard, because some unelected bureaucrat at United States Fish & Wildlife Service thinks it is "cool" to have wolves, and lots of them. Yes, wolves are iconic in nature, but their "intrinsic value", (particularly when there are tens of thousands of these wolves around the world,) should not, and must not, be placed before the safety of human lives and livestock. Nor should wolves take precedent over the vast game herds of the west, herds that took nearly 100 years to replenish, through the hard work and hard earned dollars of millions of American sportsmen, and other conservationists. I reject the idea of this oppressive, elitist government bureacracy, slowly, but surely, ruining the economy of my nation and destroying the very freedoms that so many brave Americans have died for. To be perfectly frank, what I am finding in researching this book disgusts me.

Bitterroot Valley residents tell commissioners wolves are out of control

By PERRY BACKUS Ravalli Republic
HAMILTON - The Ravalli County Commission wanted to hear about the effects wolves are having on residents' lives.

On Thursday afternoon, they got an earful.
For more than an hour and half, people waited their turn to talk

about how wolves have impacted their businesses, recreational opportunities and lives.

The meeting was part of an information-gathering drive that began at the end of June, when the commission put out a call to any resident with stories about wolf encounters over the past 16 years.

After listening to testimony Thursday, none of the commissioners offered the audience any indication just what their next step might be.

At the county level, the commission doesn't have a whole lot of authority to enact change in matters such as wolf management, Commission Chairman J.R. Iman told the crowd of about 50.

Commissioner Matt Kanenwisher said that doesn't mean the county can't try.

"I do not necessarily agree that there's nothing we can do," Kanenwisher said. "By trying everything, then we will know what we can or can't do."

For the most part, those who spoke said the wolf situation in Ravalli County was out of hand.

Judy Kline of Stevensville said she has resorted to packing a pistol whenever she leaves her house after wolves killed deer two separate times in her yard just off Kootenai Creek Road, a half mile from U.S. Highway 93.

"It's very intimidating to have wolves that close to your home," Kline said. "Now I find the need to carry a weapon whenever I walk from the garage to my house."

West Fork Lodge owner Tex Irwin said his business has been in freefall with the dramatic decline in elk numbers in the West Fork area.

From 2006 to 2010, Irwin said, he's seen an 85 percent decline in bookings for hunting season months. He has no reservations set for October this year and only two in November.
Darby outfitter Scott Boulanger said his $200,000 investment into

an outfitting business that focused on the West Fork is now worth virtually nothing.

Once considered one of the best elk hunting areas in the region, this year there are only 25 permits being offered for bull elk and none for cows.

When Boulanger purchased his business in 1998, there were no wolves in the West Fork and the elk population was doing well. He said wildlife officials told him at that time that wolves would never be allowed to decimate an ungulate population.

"They were either lying or just plain wrong," he said.

Today, the national outdoor media calls the Bitterroot Valley ground zero for wolf problems, Boulanger said. They call the West Fork the worst predator pit in the United States, he said.

Rod Knutson of Stevensville said wolves are pushing elk out the hills and local ranchers are feeling the effects on their hay meadows.

Knutson said he built an 8-foot fence around a 10-acre hayfield this year to keep the elk at bay. He harvested 432 bales last year. This year, with the fence, that number jumped to 941.

"That just goes to show you how much government livestock fed off of me in one year," he said. "When the elk are pushed down out of the hills by wolves, they quickly get accustomed and want to stay."

Dalton Christopherson's family has been ranching in the southern Bitterroot for a century.

"Wolves have disrupted my life in a major way," he said. "There have been a lot of sleepless nights and I've missed time away from my family. I have a lot of cows to take care of."

Some of those cows spend their summer on 26,000 acres of leased land. When they come home in the fall, Christopherson said, some of those don't have calves any more.

Since the reintroduction of wolves, his calf weights have declined about 30 pounds. At $1.41 a pound, that much weight loss adds up quickly with 80 calves, he said.

Bill LaCroix of Victor said that while he agreed that wolves needed to be managed, he did have concerns about the motive behind the commission's efforts to gather information.

LaCroix said he would oppose any move to weaken the federal Endangered Species Act.

Wolves haven't changed the way LaCroix spends time in the woods.

"I take my 5-year-old daughter up Sweathouse Creek all the time armed with only a fishing pole," he said.

Jim Dicken, owner of Darby's Mountain Spirit Inn, told the commission he had to use gunfire last hunting season to keep the wolves at bay.

Reading from a written statement, Dicken said he and his hunting partner had walked about 100 yards up the Tin Cup Trail about two hours before daylight when they were met with "six sets of glowing eyes" in their flashlights' beams.

His statement read: "Matt said, 'Are those coyotes?' I would estimate the animals were 15 feet in front of us. I said, "Hell no, those are wolves, start shooting.' I pulled out my SKS, which was slung over my shoulder and started firing. Matt was firing his pistol.

"I said, 'keep an eye out behind us.' The two of us walked back-to-back toward the vehicle. They were circling us, and they stayed on us all the way back. They acted in a fearless manner from us or the gunfire. It felt like two miles of walking to get back to the pickup. I went through two 30-round clips."

Once safe inside, Dicken wrote, the pair rolled down their windows a couple of inches. They could hear the wolves growling outside.

"We sat there for about an hour and a half until daylight hit, and then the wolves disappeared with the dawn."

Definition of "Anarchy:" absence or denial of any authority or established order"*

Following is an article showing how desperate things are becoming here in Idaho, Montana, and Wyoming. The same desperation I am sure the loggers felt in the Northwest, with the spotted owl, or the farmers in central California felt with the Delta Smelt, or the residents along the flooded Missouri feel with the Piping Plover. What Governor Otter did, basically, was to instruct his Idaho Wildlife agents to stop enforcing the laws, regarding the wolves and the Endangered Species Act. This amounts to a proposal of anarchy, so incredibly desperate are we here in the west to rid ourselves of the oppression of the Endangered Species Act of 1973.

Idaho Governor Rejects ESA Wolf Management

Posted on: 10/24/10

In another salvo of the wolf-wars, **Idaho's Governor Otter has ordered state wildlife managers to "relinquish their duty to arrest poachers or to even investigate when wolves are killed illegally."** Under the Endangered Species Act (ESA) Idaho wildlife officials are the "designated agent" for investigating wolf deaths in the state.

Kidk.com has a more detailed story about the Governor's orders, specifically: This means Idaho Department of Fish and Game managers will no longer perform statewide monitoring for wolves, conduct investigations into illegal killings, provide law enforcement when wolves are poached or participate in a program that responds to livestock depredations.

With U.S. District Judge Donald Molloy's ruling in August, Idaho and Montana have had to cancel public hunts. That's especially irked Otter, who contends the first legal harvest that started in 2009 and ended earlier this year demonstrated that states could manage wolves responsibly.

In an angry letter to U.S. Interior Secretary Ken Salazar, the Republican governor said withdrawing from wolf management will keep Idaho hunters and their money from subsidizing the federal program. "History will show that this program was a tragic example of oppressive, ham-handed 'conservation' at its worst," Otter wrote. **"Idahoans have suffered this intolerable situation for too long, but starting today at least the state no longer will be complicit."**

This following article was written in 2004. The wolves were introduced in 1994, and in just a decade, the elk herd had been cut in half.
As you will see, that trend continues to this day.

Elk numbers plummet; wildlife managers re-spond by regulating hunters

January 8, 2004: By Scott McMillion, Chronicle Staff Writer from Tom Adams,
Wyoming

LIVINGSTON -- Elk numbers continue to plummet in the northern
Yellowstone elk herd, according to a report released late Tuesday.

The herd is now the smallest it's been since the 1970s.

A Dec. 18 flight by state and federal biologists found 8,355 elk despite "relatively good survey conditions," which means good
weather and enough snow to make elk visible from the air.
That's a drop of at least 880 elk, 9.5 percent, from last year's count
of 9,215, when conditions were poor and biologists said they probably missed a lot of elk.

The herd has dropped by an average of 6 percent a year since 1994,
when the herd had at least 19,300 elk. That time span coincides with
the reintroduction of wolves to Yellowstone National Park in 1995.

"Wolves are certainly a primary mortality factor" for elk, said P.J.
White, a Yellowstone wildlife biologist.

Another big factor is human predation, especially in the annual Gar-
diner-area late hunt. But unlike wolves, which are protected by the
Endangered Species Act, hunter numbers can be restricted.

Regulating hunting numbers "is the only tool we have" in that area,
said Tom Lemke, wildlife biologist in Livingston for the Montana
Department of Fish, Wildlife and Parks.

The late hunt that began last weekend has already been cut in half,
and might be pared some more, Lemke said. This year, 1,400 permits were granted, compared to 2,880 in 1997.

Lemke said it's too soon to give any specific numbers, but "it's possible we will reduce them" further in coming years.

"When you have fewer elk, you harvest fewer," Lemke said.

White said the herd size probably will continue to shrink.

"I expect the population will continue to decrease in the near future," he said.

The effect of wolves on elk has become a big issue with some hunters and outfitters in the Gardiner area.

Fewer late-season hunters means fewer people renting rooms, buying meals and hiring guides in that parkside community, where the late hunt has become part of the winter economy.

"It's breaking us," said Bill Hoppe, a Jardine outfitter and a founder of the Friends of the Northern Yellowstone Elk Herd.

He said he has 40 hunters booked this year.

"I used to take 100, sometimes 150," he said. "All the outfitters you talk to are way down."

With the cuts in permits, "that's 1,000 people who didn't come to town," Hoppe said, and most hunters bring a companion.
If each spent $100 in Gardiner, that means $200,000 in lost business, plus the $200 a day charged by guides.
Last year, guided hunters took almost 50 percent of the 718 elk harvested in the late hunt, according to an FWP report.
Hoppe last year predicted a significant drop in elk numbers and said they'll continue to fall.

"What'd I say last year? That we'd be down another 1,000 elk," he said. "Like I told you last year: I told you so."

So how many elk is appropriate for the northern range? People have argued about that for most of a century.

Until 1968, rangers regularly killed hundreds of elk at a time inside the park, keeping the herd to about 3,500 animals, and critics still said the park was overgrazed.

After the National Park Service culling stopped, the herd grew quickly. And the number of hunting permits outside the park grew as well, with the goal of avoiding overgrazing outside the park.

Now, since the return of the wolf, the herd has seen a steady decline. Nobody knows how it will end.

"We'll continue to monitor it closely," White said. He noted that wolves aren't the only factor at play.

Preliminary reviews of data collected last summer show that grizzly bears are killing an increasing number of elk calves. Black bears and wolves also kill significant numbers. And weather is always a factor.

But of the three major factors affecting elk numbers -- predation, weather and hunting -- only hunting can be controlled.

White praised FWP for reducing the number of hunters. "I commend them for taking that step," he said.

By 2010, the Yellowstone Elk herd had dropped from the 9215 in 2003, to 4607, just about exactly half in just 7 short years, and this, despite mild winters, and a reduction in hunting tags from 2880 in 1997 to just 30 in 2011. For those interested in more detailed information, watch Scott Rockholm's excellent documentary **"Yellowstone is Dead."** That rumbling you hear is Teddy Roosevelt, spinning in his grave.

Yellowstone elk herd numbers down 24 percent

By MATTHEW BROWN - Associated Press RavalliRepublic.com | Posted: Wednesday, January 12, 2011

BILLINGS - Wildlife officials said Wednesday that an acclaimed elk herd in Yellowstone National Park dropped in size by 24 percent over the last year - as predators, hunters, recent drought and deep snows all took a toll.

As recently as 1994, the northern Yellowstone elk herd was the

largest in North America with almost 20,000 animals that roamed between the park and Montana's Paradise Valley.

Figures released Wednesday show it is now down to a minimum of **4,635 elk.** That compares with more than 6,000 last year. **Park biologist Doug Smith said 2010's decline was unexpected because the herd had shown signs of stabilizing in recent years.**

But he added that a smaller herd was more healthy, and that there was no reason to suspect its size will continue to plummet. Smith says deep snows also may have thrown off the count by leaving some elk uncounted if they moved into areas where they were more likely to be missed.

"Either we counted them poorly this year, predator effects were stronger, the big snow event made us miss more elk or more elk were harvested," he said. "Usually the best answer in ecology is all of the above."

The long-term decline in the herd began soon after gray wolves were reintroduced to the region in the 1990s.

Smith and other biologists say the herd was too large to begin with, forcing too many elk to compete for too little forage.

But some hunting advocates point to the decline as evidence wolves have been allowed to run amok in the region - eating their way through a herd that once supported a vibrant hunting-based economy in Yellowstone-area communities such as Gardiner.

"Smith and other biologists say the herd was too large to begin with, forcing too many elk to compete for too little forage."

This is a lie. and classic environmentalist propaganda, intimating that somehow the wolves were "balancing the ecosystem." At 19,359 elk in 1994, the Northern Yellowstone herd was <u>**13.6% below**</u> the scientifically determined Ecological Carrying Capacity, which was 22,000 elk. * There was not "too many elk to compete for too little forage." That statement is just another environmentalist lie. To the casual, un-

---

*Elk Population Processes in Yellowstone National Park Under the Policy of Natural Regulation", written by Michael B. Coughenour and Francis J. Singer, 1996, and published by the The Ecological Society of America.

suspecting American, they assume they are being told the truth, and write their favorite "green" charity another check. **Since the reintroduction of wolves into Yellowstone National Park, the northern Yellowstone elk herd has dropped by 80%.**

Thanks to wolf re-introduction, Shiras Moose are disappearing across the Northwest

We've seen how poorly the elk are doing: the Shiras moose situation is even more dire. This following, unfortunate article actually tries to blame the lack of shade, global warming, and lack of nutrition for the moose decline. Back during the devastating Fires of 1988, the biologists all claimed it was the greatest event in the history of the Yellowstone Eco-system, predicting huge benefits for the moose and elk populations. In fact, the fires did create a smorgasbord of food for the moose, which are primarily browsers. Now, rather than point the obvious finger at the wolves, they want to blame the lack of shade for the moose's demise. These people can't be serious.

> "To argue with a person who has renounced the use of reason is like administering medicine to the dead."
> Thomas Paine

My apologies to the reader for using this Thomas Paine quote twice. The fact is, when discussing the environmental movement, I could use it about every fourth page.

Moose on the decline in Jackson Hole area
Higher temperatures, lack of shade, reduction in nutrients all factor in.

By Cory Hatch, Jackson Hole, Wyo.. March 25, 2009

The number of moose in northern Jackson Hole has likely declined by more than 50 percent since the late 1980s, and researchers think wildfires, warm temperatures, competition and predators could be to blame.

The population drop will, once again, affect the availability of moose hunting licenses in the region for 2009.

About 20 years ago, wildlife managers estimated there were between 2,300 and 2,800 moose in the region, and in 1991, the Wyoming Game and Fish Department issued 495 licenses. Now, with a moose population of about 1,000, wildlife managers plan to issue 35 tags in the Gros Ventre River drainage and another 10 in the Teton Wilderness. All of the tags issued for this year will be for bull moose.

From 2007 to 2008, the calf-cow ratio in the region dropped from 23.4 calves per 100 cows to 15.3 calves per 100 cows. Wildlife managers say the ratios are a good indicator of a population's general health and that a ratio of 30 to 35 calves per 100 cows is needed to sustain a healthy population.

Scott Becker, a bear and wolf management officer in Cody, studied Jackson Hole's moose recently as a graduate student at the University of Wyoming. So far, Becker said, wildlife managers have had a difficult time bringing the moose population back to where it should be.
"Managers have continually reduced harvest, but it didn't seem to help," he said.

To investigate the cause of the population decline, Becker used global positioning system equipment and radio collars to learn about elk in Buffalo Valley, Pacific Creek, Willow Flats and the Gros Ventre. The goal was to determine what types of habitat they use, as well as their body condition and reproductive success.

In addition to following the movements of between 65 and 70 animals for each of the three years of the study, Becker collected blood, fecal and hair samples and used ultrasound to measure the animals' rump fat.

Habitat conditions worsen

Becker learned that moose prefer shrub-dominated riparian habitat in the winter while the summer habitat was much more variable.

While winter range is normally considered the most crucial habitat to protect when it comes to large game species, Becker said it's likely a combination of poor conditions on winter and summer habitat that have resulted in the moose decline.

During the summer, one important factor is temperature. While the animals typically stay about 500 feet away from the shade of conifers during the wintertime, that distance drops to about 150 feet during the summer, according to Becker's study. Game and Fish habitat biologist Steve Kilpatrick said moose typically don't tolerate temperatures hotter than 55 to 60 degrees and need lakes or ponds to cool down when temperatures reach 75 to 80 degrees.

"They are very heat sensitive," Kilpatrick said. "They expend energy to stay cool."

Becker said widespread wildfires in the Teton Wilderness in 1988, in addition to the effects of mountain pine beetle infestations, may have reduced cover in the region enough so that moose have a harder time finding shade.

"The reduction in coniferous cover likely led to a decline in [body] condition," he said.

If moose go into winter with poor body condition, they are less likely to survive and have offspring.

Kilpatrick agreed. While wildlife managers will often use prescribed burns to improve moose habitat, he said a lack of shade and increased temperatures are pushing the southern fringe of moose habitat farther north.

Diet affects reproduction

Data on moose body condition and reproductive success point to a moose population that is right on the fringe of poor nutritional health. While rump fat measurements show good results, blood tests show a decline in essential nutrients such as zinc, copper, manganese and phosphorous.

"Deficiencies in any one of those minerals could potentially have an effect on the reproductive success of an animal," Becker said.

Becker said the mineral loss could be explained by competition from elk, which might eat the nutritious young growth moose utilize during the winter to the point that only non-nutritious old growth remains.

Pregnancy rates were relatively high among the moose in Becker's study, about 92 percent, but calf survival was only about 79 percent and "twinning" rates, the rate at which a cow moose produces two calves during a pregnancy, was extremely low, only 6.7 percent. Becker said a twinning rate below 10 percent usually points to habitat problems.

Another sign of trouble was the high rate of "reproductive pauses." Only 33 percent of cows were seen with calves two years in a row. Reproductive pauses also point to poor nutrition in a given population.

In 2008, a relatively severe winter, the data show more evidence of a population that is nutritionally on edge. The pregnancy rate dropped to 75 percent, and only 24 percent of moose gave birth to live young. Further, 31 percent of adult female elk in the study died – most from starvation. Of 11 bone marrow samples studied, 10 showed signs of nutritional stress.

Wyoming Game and Fish wildlife biologist Doug Brimeyer said predators have also taken a toll.

"We did document lion, bear and wolf predation in the population," he said. "When you have predation on top of poor survival already, it really adds to the decline in the population."

Here's a newsflash for this biologist. Moose cows that are run around all winter long by excessive wolf populations are stressed to the max, and may lose their unborn calf because of it. Those moose that do actually calf, can't protect their calf from the grizzly bears, which are incredible predators on newborn moose calves. If the grizzlies don't get the calf, the wolves will.

The area of this study around Jackson Hole is just a few miles from where I lived for 10 years, Dubois, Wyoming. It is literally crawling today with grizzly bears and wolves. The moose calves don't stand a chance. Lack of shade and global warming? Give me a break. The moose were just doing just fine before the fires of 1988, and those fires were caused by a multi-year drought, extremely hot and dry weather conditions, and an ill-conceived Forest Service policy of 'Let It Burn." Because grizzly bears hibernate, the moose have a respite from predation during the winters. But in 1995, USFWS re-introduced the wolves, and its been downhill ever since for moose populations. Now, the wolves run the moose in deep snow (the moose struggle in the deep snow, while the wolves can run on top, if the snow is crusted.) The moose are dying because the wolves are killing them. The moose are not dying because they can't find any shade. That biological concept is ludicrous.

USFWS Wolf Chief Blames Moose Loss In Yellowstone On Climate Disruption

Is this a first? Climate disruption? Because the theory behind man-made global warming has been proven a fraud, has our liberal press created a new buzz word to explain away the errors, fraud, conspiracy and manipulations of "We the People"? Climate disruption? We've gone from global warming to climate change and now it's climate disruption. Is that a catch-all phrase that we can use for any excuse to place blame and pass off responsibility?

I can certainly understand how an individual, who stakes his entire life and reputation on bringing wolves back into the Yellowstone National Park area and Central Idaho, would react so emotionally when he hears that a legislator in Utah wants to kill all his wolves trying to enter the state of Utah.

Bangs is supposed to be a professional, a salaried employee of the Department of Interior/United States Fish and Wildlife Service, one whose salary is paid by the taxpayers of this country. You would expect a better response from a professional scientist.

"People who don't like them [wolves] give them supernatural powers. It's that way all over the world," Bangs says. "In reality, they're no big deal."

The tone of the article leads a reader to think that the presence of wolves is no big deal. He seems to blow off and almost ridicule anyone who doesn't subscribe to his outdated information on wolves. His reference to people "giv[ing] them supernatural powers" is almost a Farley Mowatt followers response. I wonder if he also believes wolves only eat mice and tiny rodents?

But in reality, did Bangs refer to the loss of moose in the Yellowstone area to "climate disruption" or did the author of the article do it? You decide.

Wolves have contributed to a decline of elk in and around Yellowstone, but moose loss is probably more due to climate disruption. "Moose can't handle heat at all," Bangs says. "They just lie around and don't store body fat."

Notice the quotations mark don't come in until after the use of "climate disruption" and the quiet admission by the author (I wonder where that information came from?) that wolves have contributed to elk reduction. It does however seem to fit with the quoted response by Bangs saying moose can't handle the heat – assuming he is referring to global warming. He is also saying that moose do nothing but lie around in this "climate disruption" and die. And, according to the same article, Bangs said that wolves are only a problem with some livestock.

Bangs' comments are not sitting well with many wildlife and outdoor sporting organizations. It has been slow coming but state wildlife officials in Idaho and Montana are now coming around to admit that wolves are destroying their elk, deer and moose herds far more than they thought they would. In some places, the effect is serious, posing a real threat to elk, deer and moose herds.

Don Peay of Sportsmen for Fish and Wildlife in Utah asked Bangs:

I would like some scientist to explain to me how Utah – which has a hotter climate than Wyoming, Idaho and Montana whether there is global warming, climate disruption, etc – is seeing a totally different trend in Moose, than is being experienced in the wolf inhabited areas of WY, MT, and ID.

If Climate disruption is the reason that moose are declining in the Yellowstone region – it is so hot the moose populations just lie around and don't put on fat reserves – then why are Utah moose populations increasing significantly during this same climate change phenomenon ? it would seem to me that if heat was the problem, then Utah's moose populations should be even in greater decline than the greater Yellowstone area.

Toby Bridges, a hunter and activist who administers Lobo Watch, had a much more emotional response to Bangs' comments. I won't share all of them here but here's some of what Bridges had to say:

Sportsmen here fully realize that growing wolf numbers have destroyed Yellowstone's great elk herd, not Global Warming. Likewise, elk herds all along the mountains of western Montana and northern Idaho are being decimated by out of control wolf numbers. And when addressing this issue, the best you can do is to toss out an "Oh well" attitude in the linked article, trying to use smoke and mirrors and a list of other factors to try covering up the real problem – your parasite carrying kill crazy wolves.

So while many sportsman's groups in Idaho, Montana, Wyoming, Utah, Oregon and Washington have united together to work in a proactive way to convince the courts to allow the states to manage wolves at a level that will provide a better balance between predator and prey, Bangs is still preaching the "wolves aren't the problem" mantra. Our tax dollars at work I suppose.

courtesy Tom Remington

Ed Bangs, former head of the wolf reintroduction program for the United States Fish & Wildlife Service, is either a liar, or the worst biologist in North America. There is absolutely zero chance that Bangs actually believes "climate change is the reason for the decimation of moose populations. As Don Peay clearly pointed out, Utah moose are doing just great, despite hotter weather and less shade. What's the difference? No wolves.

For those of you who still are skeptical about what I say regarding the horrendous wolf situation and the devastation of our wildlife here in the west, following is a treatise by Mr. Jim Beers, who worked for the United States Fish & Wildlife Service for 30 years.

I have never met Jim Beers, but I consider him a patriot of the first order, and I thank him for his courage to speak the truth.

> "All tyranny needs to gain a foothold is for people of good conscience to remain silent."
> Thomas Jefferson

Jim Beers is a retired US Fish & Wildlife Service Wildlife Biologist, Special Agent, Refuge Manager, Wetlands Biologist, and Congressional Fellow. He was stationed in North Dakota, Minnesota, Nebraska, New York City, and Washington DC. He also served as a US Navy Line Officer in the western Pacific and on Adak, Alaska in the Aleutian Islands. He has worked for the Utah Fish & Game, Minneapolis Police Department, and as a Security Supervisor in Washington, DC. He testified three times before Congress; twice regarding the theft by the US Fish & Wildlife Service of $45 to 60 Million from State fish and wildlife funds and once in opposition to expanding Federal Invasive Species authority. He resides in Eagan, Minnesota with his wife of many decades.

Jim Beers: Brainstorming Solutions To The Growing Wolf Calamity In The Lower 48 States

(A talk by Jim Beers on 6 July 2010 in Hamilton, Montana)

Thank you for inviting me to speak about something that more and more Americans are wondering about as wolves touch the lives of more and more Americans each day. Before we get to the all-im-

portant topic of solutions, I would like to briefly mention my qualifications to speak on this matter and then describe the current wolf
situation in the Lower 48 states.

I have a BS in Wildlife Resources from Utah State University and
an MS in Public Administration from the University of Northern
Colorado. I served in the US Navy as a Line Officer on an AKA in
the western Pacific and as a Courier Officer in the Aleutian Islands.
I am a graduate of the Minneapolis Police Academy. I served 32
years in the US Fish and Wildlife Service as a Wetlands Biologist in
Devils Lake, ND; a US Game Management Agent in Minneapolis,
MN; Grand Island, NE; New York City Port-of-Entry; and in Washington, DC as a Special Agent, Program Analyst, Congressional Fellow, Animal Damage Control Program Coordinator, Chief of
Refuge Operations, Environment and Endangered Species Administrative Officer, and as the Wildlife Biologist responsible for the
Multi-State Fish and Wildlife Agency Wildlife Projects funded by
the Pittman-Robertson excise taxes on arms and ammunition. During my final five years I represented the State Fish and Wildlife
Agencies on State Department and US Trade Representative dele-
gations negotiating with European Union bureaucracies issuing regulations designed to eliminate trapping and the international fur
industry. In 1998 the US Fish and Wildlife Service tried to force me
to retire through nefarious means and I testified twice before Congress about the theft of $45 to 60M from the Excise taxes collects for
State Fish and Wildlife Programs by USFWS managers to introduce
wolves into Yellowstone and for other illegal purposes. For a full
description of how my career intersected with Endangered Species
and wolves, see my talk titled "Criminal Activities by Federal Bureaucrats and Others Involved in the Introduction, Protection and
Spread of Wolves in the Lower 48 States" given in Bozeman Montana on 16 May 2010.

I am a wildlife biologist that believes in "managing" and "using"
renewable fish and wildlife resources. I believe in the sustainable
management and use of timber and forage resources. I believe all
such resources are for the use of human societies to enrich human
existence in myriad ways. I believe that the US Constitution and the
American Society it has created are the best human organization
man has devised to date and that until something better comes
along, it should be nourished and protected. Like you, I have religious beliefs and political experiences that flavor my views. I value

my family and I have no doubt that man is superior to other animals. I am repelled by those that would equate men with the animals or even worse, suggest that men should suffer harm because of claims that animals have "rights" equal to or superior to men. I also believe that it is a credit to our humanity that we are concerned about encouraging biodiversity and maintaining wild plant and animal communities in and around our human communities.

Wolves in America as of June 2010

Wolves have persisted in Alaska since time immemorial. There is a constant, decades-long battle between the State of Alaska and various consortiums of Lower 48 States environmental and animal rights groups (like Defenders of Wildlife) that constantly seek federal intimidation of State officials to eliminate trapping of wolves, aerial control of wolves, and all other lethal means of controlling wolves. Alaskans have long recognized the depressing effect of abundant wolf populations on moose, an important meat source and hunting object for both residents and non-residents, as well as an important source of revenue for the State Fish and Wildlife Agency. Last winter a group of four wolves killed and began consuming a schoolteacher jogging on a gravel road near her residence in a village on the Alaskan Peninsula.

Wolves have also been attacking joggers and dog-walkers in and around Anchorage and Fairbanks. Most Alaskans are very aware of the dangerous and destructive effects of wolves and are allowed to kill wolves if and when they threaten humans or their property like dogs.

Wolves were purposely and continuously exterminated from settled lands in the current Lower 48 States from Colonial times until the 1930's. After the 1930's wolves occurred only in northern Minnesota and as occasional stragglers from Canada into western Montana. Like coyotes, deer, turkeys, and other such animals; wolves were always under the primary jurisdiction of State governments and, other than as landowners (like any other landowner) of federal lands (with the exception of Yellowstone Park), the federal government had no authority over wolves. Then in the midst of the 1960's social upheaval in the US, things began to change.

1966 – The first Endangered Species Act (ESA) is passed by Con-

gress. Only US animals are me tioned. The Federal function is simply to "List" "species" so that rchase of habitat from willing sell-
ers can be requested.

1967 – The ESA is amended to low "Listing" of foreign species.
1973 – The UN Convention on International Trade in Endangered
Species (CITES, termed a "comprehensive multilateral treaty' by
lawyers) was signed (after intense US drafting and lobbying) by the
US and a coterie of European countries and "developed" nations.
Almost within days after US Senate ratification and Presidential signature on the "Convention", a revised Endangered Species Act (on
steroids regarding new federal authority, property rights, and a
wide range of other Constitutional assaults) was introduced in Congress to be passed quickly with nothing but adulation and signed by
President Nixon (as Watergate was coming to a boil). Since the
"Convention" was considered a "treaty" and therefore "the
supreme Law of the Land" per Article VI. of the US Constitution;
development of laws, regulations, and precedents by federal bureaucrats and environmental and animal rights "cooperators" established not only total federal hegemony over any "listed" plant
or animal but also five other very damaging concepts.

In total disregard for the US Constitution, and the basis on which
the ESA was "sold", the ESA:
1. Defined Endangered SPECIES as endangered SUBSPECIES,
RACES, POPULATIONS, DISTINCT POPULATIONS, and DIS-
TINCT POPULATION SEGMENTS (in other words ANY plant or
animal flock, band, or stand of plants anywhere so designated by
federal bureaucrats.
2. Authorized "taking' of private property by the government from
privately-owned real estate uses by owners to uses of privately-
owned animal property like dogs and livestock "without just compensation" as demanded by the 5th Amendment of the
Constitution.
3. Replaced the Constitutional primary legal authority and jurisdiction of State governments over the plants and animals within the
state with Federal primary legal authority and jurisdiction over any
plant or animal "race, population, etc. designated by federal bureaucrats and the academicians they employ with the "cooperation"
of various select non-government organization (NGO) "partners".
"Friendly" lawsuits and changing "targets" perpetuate this federal
authority beyond any "delisting" or "transfer to state authority" as

future bureaucratic and NGO whims dictate.

4. Evolved the arbitrary and un-American concept that bureaucrats could determine where and when any "Listed" plant or animal could be "re-introduced" in total disregard for any State or Local concerns or objections. Is it any wonder that considering bureaucrats and their "partners" could "List" what they want, did not have to pay for "taking", and were not required to consider any State or Local concerns that the ESA has grown into the rural "Godzilla" we are dealing with today?

5. Established the selective use by federal bureaucrats and their "partners" of Listing various "races, populations, etc." to selectively:
- Close public lands (public property) to uses and access.
- Stop water projects, defeat bridge and road projects, breach dams, etc.
- Impede energy developments and use.
- Eliminate public land grazing allotments and timber management.
- Destroy all forest, range, and wildlife management and use.

Wolves, termed a "charismatic megaspecies" (like bald eagles, elephants, et al) by Endangered Species enthusiasts, were "Listed" from the time of the first ESA. While wolves have always been very abundant throughout Asia (probably over a million), periodically abundant in Europe and North Africa (thousands), and very common in Canada and Alaska (100,000?): concern about their "numbers" always belied the hidden but clear intent of giving the federal government authority over wolves.

Wolf introduction and protection in the Lower 48 States would "replace" hunters and weaken hunting programs and hunting support by both killing big game animals and making hunting, fishing, trapping, camping, hiking, picnicking, etc. (especially by the young, elderly, and individuals) much more dangerous. Also, wolves would make ranching, farming, and rural living by families, retirees, and others more dangerous, expensive, and precarious thereby weakening rural opposition to environmental and animal rights agendas while lowering property values thus making rural lands more susceptible to easement and purchase offers by federal agencies and their environmental "partners" like The Nature Conservancy. Finally, since wolves were reputed to have inhabited each of the Lower 48 States federal bureaucrats and their "partners" anticipated the possibility that as wolves might inhabit more and more of all of rural America federal authority would replace State authority over everything from property rights to the human management and use of both renewable and non-renewable natural resources. Given these likely outcomes, the precedent that would authorize the federal bureaucrats to "List" an animal (the wolf) that is abundant both worldwide and nationally (Alaska) AND then to selectively "introduce" it ("them") in arbitrary locations from which they would surely spread under federal protection.

I say "them" because there is another bit of bio-political chicanery making the wolf program almost immune to any non-government influence. We are told there are "timber" wolves and "red" wolves and "Mexican" wolves and "gray" wolves "listed" as endangered and in need of "re-introduction" throughout the Lower 48 States. In fact, wolves breed successfully with and create viable offspring with coyotes, dogs, dingoes, and jackals.

"Red" wolves, recently claimed to be extinct were "rediscovered" in "captivity" and, in spite of having large amounts of dog and coyote DNA, were "re-introduced" into the Carolinas in the late 1980's and then into Tennessee. These medium-sized and mostly solitary wolves have since been killed by local folks and have bred with and been bred by dogs extensively.

"Mexican" wolves were "re-introduced" into a swath of Arizona and New Mexico in 1998. In that desert environment these wolves have killed livestock and big game herds extensively and quickly adopted the habit of stalking school kids at bus stops and the routes to and from their homes. Children are now waiting for school buses in cages that their rural parents drive them to and from. These smaller wolves demonstrate a strong tendency to kill dogs in yards and to rapidly become very brazen around rural homesteads.

Minnesota wolves (whatever the most recent "science" calls these medium-sized wolves) have spread throughout Wisconsin, the Upper Peninsula of Michigan, and have recently become established in the northern part of Lower Michigan. These wolves straggle at present into Iowa, Illinois, and even Indiana.

The wolves dumped into Yellowstone in 1995 were captured in northern Canada. These large wolves exhibit both solitary and large-pack behavior (when food is abundant) and are now established in Montana, Idaho, and Wyoming. They are spreading into

Oregon, Washington, Utah and reportedly Colorado. They have decimated big game herds of elk as well as moose and deer. Livestock losses and ranching costs are mounting as the packs increase and wild food decreases. Dogs are routinely being killed.

As we speak here, there are government plans for wolf "re-introduction" into the Grand Canyon and there is a pending request to establish wolves in New England. This latter request would ban by federal fiat any taking (shooting, trapping, etc.) of coyotes throughout New England and the trapping of bears (the most effective tool for bear management in Maine).
A word on wolf "species" is in order. Before the ESA, wolves were considered by many biologists to be one species worldwide and many even considered wolves, dogs and coyotes to actually all be one species. ESA grants, politics, and hidden agendas made it convenient to use old local names (red, Mexican, gray, timber, etc.) as rationales for the "importance" of each of these areas to "need to restore" these "different" animals.

Whether in Asia or North America or in Europe/Africa; most Northern Hemisphere mammals that occur widely from North to South exhibit size differences in addition to behavioral differences. White-tailed deer in Saskatchewan are large animals while white-tailed deer in Southern Florida (Key Deer) are small. Diet and the fact that small bodies take heat better and large bodies take cold better contribute to this. Wolves share this trait. Additionally, wolves that live on open tundra or those that live in deserts behave differently than those that live in wooded mountains or on plains or in areas where all manner of food (livestock, dogs, dumpsters, farmsteads, goats, foals, big game, etc.) is available as in the current Lower 48 States. So the fiction of these four or five wolf species "needing" to be here and over there, etc. is just that – fiction.

Since the period of the first ESA, federal and state fish and wildlife agencies began to change their programs from managing fish and wildlife to "protecting" all plants and animals. This change began an evolution of personnel from wildlife biologists, foresters, and range managers to an assortment of personnel whose primary qualifications were a "belief" in "saving" things and a righteous "higher" purpose of eliminating any human uses of natural resources by growing the power and scope of the federal government. While the agencies would never have been formed or financed originally for such programs, current state and federal bureaucrats largely believe in a future where renewable natural resource management and use, as well as private property rights, will not exist and they will be paid from federal coffers for childish "environmental" activities. In this environment, wildlife biologists like foresters and range managers have become unqualified and untrustworthy sources of information about things like wolves.

In truth, wolves cannot be censused reliably. Wolf control is very expensive to government and is not something that hunting quotas can accomplish. Wolves are very difficult to kill and they routinely cover 20 or 30 miles a day and can wander hundreds of miles on occasion. The use of traps is more and more limited as a management tool by state agencies and emotional ballot initiatives. Airplanes are ineffective in timbered and broken country and are tightly controlled by the Airborne Hunting Act. Poisons (an effective tool) are prohibited. Basic beliefs about predator control for human ends are as stubborn as political or religious beliefs in most people. Federal impositions on state management of wolves make killing a wolf to protect stock or dogs or even humans a very dangerous act for anyone suspected by bureaucrats or environmentalists or animal rights advocates of being susceptible of being made "an example" to others contemplating killing a wolf. Documenting wolf damage has been "outsourced" to an Animal Rights NGO (Defenders of Wildlife): this is somewhat akin to outsourcing the documentation of terrorist damage in the US to Al Qaeda. Wisconsin "counts" wolves by listening for howls along regular routes (a totally inadequate estimation tool for such wide-ranging animals) and then to add insult to injury uses "volunteers" from wolf advocacy organizations. Believing most of what state agencies or certainly federal "experts" say about wolves is a fool's errand. Modern state and federal natural resource agencies are like a US Defense Department composed of only Quakers or Education Departments composed entirely of unmarried and childless political appointees.

A quick review of why we are asked to believe that introduced wolves "belong" in our communities and why we must "learn to live with them" tells us much:
- Wolves are "part of the native ecosystem".
- Wolves are "apex" predators.
- Wolves "move around" (notice they don't KILL) deer and elk, thereby restoring plants.

- Wolves "create' a "natural" environment.
- Wolves provide "eco-tourism".
- Wolves are a "wilderness value".
- Wolves "were here (?) first".

NOTE: Each of the above is based on a popular myth and provides NO justification for any federal action. Note also that there is no talk of how they are "in danger of extinction" – the reason we were given as justifying the "need" for an all-powerful ESA. The REAL reason for the current wolf situation in the Lower 48 States today is – "it's the law and we (bureaucrats, politicians, professors, and radical environmental/animal rights NGO's) control the imposition of this law".

A companion list of why the current wolf situation should not be allowed to remain includes:
- State authority and Local community Constitutional authority have been captured by federal entities beholden to forces and agendas hostile to State jurisdictions and Local community standards.
- The very real danger of fatal human attacks on children, ranchers, hikers, joggers, campers, fishermen, trappers, the elderly and rural residents in general grows daily. (Read Will Graves' book, Wolves in Russia, for unvarnished and documented accounts of 150 years of wolf/human interactions in Asia and Europe. Read Stanley Young's book, The Wolves of North America, for factual accounts of Indian/settler/soldier interactions with wolves from Colonial times to the 1930's by which time wolves were effectively and purposely extirpated in the Lower 48 States.)
- Livestock losses and ranching costs are rising as wolf numbers and range increase. Not only is there the outright loss of animals and the significant loss of weight in survivors: costs of controls and compliance issues plus things like the wild behavior of cattle towards dogs (harassed cattle charge dogs during roundups that in turn flee to riders that are in
turn threatened with harm by semi-wild cattle endangering horses and riders often in isolated spots) raise annual costs to hundreds of thousands while decreasing profits as much or more for ranchers.
- Big game herds of elk and moose are being extirpated by wolves thereby destroying hunting and all the state and local revenue it generated as well as the family traditions and culture it embodied. Deer numbers and other animals like bighorn sheep are likewise being reduced and may soon be too few for hunting to continue.

- The reduction of property values as ranching becomes uneconomical; retirees and rich transplants like Californians no longer bid up land values as the killing of pets and attacks on humans become more commonplace; and even vacation properties are less enticing as attacks by wolves on residents, hunters and fishermen (etc.) are publicized and discourage vacations and traditional family get-togethers are no longer common.
- Cafes and motels experience the current increasing decline in customers as hunting and fishing decline.
- Hunting opportunity reductions breed reductions in gun-rights-defenders numbers that benefit gun control advocates.
- State fish and wildlife agencies become more and more dependent on and responsive to federal agencies as hunting and fishing license revenues decrease and excise tax availability from excise taxes on arms, ammunition,
fishing tackle, archery equipment, and motorboat fuels disappear.
- Watchdogs, house pets, bird dogs, bear dogs, rabbit dogs, cattle dogs, and guard dogs are being killed throughout wolf areas and such killings will only increase until rural people abandon dogs as pets, service animals and as PROPERTY due to government introduction and protection of the animals killing them.
- Wolves as vectors of disease, is a topic that has been purposely ignored and presents a deadly threat to rural and urban people and interests alike. Whether it is by FECES spreading tapeworm eggs, or SALIVA or BLOOD left on objects of interest to dogs, or VOMIT of hair and bones of infected prey, or PAWS or HAIR carrying Mad Cow or anthrax, or FLEAS or TICKS carrying various plagues or typhus carried miles daily by wolves and spread to many other animals, humans, and human habitations or rabid wolves biting everything they see along a 25-mile swath (as has been documented in Russia) – wolves are VERY dangerous vectors of disease.
- Wolves carry the following 31 serious infections. Those known to infect humans are followed by an (H). Those known to infect other animals, both wild and domestic, are followed by (OA)
1. Rabies (greatly feared by American Indians, Settlers, early Soldiers, etc.) (H) (OA)
2. Brucellosis (H) (OA)
3. Echinococcus granulosis (potentially deadly and debilitating tapeworm) (H) (OA)
4. Echinococcus multilocularis (a deadly tapeworm) (H) (OA)
5. Anthrax (H) (OA)
6. Encephalitis (H) (OA)

7. Great Lakes Tapeworm (H) (OA)
8. Smallpox (H) (OA)
9. Mad Cow (BSE) (H) (OA)
10. Chronic Wasting Disease (H?) (OA)
11. Anemia (carried by ticks on wolves) (H) There are 10 serious diseases in ticks carried by wolves.
12. Dermatosis (carried by ticks on wolves) (H)
13. Tick Paralysis (carried by ticks on wolves) (H)
14. Babesiosis (carried by ticks on wolves) (H)
15. Anaplasmosis (carried by ticks on wolves) (H)
16. Erlichia (carried by ticks on wolves) (H)
17. E Coast Fever (carried by ticks on wolves) (H)
18. Relapsing Fever (carried by ticks on wolves) (H)
19. Rocky Mtn. Spotted Fever (carried by ticks on wolves) (H)
20. Lyme Disease (carried by ticks on wolves) (H)
21. Plague (carried by fleas on wolves) (H) There are deadly diseases carried by fleas on wolves.
22. Bubonic Plague (carried by fleas on wolves) (H)
23. Pneumonic Plague (carried by fleas on wolves) (H)
24. Flea-borne Typhus (carried by fleas on wolves) (H)
25. Distemper (OA)
26. Neospora caninum (causes spontaneous abortions) 27. Mange (3 types including Scabies) (H) (OA)
28. GID (a deadly disease of wild and domestic sheep) (OA)
29. Foot-and-Mouth (OA)
30. Tularemia (H) (OA)
31. Helminthes (flat-worms) 2 sp. (H) (OA)
Of the 31 diseases and infections carried by wolves and listed above, only 3 are not dangerous to humans and even those (especially foot-and-mouth and distemper) are of great danger to the American Livestock Industry and the
American dog population. See my article on The Urban Threat from Wolf-Borne Diseases.

For those that understand the hidden agendas at work here and the overwhelming need to put human community needs before environmental/animal rights agendas, the political interests of career politicians, and self-serving bureaucratic interests, the following suggestions are meant to be SOLUTIONS that occur to an old bureaucrat trying hard to articulate ways to resolve this growing national disaster. While there are many valid and hopeful ongoing solution attempts to the wolf problem like lawsuits, cooperative processes, state defiance, and others: I believe that no lasting (as much as anything is "lasting" in today's environment) solution is possible until the authority and jurisdiction over plants and animals within each state are returned to State and Local control. It is with this in mind that the following solutions are offered:

1. In the current political environment (i.e. the possibility of "repealing" national healthcare and a great deal of talk about throwing out all incumbents, etc.) it is not unreasonable to consider repeal of the ESA. As this law (like Prohibition, a Constitutional Amendment, that spawned corruption and an atmosphere of defying and ignoring all law) harms more and more people and more and more of our economy and American values, the possibility of repeal of this bad law or even the UN Convention (CITES) we once signed to authorize it is no more daunting or impossible than repeal of a Constitutional Amendment. The ultimate goal should be to return authority and jurisdiction over ESA-encumbered plants and animals to State authority and jurisdiction. Control of these resources by a Constitutionally-limited central government on behalf of faraway large-city constituencies and radical organizations is deadly to rural America and should be repugnant to all Americans.

2. Absent repeal of the ESA, amend it to make Listing dependent on Worldwide status and NOT National status. Plants and animals of national concern should be addresses by voluntary cooperation of state governments with or without federal incentives.

3. Amend the ESA by limiting it to only Listing SPECIES and not any lower subdivision such as subspecies, race, population, etc.

4. Amend the ESA to force the federal government to once more PAY FOR ANY TAKING OF PRIVATE PROPERTY and that such taking is ONLY FOR A PUBLIC USE as stated clearly and succinctly for the past 219 years in the 5th Amendment to the US Constitution. Consider requiring annual payments to State governments that show a persistent loss of revenue resulting from the TAKING of State authority such as hunting license revenue and taxes from ranchers and others put out of business. This proposal and the foregoing 2 proposals (#'s 2 & 3) could be either amendments to the ESA or one or more separate laws that redirect ESA activities in a more Constitutional direction by superseding the ESA.

5. The ESA; like The Marine Mammal Protection Act, Federal Inva-

sive Species proposals, and a host of nvironmental/animal rights proposals like Wildlands, Corridors, Federal Wildernesses and Roadless Areas, and federal proposals to give animals "rights"; ultimately are created by acceptance of any federal law passed in the US Congress and these always entail a concomitant loss of State and Local authority and harm to rural communities and rural people. Such laws would be all but impossible and ratification of ruinous "Treaties" like the UN CITES, the currently proposed UN Treaty on Small Arms, or other treaties like the proposed KYOTO Treaty IF there were State's Rights' Defenders in the US Congress, especially the US Senate where treaties are ratified. At the risk of seeming the "wild extremist" I was accused of being recently on a radio program, I will mention something I have come to believe in recent years is a major cause of the drift from a Constitutional Republic to a central oligarchy. The 17th Amendment was passed in 1913 and changed the way US Senators were appointed from being "chosen by the Legislature thereof" to being "elected by the people thereof". I submit that not only are federal politicians hard to "un-elect" compared to state politicians; they have become beholden to national and international interests for money, volunteers, media support, and publicity from these interests for their re-elections. In other words, a US Senator can pass and support a treaty or law that harms state residents and their interests and still get re-elected but if he or she was "chosen by the Legislature thereof" they would not only be beholden to the state legislature (the bastion of the state's interests) but state legislators that put such bums in or re-appointed them would be very vulnerable to the state voter's wrath. Repeal the 17th Amendment and thereby return the composition of this important body (the US Senate) to true defenders of their state as opposed the "Senator from such and such" in-name-only that they have become. Today's US Senators resemble arrogant Lords of bygone and ancient oligarchies more so than anything described in our Nation's Founding Father's papers, their discussions or the US Constitution.

6. Elect state and federal politicians that will transform natural resource agencies from bastions of environmental protectionism, animal rights, and federal power-growers to educated managers of the environment responsive to the public, the public-good, and Constitutional values. Restore the Oath of Allegiance to the Constitution for new hires, reinstitute stricter requirements for serving as wildlife biologists, foresters, and range managers and eliminate programs

that serve neither the public-good nor the purposes for which the agency is funded or was founded.

7. Elect state politicians that will work to reform state universities to re-establish natural resource curriculums and Departments that support state interests and to hire professors and others that support the sustainable management and use of natural resources for the good of state residents.

8. Elect state and local politicians that are committed to strict oversight of teachers and teaching in grades 1 through 12. Where environmental and animal rights matters are in conflict with state laws and truth, teachers and curriculums should be either modified or eliminated.

9. Form partnerships with others concerned with federal power grabs, property rights, the ESA, animal use, natural resource management, and Constitutional adherence. Such groups might include – State Ranching or Livestock Organizations; Wisconsin Bear Hunters; New Mexico Ranching and Hunting Organizations; Hunting Dog Groups; San Joaquin Farmers; Klamath Farmers; Private Property Owners threatened by Military Base expansions or the expansion of Parks, Refuges, Forests, etc.; Rocky Mtn. Elk Foundation (a very recent convert); Foundation for N. American Wild heep; Gun Groups; Timber organizations; New Jersey Outdoor Alliance; Gamefowl Breeders; Big Game (foreign) Hunting Groups; Trapping Groups; Property Rights Groups; Dog Breeders; Rural Government Associations; and solid politicians running for office in need of your support.

10. Elect politicians that will work to reaffirm and protect state authority over federal properties purchased within the state. Federal management of natural resources be it for "forest" as in Forest Service, or "fish and wildlife" as in US Fish & Wildlife Service Refuge, or "cultural values" as in National Park Service, or "land" as in Bureau of Land Management should take into account local and state interests in the management and use of these public lands. From Payments-in-Lieu-of Taxes to Revenue Sharing and management and use programs; federal lands should not be simply places from which to destroy local communities and rural economies (i.e. wolf introduction) like some foreign military base on our soil from which to attack the country.

11. Work to maintain the use of traps and dogs and baiting in State and Federal regulations, on federal properties and in Federal laws to give every opportunity for state governments to utilize a licensed and regulated citizenry to maintain, control, or eliminate wolves, cougars, and bears in line with state and local community standards.

12. Openly advocate and support lethal and immediate control of dangerous animals that invade towns or homesteads. While there is a limited place for trapping and removal, the costs and likelihood of returning animals should always be considered first and foremost. This also helps to debunk the nonsensical myth that these animals are not REALLY dangerous and there are always nearby "Wildernesses" where they can be dropped in and forgotten (and if there is no nearby Wilderness the bureaucracy and radicals will help you create one).

13. Work with urban and youth organizations to explain these matters and the rationale for your positions.

14. Finally, talk to friends, relatives, associates, and co-workers about these matters. Publicize incidents and write letters to editors suggesting solutions. Appear before legislative committees and local Boards. Do not hesitate to hold federal bureaucrats, state bureaucrats, teachers and other public servants accountable and demand their replacement or firing wherever appropriate. Encourage and support friendly bureaucrats and academics. If your elected officials balk, work to elect others. Be courteous, direct, informed, and outspoken.

If you think other things like annual Social Security increases or more pay for public servants are more important than what we are discussing here, you will vote accordingly. Unless it is changed, this bad situation will simply get worse and eventually become intolerable. In my opinion, intolerable means we will be forced to either accept this dark, new way of life ("learning to live with whatever government imposes on us") or we will have to look to the only other alternative which was once described as too awful to contemplate. I vote for making the changes mentioned above before we reach that intolerable point and the abyss beyond.

Jim Beers
6 July 2010

Lichengate: Another Government Cover-up

Mysterious deaths of Wyoming elk solved; animals died after feeding on lichen

Yahoo! News ^ | Mar 22, 2004 | SARAH COOKE

CHEYENNE, Wyo. (AP) - A lichen native to the Rockies has been blamed for the deaths of at least 300 elk in southern Wyoming, a mystery that had baffled wildlife scientists and cost the state thousands of dollars, the state said Monday.

Wildlife veterinarians had suspected the lichen after finding it in the stomachs of many of the elk that died in south-central Wyoming.To confirm their suspicions, three elk were fed the lichen at research facility. One collapsed and was unable to rise Sunday, the Wyoming Game and Fish Department said. A second elk also started stumbling and a third is expected to succumb quickly, officials said. All three will be euthanized.

The ground-dwelling lichen, known as Parmelia molliuscula, produces an acid that may break down muscle tissue, said Walt Cook, a Wyoming Game and Fish Department veterinarian leading the inquiry.

Elk native to the area weren't affected by the acid, but those killed in the die-off apparently had moved in from Colorado and may have lacked microorganisms needed to neutralize the acid, state biologists said. The Colorado line is 80 kilometres south of the area where the elk died.

"Elk don't normally winter down on the ... unit where they ate the lichen," Game and Fish spokesman Tom Reed said.

"Elk are incredibly adaptable, tough animals. They'll get by on thin rations and they'll make do somehow. But this year, nearly 300 of them paid the price for that adaptability," Reed said.

The first sick elk was found on Feb. 6 and scientists quickly ruled out chronic wasting disease, the deer and elk version of mad cow disease. They also eliminated most viruses and bacteria, malnutrition, exposure to heavy metals such as arsenic, and poisoning from a leaky gas well or pipeline.

The search for the cause became expensive. For a time, researchers used a helicopter to search for afflicted elk, but the flights cost $900 US an hour. Wildlife experts also drove into the rough country near the Continental Divide and slogged through melting snow and mud to collect plant specimens and elk droppings.
Scientists still want to know more about the lichen and why it contained high amounts of the acid this year.

"There are a lot of factors we'll need to look at," Reed said. "Do elk eat this lichen in normal years? If so, why hasn't this happened before? Does a long history of drought weigh in somehow? If so, what are our management options in the future?"

The die-off killed up to five per cent of the Sierra Madre herd's breeding females, and that will affect hunting quotas this fall and could trigger wildlife policy changes, Reed said.

Other steps, such as improving range conditions to provide healthier forage, will also be considered as researchers learn more and try to prevent future die-offs.

The above is a government cover-up. I am not blaming the reporter; I am sure she reported what she was told accurately. The elk didn't die of lichen poisoning; they died from wolf predation. Win Condict, an outfitter friend, flew the blood trail in his supercub, accompanied by hunting guide Bill Nation. The Wamsutter pack of wolves had simply run these elk into the ground, killing a few along the way. Started north of Interstate 80, the elk, after having panicked and fled 30-40 miles, simply lay down and froze, totally exhausted, unable to go any further. The lichen poisoning was a government cover-up. They didn't want the Wyoming public, much of which is made up of ranchers and sportsmen, to know how far the wolves had roamed away from Yellowstone National Park.

Wolves kill Wamsutter cattle

CAT URBIGKIT Special to the Star-Tribune | Posted: Wednesday, January 7, 2004

WAMSUTTER - Federal officials say wolves killed several beef cattle near Wamsutter recently and have authorized the killing of as many as two wolves in the area.

According to the U.S. Fish and Wildlife Service, USDA Wildlife Services has confirmed that wolves killed several beef cattle in the Wamsutter area. It appears that one or two wolves were involved in the killing and Wildlife Services animal damage control specialists have been authorized to remove up to two wolves from the area, which is not far from the Colorado border.

Rancher Charlie Juare said when he began gathering cattle on the checkerboard area of the Red Desert north of Wamsutter right after Christmas, two extremely crippled cows were found, as well as other stiff and sore cattle.

Injuries to the cattle include having their tails chewed off near the backbone and severely infected wounds to their front legs at the elbow. All of the affected cattle are yearling bred heifers weighing about 900 pounds at this time of year.

One of the cows couldn't get up and subsequently died. Federal wildlife officials skinned her carcass and discovered the trauma associated with wolf predation. A second cow was killed as well, he said.

"We had two that wouldn't get up anymore," Juare said. "About 10 or so had no tails, and we've still got a few more in the barn that are hobbling along."

Trying to gather cattle that have been subject to predation has proven difficult as well, with spooky cattle that don't want to be handled, Juare said.

"They're pretty rank," Juare said.

Shane Christian of Pavillion, who runs cattle with Juare, said at least one of the cattle attacked by wolves belongs to him, but the final counts haven't been made.

"They're scattered all over creation down there," Christian said. "They don't really want to herd back up."

Juare said having wolf depredation at any time of year is a new experience, but coming close to spring it has made ranchers dread calving season with its vulnerable cows and calves. Calving season begins in April.

Juare said ranch workers have not seen nor heard of any wolves in the area.

Wamsutter, on the edge of the Red Desert Basin, is in the southern extent of the area wolves are thought to be common in Wyoming. A wolf was reported near Baggs, 50 miles south of Wamsutter, but there is talk that that may have been a released hybrid.

Look at the dates. January 7, 2004, rancher Charley Juare had wolves killing his cattle north of Wamsutter. February 6, 2004, predator hunters started finding dead & dying elk, with exactly the same symptom as Mr. Juare describes with his cattle: "We had two that wouldn't get up anymore." 300 dead elk, all from eating poisonous lichen? Those elk have lived out on those sagebrush hills for thousands of years. But these elk, according to U.S.F.W.S., had moved in from Colorado. That is a crock. Those elk move back and forth across the border all the time. There is no research describing this phenomenom anywhere else. In fact, Natural Perspective, The Fungus Kingdom* says this: "All lichens are believed to be edible (or at least not poisonous) except for Wolf Moss." Wolf Moss grows on old growth timber. The prairies of south central Wyoming are covered in sagebrush, not old growth timber.

U.S. Fish & Wildlife knew their "experiment" with wolves was coming unraveled, as the wolf populations exploded, and expanded their ranges to an area tenfold larger than what they had promised the ranchers and the general public.

| Lobo, King of the Currumpaw, trapped in NewMexico. Photo by its captor, Ernest Thompson Seton. | Timber wolf, shot in the Yukon Territory of Canada, . nearly 100 years later, and 2000 miles north. This wolf could be a litter mate to Lobo. |

Wolves have always held a special place in my heart. As a young child, I spent many days at the home of my grandparents,. My grandfather, Dr. Raymond Birch, was head of veterinary research at Cornell University, and had an extensive library in his home, much of which revolved around wildlife. My favorite book was Ernest Thompson Seton's **Wild Animals I Have Known**, a series of wildlife short stories, and my favorite story was "Lobo, King of the Currumpaw." On the wall of the library, was a famous painting of a wolf, in the moonlight, overlooking a ranch house below. Its been over half a century since I sat in that library, yet I can see it in my mind's eye like it was yesterday. It was not until I began researching for this book, that I realized the Lobo story was a true one, based on Seton's work as a government bounty hunter.

As wildlife biologist Jim Beers explains, The United States Fish & Wildllife Service wants Americans to think there are all kinds of different species of wolves: Gray Wolves, Red Wolves, Timber Wolves, Mexican Wolves, Minnesota Wolves, etc. Whatever it takes to gain more control over American lives. This is pure nonsense. Study the two photographs of wolves carefully. These wolves are virtually identical, and yet were photographed nearly a century and 2000 miles apart. Canis Lupus, all one species.

The United States Fish & Wildlife Service has allowed the wolf reintroduction program to destroy a century's worth of wildlife conserva-

http://www.perspective.com/nature/fungi/index.html

tion, destroying elk, moose, bighorn sheep, and mule deer and white-tail deer populations across the Rocky Mountain west, and in the northern midwest. As I predicted many years ago, as did many others, the reintroduction of wolves would become the greatest wildlife disaster since the slaughter of the American Bison, during the second half of the 19th century. And this wildlife disaster is brought to you courtesy of the very people, the United States Fish and Wildlife Service, that the average American citizen, thinks they are paying to enhance wildlife populations, not have them slaughtered.

> "This was the object of the Declaration of Independence. Not to find out new principles, or new arguments, never before thought of, not merely to say things which had never been said before; but to place before mankind the common sense of the subject, in terms so plain and firm as to command their assent, and to justify ourselves in the independent stand we are compelled to take. Neither aiming at originality of principle or sentiment, nor yet copied from any particular and previous writing, it was intended to be an expression of the American mind, and to give to that expression the proper tone and spirit called for by the occasion."
> Thomas Jefferson - Letter to Henry Lee, May 8, 1825

This book is not about original principles or any great new concepts. It is simply trying to bring back common sense to the governing of America and the management of our wildlife resources.

Chapter 8

Stopping America's Quest for Energy Independence

The Non-Endangered Polar Bear

It doesn't take a rocket scientist to know that America's dependence on foreign oil creates a multitude of problems for our nation, from ill-advised foreign wars and entanglements, to huge balance of payments issues. Domestically, we have incredible amounts of our own energy sources, from oil and gas, to uranium, to coal, to renewable resources such as wind and solar. The possibilities are endless, and they bode well for the future of our nation. The problem is, the Environmental Movement does not want our nation to be strong, safe and prosperous. They throw up roadblocks to every form of energy we have, regardless of how much economic sense any one particular project may make. And the tool they use, in most cases, is wildlife, and the Endangered Species Act of 1973.

Polar bear cub rescued by Oil Field Workers

Polar bears are some of the most incredibly beautiful animals on the planet, and, with cute, cuddly cubs, they are the perfect species for the Environmental Movement's fund raising machine. At one time, I was the largest hunting outfitter in the Northwest Territories of Canada. Just before the G.N.W.T. expropriated my businesses there, I had an agreement to purchase Canada North Outfitting, which would have made my companies the largest hunting outfitter in North America. Canada North, owned at the time by former wildlife biologist Jerome

Knap, arranged hunts, through various Inuit (Eskimo) Hunter and Trapper Organizations, all along the arctic coast of Canada. Species hunted included Arctic Island Caribou, Central Barrenground Caribou, Muskox, Wolves, Walrus, and Polar Bear. The vast majority of the company's revenue was derived from Polar Bear hunting, and so, as part of the due diligence of purchasing the company, I spent a lot of time researching the health of the polar bear populations.

It was very clear to me, and to any reasonably rational human being, that polar bear populations are flourishing. Although exact counts are difficult to obtain, the generally accepted numbers are that polar bear populations, worldwide, have increased from about 5,000 in the 1950s, to between 20,000 to 25,000 today. This is a four to fivefold increase. Despite scare tactics and stories of drowning bears to the contrary, the bears are doing extremely well.

Not only does the science support growing populations of polar bears, but the anecdotal evidence is also very supportive of increasing bear populations. Most of my employees in the Northwest Territories, who serve as guides, are either Inuit or First Nation peoples. The Inuit guides live on the arctic coast, in the towns of Kuglugtuk, Paulutuk, Cambridge Bay, Gjoa Haven, and Arviat. Some of the older guides, now in their mid-70s, were born on the land, and still, except for the guide wages earned in six weeks a year working for me, live a completely subsistence life style. Their knowledge of polar bears far exceeds that of the government wildlife biologists, who fly around occasionally , looking for bears. For the Inuit people, knowledge of the local wildlife is a matter of life and death, for themselves, and their families. According to these Inuit, the numbers of bears today is the highest they have seen in their lifetime, and the "problem" bear issues (bears coming into the villages) have increased dramatically.

The following CBC News article corroborates what my Inuit guides, with their "boots on the ground" knowledge, have been telling me for many years.

Arviat invaded by roaming polar bears
Bears free to roam streets while hunters limited by small hunting quota

Last Updated: Monday, November 10, 2008 | 6:03 PM CT CBC News
Residents in the central Nunavut hamlet of Arviat say they can do little but watch as an unusually high number of polar bears roam through their community.

Bears started roaming last week around Arviat, a hamlet of about 2,000, prompting local RCMP, firefighters, bylaw officers and Canadian Rangers to patrol the community's perimeter every night.

That hasn't deterred the invading polar bears, however. Mayor Johnny Mamgark told CBC News the bears are not responding to common deterrents, such as flares, bear bangers, or even gunshots fired in the air.

"All my life I've been here, and I've never seen so many polar bears coming right into town," Mamgark said in an interview.

"Back in my kid days, there was nothing, hardly any. This summer, when I went out hunting, there's bears everywhere! Like, it's different; too many polar bears."

There has been no specific estimate for the number of polar bears coming through Arviat.

Late last week, Mamgark said he saw a polar bear eating caribou meat behind someone's pickup truck in the community. "That's how close they get," he said.

Resident Stephanie Czyz said local parents are concerned about their children, as they were at a local arcade event last week.

"A lot of parents were calling, telling their children not to leave the arcade until they got there, or until someone escorted them home, because there were so many bear sightings," Czyz said.

Polar bear hunting quotas in Nunavut's Kivalliq region, where Arviat is located, have been reduced to just eight bears in the 2008-2009 hunting season — a significant cut from 38 bears last year, and 56 bears the year before.

Hunters in the region have only six more bears they can take, so they are not killing any polar bears except in emergency cases in which people's safety is being threatened.

"I don't know why they're coming into town. Maybe they know that we don't have a quota for polar bears, I guess, and they know that we're not going to kill them," Mamgark said.

"They are just crossing into town now. That's not usually like that."

The following treatise is from the National Center for Public Policy Research. .

Listing the Polar Bear Under the Endangered Species Act Because of Projected Global Warming Could Harm Bears and Humans Alike

by Peyton Knight and Amy Ridenour
Introduction and Summary

Few animals capture the imaginations of Americans quite like the polar bear. Just ask Coca-Cola, whose animated polar bear advertisement has become an annual holiday staple. Seemingly impervious to the brutal conditions of the Great White North, these mammoth bears exude an aura of cuddly invincibility.

But some environmental groups claim the polar bear is in danger of extinction due to what they believe is anthropogenic (human-caused) global warming. These groups have filed a petition with the U.S. Fish and Wildlife Service (USFWS) to list the bear as "threatened" under the Endangered Species Act, or ESA.

Listing the polar bear under the ESA because of projected future global warming would be an unfortunate mistake:

* Listing the polar bear could have adverse affects on bear conservation efforts.

* Global polar bear population levels presently are healthy.

* The anthropogenic global warming theory remains only a theory, and climate science is in its infancy. Even those who agree with the global warming theory disagree about the extent of its projected ef-

fects.

* Listing the polar bear as threatened because of estimated future global warming would most likely be extremely expensive to the U.S. economy.

* Listing the polar bear based on projected anthropogenic global warming can be expected to greatly expand federal regulatory powers under the ESA.

* Because of its great expense and controversial nature, federal policies regarding global warming should be made only by Congress with input from the Executive Branch, not by a presidential appointee charged with enforcing a 1973 law written for other purposes.

The Present State of the Polar Bear

Polar bears are the largest members of the bear family and reside exclusively on the Arctic ice cap in the Northern Hemisphere. Male bears can grow to be as large as nine feet from nose to tail and weigh upwards of 1,700 pounds. Polar bears generally live and hunt alone, relying primarily on such food sources as ringed seals, walrus, and beluga whales. They are exceptional swimmers, capable of swimming up to 40 miles without rest at a relatively brisk speed of four miles per hour.

In the 1960s and early 1970s, unregulated sport hunting was deemed a threat to the polar bear's continued existence. In the mid-1960s the total polar bear population hovered at roughly 10,000. To help bolster the bear's numbers, in 1972 Congress passed the Marine Mammal Protection Act, which prohibited polar bear hunting in Alaska, with the exception of hunting performed by natives for subsistence purposes. The following year, the U.S., Canada, Denmark, Norway and the then-U.S.S.R. signed the International Agreement on the Conservation of Polar Bears, in which the nations agreed to prohibit the unregulated sport hunting of polar bears and outlaw the practice of hunting polar bears from aircraft and icebreakers.

Over the last 40+ years, the polar bear population has more than doubled. Estimates range from 20,000 to 25,000 polar bears worldwide. In fact, according to a U.S. Geological Survey study of wildlife in the Arctic Refuge Coastal Plain, polar bear populations "may now be near historic highs." This dramatic increase in population is noteworthy, as polar bears have one of the slowest reproductive rates of any mammal.

Even the World Wildlife Fund (WWF), an environmental group that advocates listing the bear under the Endangered Species Act, notes that there are "at least 22,000 polar bears worldwide" and "the general status of polar bears is currently stable." According to a WWF study, there are "20 relatively distinct" polar bear populations. Citing data from the World Conservation Union's Polar Bear Specialist Group, WWF reports that of these 20 populations, only two are thought to be decreasing, ten are stable, two are increasing, and six are of unknown status. The same data shows there to be anywhere from 21,580 to more than 24,980 polar bears worldwide. Of this global population, a total of 3,600 bears from two populations are thought to be decreasing.

Dr. Mitchell Taylor, polar bear biologist for the Canadian province of Nunavut's Department of the Environment, has said there is no cause for alarm:

Climate change is having an effect on the West Hudson population of polar bears, but really, there is no need to panic. Of the populations of polar bears in Canada, 11 are stable or increasing in number. They are not going extinct, or even appear to be affected at present.

It is noteworthy that the neighboring population of southern Hudson Bay does not appear to have declined, and another southern population (Davis Strait) may actually be over-abundant.

I understand that people who do not live in the north generally have difficulty grasping the concept of too many polar bears in an area. People who live here have a pretty good grasp of what that is like to have too many polar bears around.

This complexity is why so many people find the truth less entertaining than a good story.12

A hearty species, polar bears have displayed past resilience and adaptability, having survived during periods warmer than the current era.

Environmental Activists Push to List the Polar Bear - And (Most Likely) Why

In February 2005 the Center for Biological Diversity (CBD), an environmental organization, petitioned the U.S. Fish and Wildlife Service to list the bear under the Endangered Species Act as a "threatened" species. Several months later, two more environmental organizations, Greenpeace and the Natural Resources Defense Council (NRDC), joined CBD in its petition.

Why the push to list an animal whose population is healthy?

Center for Biological Diversity Senior Counsel William Snape may have provided a hint to the answer in the opening line of his testimony on the subject to the U.S. Department of the Interior:

Since February 2005, when the Center for Biological Diversity first petitioned the U.S. Fish and Wildlife Service to list and protect the polar bear under the Endangered Species Act, there has been a growing political consensus in this country that global warming is a monumental environmental crisis and that humans can, indeed must, take action to combat it.

What environmental groups have been unsuccessful in accomplishing through the front door, they appear to be hoping to usher in through the back - namely, restrictions on carbon dioxide emissions similar to those mandated in the U.N.'s Kyoto global warming treaty, which the U.S. Senate has not ratified.

Indeed, the ESA is a promising method for getting global warming regulations through the back door. Section 9 of the Endangered Species Act makes it unlawful to "take" any endangered species on public or private land. In Section 3, the Act defines "take" as "harass, harm, pursue, hunt, shoot, wound, kill, trap, capture, or collect." In 1975, the U.S. Interior Department took the word "harm" in that definition and broadly expanded its meaning:

An act or omission which actually injures or kills wildlife, including acts which annoy it to such an extent as to significantly disrupt essential behavioral patterns, which include, but are not limited to, breeding, feeding, or sheltering; significant environmental modification or degradation which has such effects is included within the meaning of "harm."

This definition gives regulators wide latitude in deciding which actions can be deemed "harmful" to a listed species or its habitat. It also provides ample fodder for environmentalist lawsuits to prevent certain public or private activities. Thus, in the opinion of federal regulators, should anthropogenic global warming be deemed harmful to the polar bear or its habitat under the ESA, the mere act of emitting greenhouse gasses such as carbon dioxide, could be heavily regulated, or in some instances, outlawed entirely.

A recent action by the NRDC provides more evidence that some environmental groups are looking at the possibility of using the ESA to promote global warming-related legal restrictions on human actions and the U.S. economy. The NRDC is advocating ESA protections for another abundant species due to global warming, the Yellowstone grizzly bear. The Yellowstone grizzly was recently removed from the federal endangered species list and deemed a success story by the U.S. Fish and Wildlife Service. However, the NRDC claims global warming is an immediate threat to the Yellowstone grizzly's habitat, and thus, they argue, the bear should remain on the ESA list.

The Global Warming Theory is Not a Sound Basis for Endangered Species Policy

Under the terms of the Endangered Species Act, a species qualifies for "threatened" status if it is "likely to become endangered within the foreseeable future throughout all, or a significant portion of its range." While it is clear from population trends that polar bears are not currently endangered or threatened, environmental groups are hoping to exploit this exceedingly broad requirement by claiming that global warming could eradicate the species (in the wild) in perhaps a century's time.

The 2005 petition to the Secretary of the Interior seeking the listing of the polar bear filed by Center for Biological Diversity makes this clear:

From the Introduction, page vii: "While most [polar bear] populations are reasonably healthy and the global population is not presently endangered, the species as a whole faces the likelihood of severe endangerment and possible extinction by the end of the century... Only with prompt action to drastically reduce greenhouse gas emissions can the future of the polar bear be assured."

And on page 20, "Global warming is the primary threat to the continued survival of the polar bear..."

The case, then, for listing the bear largely rests on the theory that human activity is causing global warming and that such warming will be catastrophic within a century's time. This is problematic for several reasons. First, though opinions on global warming are easy to come by, a theory by its very definition is conjecture, not established fact, and thus makes for shaky ground on which to base policy. Furthermore, the Earth's climate is extremely complex, and human beings are far from understanding it. Mathematical models predicting global warming thus have been and as yet remain subject to severe limitations as to their likely accuracy. They are constantly being revised, and often disagree with one another. While one hesitates to put it so starkly, when it comes to knowing the temperature of the planet in a hundred years, the best policymakers can do is choose between competing educated guesses.

The use of the anthropogenic global warming theory as a basis for federal protection of the polar bear or any other living thing is problematic secondarily because of the tremendous cost involved in taking effective action to curb such warming, should we choose base federal policy on the assumption the theory is correct. Under the theory, only a massive reduction in energy use is expected to have a notable impact on global warming. Stopping such warming thus would require either a very substantial fiscal outlay by ordinary Americans both in their personal spending and in their tax expenses, or a radical reduction in standard of living, or some combination thereof. If the federal government is to mandate such sacrifices - and such is not recommended here - it should do so only after serious deliberations by the Congress, with input from the Executive, and not made solely by a presidential appointee who has been given the narrow task of enforcing of a 1973 law adopted -- interestingly, at a time when a global cooling theory was receiving media attention -- for entirely different purposes.

Listing the Polar Bear Could Hurt Polar Bear Conservation Efforts

Should the polar bear be listed as threatened under the ESA, an automatic prohibition on the importation of polar bear hides, meat and trophies into the U.S. would result, absent the adoption of special rules allowing importation to continue. A ban on importation would not only harm current "sustainable use" hunting of the bear in Canada, but also harm the conservation, management and scientific programs that benefit from such hunting.19 These programs are both funded and driven by carefully regulated sport hunting, which makes the bear a valuable resource to native economies and provides the proper incentives to keep bear population levels healthy.

As the World Conservation Union (IUCN) notes, polar bear hunting by foreigners is very important to both the health of indigenous communities and the polar bear:

A proportion of the harvest quota (varying between 12 and 15% annually) is allocated by hunter trapper organizations (HTOs) for outfitted hunts for foreign sportsmen who pay outfitting and trophy fees up to $30,000 per bear for the privilege of participating in the hunt. Approximately 2/3 of such payments makes its way directly to the local community and represent an important source of seasonal revenue and employment in these low-income regions. This added value helps sustain the hunter/wildlife relationships that benefit customary conservation values and practices. The small proportion of the total number of tags allocated by Inuit hunters to sport hunting reflects the high value placed on polar bear hunting by native hunters.20

Furthermore, each time the U.S. Fish and Wildlife Service issues a permit to import a polar bear trophy into the United States, $1,000 of the import fee goes "to develop and implement cooperative research and management programs for the conservation of polar bears in Alaska and Russia under section 113(d) of the Marine Mammal Protection Act."

According to the IUCN, between April 1997 and December 2004, the U.S. Fish and Wildlife Service issued 705 permits to allow the importation of polar bear trophies, generating $705,000 for conservation programs.

The Alaskan government recently warned against listing the polar bear under the ESA, stressing the danger such a listing would pose to polar bear conservation and local economies:

The ability for polar bears to be hunted and hides legally imported into the United States creates a unique economic incentive for Nunavut [Canada] residents and their communities to benefit economically and socially as well as for scientists to gain cooperation in the monitoring and conservation through setting of harvest quotas.

As significant portion of the world population of polar bears is subject to Canadian and Nunavut management authorities and only a small portion of polar bear habitat occurs in the United States. A listing as "threatened" under the Endangered Species Act would automatically trigger a "depleted" designation under the Marine Mammal Protection Act. Such a designation prohibits take of polar bear, which will prevent import of hides and prohibits subsistence harvest by Alaska Natives. Although the Service professes intent to write regulations to allow Alaska Natives to continue to harvest polar bears and to allow the import of hides, the likelihood of subsequent litigation to eliminate all hunting is nearly certain.

The sustainable management of hunting programs in Canada is largely tied to the economic incentives for its governments to implement and adhere to polar bear harvest quotas, which are otherwise entirely voluntary under the act establishing Nunavut. The conservation management includes establishment of male/female harvest ratios, protection of cubs, and others in co-management agreements. It also results in cooperative establishment of carrying capacity and programs that significantly reduce nuisance kills near communities and hunting camps. Elimination of these conservation measures by depriving the managers of incentives would result from a listing under the Endangered Species Act that prohibits the import of hides and will not benefit polar bears in Canada and other countries. It will also deprive Alaska Natives of traditional uses without benefiting polar bear populations or their habitat in Alaska.

Safari Club International has also warned that listing the polar bear would harm the management and conservation of the animal:

Listing would undermine conservation by curtailing the involvement of U.S. hunters in Canadian sport hunting of the polar bear, disrupting an important source of funds to support polar bear management and conservation. Since the ESA listing would not stop polar bear hunting, but merely the ability of U.S. citizens to import polar bears, the listing would accomplish nothing in terms of reducing the number of polar bears taken. Instead, native subsistence hunters and/or sport-hunters from countries other than the U.S., who will likely pay much less for the polar bear hunt than U.S. citizens, will fill the market. The result of listing likely will be continued take at current levels, with less revenue for polar bear management and conservation. The $1,000 per import permit for research and conservation also would be lost.

In a letter to their colleagues in the U.S. House of Representatives, the leaders of the Congressional Sportsmen's Caucus warned that a ban on the importation of polar bear trophies into the U.S. would "deprive the Nunavut of a critical source of revenue and deplete global funds for polar bear conservation."
The letter further states:

The Government of Nunavut and the Nunavut Wildlife Management Board together contribute about $1,000,000 per year to polar bear conservation, in addition to providing local conservation staff. Another $100,000 is generated in license fees, which is put toward international polar bear conservation efforts. Sport hunts bring in a total of $2.5 million for Nunavut communities, many of which have little other economic activity.

The Congressional Research Service notes in a March 2007 report: "Such an import ban, effectively stopping U.S. participation in conservation hunting programs, is likely to seriously compromise successful Canadian community-based conservation programs."

The Association of Fish and Wildlife Agencies told Congress that a ban on the importation of polar bear trophies into the U.S. "would not result in the taking of fewer polar bears; it will just complicate the work of those trying to conserve them."

A study conducted by the University of Calgary's Arctic Institute of North America found that polar bear hunting in Canada helps ensure the short and long-term health of the population because it provides the necessary incentives to monitor, manage and protect the bear's population and habitat.
Listing the Polar Bear Could be Costly

Listing the polar bear as "threatened" under the Endangered Species Act could have far-reaching negative consequences on virtually all sectors of the American economy, as virtually all are dependent on energy use. In the past, regulatory actions undertaken under the ESA have been limited to the general vicinity of a species' declared habitat. However, if man-made carbon dioxide emissions are deemed harmful to the polar bear's existence, regulators may not deem it significant if those emissions originate in Kansas or in Alaska.

According to Stoel Rives Environmental Group:

[I]f the polar bear were listed and critical habitat designated based on environmental impacts attributed to GHG [greenhouse gas] emissions, the consequences of such a finding for all major U.S.-based GHG emission sources and to planned energy and industrial facilities could be significant. Action agencies permitting or authorizing such facilities may be required to consult with FWS under Section 7 of the ESA each time they issue a Title V permit under the Clean Air Act, or take other actions that 'may affect' listed polar bears. Such ESA consultations would address whether the direct, indirect and cumulative effects of the proposed action jeopardize the survival or recovery of polar bears, and whether the proposed action adversely modifies designated critical habitat.

According to the U.S. Department of Energy, America's dependence on foreign oil negatively "affects our economy and our national energy security." This dependence is likely to be exacerbated should the polar bear be listed under the ESA, as such a listing would present an additional barrier to oil exploration in the Arctic National Wildlife Refuge (ANWR), the most promising unexplored oil reserve in North America, and in other areas as well.

Under Section 7 of the ESA, federal agencies are required to work with the U.S. Interior Department to ensure that any action they undertake does not "jeopardize the continued existence of any endangered or threatened species or result in the destruction or adverse modification of habitat of such species."33 The Section 7 Consultation Handbook, produced by the Clinton Administration in 1998, is over 300 pages long.

As the U.S. Government Accountability Office reports, Section 7 consultations can have a crippling effect:

After several fish species in the Pacific Northwest were listed in the late 1990s, the Services' consultation workload increased significantly in Idaho, Oregon, and Washington, and the Services were unable to keep up with requests for consultation. As a result, many proposed activities were delayed for months or years. Even under normal workload conditions, the consultation process can be difficult, in part because decisions about how species will be protected must often be made with uncertain scientific information using professional judgment.

The ESA's regulatory supremacy over a wide range of federal actions is well documented, as are the legal provocations from the environmental community. Both would be vastly expanded should carbon dioxide emissions be deemed to fall under the Act's authority.

For example, future power plant construction necessary to feed our growing economy, as well as energy use in general, could be threatened by activists' lawsuits that claim CO_2 emissions are harmful to the "threatened" polar bear. As primary energy use in the United States (including residential, commercial, industrial and transportation) is projected to increase 31 percent from 2005 levels by 2030, the need for new energy generating capability is obvious.36

Vital public works and defense projects, as well as private economic activity important to the livelihood of large numbers of Americans could likewise be stymied by litigation and regulation, as the federal agencies responsible for such projects could be required to clear their activities with the Interior Department under Section 7 prior to acting.

Such scenarios are not without precedent.

For example, in response to lawsuits filed by environmental groups, the federal government denied water to 1,500 farmers and over 200,000 acres of the Upper Klamath Lake region of Oregon in 2001, citing the need to protect two fish listed under the ESA.

Likewise, in 2003 a federal judge ordered a reduction in the amount of dammed water that would be permitted to flow into the Missouri River despite the detrimental effect such an action posed to people along the river. This, too, was in response to environmentalist lawsuits filed under the ESA. According to Missouri Attorney General Jay Nixon, "Water for the Missouri is like blood for our bodies; the flow of the Missouri River helps keep our economy alive." As written, however, the ESA does not make distinctions between protections that harm human beings, and those that do not.

Not even military readiness and training is immune from the long grasp of the ESA. Marine training exercises at Camp Pendleton, California have been hampered to accommodate the tidewater goby, a species of fish listed under the ESA.

According to the U.S. Energy Information Administration, energy use by the U.S. military accounted for roughly 81% of all energy consumption by federal agencies in 2005. Should energy use be restricted under the ESA to protect the "threatened" polar bear, military operations and readiness could conceivably be impaired.
If restrictions on carbon dioxide emissions are imposed to protect the bear's critical habitat under the ESA, it could prove extremely costly across the U.S. The Department of Energy determined that emissions restrictions like those prescribed in the Kyoto Protocol would have reduced U.S. gross domestic product (GDP) $397 billion by 2010. In addition, the regulatory and tax costs of complying with such restrictions could be as high as $338 billion (1992 dollars) annually from 2008 to 2012. Such restrictions were predicted to raise electric utility bills by an estimated 86 percent, the cost of heating oil by 76 percent and gasoline prices by 66 cents per gallon.

The threat of regulatory actions and activists' lawsuits would not be limited to federal activities. If carbon dioxide emissions are deemed legally harmful to the polar bear or its habitat, then the act of emitting carbon dioxide, or perhaps "too much" of it, anywhere in the U.S., could be considered an illegal activity for private individuals under the ESA's broad "take" provision in Section 9. Certain private activities in which CO_2 is emitted could trigger environmental lawsuits and adverse regulatory actions for U.S. citizens and property owners.

Should the polar bear be listed, the possibilities for an expansion of federal regulatory power combined with lawsuit abuse are nearly endless. They also could be pointless, as even a radical reduction in energy use by the United States would not be sufficient to forestall alleged anthropogenic global warming in light of increased greenhouse gas emissions in Europe, China, India and elsewhere.

Listing the Polar Bear because of Projected Future Global Warming Could Set an Expansive New Precedent for Future ESA Listings

The polar bear could become the first species to be listed under the ESA specifically due to the effect climate fluctuation is projected to have on its habitat. This would establish a wildly broad standard for listing species, as the climate is in constant flux, and whether warming or cooling, is bound to have both positive and negative effects on many species and their habitats.

It should be noted that some environmental activists have claimed that two corals listed as threatened under the ESA in 2006 already establish a "global warming" precedent for listing species.

In May 2006, the National Oceanic and Atmospheric Administration (NOAA) Fisheries Service, in response to a petition filed by the Center for Biological Diversity, listed both the staghorn and elkhorn corals as threatened under the ESA. In its petition the CBD claims "global warming" is one factor afflicting the species.
However, the listing determination for both corals found in the Federal Register lists "elevated sea surface temperature" as one of many factors with the "potential to impact" the coral, and does not attribute the cause of temperature rise to anthropogenic activities.46 Furthermore, the determination states:

We determined that neither elkhorn nor staghorn corals are currently in danger of extinction throughout their entire ranges and neither meets the definition of endangered under the ESA...

Additionally, as evidenced by the geologic record, both elkhorn and staghorn corals have persisted through climate cooling and heating fluctuation periods over millions of years, whereas other corals have gone extinct.

The Center for Biological Diversity apparently agrees the coral listings do not establish a "global warming" listing precedent. As CBD staff attorney Kassie Siegel wrote in an op-ed piece for the Los Angeles Times: "The corals were listed as threatened species in May, but with far less fanfare than the polar bear and without an explicit recognition of global warming as a cause of their decline."

Siegel also writes that the U.S. Interior Department's proposal to list the polar bear "marks the first legally binding admission by the Bush administration of the reality of global warming." If the CBD considers the mere proposal to list the polar bear as significant precedent, then the actual listing of the two coral species by the Bush administration, at least in the eyes of Siegel and the CBD, did not establish such precedent.

It is by the listing of the polar bear that Siegel and her colleagues apparently hope to achieve "explicit recognition of global warming." As Siegel herself writes, "Once protection for the polar bear is finalized, federal agencies and other large greenhouse gas emitters will be required by law to ensure that their emissions do not jeopardize the species. And the only way to avoid jeopardizing the polar bear is to reduce emissions."

Indeed, two unfortunate precedents could be established by listing the polar bear under the ESA: 1) The precedent whereby species may be listed as threatened under the ESA because third parties have predicted future climate fluctuations, which, if they come to pass, could be threatening to the species, and 2) a precedent in which greenhouse gas emissions are regulated not based upon the perceived benefits of such regulations to human beings after due consideration of pros and cons, but automatically, even if (as seems likely) human beings and other species are adversely affected.

Conclusion
The global polar bear population is healthy, and the estimated total number of bears is more than double the amount thought to exist four decades ago. The charge from some environmental groups that the polar bear is threatened by anthropogenic global warming, which they say could cause the bear's extinction in the wild within a century, is unsubstantiated. Their claim rests on the theory that man is largely responsible for recent increases in global temperature and that these increases will continue unabated unless radical decreases in global greenhouse gas emissions are mandated and accomplished. Expert opinion, however, disagrees on this point, and climate science, which is extremely complex, remains in its infancy.

Furthermore, listing the polar bear under the Endangered Species Act could harm bear conservation efforts by eliminating revenues from the carefully-regulated   rt hunting of polar bears by Americans and the importation of   ar bear meat and trophies into the U.S. As hunting by non-A   ricans would replace hunting by Americans, nothing would b   ccomplished in terms of reducing the number of polar bears ta   , but the revenue currently generated by American sport hun   for conservation and research efforts would be eliminated.

Listing the polar bear as threa   ned due to projected global warming also could be enormously costly to the U.S. economy and could create a precedent for massively expanded federal regulatory powers under the ESA. It is very likely to harm indigenous cultures in the arctic while increasing the number of lawsuits filed for the purpose of blocking economic activity in the U.S.

One thing it is unlikely to do is help the polar bear.

-Footnotes:

1 U.S. Fish and Wildlife Service, "Polar Bears and the Endangered Species Act," February   2007,   available   at http://alaska.fws.gov/fisheries/mmm/polarbear/pdf/Polar_Bear_Fact_Sheet.pdf as of March 26, 2008.

2 U.S. Fish and Wildlife Service - Alaska, "Marine Mammals Management: Polar Bear Natural History," January 2004, available at http://alaska.fws.gov/fish-

Photo by Jeff Vanuga

eries/mmm/polarbear/facts.htm as of March 26, 2008.
3 Ibid.

4 San Francisco Zoo, "Polar Bear," available at http://www.sfzoo.org/cgi-bin/animals.py?ID=18 as of April 6, 2007.

5 International Union for the Conservation of Nature and Natural Resources, "Red Data Book," Vol. 1 - Mammalia, 1966, available at http://www.animalinfo.org/species/carnivor/ursumari.htm as of April 6, 2007.

6 U.S. Fish and Wildlife Service - Alaska, "Marine Mammals Management: Polar Bear Population History," January 4, 2004, available at http://alaska.fws.gov/fisheries/mmm/polarbear/phistory.htm as of March 26, 2008.
7 Polar Bears International, "Polar Bear Status Report," available at http://www.polarbearsinternational.org/bear-facts/, as of April 6, 2007.

8 Steven C. Amstrup, "Section 8: Polar Bears: Movements and Population Dynamics of Polar Bears," Arctic Refuge Coastal Plain Terrestrial Wildlife Research Summaries, U.S. Department of Interior and U.S. Geological Survey, 2002, available at http://www.absc.usgs.gov/1002/section8.htm as of March 26, 2008.

9 Polar Bears International, "Polar Bear FAQ," available at http://www.polarbearsinternational.org/faq/ as of April 6, 2007.

10 World Wildlife Federation, "Save the Polar Bear," July 13, 2006, available at http://www.panda.org/about_wwf/where_we_work/europe/what_we_do/arctic/polar_bear/threats/hunting/index.cfm as of April 6, 2007.

11 Stefan Norris, Lynn Rosentrater, and Pål Martin Eid, "Polar Bears at Risk," World Wildlife Federation, May 2002, available at http://worldwildlife.org/polarbears/pubs/polar_bears_risk.pdf as of April 6, 2007.

12 Dr. Mitchell Taylor, "Silly to Predict Their Demise," Toronto Star, p. A19, May 1, 2006.

13 Steven Milloy, "Polar Bear Meltdown," FOXNews.com, December 28, 2006, available at http://www.foxnews.com/story/0,2933,239697,00.html as of April 6, 2007.

14 William J. Snape, III, "Testimony of William J. Snape, III," Hearing on a Proposal to List the Polar Bear Under the ESA, Interior Department, Washington, DC, March 5, 2007.
15 Jeffrey A. Michael, "The Endangered Species Act and Private Landowner Incentives," available at http://www.aphis.usda.gov/ws/nwrc/symposia/economics/michael.pdf as of April 6, 2007.

16 Allison Winter, "Yellowstone Grizzlies Lose ESA Protection," E&E News PM, E&E Publishing, LLC, March 22, 2007, available at http://www.eenews.net/eenewspm/2007/03/22/#7 as of April 6, 2007.

17 United States Department of Agriculture Forest Service Northeastern Area, "Threatened and Endangered Species and the Private Landowner," available at http://www.na.fs.fed.us/spfo/pubs/wildlife/endangered/endangered.htm as of April 6, 2007.

18 "Before the Secretary of the Interior, Petition to List the Polar Bear (Ursus maritimus) as a Threatened Species Under the Endangered Species Act," Center for Biological Diversity, February 16, 2005.

19 Ralph Cunningham, "Comments on Proposed Rule to List the Polar Bear as Threatened," Safari Club International, April 9, 2007, page 2.

20 Dr. Lee Foot, Dr. Milton Freeman, "U.S. Endangered Species Act: Polar Bear Listing," World Conservation Union, May 2006, available at http://www.iucn.org/themes/ssc/susg/news/may06polarbear.htm as of May 15, 2007.

21 50 C.F.R. § 18.30(g)(2), current as of May 11, 2007, available at http://ecfr.gpoaccess.gov/cgi/t/text/text-idx?c=ecfr&sid=c0b16ccd693b08320cf751b315b3142&rgn=div5&view=text&node=50:6.0.1.1.1&idno=50 as of May 15, 2007.

22 Jon Aars, Nicholas J. Lunn, Andrew E. Derocher, "Polar Bears: Proceedings of the 14th Working Meeting of the IUCN/SSC Polar Bear Specialist Group, 20-24 June 2005, Seattle, Washington, USA," page 74.

23 State of Alaska, "State of Alaska's consolidated state agency comments, additional data, and analyses as requested in the January 9, 2007, (Federal Register Vol. 72, No. 5) proposal to list the polar bear as threatened throughout its range pursuant to the Endangered Species Act," April 9, 2007, page 13, available at http://www.adfg.state.ak.us/special/esa/polarbears/state_comments4-9-07.pdf as of April 24, 2007.

24 Ralph Cunningham, "Comments on Proposed Rule to List the Polar Bear as Threatened," Safari Club International, April 9, 2007, pp. 4-5..

25 Rep. Ron Kind (D-WI), Rep. Paul Ryan (R-WI), Rep. Dan Boren (D-OK), Rep. Steve Pearce (R-NM), "Help Conserve Polar Bears: Oppose H.R. 2327," Letter to Colleagues.

26 Ibid.

27 Eugene H. Buck, "Polar Bears: Proposed Listing Under the Endangered Species Act," Congressional Research Service, March 30, 2007, page 11, available for download at http://opencrs.cdt.org/document/RL33941 as of June 27, 2007.

28 Matt Hogan, Letter to Members of Congress, Association of Fish and Wildlife Agencies, June 22, 2007.

29 M.M.R. Freeman, G.W. Wenzel, "The Nature and Significance of Polar Bear Conservation Hunting in the Canadian Arctic," Arctic Institute of North America of the University of Calgary, March 1, 2006, available at http://www.accessmylibrary.com/coms2/summary_0286-14795316_ITM as of June 28, 2007 (Note: Free subscription required to view full study).

30 Stoel Rives Environmental Group, "Endangered Species Act Alert - Petition to List the Polar Bear Threatens Major U.S. Emission Sources and Alaska Oil and Gas

Development," available at http://www.stoel.com/showarticle.aspx?Show=847 as of April 6, 2007.

31 "Strengthen Energy National Security," undated U.S. Department of Energy document, available at http://www.fueleconomy.gov/feg/oildep.shtml as of April 6, 2007.

32 Alaska Governor Frank Murkowski, Testimony before the House Energy and Commerce Subcommittee on Energy and Air Quality, on Energy Legislation," February 10, 2005, available at http://www.nga.org/portal/site/nga/menuitem.0f8c660ba7cf98d18a278110501 010a0/?vgnextoid=60387618c4042010VgnVCM1000001a01010aRCRD as of April 6, 2007.

33 U.S. Fish and Wildlife Service, "The Endangered Species Act of 1973," available at http://www.fws.gov/endangered/esa.html#Lnk07 as of April 6, 2007.

34 U.S. Fish and Wildlife Service, "Section 7 Consultation Handbook," available at http://www.fws.gov/endangered/consultations/s7hndbk/s7hndbk.htm as of April 6, 2007.

35 U.S. Government Accountability Office, "Endangered Species: Despite Consultation Improvement Efforts in the Pacific Northwest, Concerns Persist about the Process," Summary, June 25, 2003, available at http://www.gao.gov/docdblite/details.php?rptno=GAO-03-949T as of April 6, 2007.

36 U.S. Energy Information Administration, "Annual Energy Outlook 2007 with Projections to 2030," p. 73, February 2007, available at http://www.eia.doe.gov/oiaf/aeo/index.html as of April 6, 2007.

37 John P. McGovern MD Center for Environmental and Regulatory Affairs, "Shattered Dreams: One Hundred Stories of Government Abuse, Fourth Edition," The National Center for Public Policy Research, p. 28, 2003, available at http://www.nationalcenter.org/ShatteredDreams.pdf as of April 6, 2007.

38 Center for Environmental and Regulatory Affairs, "Shattered Dreams: One Hundred Stories of Government Abuse, Fifth Edition," The National Center for Public Policy Research," p. 42, 2007, available at http://www.nationalcenter.org/ShatteredDreams.html as of April 6, 2007.

39 Dana Joel Gattuso, "Rules Protecting Endangered Species Endanger Defense Readiness Instead," National Policy Analysis, The National Center for Public Policy Research, July 2003, available at http://www.nationalcenter.org/NPA475.html.

40 U.S. Energy Information Administration, "U.S. Government Energy Consumption by Agency, Fiscal Years 1975-2005," Table 1.11, available at http://www.eia.doe.gov/emeu/aer/overview.html as of April 6, 2007.

41 Energy Information Administration, "What Does the Kyoto Protocol Mean to U.S. Energy Markets and the U.S. Economy?," Department of Energy, October 1998, available at http://www.eia.doe.gov/oiaf/kyoto/kyotobtxt.html as of April 6, 2007.

42 Ibid.

43 John Carlisle, "President Bush Mu... Kill Kyoto Global Warming Treaty and Oppose Efforts to Regulate Carbon Diox... The National Center for Public Policy Research, February 2001, available at http://www.nationalcenter.org/NPA328.html.
44 National Oceanic and Atmospheric Administration, "Elkhorn and Staghorn Corals Listed in Threatened Status," May 5, 2006, available at http://www.noaanews.noaa.gov/stories2006/s2627.htm as of May 15, 2007.

45 Center for Biological Diversity, "Petition to List Acropora Palmata (Elkhorn Coral), Acropora Cervicornis (Staghorn Coral), and Acropora Prolifera (Fused-Staghorn Coral as Endangered Species Under the Endangered Species Act," March 3, 2004.

46 Federal Register, "Rules and Regulations," Vol. 71, No. 89, May 9, 2006, page 26,858.

47 Ibid, page 26,856.

48 Kassie Siegel, "Don't Wait to Save the Polar Bear," Los Angeles Times, January 8, 2007, available at http://www.latimes.com/news/opinion/la-oe-siegel8jan08,0,2035118.story?coll=la-opinion-rightrail as of May 15, 2007 and http://www.commondreams.org/v...s07/0108-23.htm as of March 26, 2008.

49 Ibid.

50 Ibid.

Despite the clear evidence that polar bears are not threatened or endangered, the U.S. Fish & Wildlife Service, seeking ever more and more control over our nation' sources and economic engine, went ahead and listed the Polar Bear n November 24, 2010. To put the size of the area in perspective, it is 1..% larger than the states of Alabama, Connecticutt, Maine, Delaware Maryland, Massachusetts, Rhode Island, Vermont, Hawaii, New Jersey, and West Virginia **combined.** And it is now under the direct control of unelected "green" bureaucrats, that hate the idea of America drilling for oil and natural gas.

187,157 Square Miles of Critical Habitat Designated for Polar Bear

Posted on December 3, 2010 by Robert Horton

On November 24, 2010, the U.S. Fish and Wildlife Service announced a final rule (PDF) designating 187,157 square miles of on- and off-shore habitat in northern Alaska as critical habitat for two populations of polar bear listed as threatened under the Endangered Species Act.

The Service originally proposed to designate 200,541 square miles of critical habitat. However, the final designation removed land that turned out to lie beyond the U.S. territorial waters, the U.S. Air Force (USAF) radar sites, the Native communities of Barrow and Kaktovik, and all existing man-made structures. According to the Service, the radar sites are already subject to Integrated Natural Resource Management Plans, and the Native communities have a history of coordinating with the Service regarding polar bear management and conservation.

Because approximately 95% of the designated habitat consists of sea ice in the Beaufort and Chukchi Seas where oil and gas development occurs, there has been significant concern about the new rule's economic impact on industry, landowners, Alaska Native Regional Corporations, and other stakeholders. According to the Service's economic analysis (PDF 10MB), the designation of critical habitat will not result in any significant incremental economic impact because the polar bear is already protected under the Endangered Species Act as a threatened species, under the Marine Mammal Protection Act of 1972 (MMPA), and under the Convention on International Trade in Endangered Species of Wild Fauna and Flora (CITES) signed in 1973. Thus, activities such as oil and gas exploration and production that require federal permits or other approvals are already subject to incidental take regulations. As a result, the Service has determined that designation of critical habitat will not result in additional polar bear conservation measures, and thus economic impacts are forecast to be limited to additional administrative costs.

Nevertheless, stakeholders are concerned that the designation of critical habitat will spur litigation, which creates regulatory uncertainty and discourages investment.

The final rule will become effective 30 days after it appears in the Federal Register.

"A long habit of not thinking a thing wrong, gives it a superficial appearance of being right, and raises at first a formidable outcry in defense of custom. But the tumult soon subsides. Time makes more converts than reason."
Thomas Paine

Comment by the National Center for Public Policy Research Center President Amy Ridenour on Announcement Regarding Listing the Polar Bear Under the Endangered Species Act

The decision to list the polar bear as "threatened" announced today by Interior Secretary Dirk Kempthorne was probably the best that could be expected from a government agency operating under a severely-flawed Endangered Species Act, but it is a regrettable decision nonetheless.

The Secretary's clear intent to deny environmental organizations the power to regulate the energy use of the American people through Endangered Species Act-related lawsuits is commendable, but it is only through a failure of lawmaking that such a threat to representative government is even possible.

It remains to be seen if the Secretary's effort to keep the development of climate policies where it belongs -- with Congress -- will succeed.

Environmental organizations will continue to try to use the Endangered Species Act to impose energy-use restrictions on the American public, but no climate policy should be adopted without the consent of the public as expressed through the votes of their the elected representatives in Congress.

Those politicians who support the effort to impose climate policy without public consent are doing so due to political expediency. The present majority leadership of the House and Senate claim to be persuaded that the theory that human beings are causing significant climate change is correct, yet it is unwilling to push energy-use restrictions through Congress because the public does not support this action. The Congressional leadership is taking the coward's way out.

The Endangered Species Act was never intended to govern the energy policy of our entire nation. To reduce the threat that it can be used in this way, and for other reasons, the Endangered Species Act must be reformed.

The American public should never allow elected officials to put their political fortunes ahead of the public's right to be governed by people it elected.

Polar Bear Scare on Thin Ice

Friday, November 12, 2004
By Steven Milloy

This "Global warming could cause polar bears to go extinct by the end of the century by eroding the sea ice that sustains them," is the dire warning contained in a new report from an international group of "researchers" called the Arctic Climate Impact Assessment.

I'm not quite sure what the future holds for polar bears (search), but it doesn't appear that any alleged manmade global warming has anything to do with it.

The report, entitled "Impacts of a Warming Arctic," pretty much debunks itself on page 23 in the graph labeled, "Observed Arctic Temperature, 1900 to Present."

The graph shows that Arctic temperatures fluctuate naturally in regular cycles that are roughly 40 years long. The Arctic seems currently to be undergoing a warming phase — similar to one experienced between 1920-1950 — which will likely be followed by a cooling phase — similar to the one experienced between 1950-1990.

The report's claim that increased manmade emissions of greenhouse gases (search) are causing Arctic temperatures to rise is debunked by the same graph, which indicates that the near surface Arctic air temperature was higher around 1940 than now, despite all the greenhouse gas emissions since that time.

Also self-debunking is the report's statement, "Since the start of the industrial revolution, the atmospheric carbon dioxide concentration has increased by about 35 percent and the global average temperature has risen by about 0.6 degrees Centigrade."

So despite all the greenhouse gases emitted by human activity over a period of 200 years — we're supposed to worry, and even panic, about a measly 0.6 degree Centigrade rise in average global temperature during that time?

Even if such a slight temperature change could credibly be estimated, it would seem to be well within the natural variation in average global temperature, which in the case of the Arctic, for example, is a range of about degrees Centigrade. Remember, global climate isn't static — it's always either cooling or warming.

Even though manmade greenhouse gas emissions and warmer temperatures don't seem to be a problem in the Arctic according to their own data, the researchers nevertheless blamed them for causing supposed 15 percent declines in both the average weight of adult polar bears and number of cubs born between 1981 and 1998 in the Hudson Bay region.

The 1999 study in the science journal Arctic that first reported apparent problems among the Hudson Bay polar bear population (search) suggested that their condition may be related to the earlier seasonal break-up of sea ice on western Hudson Bay —a phenomenon that seems to correlate with the 1950-1990 Arctic warm-up. But, as mention previously, the 1950-1990 Arctic warming period seems to be part of a natural cycle and not due to manmade emissions of greenhouse gases.

Moreover, the notion of a declining polar bear population doesn't square well available information.

A Canadian Press Newswire story earlier this year reported that, in three Arctic villages, polar bears "are so abundant there's a public safety issue." The local polar bear population reportedly increased from about 2,100 in 1997 to as many as 2,600 in 2004. Inuit hunters (search) wanted to be able to kill more bears because they are "fearsome predators."

An aerial survey of Alaskan polar bears published in "Arctic" (December 2003) reported a greater polar bear density than previous survey estimates dating back to 1987.

If polar bears really are getting skinnier as the 1999 study suggested, it may actually be due to an increased population subsisting on the same level of available food. After all, the harvesting of Alaskan polar bears has been limited by the Marine Mammal Protection Act (search) and international agreements since 1972.

The Arctic Climate Impact Assessment report has spurred a new round of calls for a clamp-down on carbon dioxide emissions. Sens. John McCain, R-Ariz., and Joe Lieberman, D-Conn., told the Associated Press that the "dire consequences" of warming in the Arctic underscore the need for their proposal to require U.S. cuts in emissions of carbon dioxide and other heat-trapping greenhouse gases.

Fortunately their call will likely get a chilly response from President Bush, who reiterated through a spokesman last weekend that he continues to oppose the international global warming treaty known as the Kyoto Protocol (search).

Steven Milloy is the publisher of JunkScience.com, an adjunct scholar at the Cato Institute and the author of "Junk Science Judo: Self-Defense Against Health Scares and Scams" (Cato Institute, 2001).

Polar bears in danger? Is this some kind of joke?*

James Delingpole: Thunderer

Why don't polar bears eat penguins? Because their paws are too big to get the wrappers off, obviously. It's not a joke you hear so often these days, though, because polar bears are now a serious business. They're the standard-bearers of a tear-jerking propaganda campaign to persuade us all that, if we don't act soon on climate change, the only thing that will remain of our snowy-furred ursine chums will be the picture on a pack of Fox's glacier mints.

First there came the computer-generated polar bear in Al Gore's An Inconvenient Truth; then that heartrending photo, syndicated everywhere, of the bears apparently stranded on a melting ice floe; then the story of those four polar bears drowned by global warming (actually, they'd perished in a storm).

*http://www.timesonline.co.uk/tol/comment/columnists/guest_contributors/article2852551.ece

Now, in a new cinema release called Earth – a magnificent, feature-length nature documentary from the makers of the BBC's Planet Earth series – comes the most sob-inducing "evidence" of all: a poor male polar bear filmed starving to death as a result, the quaveringly emotional Patrick Stewart voiceover suggests, of global warming.

Never mind that what actually happens is that the bear stupidly has a go at a colony of walruses and ends up being gored to death.

The bear wouldn't have done it, the film argues, if he hadn't been so hungry and exhausted. And why was he hungry and exhausted? Because the polar ice caps are melting, thus shortening the polar bears' seal-hunting season.

Having been up to the bears' habitat in Svalbard, I do have a certain amount of sympathy with these concerns. To claim, however, that they are facing imminent doom is stretching the truth. In 1950, let us not forget, there were about 5,000 polar bears. Now there are 25,000.

No wonder Greenpeace had trouble getting polar bears placed on the endangered species list. A fivefold population increase isn't exactly a catastrophic decline.

But never let the facts get in the way of a good story. The doom-mongers certainly won't. Despite evidence from organisations such as the US National Biological Service that in most places polar bear populations are either stable or increasing, Ursus maritimus will continue to top the eco-hysterics' list of animals in danger because it's so fluffy and white and photogenic.

If you're really that worried about their demise, I'd book yourself a ticket to Churchill, Manitoba, where the evil buggers (about the only creature, incidentally, that actively preys on humans) are so rife they're almost vermin.

And if things get really bad, we can always ship the survivors off to Antarctica where, unlike the North Pole, the ice shelf appears to be growing. Then the joke would be even less comprehensible. Why don't polar bears eat penguins? But they do, actually!

Unfortunately, folks, it is not a joke. The Environmental Movement, with the help of our own U.S. Government, through the U.S. Fish & Wildlife Service, is shutting down industry after industry. Ask the farmers in California, or the loggers in the Northwest, or the ranchers in Montana, or the shrimpers in Louisiana, or the contractors across the country. Believe me, speaking from very personal experience, losing one's livelihood because of environmentalist lies, is anything but funny. Worst yet, some of our activist judges support this nonsense.

Polar bears' threatened status upheld in court*

WASHINGTON (Reuters) - A U.S. federal judge upheld the status of polar bears as a species threatened by climate change, denying challenges by a safari club, two cattlemen's organizations and the state of Alaska.

The ruling on Thursday by District Judge Emmet Sullivan confirmed a 2008 decision that polar bears need protection under the U.S. Endangered Species Act because their icy habitat is melting away.

The legal challenges -- some contending polar bears don't need this protection, others maintaining the big white bears need more -- were launched after the U.S. Fish and Wildlife Service included this Arctic mammal on its list of threatened species.

The state of Alaska, Safari Club International and two cattlemen's groups claimed the federal government's decision to list the polar bear was "arbitrary and capricious and an abuse of agency discretion," according to a memorandum opinion released with the ruling.

On the other side, environmental groups including the Center for Biological Diversity, urged that polar bears be listed as endangered, which offers greater protection than that provided for wildlife classified as threatened.

RATIONAL DECISION

The heart of the judge's decision was whether the Fish and Wildlife Service had made a rational decision in its 2008 listing.

*http://www.reuters.com/article/2011/06/30/us-climate-polarbears-idUSTRE75T6CK20110630

The judge noted that the wildlife agency took three years to "evaluate a body of science that is both exceedingly complex and rapidly developing," considering 160,000 pages of documents and some 670,000 comments from a wide range of interested parties."

"The court finds that plaintiff (who challenged the listing) have failed to demonstrate that the agency's listing determination rises to the level of irrationality," Sullivan wrote.

"... the Court finds the (wildlife) service's decision to list the polar bear as a threatened species ... represents a reasoned exercise of the agency's discretion based upon the facts and the best available science as of 2008 when the agency made its listing determination," the judge wrote.

Environmental activists gave the decision measured praise.

Greenpeace called it "bittersweet," the Natural Resources Defense Council and the Center for Biological Diversity said stronger protections were warranted.

However, Kassie Siegel of the Center for Biological Diversity's Climate Law Institute said in a statement: **"This decision is an important affirmation that the science demonstrating that global warming is pushing the polar bear toward extinction simply cannot be denied."**

> **"Make the lie big, make it simple, keep saying it, and eventually they will believe it."**
> Adolf Hitler

Like the debate on global warming, the Environmental Movement tells a big lie, then declares the debate over. How dare anyone have the temerity to question these people! "Affirmation of the Science"??? The judge didn't even look at the science!

Below is an excerpt from the court decision:

> ("[The court] must look at the decision not as the chemist, biologist or statistician that [it is] qualified neither by training nor experience to be, but as a reviewing court exercising [its] narrowly defined duty of holding agencies to certain minimal standards of rationality."). **Specifically, with regard to FWS decisions, this Court has previously recognized that "given the expertise of the FWS in the area of wildlife conservation and management and the deferential standard of review, the Court begins with a strong presumption in favor of upholding decisions of the [FWS]."** Am. Wildlands v. Kempthorne, 478 F. Supp. 2d 92, 96 (D.D.C. 2007) (citing Carlton v. Babbitt, 900 F. Supp. 526, 530 (D.D.C. 1995))."

The State of Alaska, two cattlemen associations, and Safari Club International had biologists presenting testimony that disagreed with the positions of the United States Fish & Wildlife Service. The judge here has abdicated his responsibility, stating **"the Court begins with a strong presumption in favor of upholding decisions of the (FWS)."**

In other words, ordinary citizens (as represented by the cattlemen, the residents of Alaska, and conservationists), are virtually powerless against the decisions of the United States Fish & Wildlife. This a department made up of unelected bureaucrats, unaccountable even to Federal judges, who, obviously, have decided to demure to their "expertise" in the management of wildlife. Is it written somewhere that U..S. Government always hires the best and the brightest? Has government proven, over the course of centuries, to be the beacon of brilliance among men? Why is the expertise of the U.S.Fish & Wildlife Service a "given", when any reasonable person, looking at their record, would find error stacked upon error?

Is this what Congress intended when it passed the Endangered Species Act of 1973, to put our nation's welfare into the hands of these bureaucrats and their "expertise"? If so, they have clearly done a great nation a great disservice.

"The liberties of our country, the freedom of our civil Constitution, are worth defending at all hazards; and it is our duty to defend them against all attacks. We have received them as a fair inheritance from our worthy ancestors: they purchased them for us with toil and danger and expense of treasure and blood, and transmitted them to us with care and diligence. It will bring an everlasting mark of infamy on the present generation, enlightened as it is, if we should suffer them to be wrested from us by violence without a struggle, or to be cheated out of them by the artifices of false and designing men."
Samuel Adams

The critical, but false, assumption made by the Environmental Movement, or at least presented by them as fact, is that oil drilling and pipelines somehow hurt polar bears and other arctic species. I have watched tens of thousands of caribou, and dozens of grizzly bears and wolverines walk within a few yards of my hunting camps. They don't fall over and die, and the same is true when they apporach pipelines and oil rigs. They simply walk around them. The critical component of all wildlife management is mortality rates, and what causes them. Man's activity in the arctic regions don't kill polar bears, caribou, wolves, or any other species. And don't let the government biologists try to fill you with the "Cumulative Affects" nonsense. The science behind that theory is pure rubbish.

I live in the Bitterroot Valley of western Montana, in a subdivision of 15 acre lots. It is the ultimate area of "cumulative affects", with roads, joggers, bikers, and barking dogs. On a daily basis, I see whitetail deer, mule deer, elk, black bear, bighorn sheep, and wild turkeys. A mountain lion was treed not long ago in my front yard. Smaller game, birdlife, and plantlife abounds. Wildlife can, and does, adapt to human encroachment. It is what actually kills them that counts, not close association to human beings.

Investing in America and the Lack of Certainty

America has been built by entrepeneurs, who have accepted Thomas Paine's Entrepeneur's Credo- *"to dream and to build. To fail and to succeed."* And the reason those entrepeneurs were willing to gamble all, was, paradoxically, because of "**certainty**".*

*www.merriam-webster.com/dictionary/certainty

Entrepreneur's Credo

I do not choose to be a common man,
It is my right to be uncommon ... if I can,
I seek opportunity ... not security.
I do not wish to be a kept citizen.
Humbled and dulled by having the
State look after me.
I want to take the calculated risk;
To dream and to build.
To fail and to succeed.
I refuse to barter incentive for a dole;
I prefer the challenges of life
To the guaranteed existence;
The thrill of fulfillment
To the stale calm of Utopia.
I will not trade freedom for beneficence
Nor my dignity for a handout
I will never cower before any master
Nor bend to any threat.
It is my heritage to stand erect.
Proud and unafraid;
To think and act for myself,
To enjoy the benefit of my creations
And to face the world boldly and say:
This, with God's help, I have done
All this is what it means
To be an Entrepreneur."

Thomas Paine

"Certainty": the quality or state of being certain, especially on the basis of evidence"*

It was certainty that America, and America's government, gave them. Not the certainty of success, but the certainty of a level playing field and a non-intrusive government. The certainty of the Constitution, that guaranteed certain, inalienable rights. Whether a small businessman or a large, multinational corporation, before plunking down your hard earned capital in an entrepeneurial venture, they will examine the evidence regarding the certainty of the environment in which that venture will operate. It is the task of good government to create this environment of certainty.

What a prospective business most wants to avoid is the proverbial (and adjusted for politcal correctness) "Negro in the Wood Pile." (The term dates back to the 1850s, when the Underground Railroad was flourishing, helping runaway slaves to freedom in the north.) The expression came to mean: ."some fact of considerable importance that is not disclosed."

And what has happened, and continues to happen, is that the Government of the United States of America, through the Endangered Species Act of 1973, is no longer protecting private property rights (despite the guarantees of the Fifth Amendment) and is creating an atmosphere of uncertainty, the proverbial "Negro in the Woodpile"*. As the Domenigoni family discovered, even after having farmed their land for five generations, there is no certainty that the United States Fish & Wildlife Service won't decide that, all of a sudden, you've got Stephen's Kangaroo Rats, and you can no longer utilize your investment of treasure, blood, sweat, tears, and heartache.

And that is the reason, or certainly one of them, that American companies are moving overseas, and international companies are choosing to invest elsewhere.

Will A Lizard Stop West Texas Oil?

Posted 04/27/2011 06:27 PM ET

Species: After the harm done by the spotted owl and delta smelt, the listing of a tiny reptile as endangered may be the latest salvo in the war on domestic energy.

* Wikipedia On-line Encyclopedia

As Yogi Berra would say, it's deja vu all over again. If the dunes sagebrush lizard is listed by the U.S. Fish and Wildlife Service as an endangered species, another key part of the American economy will fall prey to the eco-extremist mantra that every little critter's well-being trumps that of the American people and economy.

Last December, the Fish and Wildlife Service announced that the lizard, a three-inch-long reptile native to the American Southwest, "faces immediate and significant threats due to oil and gas activities and herbicide treatments" and initiated the process to get it listed under the Endangered Species Act.

In 2002, the Center for Biological Diversity first petitioned to have the lizard, originally considered a subspecies of the common sage-brush lizard, listed as endangered. The Bush administration delayed consideration for six years. Last year, the Obama administration put it back on the fast track.

And why not? This is an administration that has ignored a judge's order to remove restrictions on oil drilling in the Gulf of Mexico and designated vast areas in and off Alaska as protected habitat for the caribou and the polar bears, species whose only problem is one of overpopulation.

As director of the Lawrence Berkeley National Laboratory, Steven Chu, Obama's secretary of energy, expressed a fondness for high European gas prices as a means of reducing consumption of fossil fuels. In a September 2008 newspaper interview, he said, "Somehow we have to figure out how to boost the price of gasoline to the levels in Europe." Gas prices in Europe then averaged about $8 a gallon.

As gas prices here soar toward $5 a gallon, Chu's friends at the Interior Department may help him and President Obama get the rest of the way toward their goal. If the dunes sagebrush lizard, now considered a separate species, is granted endangered status, oil and gas production in the Permian Basin in New Mexico and Texas may have to be shut down.

When Obama recently addressed the current energy crisis, he told Americans not to worry: "We've been down this road before." But we should worry — and for that very reason. We've seen the spotted owl kill logging and create ghost towns in the Northwest. The ESA's listing of the delta smelt created 40% unemployment in California's San Joaquin Valley and turned America's food basket into a dust bowl.

The Department of Energy says the Permian Basin has a quarter of the nation's proven reserves and 20% of the nation's daily production comes from there. It has a quarter of the nation's active oil and gas wells and is home to 21% of the rigs actively drilling in the U.S.

Gulf oil production is expected to be down 20% in 2011, meaning the loss of 375,000 jobs. But that's a drop in the barrel compared with the loss of production and jobs if America's biggest oilfield is shut down to make a lizard's life more comfortable.

So the day when you pump Secretary Chu's expensive gas, it won't be the fault of those big bad oil companies charged by President Obama with conspiring to boost oil prices by restricting supply. It'll be the administration restricting supply as part of its plan to make domestic energy prices "necessarily skyrocket" so that green energy looks more attractive and necessary.

Dunes Sagebrush Lizard Might Stop Oil Drilling Hot Air

Will oil industry become an endangered species in West Texas?
By Ed Morrissey

It might, if the US Fish and Wildlife Service puts the Dunes Sagebrush Lizard on the endangered-species list. USFWS has an open period for public comment at the moment on the proposal, which if adopted could force oil companies in West Texas and New Mexico to close up shop. The industry argues that USFWS is relying on bad data and faulty methodology:

A three-inch lizard that thrives in desert conditions could shut down oil and gas operations in portions of Southeast New Mexico and in West Texas, including the state's top two oil producing counties.

Called the Dunes Sagebrush Lizard, it is being considered for inclusion on the federal Endangered Species listing by the U.S. Fish and Wildlife Service. A public rally to oppose this move is being sponsored by the Permian Basin Petroleum Association on Tuesday, April 26 at Midland Center beginning at 5 p.m. Congressman Mike Conaway will speak, as will Land Commissioner Jerry Patterson; other public officials have been invited.

"We are very concerned about the Fish and Wildlife Service listing," said Ben Shepperd, president of the PBPA, noting the service also has proposed listing the Lesser Prairie Chicken next year. "The wolf at the door is the lizard; we're concerned listing it would shut down drilling activity for a minimum of two years and as many as five years while the service determines what habitat is needed for the lizard. That means no drilling, no seismic surveys, no roads built, no electric lines."

Well, thank goodness we overproduce into big surpluses of domestic oil, and fuel is so cheap. Otherwise, killing off the oil industry in West Texas might really hurt consumers with higher prices on everything, starting with gasoline and quickly inflating food prices. What's that — huh? Oh, yeah.
My friend Hugh Hewitt, who practices in environmental law when not hosting his excellent talk-radio show, explains the mischief behind abuses of the Endangered Species Act:

This lizard isn't protected under the Endangered Species Act ("ESA") — yet. But if the industry, lessees and land owners, and affiliated businesses and communities do not rally to present the necessary science and defend against the typically hyperbolic claims of the species' imminent demise due to "habitat fragmentation" presented by anti-growth, anti-energy environmental extremists, the lizard will soon add another burden to the business of energy production, just as scores of species listings in other states have diminished economic growth across a number of industries.

The abuse of the ESA is more than two decades old, but is now something of a science on the left, and the sporadic attempts to amend the ESA over the years have all come to naught. I have battled such listing for 20 years and it is crucial not just for the soon-to-be-impacted property-owners and industry interests to organize, but also for the House Natural Resource Committee to exercise oversight on this proposed listing and all new listings and to make sure that the administrative record is full of arguments against the listing and especially against the entire theory of "habitat loss" as a rationale for a listing.

This issue must be raised in Congress. It's just as important to curtail the abuse of the ESA as it is to rein in the EPA. The dry lands of the formerly-productive California Central Valley and the thousands out of work over the Delta smelt can attest to these dynamics.

Lizard Stops Oil Drilling in America!

In a previous article entitled: Enviro's Shut Down a Solar Plant in the Desert I wrote about how the enviro's shut down a solar plant in the Mojave desert because 164 turtles live on the land. Now they have switched tactics by petitioning the Government to declare the Dunes Sagebrush Lizard an Endangered Species and effectively shutting down new drilling in West Texas and Southeast New Mexico! I kid you not!

The new tool of the Obama administration is the U.S. Fish and Wildlife Service. Because they weld great power over animals like the turtle, the spotted owl, and the lizard, they can control which areas we can drill for oil. Isn't it amazing that wherever we drill, the U.S. Wildlife service shows up unannounced to save the animals?

Ben Sheppard, president of the Permian Basin Petroleum Association said this:

"This is the most prolific oil-producing region in onshore America. If you knock out a big portion of that, it clearly will drive prices up at the gas station."

Because oil creates jobs in America, New Mexico's governor, Susana Martinez, who just happens to be Republican, wrote in a letter to the U.S. Fish and Wildlife, "the future of our state's livelihood of so many employers and hardworking New Mexicans are at stake."

Fish and Wildlife folks say they are using the best available science and is working with companies. Yeah and global warming scientists never lie! The scientist have determined that the Sagebrush Lizard cannot live anywhere else! Come on... you mean if you move them a mile away, they can't adapt? I am not that gullible! They tried that argument on the Alaskan Pipeline, and today the animals are thriving more than ever! Why? Cause the pipeline is heated and animals in the cold like that!

But the oil industry has made deals with have agreed to pay $10,000-$20,000 per well (aka blackmail) to return the land back into its original state, thereby allowing the lizard to thrive. Odds are it will be doing just fine down the road and this is enviro-terrorisim, which all of us pay at the pump.

We must drill for oil in America if we ever want to get this country up and running again. Now the U.S. Fish and Wildlife in conjunction with the environmentalist wacko's are going to declare any species "endangered" and stop any new production.

How far will this go? Invest in torches folks, cause that is where we are headed!

Paul Smith Owner: WWW.SmithHeggumReport.com

Could a three-inch lizard collapse the West Texas oil industry?

A three-inch lizard that thrives in desert conditions could shut down oil and gas operations in portions of Southeast New Mexico and in West Texas, including the state's top two oil producing counties.

Called the Dunes Sagebrush Lizard, it is being considered for inclusion on the federal Endangered Species listing by the U.S. Fish and Wildlife Service. A public rally to oppose this move is being sponsored by the Permian Basin Petroleum Association on Tuesday, April 26 at Midland Center beginning at 5 p.m. Congressman

Mike Conaway will speak, as will Land Commissioner Jerry Patterson; other public officials have been invited.

"We are very concerned about the Fish and Wildlife Service listing," said Ben Shepperd, president of the PBPA, noting the service also has proposed listing the Lesser Prairie Chicken next year. "The wolf at the door is the lizard; we're concerned listing it would shut down drilling activity for a minimum of two years and as many as five years while the service determines what habitat is needed for the lizard. That means no drilling, no seismic surveys, no roads built, no electric lines."

The move would impact activity in Andrews, Crane, Gaines, Ward and Winkler counties in Texas and Chaves, Eddy, Lea and Roosevelt counties in New Mexico.

Not only would the move impact oil and gas operations but agriculture, Shepperd noted, shutting down agricultural activities like grazing and farming -- "anything that disturbs the habitat." While the industry is perfectly willing to undertake conservation measures to protect the lizard's habitat, he said, naming it an endangered species "would shut down activity and be devastating not only to Permian Basin economies but to the national economy. We are the one bright spot month after month; in our economic turnaround, the main driver is the oil and gas industry."

The concern is, he said, that the Fish and Wildlife Service lacks enough data to conclude that the tiny lizard is endangered and is basing its action on flawed methodology. "They didn't spend enough time looking for them or the right technique to find them," he said.

In New Mexico, where the lizard can be found on both private and public lands, Shepperd said a number of companies have entered into voluntary agreements to help conserve the lizard's habitat, mitigate threats to the lizard and remediate any damage while continuing to operate. He said he wants the same to happen in Texas. The association favors such joint agreements between the federal government and landowners to protect the lizard's habitat while allowing drilling operations to continue responsibly.

"The point is, we think the best way is for land owners and industry actually on the ground where the lizards are, who know how to protect the lizard, to be in charge instead of the feds putting up 'Do Not Enter' signs on every gatepost," Shepperd said.

A sign of hope is that four counties -- Lea, Andrews, Ward and Winkler, and the town of Monahans, have passed resolutions demanding to have standing during the comment phase, which ends May 16. Under the National Environmental Protection Act, or NEPA, Shepperd said, the federal government is required to work with local governmental entities when they make such a request.
"This will enable them to bring in the economic impact," he said. "We feel like the counties demanding to be part of the process should require the Fish and Wildlife Service to work with them to develop a reasonable conservation process that we all can live with." He said he hopes those attending Tuesday's rally "will be inspired and better prepared to testify at the public hearing" being held by the Fish and Wildlife Service on Wednesday, April 27. The public hearing will also be at Midland Center, beginning at 6:30 p.m.

It can't happen, right? Nobody believed they would shut down logging all across the Northwest, just to save a subspecies of owl, the Northern Spotted Owl. But it happened.

Nobody believed they would shut down millions of acres of farmland in California, to save the Delta Smelt. But it happened.

Nobody believed they would risk flooding thousands of homes along the Missouri River, to save piping plover nests. But it happened.

Nobody believed they would arrest a Taiwanese immigrant for plowing his own fields. But it happened.

Nobody believed they would introduce wolves into the west, decimating deer, elk, moose, and bighorn sheep herds, effectively wiping out a hundred years of excellent conservation work. But it happened.

Nobody believed they would deny water to four young firefighters because of endangered salmon, putting their lives in jeopardy. But it happened. And they died.

Nobody believed a California rancher would be arrested for disking a firebreak around his home, to save it from wildfire. But it happened.

"When the Nazis came for the communists,
I remained silent;
I was not a communist.

Then they locked up the social democrats,
I remained silent;
I was not a social democrat.

Then they came for the trade unionists.
I did not speak out; I was not a trade unionist.

Then they came for the Jews.
I did not speak out;
I was not a Jew.

When they came for me,
there was no one left to speak out for me."

Martin Niemoller, on why the German people didn't resist the
Nazis

"What, me worry?"

Global warming, drowning polar bears, disappearing lizards, dying kangaroo rats, are all the same, really. Simply tools of the Environmental Movement to bring all Americans to the least common denominator. Energy use creates human productivity, and, in turn, creates wealth. The simple reality is, the Environmental Movement is against the creation of wealth, and sees most human endeavors as evil. It is not breaking news that the environmental movement is against the use of oil and gas, but what about other forms of energy?

The following articles are self-explanatory.

Just Say "No" to Solar Power

Groups sue to stop SunPower plant in California

Thu Jun 2, 2011 3:39pm EDT

By Nichola Groom

LOS ANGELES, June 2 (Reuters) - Two conservation groups and a California resident have sued to stop construction of a SunPower Corp (SPWRA.O) solar power plant, saying the project would harm the rural area's wildlife, air quality and natural beauty.

San Luis Obispo county community groups Carrizo Commons and North County Watch and local farmer and auto repair shop owner Michael Strobridge filed the lawsuit on May 20 in California state court.

In court papers, the plaintiffs said county officials did not adequately analyze the 250-megawatt California Valley Solar Ranch's impact on the area's aesthetics, air quality, biological resources, noise, traffic, greenhouse gas emissions and agricultural resources. The suit asks that the county be ordered to set aside its approval of the California Valley Solar Ranch and that the project be declared unlawful.

In addition to SunPower, the lawsuit names San Luis Obispo county, its Board of Supervisors, NRG Energy Inc (NRG.N), utility PG&E Corp (PCG.N) and several others as defendants. NRG last year said it would buy the project, though SunPower will develop it.

A SunPower spokeswoman said the company does not comment

on pending litigation, but called the county's review process "very thorough... the California Valley Solar Ranch is designed to minimize environmental impacts and maximize economic benefits to the County."

The project was approved by the county's planning commission in February after a string of hearings during which the five-member panel weighed the project's economic and environmental benefits against its impact on native species, local residents and the region's landscape. [ID:nN2496103]

Several challenges to that approval were rejected by the county's Board of Supervisors in April. [ID:nWEN1430]

SunPower in April received a conditional commitment for a $1.187 billion loan guarantee from the U.S. Department of Energy to fund construction of the plant.

Another, larger, solar project is also planned for the same area. First Solar Inc's (FSLR.O) 550 MW Topaz Solar Farm won approval from the county's planning commission last month. Three appeals to that approval have already been filed by Strobridge, landowner Jody Stegman, and a group of conservation groups including North County Watch, Carrizo Commons, the Center for Biological Diversity and Defenders of Wildlife.

Just Say "No" to Nuclear Power

Riverkeeper Challenges NRC on Endangered Sturgeon Impacts*

New Legal Filing attacks adequacy of Final Environmental Assessment by NRC

OSSINING, NY – February 7, 2011 – Riverkeeper today filed a new claim with the Nuclear Regulatory Commission (NRC) in the ongoing Indian Point relicensing battle. This latest legal challenge faults the Federal oversight agency for failing to consider vital information from the National Marine Fisheries Service (NMFS) about affects on endangered and threatened aquatic life in the Hudson River prior to issuing its determination this past December that

*Tina Posterli, Riverkeeper, 914-478-4501 x 239 tposterli@riverkeeper.org

there are no environmental impacts that would preclude license renewal for the Indian Point nuclear power plant.

The Endangered Species Act (ESA) requires Federal agencies to consult with NMFS whenever a proposed action will impact endangered or threatened species. NRC learned from NMFS as early as October 2007 that the license renewal of Indian Point could adversely affect two federally protected sturgeon species present in the Hudson River. Under the ESA, the NRC then became obligated to prepare a biological assessment for NMFS to review, in order for NMFS to be able to issue an official biological opinion regarding whether relicensing Indian Point will improperly jeopardize endangered species. NMFS' opinion will contain critical information about impacts to endangered species in the Hudson River, including any necessary mitigation measures or project alternatives.

However, NRC delayed for three years in giving NMFS all the information necessary for NMFS to perform its required consultation duties. As a result, the NRC ultimately issued a Final Supplemental Environmental Impact Statement (FSEIS) recommending license renewal before NMFS could perform its required analysis and inform NRC's assessment with crucial input.

"NRC's failure to consider feedback from NMFS completely flouts the whole purpose of the Endangered Species Act, and leaves the FSEIS blatantly inadequate," said Riverkeeper Staff Attorney, Deborah Brancato. "Without the benefit of NMFS' biological opinion, it is hard to fathom how NRC's conclusions about impacts to endangered species, and ultimately, the appropriateness of relicensing Indian Point were fully-informed and accurate."

Riverkeeper's new filing comes on the heels of a challenge filed by Riverkeeper and Hudson River Sloop Clearwater calling for NRC to fully assess the environmental impacts of long-term nuclear waste storage at Indian Point prior to its relicensing. Since the NRC issued its FSEIS, Riverkeeper has been concerned about the scientific information in the report contradicting the agency's conclusions.

These new claims are yet further examples of NRC's flawed environmental review process in the Indian Point license renewal proceeding. NRC has overlooked serious environmental issues in reaching the conclusion that Indian Point should be relicensed. NRC's conclusions continue to be unsupported by the facts and raise serious questions about the agency's willingness to objectively assess Indian Point's true impact on the Hudson River.

A panel of independent NRC judges will now determine whether Riverkeeper's new claim will be admitted into the ongoing license renewal proceedings. Riverkeeper currently is preparing for a hearing on three issues challenging the safety and environmental impacts of relicensing Indian Point. A federal hearing is tentatively scheduled for summer 2011.

Just Say "No" to Coal Power

'Right Out of Atlas Shrugged': Hear an Exasperated Alabama Businessman Tell the Feds – 'I'm Just Quitting'

Posted on July 26, 2011 at 8:50am by Dave Urbanski
Ronnie Bryant was vastly outnumbered.

Leaning against a wall during a recent Birmingham, Alabama, public hearing, Bryant listened to an overflow crowd pepper federal officials with concerns about businesses polluting the drinking water and causing cases of cancer.

After two hours, Bryant—a coal mine owner from Jasper—had heard enough and, in a moment being described as "right out of Atlas Shrugged," took his turn at the microphone:
"Nearly every day without fail...men stream to these [mining] operations looking for work in Walker County. They can't pay their mortgage. They can't pay their car note. They can't feed their families. They don't have health insurance. And as I stand here today, I just...you know...what's the use? I got a permit to open up an underground coal mine that would employ probably 125 people. They'd be paid wages from $50,000 to $150,000 a year. We would consume probably $50 million to $60 million in consumables a year, putting more men to work. And my only idea today is to go home. What's the use? I see these guys—I see them with tears in their eyes—looking for work. And if there's so much opposition to these guys making a living, I feel like there's no need in me putting out the effort to provide work for them. So...basically what I've decided is not to open the mine. I'm just quitting. Thank you."

The Blaze contacted Bryant, and he remains as resolute as he was at last week's public hearing. To him, it's just not worth the time, money, and regulatory hassle to open up a new mine—even one located in a remote area with less environmental impact.

"If they want to create jobs, provide health insurance, and increase revenue," Bryant said in reference to the federal government, "they need to back down on the regulatory burden. It's like pulling an iron ball with a chain. I'm not saying to make it go away—just the stuff that's not pertinent or useful."

Terry Douglas, who owns two mines in Jasper with Bryant, said it costs them about $250,000 per mine in permit fees alone and that paperwork and regulatory inspections are a constant presence (as well as an additional revenue strain). When asked about typical concerns surrounding coal mining—including companies skirting health and safety regulations—Douglas said it "doesn't make sense" to let safety lapse and risk losing miners to illness or injury when it would only cost more to train new personnel.

"We take care of our equipment and take care of our people," Douglas said. "The regulations make coal miners out to be criminals; but we're not outlaws. Coal mining is an art. I have a civil engineering degree; Ronnie has a mining engineering degree. It's not wildcat whiskey we're making; this is drinking whiskey we got."

Bryant pointed to less stringent environmental regulations in countries such as China, saying that the U.S. is falling behind even though it has abundant resources. "But you can't get to them," he said, adding that while there are concerns over dwindling wildlife populations, "people are becoming the endangered species."

Gwendolyn Keyes Fleming, regional administrator for EPA's Southeast Region, attended the Birmingham public hearing but could not be reached for comment.
(h/t David McElroy)

Just Say "No" to Wind Power

Ohio Agricultural Law Blog

The Indiana bat, an endangered species with the power to stop a wind development project. The Beech Ridge wind energy project involves construction of 122 wind turbines along the ridgeline of the Appalachian mountains in Greenbrier County. About forty of the turbines are currently in the construction phase, but the federal court has issued an injunction stopping construction of any additional turbines and limiting existing turbine use to the bat's winter hibernation period. The reason project developers failed to take seriously the issue of harm to the Indiana bat. The Indiana Bat is on the list of "endangered" species, and interference with the animal or its habitat is prohibited by the federal Endangered Species Act (ESA). The wind project developers did hire an environmental consultant to examine the situation, but the consultant repeatedly disregarded information and advice from the U.S. Fish and Wildlife Service (FWS) that would have more accurately identified the Indiana bat population. The court criticized the consultant's efforts, stating that "[s]earching for bats near proposed wind turbine locations for one year instead of three, looking in one season rather than three, and using only one method to detect bats was wholly inadequate to a fair assessment." Later surveys revealed the existence of two caves within ten miles of the project that are home to hundreds of bats, including Indiana bats, and evidence suggested that nearly 7,000 bats would die each year because of the project.

Despite the existence of the bats near the project, however, the court pointed out that Beech Ridge's developers could have requested an "incidental take permit" (ITP) pursuant to the ESA. The ESA's incidental take permit mechanism could have allowed the project to proceed, but with preparation of an FWS approved Habitat Conservation Plan demonstrating that measures would be taken to minimize or mitigate adverse effects on the Indiana bat. "Indeed, the tragedy of this case is that Defendants disregarded not only repeated advice from the FWS but also failed to take advantage of a specific mechanism, the ITP process, established by federal law to allow their project to proceed in harmony with the goal of avoidance of harm to endangered species," said the court.

The Animal Welfare Institute and Mountain Communities for Responsible Energy filed the lawsuit, and produced expert testimony indicating that Indiana bats exist near the project site and that there was a very high likelihood that the turbines would kill and injure the bats. The court drew upon Benjamin Franklin in its response to the expert testimony, stating ". . . the Court concludes, by a preponderance of the evidence, that, like death and taxes, there is a virtual certainty that Indiana bats will be harmed, wounded, or killed imminently by the Beech Ridge Project . . ."

The difficulty of rendering such a decision is apparent in the court's opinion. Judge Titus expresses disappointment and frustration with the project developer's approach to the bat issue, and "reluctantly" orders the injunction. But unlike many in the wind development arena, the court does not hesitate to give credibility to the interference of wind turbines with the bat population. He recognizes that the case illustrates a clash between two federal policies: protection of species and encouragement of renewable energy development, but insists that the two policies are not necessarily in conflict because of the ESA's incidental take option and the opportunity for harmonious development. Seeking an incidental take permit is the only avenue available to help project developers resolve their "self-imposed plight," states the court. "The development of wind energy can and should be encouraged," says Judge Titus, "but wind turbines must be good neighbors."

As the Indiana bat did years ago, wind development has made its way to Ohio. The Ohio Power Siting Board is currently considering approval of several wind projects including the Buckeye Wind Project, a 70 turbine project in Champaign County that would be Ohio's largest wind development. Testimony by an environmental consultant at last month's hearings before the board focused on potential impacts of the project on the Indiana bat. According to the consultant, studies revealed no evidence of the Indiana bat in the project area. Studies in nearby Logan County in 2008 revealed the existence of Indiana bats in an area that has since been removed from the project, and another wind developer reported finding an Indiana bat in Champaign County earlier this year. The Ohio Power Siting Board may take months to decide whether to approve the Buckeye Wind Project and to indicate its conclusions about impacts on Indiana bats.

In accordance with state policy promoting renewable resource development, the Ohio Department of Natural Resources encourages wind developers to enter into a voluntary agreement to cooperatively address wildlife issues. In the agreement, ODNR promises not to pursue liability against the developer for any incidental takings of endangered or threatened species. However, ODNR's agreement cannot prevent private groups from challenging the turbines

U.S.A. vs. E.S.A.

in federal court using the approach of the Beech Ridge Energy case. Should the Ohio Power Siting Board approve a project like the Buckeye Wind Project, Ohio may see its own federal court case on Indiana bats and wind development.

Just Say "No" to Hydro Power

Will dam breaching happen in the Pacific Northwest?

Author: Damien M. Schiff

We're one step closer to an affirmative answer to my title question in the wake of this week's ruling from Judge James Redden in National Wildlife Federation v. National Marine Fisheries Service. This is a lawsuit with a long, long, history (we've been covering it here for as long as the blog has been in existence) but it now boils down to whether the feds can put together a plan that satisfies what Judge Redden understands to be legally required for sustaining a variety of salmon populations protected under the Endangered Species Act. The feds have tried to do that by allowing more water to pass through the dams, but the court's recent ruling seems to indicate that the judge won't be happy unless more drastic steps are taken.

US Representative Doc Hastings, chairman of the House's Natural Resources Committee, has a statement out contending that the judge would have no authority to order any dams to be breached and that, even if he did, Congress would act to countermand it. I'm fairly confident that Congress would not allow the dams to be breached, but the judge probably would have the authority otherwise to breach the dams. After all, in TVA v. Hill the Supreme Court held that federal courts have the power and duty to protect endangered species, and that such power and duty required that a multi-million-dollar dam project be stopped. If the courts can stop it, they likely can pull it down, too.

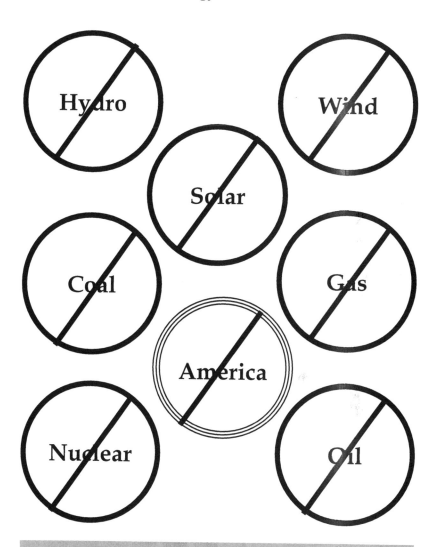

Tucson-based advocacy group makes industry of suing on behalf of wildlife

By Grant Martin, Cronkite News Service

(Kieran Suckling, executive director of the Tucson-based Center for Biological Diversity, discusses the center's efforts on behalf of wildlife. Some government officials fault the center's emphasis on litigation over working toward consensus, but Suckling says the aggressive tactics are proper and effective.)

Wearing a rakishly unbuttoned short-sleeved shirt and two days' worth of stubble, Kieran Suckling looks more like an auto mechanic than one of the most influential and polarizing wildlife conservationists in the country.

But when he talks about how he came to devote a career to animal advocacy, he betrays an academic career steeped in philosophy and biological diversity.

"All humans very naturally love all wildlife," Suckling explains. "The oldest version of the Noah's Ark story is 1,600 years older than the Old Testament. And so from the very dawn of Western culture we have believed and acted on the belief that we should protect all species."

It's a philosophy that has catapulted Suckling – and the Tucson-based group he co-founded and now directs, the Center for Biological Diversity – to the forefront of the 21st century conservation movement.

The group has achieved its high profile in part through its litigation-based approach to conservation. Since July 1, for example, the center has filed 12 lawsuits to prevent development around the country that it contends would threaten various endangered species.

It's an approach that has earned Suckling a reputation as an agitator, a description that Andrew Smith, a longtime conservationist and biology professor at Arizona State University, calls accurate.

"They like to be a thorn in the side," Smith says. "At a convention for the Society of Conservation Biology I attended in July," Smith adds, "I heard more than a few people refer to Suckling as a renegade."

Even the center's detractors, however, concede that it is remarkably successful at effecting change through litigation. Suckling boasts that the center has achieved a favorable outcome in 93 percent of the lawsuits in which it has participated.

Those wins include a legal settlement earlier this year to preserve 1,100 acres of habitat for the endangered Stephens' kangaroo rat in California from planned development. The center negotiated a 2008 settlement with the U.S. Fish and Wildlife Service that designated nearly 9,000 acres of critical habitat for picture-wing flies in Hawaii. "They've always been very active, very successful when it comes to filing cases," says Jeff Humphrey, a spokesman for Arizona Ecological Services, a federally funded conservation agency. "But there's more to protecting wildlife than just a good win-and-loss record in the courtroom."

Humphrey says that Arizona Ecological Services, a subsidiary of the U.S. Fish and Wildlife Service, is a frequent target of litigation brought by the center.

"They require and ask of us much more than we can provide," says Humphrey, explaining the center's success in court. "Compared to them, we're understaffed and underfunded, and we can't keep up with their demands."

Speaking at the center's headquarters, Suckling smiles when asked to elaborate on his organization's legal record.

"Being able to file litigation successfully is a very complicated matter, and we've been lucky to figure out we have a really good knack for it," he explains.

Suckling grows animated when explaining the nature of his group's negotiations with the federal government, characterizing it as a complex process of give and take.

"A boxing match doesn't take place [with] two guys standing in the middle of the ring and taking turns whacking each other," he says, swinging his fist for emphasis. "It's much more like a dance, and a rhythm, and it's about moving the other person around the ring and following and responding and planning where you're going."

The center employs about 20 staff attorneys, and Suckling estimates an additional 40 take cases on a pro bono basis. Asked how a non-profit organization pays for so many legal battles, Suckling explains that the center derives roughly equal funding from three bases: donations from a membership of nearly 300,000, foundation grants and funding from "a small group of very wealthy individuals."

According to the center's 2009 annual report, it had an operating budget of approximately $7.5 million, of which nearly $5 million was donated by its membership. Suckling referred to these members as part of a "communication network" that receives solicitations for donations whenever the center decides to file new litigation.

Part of what sets the center apart from other conservation agencies is its advocacy for all endangered animals, not just those most conventionally embraced by a sympathetic public.

"So many groups really just spend their life pandering to the panda," Suckling says. "We believe all living things are sacred, all living things are an amazing product of 4 billion years of evolution." Suckling and two others founded the center in 1989 after discovering an endangered Mexican spotted owl in land the Forest Service had intended to lease to timber companies. After successfully lobbying the agency to preserve the land, the trio founded the Greater Gila Biodiversity Project.

The name was later changed to reflect the broadening scope of its influence, and today the center's focus has moved – both ideologically and geographically – away from its roots defending land-based animals in the Southwest.

Particularly emblematic of this shift was the center's vociferous advocacy for aquatic species threatened by this summer's oil spill in the Gulf of Mexico.

"We came in there and descended on the Gulf like a chapter out of the Old Testament," Suckling says. "We filed seven lawsuits very, very rapidly, including the biggest clean water suit ever filed in history."

Looking ahead, Suckling anticipates increasing the size of his staff from 68 to about 150 in the next decade and acknowledges that the center's biggest challenge will be its commitment to its uniquely aggressive form of advocacy.

"We need to get out there and protect as much as possible," Suckling says. "We have to guard against viewing our work as a long-term mission where what's not done today will get done tomorrow, because sometimes things have to get done today. Tomorrow is too late."

Some cases involving the Center for Biological Diversity:

Jaguar – The center sued the U.S. Fish and Wildlife Service three times to obtain a recovery plan and critical habitat designation for the jaguar. When the last known American jaguar was captured and later euthanized by the Arizona Game and Fish Department in 2009, the group called on Fish and Wildlife to perform an independent investigation of the incident. The investigation revealed that the state agency's actions had been unlawful.

Kangaroo Rat – In April 2010, the center won a legal settlement to stop the proposed large-scale development of a 1,100-acre habitat for the Stephens' kangaroo rat in California's Riverside County.

Picture-Wing Flies – In 2008, the center reached a settlement with the U.S. Fish and Wildlife Service designating nearly 9,000 acres of critical habitat for picture-wing flies throughout four counties in Hawaii.

Spotted Owl – In 2007, the center successfully battled a proposal by then-President George W. Bush to reduce by one-fifth the area designated as "critical habitat" for the endangered spotted owl in the Pacific Northwest.

Shutting down America, and lining their own pockets at the same time, is the real goal for the Center for Biological Diversity and many other Environmental Organizations that hide behind the "Conservation" label. As you can see from the cases above, even the President of the United States is virtually powerless against the Endangered Species Act of 1973.

"We came in there and descended on the Gulf like a chapter out of the Old Testament," Suckling brags. "We filed seven lawsuits very, very rapidly, including the biggest clean water suit ever filed in history."

There a tragic, deadly explosion, and oil spill, in the Gulf of Mexico, and these vultures immediately descend on the area with lawsuits, and are proud of it. And in the end, who is footing the ultimate bill for these lawsuits? The average American taxpayer and consumer. It's not the wildlife these people care about, its the money they earn by using wildlife as a tool.

I do not believe the Endangered Species Act of 1973 should be amended. Repeal of the act is the only sensible action. Repeal the act, and start over again, from scratch. Return complete management of wildlife to the state level and then begin to construct a law that makes sense for America, and abides strictly by the Constitution. Under the current act, humans and their habitat have fewer rights than such iconic species as the San Bernardino Kangaroo Rat, the Government Cave Loving Spider, and the Delhi Sands Flower Loving Fly. That is ridiculous.

The Environmental Movement, naturally, will cry "Bloody Murder", insisting all kinds of terrible things will immediately begin to happen to endangered species all across America and around the world. Polar Bears will drown, Moose will die from lack of shade, Piping Plovers will get stomped by beachcombers. This is all nonsense. As we've shown, the Environmental Movement is much more interested in raising money and stopping human development than saving wildlife. Repealing the Endangered Species Act will simply take away the Number One tool in their arsenal.

The repeal of the Endangered Species Act will not cause the demise of a single, true species. The day after Congress repeals the law, not a single animal will die. Eventually, some species will become extinct, a process that has been going on or billions of years, as the strong survive, and the weak do not. As Stephen J. Obrien states in <u>Tears of the Cheetah, And Other Tales From the Genetic Frontier</u> :

" The history of life on earth is dominated by extinction events so numerous that more than 99.9 percent of the species ever to have existed are gone forever."

I am much more concerned with the extinction of freedom: freedom to grow food for my family, freedom to build shelter for my children, freedom to walk a beach, freedom to defend my country, than I am about the extinction of the Mexican Burrowing Toad.(That's a real species, not an illegal immigrar) As proven over the last few billion years, not all species will survive. I am rooting for the Toad (and all other species) , but I am rooting harder for my grandchildren.

The Environmentalist's Vision for America

"Big Ag"

Mass Transit

Ford F-150

Manufacturing

National Defense

Home Construction

National Rifle Association

Chapter 9

Flooding the Missouri River Valley to Save the Piping Plover

"The difference between animals and humans is that animals change themselves for the environment, but humans change the environment for themselves."
Ayn Rand

Are Thousands of People Flooded on the Missouri Because of Fish and Bird Habitats?*

Thousands of people, businesses and farms along the Missouri River from Montana to Missouri are being submerged or heavily flooded by the run-off from record heavy snows and torrential spring rainfall. But there is a question now up and down the 530,000 square mile drainage zone: Could this flooding have been prevented by better management of the Missouri River dam system?

Missouri River Basin

The Missouri River is our nation's longest river, and is "managed" by the Army Corps of Engineers through a series of dams. It turns out there is a Missouri Water Control Manual, a document forged by the Corps but with input of Congress, the federal courts, sports, navigation, and environmental groups and carrying the force of law.

See photos of flood damage between Yankton, SD and Iowa here.

The question of 2011 as people who have never before been flooded lose their homes and livelihoods to the huge crest of the Missouri River: Is this happening because fish and birds were considered more important than people by some policy manual? If yes, why is flood control to preserve PEOPLE not the top priority of the network of dams constructed by taxpayers?

Matt Bunk of the Great Plains Examiner first wrote June 9 about the growing suspicion of hard-hit residents of Bismarck, North Dakota is that concern over spring fish and bird habitats outweighed the safety of homes, farms and businesses. Bismarck has suffered a minimum of $15 million damage:

"The period between late March and early May is something the Army Corps of Engineers has been trying really hard not to talk

*http://www.uncoverage.net/2011/06/are-thousands-of-people-flooded-on-the-missouri-because-of-fish-and-bird-habitats/

Flooding on the Missouri River, 2011

about. During that 45-day period, the agency's water managers stored near-record amounts of water in the reservoir behind Garrison Dam while keeping river levels low, despite evidence that there was about 30 percent more snow in the mountains than normal.

Instead of explaining what their strategy was during the months leading up to the flood, top officials with the Corps of Engineers have offered cryptic answers while pointing to their operations manuals.

"We were operating the mainstem reservoirs in compliance with our master manual," said Jody Farhat, chief of Missouri River basin water management for the Corps of Engineers. When asked to elaborate, she repeated the same line.

Without answers, people who live along the river have done a bit of their own detective work. Many of them suspect the Corps of Engineers was trying to protect the habitat of federally protected birds. Others are convinced spring floods in the lower basin of the Missouri River may have prompted the Corps to hold more water behind the dams farther north.

Corps of Engineers officials denied both of those assertions and insisted that they have been operating in "flood-control mode" at

Garrison Dam since the beginning of the year. But public records maintained by the agency tell a different story about the way the dam was managed during the two months prior to the flood.

To gather the information for this report, the Great Plains Examiner spent nearly two weeks comparing sets of data on release rates and storage levels recorded by the Corps of Engineers as far back as 1967 when the dam began operating. Additional research included studying operations manuals that guide the agency's decisions and interviewing dozens of local leaders, federal officials, biologists and hydrologists from North Dakota and across the U.S.
Daily logs kept by the Corps of Engineers show that the agency began 2011 on an aggressive schedule to draw down the levels at Lake Sakakawea, releasing high amounts of water through the dam in January, February and the beginning of March. The average release of about 25,000 cubic feet per second during the first two-and-a-half months was almost twice as much as the average rate for that time of year.

Instead of continuing that pattern, though, the agency curtailed the releases from March 20 until May 5, allowing the reservoir to rise to about eight feet above average for that time of year while the river ran through Bismarck at its seasonal low point. Prior to slowing the release rate, the Corps had received data showing above-average snowpack in the mountains overlooking the upper river basin.

Everything changed rapidly in mid-May when heavy rain in Montana forced the Corps of Engineers to start draining Lake Sakakawea to avoid overflowing the dam. But each time the agency pushed more water through the dam, the rain came down even harder; statistics for the month show the amount of water that flowed into the reservoir was nearly double the amount that was released into the river.

Farhat said a year's worth of rain flowed into Lake Sakakawea at the end of May. "The game-changer was the rain," she said.

In June, the agency opened the Garrison Dam spillway gates for the first time ever as the rate of release ramped up to more than 120,000 cubic feet per second, about twice as much water as the previous record. Within days, floodwaters overtook communities along the river from Montana to Missouri and forced thousands of residents to evacuate their homes. In Burleigh and Morton counties, more than 700 households were given notice to evacuate and thousands of other houses are in jeopardy as the rate of release is expected to reach 150,000 cubic feet per second by mid-June.

Many residents of Bismarck-Mandan have questioned why the Corps of Engineers didn't release more water earlier in the spring, especially considering there was so much snow in the mountains.

"The river could have handled more water early this spring," said Brent Hanson, a Bismarck resident who works at a boat dealership and marina next to the river. "They could have raised it more than five feet without causing any flooding here, then maybe we wouldn't have had to deal with as much water now."

Unterseher said the Corps of Engineers screwed something up, no matter how a person looks at it.

"It's hard to blame somebody for this," he said. "But it has to be mismanagement. This is pathetic."

Water-management experts said the Corps of Engineers eventually will have to explain why so little water was released in the months leading up to the flood.

"What were they doing in the winter months and early spring when this was building?" asked Larry Larson, executive director of the Association of State Floodplain Managers. "Were they preparing for it, or were they playing the odds and then found themselves caught in a box?"

Farhat said flooding was unavoidable because the amount of rain in May made it impossible to store all the water flowing into Lake Sakakawea. She said higher releases through the Garrison Dam during early spring may have caused ice jams and flooding, similar to what Bismarck-Mandan experienced in 2009. But neither of those statements explains what the Corps of Engineers was doing in April after the ice had receded from the river.

"The main stem reservoir system has been operated in full flood-control mode since the high water of 2010," she said. "We have not made any operational decisions this year for anything other than flood control."

Col. Robert Ruch, commander of the Omaha division of the Corps of Engineers, took it one step further, saying "In hindsight, I can't imagine doing anything differently."

Despite daily press conferences and several appearances at community meetings, officials with the Corps of Engineers have not explained what, if anything, went wrong other than several unpredictable rainstorms. However, a review of the agency's master manual for the Missouri River system and its 2011 operating plan shows the agency was directed to follow regulations that encourage water storage in the reservoirs in the upper basin of the Missouri River during early spring for several reasons.

The Corps of Engineers has been instructed to save water in the reservoirs during spring so it can be sold to agricultural and industrial interests year-round; to ensure enough water is available during the summer to keep the river high enough for navigation and recreation; to maintain consistent production of hydropower during all seasons; and to limit releases during spring and summer to protect habitat for federally protected birds.

It's that last item that really grinds on people like Unterseher.

"The birds had something to do with it," he said. "That's what I believe anyway."

Two bird species, the piping plover and the least tern, migrate to the Missouri River basin during the spring nesting season, which starts in early May. In the past, the Corps of Engineers has taken steps to protect the birds, including dredging parts of the river to create sandbars and cutting down vegetation on existing sandbars to give the birds an unobstructed view of predators.

"As in previous years, releases from Garrison will follow a repetitive daily pattern during the (threatened and endangered birds) nesting season to limit peak stages below the project for nesting birds," officials noted in the Corps of Engineers' 2011 operating plan for the Missouri River. "All reasonable measures to minimize the loss of nesting (threatened and endangered) bird species will be used."

The Corps of Engineers has been falling short of its bird-habitat requirements in recent years and was under pressure from the U.S.

Fish and Wildlife Service to create and maintain more acreage of sandbars. Most of the piping plovers and least terns choose nesting grounds south of Gavins Point Dam, but some migrate to the area between Garrison Dam and Lake Oahe.

Ruch, Farhat and other officials with the Corps of Engineers have said repeatedly that the agency at the beginning of the year abandoned all plans to protect the sandbar habitat for piping plovers and the least terns.

"There has been zero water managed for endangered species this year," Ruch said.

Henry Maddux, geographic supervisor of the Missouri River for U.S. Game and Fish, said the Corps of Engineers notified his office that the conditions this spring made it impossible to protect habitat for endangered and threatened birds. He said that notification was given in late April, just before nesting season.

"There was nothing done for our species this year," he said. "They didn't hold water back for us."

So as Bunk's reporting shows, some of the Missouri dams WERE kept very full from March to May, which may be why there is TOO MUCH water to get rid of now:

In an interview on NPR last week, the Army Corps of Engineers hinted for the first time that they may have had "other" priorities other than people in mind for several critical weeks this spring :

"Jody Farhat, the chief of the Missouri River Basin Water Management Office in Omaha, is in charge of water management for the area.

"It's difficult to see the impacts of these historic releases on individuals and communities," Farhat says. "My staff and I are making those release decisions based on the information coming in every day."

These decisions are also made according to the Missouri Water Control Manual, referred to as the "master manual." It's a handbook written by the Corps with input from Congress, and it dictates the Corps' priorities. Some are easy to follow, like flood control, but others are more difficult to navigate, like keeping reservoirs full even when there's heavy snowpack, so tourists can take boats out and power companies can use water flow.

Too Many Priorities

That manual makes life tough for the Corps, which is bound by law to follow its recommendations, former Corps head Mike Parker says.

"It's a political document," he says. "Several years ago, Congress decided you have a lot of interests out there, and these interests got together and said, 'We're not getting represented.' So instead of having navigation and flood control as being the two primary things that the Corps was looking at, they had a list of eight things that they had to consider."

In addition to navigation and flood control, this list of priorities includes irrigation, water supply, hydropower, fish and wildlife, recreation and water quality. Parker says that some of these priorities run counter to each other. "If the Corps only had to take care of navigation and flood control, I guarantee you those levels [in the Missouri River reservoirs] would have been much lower," he says. The choices the Corps has made in recent months have impacted millions of lives along the Missouri and Mississippi rivers. Parker says that the decision to open the Morganza Spillway in Louisiana last month came at a cost.

"Gen. Mike Walsh had to stand in front of people and say, 'People, I'm opening these floodgates and by the way, I'm going to flood your homes. We're going to flood your businesses; we're sorry.'"

Lawmakers slash Missouri River ecosystem plans in name of flood control*

By Robert Koenig, Beacon Washington correspondent
Posted 6:12 pm Tue., 7.19.11

WASHINGTON - In the wake of this summer's severe flooding, members of Congress from Missouri have been mounting what ap-

*http://stlbeacon.org/index.php

pears to be a systematic effort to slash studies and efforts that aim to restore the ecosystems along the now-swollen Missouri River -- even though many analysts feel that such restoration can help lessen future flooding.

Last week, U.S. Rep. Blaine Luetkemeyer, R-St. Elizabeth -- arguing that "it is preposterous to think that environmental projects are more important than the protection of human life" -- convinced the U.S. House to approve his amendment to cut funding for the Missouri River Ecosystem Restoration Plan, or MR-ERP.

A few days earlier, Rep. Sam Graves, R-Tarkio -- saying that "we spend too much to protect fish at the expense of people" -- added an amendment to the same bill that would transfer $1 million from the related Missouri River Recovery Program to an Army Corps of Engineers account to be used to maintain levees. The same legislation added an extra $1 billion for the Corps to repair levees and other flood-control systems nationwide.

(The Senate has not yet taken up the bill to which these amendments were added.)

In a letter sent this month to the head of the Corps' Kansas City district, Missouri Farm Bureau President Blake Hurst contended that "the Missouri River has been hijacked by those who believe recreation and endangered species are more important than protecting lives and property."

The assault on longstanding efforts to restore Big Muddy's ecosystem -- devastated by decades of structural flood-control changes that some experts contend have raised river levels and worsened some floods -- has led to pushback from environmental groups, academics and some government river experts.

"We can develop win-win solutions that can help reduce the risks of flooding, benefit people in the floodplain and, at the same time, benefit wildlife and the ecosystem," said Wayne Nelson-Stastny, a program manager who helps coordinate the MR-ERP study for the U.S. Fish and Wildlife Service (FWS). He told the Beacon that the study involves efforts to find sustainable ways to improve flood control on the Missouri.

Many environmental and flood-plain management groups contend that building higher levees that straightjacket the river can worsen floods; they argue for solutions that allow the river to flood some bottomlands, including wildlife refuges and wetlands.

"Millions of acres of farmland and an estimated $18 billion of residential and other property are subject to flooding along the Missouri River," said Andrew Fahlund, vice president for conservation of American Rivers, an environmental group that supports better flood-plain management.

Instead of rebuilding old levees and returning to failed river-management strategies, Fahlund told the Beacon, "the record breaking flooding along America's longest river [with a basin] covering one-sixth of the United States demands flood-control efforts that move people out of harm's way, sets levees back allowing more room for rivers to roam."

Among the academic experts who question the Corps' techniques and agree with the need for more wetlands is Robert Criss, a professor in Washington University's earth sciences department and author of "At the Confluence: Rivers, Floods and Water Quality in the St. Louis Region."

Calling the initiatives to defund Missouri River studies "absolutely absurd," Criss said lawmakers were using the flood "as an excuse to scale back environmental protections. It's more of the same of our Congress doing its darndest to reward failure" of existing flood-control systems that rely too much on levees.

Kathleen Logan Smith, executive director of the St. Louis-based Missouri Coalition for the Environment, told the Beacon on Tuesday that it is "disingenuous" for members of Congress to de-fund river studies in the name of flood control when such studies may offer sustainable -- and less expensive -- solutions to limit the impact of future floods.

"We don't have the money to continue to build and build levees and other structures to contain rivers" [like the Missouri], Smith said, adding that "it's cheaper and more practical to give the rivers more space."

While Smith agrees that "we do need to find ways to protect our farmland," she also contends that "we also need to allow some flood-plains to behave like floodplains. That's why we need to find middle ground."

The following paper below is where the problem begins.

"We recommend a review of annual operating plans of managed rivers to account for the effects of dam discharges on Least Terns and Piping Plovers. "

Flooding: Mortality and Habitat Renewal for Least Terns and Piping Plovers

John G. Sidle and David E. Carlson

U. S. Fish and Wildlife Service
203 West Second Street, Grand Island, Nebraska 68801

Eileen M. Kirsch

Division of Biological Sciences, University of Montana,
Missoula, Montana 95812
Present Address: U.S. Fish and Wildlife Service, Northern Prairie Wildlife Research Center,
P.O. Box 818, LaCrosse, Wisconsin 54602

John J. Dinan

Nebraska Game and Parks Commission, P.O. Box 30370,
Lincoln, Nebraska 68503

Abstract.—We observed extensive mortality (eggs and chicks) of the endangered interior population of the Least Tern (*Sterna antillarum*) and threatened Piping Plover (*Charadrius melodus*) caused by natural flooding during the 1990 breeding season along the Platte River, Nebraska. Aerial videography of the Platte River before and after the flood revealed a 78% reduction of perennial vegetation on sandbars. The flood scoured vegetation from sandbars and greatly increased the amount of barren sandbar habitat that nesting Least Terns and Piping Plovers use. A review of river gauging station data indicated that flooding of the 1990 magnitude or greater can be expected to occur about once every nine years. We recommend a review of the annual operating plans of managed rivers to account for the effects of dam discharges on Least Terns and Piping Plovers. *Received 3 June 1991, accepted 7 November 1991.*

Key words.—*Charadrius melodus*, flooding, habitat, Least Tern, mortality, Piping Plover, *Sterna antillarum*.

Colonial Waterbirds 15(1): 132-136, 1992

Least Terns and Piping Plovers nest and rear their young on barren to sparsely vegetated sandbars along large rivers of the northern Great Plains (U.S. Fish and Wildlife Service (USFWS) 1988, 1990a). Although untimely discharges of water from dams frequently inundate their nests along the Missouri River and elsewhere, flooding due to local precipitation also causes egg and chick mortality (Schwalbach 1988, Mayer and Dryer 1989, Dirks 1990, USFWS 1990a, b, U.S. Army Corps of Engineers 1991). High flows, however, also scour vegetation from sandbars creating barren islands of sand and gravel, ideal nesting habitat for Least Terns and Piping Plovers (Currier et al. 1985, USFWS 1990a, b).

We observed the Platte River, Nebraska before and after flood events during June and July 1990 and recorded the mortality of Least Tern and Piping Plover eggs and chicks caused by flooding. We also recorded the removal of vegetation by scouring river flows and the subsequent increase of sandbar habitat suitable for nesting Least Terns and Piping Plovers.

STUDY AREA AND METHODS

We videotaped the lower Platte River (mouth of Loup River to mouth of Platte River) (Fig. 1) from an aircraft on 11 June 1990 before the flood, and on 4

Figure 1. The Lower Platte River, Nebraska from the confluence of the Loup River to the Platte's confluence with the Missouri River.

Please note that the paper is written by John Sidle and David Carlson, of the United State Fish and Wildlife, and Eileen Kirsch, of the University of Montana, who then goes to work for the U.S. Fish and Wildlife Service. Completed in 1992, the Missouri River basin experienced record floods in 1993. That is a pretty strange coincidence, since the previous catastrophic flood occurred all the way back in 1927, before all the flood control dams were built.

Missouri River Flooding

Great Mississippi and Missouri Rivers Flood of 1993*

"The Great Mississippi and Missouri Rivers Flood of 1993 (or "Great Flood of 1993") occurred in the American Midwest, along the Mississippi and Missouri rivers and their tributaries, from April to October 1993. The flood was among the most costly and devastating to

*Wikipedia On-line Encyclopedia

ever occur in the United States, with $15 billion in damages. The hydrographic basin affected cover around 745 miles (1200 km) in length and 435 miles (700 km) in width, totaling about 320,000 square miles (840,000 km²).[1] Within this zone, the flooded area totaled around 30,000 square miles (80,000 km²)[2] and was the worst such U.S. disaster since the Great Mississippi Flood of 1927, as measured by duration, square miles inundated, persons displaced, crop and property damage, and number of record river levels. In some categories, the 1993 flood even surpassed the 1927 flood, at the time the largest flood ever recorded on the Mississippi.

Missouri River Plan Hurt Local Residents
by Amy Ridenour, National Center for Public Policy research

In an effort to protect endangered birds and fish, a federal judge restricted the amount of dammed water allowed to flow into the Missouri River. As a result, water levels became too shallow for regional farmers to ship goods by barge, forcing them to use more costly transportation alternatives.

Missouri River Plan Hurt Local Residents

Citing the need for lower water levels to protect the endangered Least Tern, Piping Plover and Pallid Sturgeon, a coalition of environmental groups sued the government to restrict the amount of dammed water that would be permitted to flow into the Missouri River.

Missouri Attorney General Jay Nixon, commenting on the region's economic reliance on the river, noted that "water for Missouri is like blood for our bodies; the flow of the Missouri River helps keep our economy alive."

Though she acknowledged the economic hardship that would result, a federal judge ruled the well-being of these protected birds and fish outweighed human concerns.

Noting, "there is no dollar value that can be placed on the extinction of an animal species," U.S. District Court for the District of Columbia Judge Gladys Kessler ordered a reluctant U.S. Army

The Piping Plover   The Least Tern

Corps of Engineers to reduce the flow of the Missouri River beginning in July of 2003. While the Corps initially refused to obey
the order and was cited in contempt of court, Kessler's decision was
later sustained on appeal and water levels were dropped in August.

Almost immediately, the reduction in flow caused the river level in
Kansas City, Missouri to fall by six feet. This virtually eliminated
the ability of barges to operate on the Missouri River and forced
local farmers to seek more costly alternatives, such as air, rail and
road, to transport their products. Transporting goods by barge
makes good economic sense for farmers. An average 15-ton barge
can carry the equivalent of 870 truck payloads.

In the spring of 2004, towing companies normally serving Sioux
City, Iowa announced they would not be able to deliver the 50 to 60
regular bargeloads of fertilizer due to uncertain river depths. Big
Soo Terminal manager Kevin Knepper lamented: "We have lost our
spring and the most profitable season. It's just too late to get up and
running and make any money... [W]e're [now] concerned the rail
industry will not be able to service the additional tonnage that we're
going to need to move this spring."

As a result of a diminished Missouri River, pollution and other environmental harm became an unintended and pressing concern for
the region. Nixon predicted "the increased congestion and air pollution stemming from the loss of river transportation [will] be im-
mense." Within weeks of the river dropping to levels not seen since
the dustbowl era, water temperature rose to a point nearly exceed-

ing Missouri water quality standards.

Although Kessler's decision in 2003 had been upheld, a different federal judge assigned to the river litigation has since ruled differently. In June 2004, U.S. District Judge Paul Magnuson in Minneapolis ruled in favor of the Corps and blocked the contempt citation.

The judge noted:

"there is no dollar value that can be placed on the extinction of an animal species."

Missouri's Piping Plover*
The issue of the election year...and Gore is AWOL.
By Michael Catanzaro, a reporter for Robert Novak, 10/18/00

Few political pundits could have predicted that endangered species would decide which presidential candidate carries Missouri this year. But thanks to Bill Clinton's veto of a $23.6 billion appropriations bill, the piping plover, the least tern, and the pallid sturgeon may become Texas Gov. George W. Bush's best friends.

Clinton's veto on October 7 was wildly unpopular in the state and augurs poorly for Vice President Al Gore in November. "This issue is the script of how Al Gore will lose Missouri," said a GOP source. **The veto stems from a decision in July by the U.S. Fish and Wildlife Service ordering the Army Corps of Engineers to manipulate the Missouri's water levels to save three endangered species.** In effect, the Corps proposed a plan that would decrease water flow each summer and then increase it every third spring.

Sen. Kit Bond (R., Mo.) responded recently by inserting language into the Energy and Water appropriations bill blocking the Corps from implementing the plan for one year. Bond's effort cut across partisan lines: Nearly ever member of the Missouri congressional delegation supported him, including House minority leader Dick Gephardt.

It's not hard to understand why. Barge owners bitterly complained

*http://old.nationalreview.com/battleground/battleground-missouri101800a.shtml

that low water flow could stop barge traffic for six weeks at a time, decimating river commerce. The Missouri Farm Bureau said artificial increases would induce rampant flooding, already a serious and frequent problem along the banks of the river. (**Note: the Army Corps of Engineers tried unsuccessfully to prevent Missourians from rebuilding levees after the disastrous 1993 flood**).

Farmers, an important constituency in the state, are unequivocally ticked at Gore. "**The Clinton-Gore Administration is continuing to ignore the pleas of Missourians not to threaten their lives and property with this ill-conceived plan**," said Charles Kruse, president of the Missouri Farm Bureau. "I think this gives our members and the people of Missouri a stark choice in November."

The Democratic mayors of St. Louis and Kansas City both urged Clinton to rescind the order. Even the Missouri Department of Natural Resources argued that the ebb-and-flow plan "will produce meager, if any gains for the (endangered) species."

The issue has serious implications for a very competitive open seat in the House. The Missouri River cuts through the 6th congressional district, where state senator Sam Graves is battling former Democratic state senator Steve Danner. The seat, now held by Danner's mother, Rep. Pat Danner, is prime pickup territory for Republicans.

The tragic death yesterday of Democratic governor Mel Carnahan effectively means Republican senator John Ashcroft will be re-elected. The only possibility for a new challenger to enter the race will be through a write-in campaign, which is highly unlikely. Carnahan's name will remain on the ballot Nov. 7.

Congressional leaders tried to squeeze as much political mileage from the issue as they could. The House voted last week 315 to 98 to override Clinton's veto, as all Missouri House members, with the exception of Democratic representative Karen McCarthy, voted in favor of the override. Republicans senators, however, failed to garner the necessary two-thirds, and the override languished in the Senate.

To appease Clinton, negotiators were forced to strip the Bond language from the bill, essentially allowing the Corps to begin planning the timing and implementation of the plan. Bond, meanwhile, has campaigned across the state to remind voters of the Clinton-Gore environmental agenda for Missouri.

The Farm Bureau launched a $10,000, three-day radio ad campaign attacking Gore for his failure to stop it. **"The White House is threatening to veto legislation designed to prevent flooding on the Missouri River," according to one ad. "Don't they know the damage flooding does to families, communities, jobs, and property?"**

Over the last several weeks, the momentum has clearly been with Bush in Missouri, and this issue has undoubtedly been a key rea-

George W. Bush carried Missouri in 2000 by three percentage points, and double that in 2004. I hope the politicians out there are paying attention. They need to understand that people will vote to protect their property, their lives, and their freedoms. For Americans, these have a lot more "intrinsic value" than the Pallid Sturgeon or the Piping Plover.

Without answers from Corps, public blames flood on plovers*
June 9, 2011
Written by: Matt Bunk

A month ago, Mark Unterseher was fishing off sandbars near his home on the heavily wooded shoreline less than two miles northwest of Bismarck city limits. He says he was doing the same thing in April while the Missouri River was flowing lazily past his neighborhood at a depth of just more than six feet.

Unterseher, 44, said it's hard not to think about those days now that the river is nearly three times deeper and his home is filling up with water.

"It shouldn't have been this way," he said Tuesday while piling sandbags in front of his neighbor's home. "For most of the spring there were sandbars over the whole damn river."

The period between late March and early May is something the Army Corps of Engineers has been trying really hard not to talk about. During that 45-day period, the agency's water managers stored near-record amounts of water in the reservoir behind Gar-

*http://www.greatplainsexaminer.com/2011/06/09/without-answers-from-corps-public-blames-flood-on-plovers/

rison Dam while keeping river levels low, despite evidence that
there was about 30 percent more snow in the mountains than normal.

Instead of explaining what their strategy was during the months
leading up to the flood, top officials with the Corps of **Engineers**
have offered cryptic answers while pointing to their operations
manuals.

"We were operating the mainstem reservoirs in compliance with
our master manual," said Jody Farhat, chief of Missouri River basin
water management for the Corps of Engineers. When asked to elaborate, she repeated the same line.

Without answers, people who live along the river have done a bit
of their own detective work. Many of them suspect the Corps of
Engineers was trying to protect the habitat of federally protected
birds. Others are convinced spring floods in the lower basin of the
Missouri River may have prompted the Corps to hold more water
behind the dams farther north.

Corps of Engineers officials denied both of those assertions and insisted that they have been operating in "flood-control mode" at Garrison Dam since the beginning of the year. But **public records**
maintained by the agency tell a different story about the way the
dam was managed during the two months prior to the flood.

To gather the information for this report, the Great Plains Examiner
spent nearly two weeks comparing sets of data on release rates and
storage levels recorded by the Corps of Engineers as far back as 1967
when the dam began operating. Additional research included
studying operations manuals that guide the agency's decisions and
interviewing dozens of local leaders, federal officials, biologists and
hydrologists from North Dakota and across the U.S.

Daily logs kept by the Corps of Engineers show that the agency
began 2011 on an aggressive schedule to draw down the levels at
Lake Sakakawea, releasing high amounts of water through the dam
in January, February and the beginning of March. The average release of about 25,000 cubic feet per second during the first two-and-
a-half months was almost twice as much as the average rate for that
time of year.

Instead of continuing that pattern, though, the agency curtailed the releases from March 20 until May 5, allowing the reservoir to rise to about eight feet above average for that time of year while the river ran through Bismarck at its seasonal low point. Prior to slowing the release rate, the Corps had received data showing above-average snowpack in the mountains overlooking the upper river basin.

Everything changed rapidly in mid-May when heavy rain in Montana forced the Corps of Engineers to start draining Lake Sakakawea to avoid overflowing the dam. But each time the agency pushed more water through the dam, the rain came down even harder; statistics for the month show the amount of water that flowed into the reservoir was nearly double the amount that was released into the river.

Farhat said a year's worth of rain flowed into Lake Sakakawea at the end of May. "The game-changer was the rain," she said.

In June, the agency opened the Garrison Dam spillway gates for the first time ever as the rate of release ramped up to more than 120,000 cubic feet per second, about twice as much water as the previous record. Within days, floodwaters overtook communities along the river from Montana to Missouri and forced thousands of residents to evacuate their homes. In Burleigh and Morton counties, more than 700 households were given notice to evacuate and thousands of other houses are in jeopardy as the rate of release is expected to reach 150,000 cubic feet per second by mid-June.

Many residents of Bismarck-Mandan have questioned why the Corps of Engineers didn't release more water earlier in the spring, especially considering there was so much snow in the mountains.

"The river could have handled more water early this spring," said **Brent Hanson, a Bismarck resident who works at a boat dealership and marina next to the river.** "They could have raised it more than five feet without causing any flooding here, then maybe we wouldn't have had to deal with as much water now."

Unterseher said the Corps of Engineers screwed something up, no matter how a person looks at it.

"It's hard to blame somebody for this," he said. **"But it has to be**

mismanagement. This is pathetic."

Water-management experts said the Corps of Engineers eventually will have to explain why so little water was released in the months leading up to the flood.

"What were they doing in the winter months and early spring when this was building?" asked Larry Larson, executive director of the Association of State Floodplain Managers. "Were they preparing for it, or were they playing the odds and then found themselves caught in a box?"

Farhat said flooding was unavoidable because the amount of rain in May made it impossible to store all the water flowing into Lake Sakakawea. She said higher releases through the Garrison Dam during early spring may have caused ice jams and flooding, similar to what Bismarck-Mandan experienced in 2009. But neither of those statements explains what the Corps of Engineers was doing in April after the ice had receded from the river.

"The main stem reservoir system has been operated in full flood-control mode since the high water of 2010," she said. "We have not made any operational decisions this year for anything other than flood control."

Col. Robert Ruch, commander of the Omaha division of the Corps of Engineers, took it one step further, saying "In hindsight, I can't imagine doing anything differently."
Despite daily press conferences and several appearances at community meetings, officials with the Corps of Engineers have not explained what, if anything, went wrong other than several unpredictable rainstorms. However, a review of the agency's master manual for the Missouri River system and its 2011 operating plan shows the agency was directed to follow regulations that encourage water storage in the reservoirs in the upper basin of the Missouri River during early spring for several reasons.

The Corps of Engineers has been instructed to save water in the reservoirs during spring so it can be sold to agricultural and industrial interests year-round; to ensure enough water is available during the summer to keep the river high enough for navigation and recreation; to maintain consistent production of hydropower during all seasons; and **to limit releases during spring and summer to pro-tect habitat for federally protected birds.**

It's that last item that really grinds on people like Unterseher.

"The birds had something to do with it," he said. "That's what I believe anyway."

Two bird species, the piping plover and the least tern, migrate to the Missouri River basin during the spring nesting season, which starts in early May. **In the past, the Corps of Engineers has taken steps to protect the birds, including dredging parts of the river to create sandbars and cutting down vegetation on existing sandbars to give the birds an unobstructed view of predators.**
"As in previous years, releases from Garrison will follow a repetitive daily pattern during the (threatened and endangered birds) nesting season to limit peak stages below the project for nesting birds," officials noted in the Corps of Engineers' 2011 operating plan for the Missouri River. **"All reasonable measures to minimize the loss of nesting (threatened and endangered) bird species will be used."**

The Corps of Engineers has been falling short of its bird-habitat requirements in recent years and was under pressure from the U.S. Fish and Wildlife Service to create and maintain more acreage of sandbars. Most of the piping plovers and least terns choose nesting grounds south of Gavins Point Dam, but some migrate to the area between Garrison Dam and Lake Oahe.

Ruch, Farhat and other officials with the Corps of Engineers have said repeatedly that the agency at the beginning of the year abandoned all plans to protect the sandbar habitat for piping plovers and the least terns.

"There has been zero water managed for endangered species this year," Ruch said.

Henry Maddux, geographic supervisor of the Missouri River for U.S. Game and Fish, said the Corps of Engineers notified his office that the conditions this spring made it impossible to protect habitat for endangered and threatened birds. He said that notification was given in late April, just before nesting season.

"There was nothing done for ☐r species this year," he said. "They didn't hold water back for u☐"

The Corps of Engineers also ☐nceled the two "pulses" planned for March and May that would ☐ mally have called for higher, short-term releases from Garrison ☐m to create more suitable conditions downstream for the pallid s☐rgeon. Those operations were canceled because the Corps' w☐r managers were concerned about worsening the flood conditi☐s in lower-basin states such as Nebraska, where the river had r☐ed flood stage in early April, Maddux said.

So was the Corps of Engineers ☐eping water releases low at Garrison during April to prevent more severe flooding in the lower reaches of the Missouri River or even the Mississippi River? **The Corps of Engineers, once again, avoided anything resembling a real answer.**

"We coordinate our releases with our sister district along the Mississippi River, but we do not make release decisions based on conditions along the Mississippi River," Farhat said.

The public isn't alone in its frustration with the Corps of Engineers' water-management techniques. On Tuesday, U.S. Sen. John Hoeven joined several other elected ☐fficials in states along the Missouri River to call for a thorough a☐r-action review of this year's event, including a review of the mas☐r manual, the Corps' principal guide to managing river operation☐

"Taking a hard look at this ye☐'s flooding and the Corps' response to it could help us improve o☐ mitigation efforts in the future," Hoeven stated. "That has to b☐ part of our larger response to this flood."

Research shows that the annu☐ "incidental take" of Piping Plovers, caused by the United States Ar☐y Corps of Engineers, may not have any effect whatsoever on the lo☐g term viability of the Piping Plover. In the 2009 paper, entitled: "<u>A ☐antitative framework to evaluate incidental take and endangered ☐ecies population viability</u>," the authors, C.P. McGowan and M.☐ Ryan, of the Department of Fisheries and Wildlife Sciences, Universit☐ of Missouri, stated:

"After these extensive population modeling exercises the question still remains: Does incidental take of eggs and chicks in the Missouri River cause jeopardy for Piping Plovers in the Great Plains? Our population model predicts that even with incidental take components set to zero, the population was still declining by over 7% annually. It could be argued that the actions by the USACE do not cause jeopardy because the population faces such a high level of jeopardy in the absence of this specific take."

The following letter appeared in the Sioux City Journal

'I hope the plover are happy'*

Friday, July 29, 2011

NORTH SIOUX CITY - A year or so ago, I talked to a park ranger in Yankton, S.D., while watching the Missouri River from an overlook near Yankton. **I casually asked the ranger why the Corps was holding back so much water in the spring. "To protect the plover,"** he replied, as if it were common knowledge. "The what?" I inquired. "The plover - it is a shore bird that nests along the Missouri. If they let out too much water in the spring, it drowns out their nests and kills the baby birds. So the Corps holds it back to allow the birds to hatch." How noble, I thought - we hold back mighty waters to protect bird life.

Fast forward to the spring of 2011. **As I watched my friends in Dakota Dunes frantically trying to escape the mighty floodwaters released in record amounts by the Corps, while their houses are ruined by the Muddy Mo, and my friends, neighbors, and family members worked feverishly to protect our own homes and each others' homes in Wynstone - up river a ways - I thought a lot about the plover.**

Folks around here are asking: **"Why is the Corps just now releasing record amounts of water, thereby creating a flood of epic proportions, the likes of which have never been experienced in recorded history?"** If purposely flooding the folks on the Missouri River from Yankton down to Omaha and below is "flood control," [sic] then **"flood control" is the biggest and cruelest oxymoron ever.** Given that the United States experienced record amounts of snow and moisture last winter and this spring, it is certainly fair to ask: Did the Corps not anticipate that the reservoirs upstream in

*http://www.siouxcityjournal.com/news/opinion/mailbag/article_0ad77a79-1bcd-5653-bddd-e05e33750417.html

South Dakota would be brim full? Was there no thought given to the idea of releasing water incrementally over the past many months so as to avoid the largest single release of waters in history and the horrendous man-made catastrophe that has befallen our friends and neighbors along the Missouri?

Perhaps this is about the plov... or perhaps this is just about a government agency asleep at the switch. **Perhaps it is a little of both. Either way the result is just the same - misguided government policy, and failure to anticipate that which any reasonable person would anticipate, has caused and continues to cause needless destruction of property and liv... tragically interrupted.**

If this example of "flood con... " [sic] is any indication of how the government is going to run o... health care system, God help us all. I hope the plover, at least, a... appy. **It does not look so good for us humans right now.**

- William Kevin Stoos

Americans are not stupid. Naive, perhaps, but not stupid. Most of us go about our daily lives, working hard, raising our children and spoiling our grandchildren. In most cases, we choose to ignore the government, knowing full well they don't operate with any sort of high efficiency, but at least thinking they are trying to do the right thing.

Every once and a while, though, the people have to wake government up, and get them pointed back in the right direction. I believe that time has arrived. As Mr. Stoos points out clearly:

"It does not look good for us humans right now."

It is time for Congress to act, and act decisively.

"True patriotism hates injustice in its own land more than anywhere else."
Abraham Lincoln

Missouri River Flood May Aid Protected Birds, Fish

By JAMES MacPHERSON Associated Press
BISMARCK, N.D. June 6, 2011 (AP)

The swollen Missouri River that promises to be a prolonged headache for small towns and farmers along its path is likely to be a boon for several protected and endangered species living in or near its basin, biologists say.

The piping plovers and interior least terns that lay eggs on the river's sandbars are likely to find more room to do so once the river recedes. The pallid sturgeon, a fish also classified as endangered, is likely to benefit from increased nutrients and organic matter carried and deposited by the high water, which mimics the Missouri's flow before it was dammed starting some 60 years ago, said Greg Pavelka, a U.S. Army Corps of Engineers wildlife biologist at Yankton, S.D.

It could leave behind a more natural habitat than the area's native species have seen in decades.

"The former function of the river is being restored in this one-year event," Pavelka said. "In the short term, it could be detrimental, but in the long term it could be very beneficial."

Flood concerns are high along the Missouri as massive amounts of water are released far upstream from dams along the river's length. Last month's heavy rains in the Northern Plains prompted corps to let water out faster, and heavy snowpack in the Rocky Mountains still must make its way down the river. Authorities are re-enforcing levees and evacuating some low-lying areas near the river from the South Dakota capital of Pierre to the Iowa-Missouri border, where crews dropped massive sandbags Monday to after several small breaches along earthen flood walls.

The swollen Missouri River is causing headaches for cities and homeowners but the river's swift run is likely to be a boon for the piping plover, an endangered species, that will likely find more room to nest on the river's sandbars once it recedes. Wildlife near the river is coping with disruption, too.

A stretch of the river between Fort Peck, Mont., and Sioux City, Iowa, is designated as critical habitat for the plover and least tern, whose sand-colored eggs are tougher for predators to spot on sandbars. Yet most of that habitat is either under water or will be soon, said Kelly Crane, a corps biologist in Omaha, Neb.

Some piping plovers have been spotted building their nests on gravel boat ramp parking lots near the Garrison Dam, about 75 miles upstream of Bismarck. No nests have been detected this spring for the least tern.

The corps, which manages dams and reservoirs along the 2,341-mile river, has spent $40 million since 2004 building habitat for birds in the upper portion of the river because the reservoir system restricts the natural creation of sandbars, said Crane, who manages the corps' sandbar restoration project.

Crane said the sandbar work won't be wasted. The deep water and high river flows should deposit more sediment on the sandbars and expand them.

I realize America is an affluent nation, but $40,000,000.00 on sandbars for Piping Plovers is a bit much, from my point of view. How many starving children in Africa can you save with $40,000,000.00? Kelly Crane, the corps biologist, says " **the sandbar work won't be wasted, the deep water and high river flows should deposit more sediment on the sandbars and expand them."** Some Americans, myself included, might argue that the money has already been wasted. As far as the sandbars still being there after the flood, last time I checked, high river flows can also wash away sandbars.

In addition to the 40 million dollar Sandbar Project, the U.S. Army Corps of Engineers, also has a multi-million dollar Predator Control Program* for the Piping Plover. It also mows the 40 million dollar sandbars, so that the Piping Plovers can see the wily predators approaching. Having personally spent hundreds of hours behind a mower on the family farm, and seen dozens of bird and rabbit nests go shooting out the mower discharge, I wonder if it occurred to the United States Army Corps of Engineers that maybe this mowing is why the Piping Plover populations are dropping 7% a year? You don't need a degree in biology to tell that, once hit with a mower, birds and rabbits are pretty well done "populating."

*Predator Management Plan for the Least Tern and Piping Plover along the Missouri River

Grill serving Missouri River endangered species in flood-threatened Hamburg?**

Hamburg, Ia. — Vicky Shin isn't really serving up endangered species at her Blue Moon Bar & Grill in Hamburg despite the sign up front offering to grill or fry them.

But she is dishing up a lot of hamburgers to workers finishing a levee intended to stop the raging Missouri River from washing over the southern end of this town of 1,100 in extreme southwest Iowa. Residents living on high ground also have helped boost business so much, the restaurant added Sunday hours.

"Now serving pallid sturgeon, piping plover. Any way you want," the sign reads, offering a side of tongue in cheek, and a dash of frustration.

The sturgeon is a prehistoric fish and the piping plover is a shore bird. Both are on the federal endangered species list. The U.S. Army Corps of Engineers has been required to manage the Missouri River to protect the species while also trying to prevent floods and to keep boaters happy.

Many in Hamburg and other spots up and down the Missouri River say people should get more protection than the imperiled fish and bird.

That's a debate for another day. On Saturday, city workers downtown said they were heading out to the levee to apply plastic to the top after a private crew left. Most large equipment sat idle near the levee.

The nearly 3-mile-long berm appeared to be holding strong, as did another levee under an Interstate Highway 29 bridge on the south edge of town.

Esther Barrett — Shin's aunt — sat outside the Blue Moon puffing a cigarette and reveling in her niece's good fortune. Barrett and Shi 43, both live on high ground, and Blue Moon is doing better business than ever, even with several hundred residents gone to higher ground in case the flood creeps into town.

A block to the north, the Harvest Inn's sign advertises a Sunday fish

**http://blogs.desmoinesregister.com/dmr/index.php/2011/06/18/grill-serving-missouri-river-endangered-species-in-flood-threatened-hamburg/

fry. But no endangered species are mentioned, and the place is closed due to the flood.

"We're the only place open in town," save a Casey's convenience store that is moving a lot of pizza, chicken nuggets, and other goodies, said Barrett, 76. "It's been lively around here."

Shin wasn't around, but Barrett said the sign was Shin's idea. "She put that out there," Barrett said.

Customers pass through a gap in a huge sandbag and dirt berm to get to the restaurant, stepping over a low string of sandbags soaked by rain Friday night.

In Council Bluffs, there were still a few flood-related detours around town, but people mainly went about their business. Near the Horseshoe casino, electrical equipment along the road had been sandbagged but the facade of Hooters restaurant remained bare.

Harrah's casino did its own rumor control. "We're open," an electronic sign flashed in huge letters along Interstate Highway 29.

The National Weather Service reported the river was at a steady height, more or less, and could drop slightly over the next few days.

The U.S. Army Corps of Engineers indicated Friday that rainfall would have to become extreme to change the flow of the river much. The releases from Gavins Point Dam near Yankton, S.D., still running at twice the previous record, are the big driver now.

The mighty Missouri River: the flooding and the damage done

Reuters, by David Bailey and David Hendee | Reuters – Sat, Sep 3, 2011

MINNEAPOLIS/COUNCIL BLUFFS, Iowa (Reuters) - **The cost of America's quiet billion dollar disaster in the Upper Midwest keeps rising as floodwaters decline.**

Shortly before Memorial Day, a summer of unprecedented flood-

ing from Montana to Missouri along the Missouri River started
washing away interstate highway lanes and swamping rail lines as
it routed thousands of people from their homes.

Flooding continues this Labor Day weekend and is expected not to
end for several more weeks. As the water recedes, the extent of damage from three months of flooding is showing up.

In cities such as Pierre, South Dakota's capital, the receding floodwaters have left behind sinkholes in roads and parks and begun to
reveal widespread damage to storm sewer systems, public softball
fields and a city golf course.

"We are just now, as the river is going back, really seeing what the
damage is," Pierre Mayor Laurie Gill said.

**Along the riverbanks, the U.S. Army Corps of Engineers estimates
the cost of repairing its levees and patching up its dams from
Montana to Nebraska could top $1 billion.**

Behind breached levees and across the floodplains, the estimated
cost of fixing damaged roads, rail lines, bridges and other infrastructure is swelling in time and dollars.

States in the Midwest are competing for attention, and for federal
dollars, with other disasters that have struck since the flooding, including Hurricane Irene on the East Coast at the end of August.

Heavy rains and snow melt in the Northern Plains this spring forced
the Corps to release record volumes of water out of its reservoirs,
causing historic and persistent flooding.

Along the Nebraska-Iowa border, the three-mile-long Interstate 680
link between Omaha, Nebraska, and Interstate 29 north of Council
Bluffs in western Iowa was destroyed.

The south-flowing current reduced the east-west-aligned lanes to
rubble. Rebuilding the highway is expected to take until at least November 2012.

Debris and floodwater still covers most of the 22 miles of I-29 north
of Council Bluffs to Missouri Valley, Iowa. Iowa officials hope to

open that stretch of road this fall.

Floodwater is undermining and scouring I-29 near Hamburg in southwest Iowa. The Interstate -- the main route from Kansas City, Missouri, to Canada -- has been closed in southwest Iowa most of the summer.

RAIL AND ROAD DIVERSIONS
Iowa road officials don't expect floodwater to recede enough to assess damage along all of I-29 until mid October.
Floodwater flowed across Iowa Highway 2 between I-29 and Nebraska City, Nebraska, all summer. Engineers expect to find nothing but concrete debris when the water goes down.

The cost of I-29 repairs alone could be tens of millions of dollars, according to the Iowa Department of Transportation, but they hope to open the route by the end of the year.

The damage to I-29 extends into northwest Missouri, where some 65 miles of mainly lower volume roads are water-covered. Many roads have been inundated for more than two months.

Missouri hopes to have the majority of road repairs completed by the end of the year, said Rick Bennett, a traffic liaison engineer coordinating Missouri efforts. Shoulder damage could be repaired by October or November, he said.

Inspections have found holes in roads, at least one up to 30 feet deep, that will take longer to repair, he said.

This is the worst flood damage to roads in Missouri in the last four to five years, but: "The flood of 93 was a magnitude worse than this one," Bennett said.

The major river bridges into Missouri from Nebraska and Kansas that are closed were not damaged on the Missouri side, but there is some significant damage to pavement leading to bridges on Highways 136 and 159, officials said.

While highways in the region took the brunt of flooding, railroads have poured hundreds of millions of dollars into raising tracks in an often-futile race with floodwaters.

BNSF Railway, based in Fort Worth, Texas, expects to spend more than $300 million to restore and harden its rail network, said John P. Lanigan Jr., executive vice president.

Flooding severed BNSF's busy St. Joseph, Missouri, corridor. It was scheduled to reopen September 3, but persistent high water was expected to keep nearby lines in the Omaha area out of service until late September or early October.

BNSF raised miles of track by up to eight feet, built levees and berms to protect rails and repaired and replaced hundreds of miles of damaged track, bridges and structures.

The railroad also rerouted up to 40 percent of its trains and shifted nearly 500 BNSF employees temporarily to handle the change.

Union Pacific Railroad, based in Omaha, spent about $14 million on materials and other flood-related efforts, spokesman Mark Davis said.

The railroad lost about $20 million in coal revenue during the first month of flooding alone, he said. Crews raised nearly 75 miles of track and nine bridges in northeast Kansas and northwest Missouri.

2011 Missouri Flooding

A multi-billion dollar catastrophe that maybe didn't have to happen. Was it caused by holding back water to protect the Piping Plover? I can't say with certainty. The above articles are all written by local people and reporters, on the scene. I have a propensity to believe them, and will be very leery of governmental reports and coverups. I do know with certainty it wasn't the first time this sort of thing has happened.

> "Those who don't know history are destined to repeat it."
> Edmund Burke

Flood, Deaths Blamed on Endangered Species Act*

Delays in repairing California's Feather River levee system due to **Endangered Species Act (ESA) regulations contributed to a severe flood that caused three deaths and forced 32,000 people to flee from their homes.** For six years prior to the 1997 flood, the Army Corps of Engineers and local flood control officials had warned that the levee in the town of Arboga needed repairs. The Corps of Engineers report specifically stated that **"Loss of human life is expected under existing conditions** (without remedial repairs) for major flood events." Despite this warning, **the United States Fish and Wildlife Service insisted that lengthy studies had to been done to determine the impact repair work would have on the Valley Elderberry Longhorn Beetle - a protected species.** The Valley Elderberry Longhorn Beetle lives in elderberry bushes. Since 43 bushes would be cleared away on the levee, **federal regulators forced local officials to spend $10 million replanting 7,500 elderberry stems on an 80-acre site.** In addition, the local flood control authority, California Reclamation District 784 (RD 784), complained it was prevented from performing necessary maintenance tasks such as clearing brush and controlling rodents that burrow in the earthen dams because of ESA regulations. Officials also objected to the requirement that they build a wetland within 600 feet of the levee over concerns that water from the 17-foot-deep pond would seep into the levee and weaken it. **When the levee broke on January 2, 1997, 25 square miles of property and habitat were flooded.** Ironically, the 80-acre plot of newly-planted elderberry bushes was also destroyed. RD 784 officials and local congressmen said that the ESA red tape that delayed the vital repair work for so long contributed to the collapse of the levee.
Source: Testimony of Rep. Wally Herger before the U.S. House of Representatives Committee on Resources, April 10, 1997

*Shattered Dreams, 100 Stories of Government Abuse, National Center for Public Policy Research

Three people are dead because of the Valley Elderberry Longhorn Beetle, one of 350,000 species of beetles worldwide. That is a a heinous crime against humanity.

$10,000,000.00 to plant 7500 elderberry stems ($1,333.33 per stem)? That is heinous crime against the American taxpayer, by a Federal bureaucracy, that has, clearly, lost all sense of reality. I found elderberry stems for sale on the web for $7.00/stem. I once was a commercial rose grower. We used to plant 12,000 rose bushes in a day, with a crew of twenty men, all earning minimum wage plus $1.00, which is (today) $8.25 an hour. Let's say it took myself and the crew 6 hours to plant the 7500 elderberry stems. Being 115 degrees in the greenhouses in the middle of July, and having just completed our task for the day, I decide we're going to have a cold beer for the crew (think <u>Shawshank Redemption</u>). It's a government project, right? How much money do we have left for beer?

$10,000,000.00 minus $52,500 (for the elderbeery stems) minus $1320.00 (for planting labor,) leaves $9,946,180.00 to buy the beer.

Mmmm. Maybe these bureaucrats aren't so dumb after all.

Valley Elderberry Longhorn Beetle

The Purposeful Flooding of America's Heartland*

By Joe Herring

The Missouri River basin encompasses a vast region in the central and west-central portion of our country. This river, our nation's longest, collects the melt from Rocky Mountain snowpack and the runoff from our continents' upper plains before joining the Mississippi river above St. Louis some 2,300 miles later. It is a mighty river, and dangerous.

Some sixty years ago, the U.S. Army Corps of Engineers (USACE) began the process of taming the Missouri by constructing a series of six dams. The idea was simple: massive dams at the top moderating flow to the smaller dams below, generating electricity while providing desperately needed control of the river's devastating floods.

The stable flow of water allowed for the construction of the concrete and earthen levees that protect more than 10 million people who reside and work within the river's reach. It allowed millions of acres of floodplain to become useful for farming and development. In fact, these uses were encouraged by our government, which took credit for the resulting economic boom. By nearly all measures, the project was a great success.

But after about thirty years of operation, **as the environmentalist movement gained strength throughout the seventies and eighties, the Corps received a great deal of pressure to include some specific environmental concerns into their MWCM (Master Water Control Manual, the "bible" for the operation of the dam system). Preservation of habitat for at-risk bird and fish populations soon became a hot issue among the burgeoning environmental lobby.** The pressure to satisfy the demands of these groups grew exponentially as **politicians eagerly traded their common sense for "green" political support.**

Things turned absurd from there. An idea to restore the nation's rivers to a natural (pre-dam) state swept through the environmental movement and their allies. Adherents enlisted the aid of the U.S. Fish and Wildlife Service (FWS), asking for an updated "Biological Opinion" from the FWS that would make ecosystem restoration an "authorized purpose" of the dam system. The Clinton administra-

*http://www.americanthinker.com/2011/06/the_purposeful_flooding_of_americas_heartland.html

tion threw its support behind the change, officially shifting the priorities of the Missouri River dam system from flood control, facilitation of commercial traffic, and recreation to habitat restoration, wetlands preservation, and culturally sensitive and sustainable biodiversity.

Congress created a committee to advise the Corps on how best to balance these competing priorities. The Missouri River Recovery and Implementation Committee has seventy members. **Only four represent interests other than environmentalism.** The recommendations of the committee, as one might expect, have been somewhat less than evenhanded.

The Corps began to utilize the dam system to mimic the previous flow cycles of the original river, holding back large amounts of water upstream during the winter and early spring in order to release them rapidly as a "spring pulse." The water flows would then be restricted to facilitate a summer drawdown of stream levels. This new policy was highly disruptive to barge traffic and caused frequent localized flooding, but **a multi-year drought masked the full impact of the dangerous risks the Corps was taking.**

This year, despite more than double the usual amount of mountain and high plains snowpack (and the ever-present risk of strong spring storms), the true believers in the Corps have persisted in following the revised MWCM, **recklessly endangering millions of residents downstream.**

Missouri Senator Roy Blunt agrees, calling the management plan "flawed" and "poorly thought out." Sen. Blunt characterized the current flooding as "entirely preventable" and told reporters that he intends to force changes to the plan.

Perhaps tellingly, not everyone feels the same apprehension toward the imminent disaster.

Greg Pavelka, a wildlife biologist with the Corps of Engineers in Yankton, SD, told the Seattle Times that this event will leave the river in a "much more natural state than it has seen in decades," describing the epic flooding as a "prolonged headache for small towns and farmers along its path, but a boon for endangered species." He went on to say, "The former function of the river is

A few images of what a U.S. government biologist callously describes as "prolonged headache for small towns and farmers along its path, but a boon for endangered species."

being restored in this one-year event. In the short term, it could be detrimental, but in the long term it could be very beneficial."

At the time of this writing, the Corps is scrambling for political cover, repeatedly denying that it had any advance warning of the potential for this catastrophe. The official word is that everything was just fine until unexpectedly heavy spring rains pushed the system past the tipping point.

On February 3, 2011, a series of e-mails from Ft. Pierre SD Director of Public Works Brad Lawrence sounded the alarm loud and clear. In correspondence to the headquarters of the American Water Works Association in Washington, D.C., Lawrence warned that "the Corps of Engineers has failed thus far to evacuate enough water from the main stem reservoirs to meet normal runoff conditions. This year's runoff will be anything but normal."

In the same e-mail, he describes the consequences of the Corps

failure to act as a "flood of biblical proportions." His e-mails were forwarded from Washington, D.C. to state emergency response co-ordinators nationwide. The Corps headquarters in Omaha, NE which is responsible for the Missouri river system, claims they heard no such warning from Lawrence or anyone else. Considering the wide distribution of this correspondence, and the likely reactions from officials in endangered states, **their denials strain credulity.**

Whether warned or not, the fact remains that had the Corps been true to its original mission of flood control, the dams would not have been full in preparation for a "spring pulse." The dams could further have easily handled the additional runoff without the need to inundate a sizeable chunk of nine states. The Corps admits in the MWCM that they deliberately embrace this risk each year in order to maximize their re-ordered priorities.

MWCM (Sec 7-07.2.6):

" **Releases at higher-than-normal rates early in the season that cannot be supported by runoff forecasting techniques is inconsistent with all System purposes other than flood control.** All of the other authorized purposes depend upon the accumulation of water in the System rather than the availability of vacant storage space. [Emphasis added.]"

Perhaps the environmentalists of the Corps grew tired of waiting decades to realize **their dream of a "restored Missouri River."** Perhaps these elements heard the warnings and saw in them an opportunity to force an immediate re-naturalization of the river via epic flood. At present, that is impossible to know, but to needlessly imperil the property, businesses, and lives of millions of people constitutes criminal negligence. Given the statements of Corps personnel, and the clear evidence of their mismanagement, the possibility that there is specific intent behind their failure to act must be investigated without delay.

In recent decades, many universities have steeped their Natural Sciences curriculum in the green tea of earth-activism, producing radically eco-centric graduates who naturally seek positions with the government agencies where they can best implement their theories. Today, many of these men and women have risen high

in their fields, hiring fellow t[...]velers to fill subordinate positions and creating a powerful echo chamber of radical environmentalist theory.

The U.S. Army Corps of Engineers is a victim/tool of the above-described process. The horrifying consequence is water rushing from the dams on the Missouri twice as fast as the highest previous releases on record. Floodgates that have not been opened in more than fifty years are in full operation, discharging water at a rate of 150,000 cubic feet per second toward millions of Americans downstream.

This is a mind-boggling rate of release. Consider that 150,000 cubic feet of water would fill a football field instantly to a depth of four feet. **This amount of water, being released every second, will continue unabated for the next several months.** The levees that protect the cities and towns downstream were constructed to handle the flow rates promised at the time of the dam's construction. None of these levees have ever been tested at these levels, yet they must hold back millions of acre-feet of floodwater for the entire summer without failing. In the flood of 1993, more than a thousand levees failed. This year's event will be many orders of magnitude greater.

There are many well-publicized examples of absurd obeisance to the demands of radical environmentalists resulting in great economic harm. The Great Missouri River Flood of 2011 is shaping up to be another -- only this time, the price will likely be paid in lives lost as well as treasure. Ayn Rand said, "You can avoid reality, but you cannot avoid the consequences of avoiding reality."

We need to begin the investigations immediately. It seems that it is sanity, and not the river, that needs to be restored.

I asked former U.S. Fish and Wildlife Service officer Jim Beers about the makeup of personnel in that agency. I said to him, "Jim, I do not want to harm the many good people that have to be working in that department." He said to me:

"John, this is what I explain to people when I am out on the lecture tour. Suppose the United States Department of Defense were to hire a young Quaker lad. Over a period of time, he would encourage his

friends to also come work in the Defense Department. They, in turn, would encourage their friends. After 30 years of this, what kind of Defense Department would we have?"

And so it is with the U.S. Fish & Wildlife Service (and other governmental agencies.) Years ago, sportsmen dominated this service, encouraging hunting, fishing, outdoor recreation, forestry, proper wildlife management, and the wise use of our nation's natural, renewable resources. Now, instead of sportsmen and conservationists, we have "tree huggers", intent on stopping all use of America's resources, and consequently, destroying our economy.

The final bills for this year's flooding has not yet been tallied, as the day of this writing is September 21, 2011, and much of the flood waters are still receding. The article "**The mighty Missouri River: the flooding and the damage done**", quoted earlier and dated September 3, 2011, put the damage to the levees at 1 billion dollars. Just two weeks later, September 19, 2011, the Corps changed its mind, and decided to double the damage estimate to $2,000,000,000.00.

Corps Pegs 2011 Flood Damage to Levees at $2B*

By Heather Hollingsworth | September 19, 2011

The U.S. Army Corps of Engineers estimates it will cost more than $2 billion to repair the damage to the nation's levees, dams and riverbanks caused by this year's excessive flooding, a sum that dwarfs $150 million it currently has to make such repairs and that doesn't account for damage from Hurricane Irene or Tropical Storm Lee.

Floodwaters that raged down the nation's rivers this year have strained dams, eroded riverbanks, filled harbors with silt and ripped football field-sized holes in some earthen levees protecting farmland and small towns. The damage estimate, confirmed to The Associated Press by corps officials, promises to be more significant than with a typical flood in which high water recedes quickly.
The estimate does not factor in flood damage caused by Hurricane Irene and Tropical Storm Lee, and the corps does not have an estimate of the damage from those storms yet.
Along some stretches of the Missouri River, levees have been hold-

http://www.google.com/hostednews/ap/article/ALeqM5gkLn7cjZwg385lld7y8GACwMmaBQ?docId=6eb66f48718e4d0d83f22e5db8598e53

ing back floodwaters since June 1 as the corps lowered water levels from upstream dams that had filled to overflowing with record runoff from rain and winter snows. That water ultimately proved too much for many levees downstream in states such as Iowa and Missouri. Record high water levels also created havoc along the lower Mississippi from Missouri to Louisiana.

"I'm really nervous about it," Tom Waters, chairman of the Missouri Levee and Drainage District Association, said of the limited resources. "I think the corps is real nervous about it, too."

The Senate is considering a $7 billion emergency disaster relief bill, but only $1.3 billion of that would go to the corps. A competing House bill would allocate $3.7 billion to overall disaster aid, $226 million of it to the corps, although Congress could provide more money in future legislation.

Iowa Sen. Tom Harkin said he is working with senators in neighboring states to urge support for the emergency relief.

"I have seen firsthand some of the devastation along these rivers and local communities need financial assistance to recover," Harkin said.

Sensing it might not get all the money it needs, the corps is racing to repair the most essential damaged flood barriers before the spring runoff. Priority is being given to repairing damaged infrastructure that if left unfixed would put lives at risk when the snows start melting and the 2012 flood season begins. Repairs only meant to safeguard property from future damage would get second billing.

"We are trying to rack and stack them and see which projects need to be done quickly and which ones can be delayed for some time," said Jud Kneuvean, emergency management chief for the corps' Kansas City district. "And honestly some of them can't be delayed. There is a high likelihood for failure. The consequences associated with failure are high."

Crews have been bulldozing earth back into place along the Mississippi River's damaged floodwalls, but repairs along much of the Missouri River will have to wait until the water level fully re-

cedes, likely by October. A dry winter would allow repair work to continue, but ice and snow could force them to shut down temporarily.

"We've got to be ready to roll when the water recedes because time is our enemy," said Jud Kneuvean, emergency management chief for the corps' Kansas City district. "I will cross my fingers that it will be dry through the winter and spring."

In northwest Missouri's Holt County, more than 30 levee breaks inundated more than 230 square miles. Presiding commissioner Mark Sitherwood, whose own corn and soybean crops were ruined, said the levee damage will be in the millions.

"A lot of these little levee districts are sitting here with $20,000 in the bank," Sitherwood said. "They don't have that kind of money and the county certainly doesn't have the kind of money it's going to take to fix this. So Congress is going to have to step up."

Waters that overflowed their banks from coast to coast will make 2011 among the costliest years of flooding in U.S. history, yet will still fall far short of the damage caused by other large-scale events, such as Hurricane Katrina.

But the floods came in a year packed with disaster. In Missouri alone, historic flooding along the Mississippi River forced the intentional break of a levee that protected thousands of acres of prime farmland. In May, a monster tornado blamed for 162 deaths wiped away much of Joplin. Storms also devastated parts of the South, and Irene and Lee caused heavy flooding in parts of the Northeast.

"This year, as far as weather anomalies, has been unlike anything we've seen in a while," said corps spokeswoman Monique Farmer. "There is only so much money available to be spent on repairs from damages from all of the disasters that have taken place this year."

Kneuvean, who supervises a span of the Missouri River from Rulo, Neb., to St. Charles, Mo., has identified 53 repair projects, mostly levees, that need to be completed to restore the river to its pre-flood condition. He estimates it would cost $35 million to complete the projects, which amounts to a quarter of the money the corps currently has for repairs.

The corps estimates it would cost $460 million to repair the damage along the entire Missouri River, and rivers in the Pacific Northwest, including the Columbia, that overflowed their banks this spring.

Kneuvean said the potential funding shortfall could force branches of the corps that oversee different parts of the country to compete with each other for money.

"It's a tough spot to be in," Kneuvean said. "It's not a spot we wish we were in and it's one we wish we didn't have to put our stakeholders through."

Steve Wright, a corps spokesman, cautioned that Missouri River damage estimates are extremely preliminary and won't be complete until the water recedes to normal levels along the entire river.

Along the Mississippi, where floodwaters receded months ago and estimates are more solid, the preliminary repair total is about $780 million, including nearly $32 million for levee repair. The corps also must fix damage on small rivers including the Souris in North Dakota, which rose so high this year that it temporarily pushed 11,000 people from their homes and damaged hundreds of businesses.

Steve Ellwein, owner of an ice making company in Pierre, S.D., said he is confident the corps will find money to make the necessary repairs. The 61-year-old was forced to move back to his parents' home this summer as he waited to see if sandbags and pumps would keep water out of his house on the riverbank upstream from Fort Pierre.

"If they don't fix it — they're not that stupid. You would think they're not that stupid," he said. "I just don't believe they won't come up with the money to fix the reservoirs because then, if they don't, it makes all the problems worse."

Associated Press writer Kristi Eaton in Sioux Falls, S.D., contributed to this story

The government "not that stupid"? Unfortunately, as demonstrated throughout this book, that is wishful thinking. The following statement is from the United States Fish & Wildlife Service Recovery Plan for the Salt Creek Tiger Beetle.

RECOVERY OUTLINE
for the
Salt Creek tiger beetle
(Cicindela nevadica lincolniana)
Nebraska Ecological Services Field Office
February 2009

"Construction of levees, reservoirs, and additional channelization of Salt Creek resulted in the degradation and loss of saline wetlands and seeps and entrenchment of associated tributaries (Murphy 1992)."

As seen previously, the repair of life-saving levees was fought by the environmentalists in California, to save the Valley Elderberry Longhorn Beetle. Three people died because of it. In the floods of 2011, 368 people died.** Are the environmentalists any less enamored with the Salt Creek Tiger Beetle, found near Lincoln, Nebraska? The environmental movement got the flood it was hoping for. As they said, just a "headache" for the local residents, but a "boon for endangered species."

Does anyone think for a single minute that environmentalists won't try to delay the rebuilding of these levees, so that the Missouri River can return to its "natural" state?

The Disastrous Flood of 2011   **Salt Creek Tiger Beetle**

Army Corps sue over levee-building*

by Walter Olson on September 9, 200

Over the years the U.S. Army Corps of Engineers has proposed numerous levee and other public works projects aimed at reducing hurricane dangers to New Orleans and elsewhere in the Mississippi/Missouri river system. **nvironmental groups have sued, and sued, and sued, and sue and their lawsuits have often succeeded in stopping these flood-control measures.** (John Berlau, "Greens Vs. Levees", National Review Online, Sept. 8; Michael Tremoglie, "New Orleans: A Green Genocide", FrontPage, Sept. 8). Plus: Prof. Bainbridge (Sept. 9) has more details and spots a Los Angeles Times article raising the issue (Ralph Vartabedian and Peter Pae, "A Barrier That Could Have Been", Sept. 9). The article's summary line: **"Congress OKd a project to protect New Orleans 40 years ago, but an environmentalist suit halted it. Some say it could have worked."**

How much damage to our nation do we have to tolerate, in the name of "environmental protection" and "species diversity"? Why should we have to pay, over and over again, to rebuild levees, roads, homes, schools, churches, factories, and farmsflooded across the Midwest? Build the dams that will control the floods, and then use the dams as they were intended. Sandbars for Piping Plovers? They will find sandbars on their own, or learn to nest elsewhere. It is called adaptation.

There were at least 383 people killed** in the 2011 Missouri flooding. I am not a prosecuting attorney, but the actions of the U.S. Army Corps of Engineers appear to me to border on Criminally Negligent Homicide. Were the human beings living along the Missouri River told that protection of Piping Plover habitat was going to take precedent over the protection of human habitat? Was that decision ever voted on, or was it just shoved down the throats of the American people?

*http://overlawyered.com/2005/09/army-corps-sued-over-levee-building/
**http://en.wikipedia.org/wiki/2011_Mississippi_River_floods

Chapter 10

Environmental Totalitarianism

"Now observe that in all the propaganda of the ecologists—amidst all their appeals to nature and pleas for "harmony with nature"—there is no discussion of man's needs and the requirements of his survival. Man is treated as if he were an unnatural phenomenon. Man cannot survive in the kind of state of nature that the ecologist envision—i.e., on the level of sea urchins or polar bears....

In order to survive, man has to discover and produce everything he needs, which means that he has to alter his background and adapt it to his needs. Nature has not equipped him for adapting himself to his background in the manner of animals. From the most primitive cultures to the most advanced civilizations, man has had to manufacture things; his well-being depends on his success at production. The lowest human tribe cannot survive without that alleged source of pollution: fire. It is not merely symbolic that fire was the property of the gods which Prometheus brought to man. The ecologists are the new vultures swarming to extinguish that fire."
Ayn Rand (The Return of the Primitive: The Anti-Industrial Revolution)

Defintion of Totalitarianism: a political system where the state recognizes no limits to its authority and strives to regulate every aspect of public and private life wherever feasible.*

Call it Totalitarianism, Communism, Fascism, Naziism, Environmental Extremism, the Far Left. The ultimate goal is the elimination of individual freedoms and placing power in the hands of the governing few, usually under the guise of enriching everyone equally. The concept that Communism has gone underground into the Environmental Movement is not new. Sadly, it becomes abundantly clearer with each passing day, that this assessment is absolutely accurate. The implementer of this environmental extremism is our own U.S. governmental agency, the United States Fish and Wildlife Service. If allowed to continue unchanged and unchallenged, this law and this governmental department has the power to destroy our nation, as we know it. It is their viewpoint that they know what is best for the American people, and the entire planet.

*Wikipedia On-line Dictionary

"We are fast approaching the stage of the ultimate inversion: the stage where the government is free to do anything it pleases, while the citizens may act only by permission; which is the stage of the darkest periods of human history, the stage of rule by brute force."
Ayn Rand

The following is courtesy of DiscoverThe Networks.org, A Guide to the Political Left

DEFINING AND UNDERSTANDING THE LEFT

"The origins of the modern left can be traced back to the famous passage in Rousseau's Discourse on the Origin and Foundations of Inequality, in which he condemned the institution of private property:

"The first man, who after enclosing a piece of ground, took it into his head to say, 'this is mine,' and found people simple enough to believe him, was the real founder of civil society."

Added Rousseau: "How many crimes, how many wars, how many murders, how many misfortunes and horrors, would that man have saved the human species, who pulling up the stakes or filling up the ditches should have cried to his fellows: Beware of listening to this impostor; you are lost, if you forget that the fruits of the earth belong equally to us all, and the earth itself to nobody!"

Around the 1830s, a faction of French liberals gravitated toward Romanticism and the philosophy of the late Rousseau, proclaiming that capitalism, private property, and the increasing complexity of modern society were agents of moral decay -- both for the individual and for society at large. This is essentially the worldview that has made its way, through history, into the collective mind of the modern left; it is a worldview calling for a revolution that not only will topple the existing capitalist order and punish its corrupt leaders, but that also will replace that order with a socialist regime where the utopian ideals of perfect justice and equality will reign. Such an ambition can be put into effect only by a totalitarian state with the authority to micromanage every facet of human life, precisely the end-point toward which the policies and crusades of the modern left are directed.

The contemporary left hold that non-socialist societies are composed largely of dominators and the dominated, oppressors and the oppressed. The alleged cause this social arrangement is the economic system of free-market capitalism, which is viewed by the left as the root of all manner of social ills and vices -- racism, sexism, alienation, homophobia, imperialism. In the calculus of the left, capitalism is an agent of tyranny and exploitation that presses its boot upon the proverbial necks of a wide array of victim groups -- blacks and other minorities, women homosexuals, immigrants, and the poor, to name but a few. This is why according to the left, the United States (historically the standard-bearer of all capitalist economies) can only do wrong.

To eliminate America's inherent injustices, the left seeks to invert the power hierarchy, so that the groups now said to be oppressed become the privileged races and classes (and gender) of the new social order. The left's quest to transform the "dominated" into dominators, and vice versa, draws its inspiration from the Communist Manifesto, which asserts that "[t]he history of all hitherto existing society is the history of class struggle." The struggle identified by the Manifesto was that of the proletarians and their intellectual vanguard, who, armed with the radical utopian vision of socialism, were expected to launch a series of civil wars in their respective countries -- battles that would topple the "ruling classes" and the illegitimate societies they had established.

According to Marxist theory, these conflicts would rip each targeted society apart and create a new revolutionary world order from its ruins. In an effort to bring about this utopia, the contemporary left has formed a broad alliance, or united front, composed of radicals representing a host of demographic groups that are allegedly victimized by American capitalism and its related injustices. Each constituent of this alliance -- minorities, homosexuals, women, immigrants, the poor -- contributes its voice to a chorus that aims to discredit the United States specifically -- and Western culture generally -- as abusers of the vulnerable. **Nor is the left's list of victim groups limited only to human beings; in the worldview of left-wing environmentalists and animal rights activists, even certain species of shrubs, trees, insects, and rodents qualify as victims of capitalism's ravages."**

Capitalism, private property, and individual freedom is what has made America great. The Founding Fathers, believed in **equality of men at birth**, each born with certain inalienable rights. In establishing our nation's independence, and our Constitution, their goal was to create a governmental system where all men could pursue equally, "Life, Liberty, and the Pursuit of Happiness." As free individuals, how we pursue these lofty goals is up to us. Some run faster, work harder, are more gifted, and therefore, achieve more, than others. Nowhere in the writings of Thomas Jefferson, Thomas Paine, Samuel Adams, or John Adams, have I found a statement where the goal of the new American government was to create **the equality of men at the time of their death.** That is the goal of Marxism and Environmentalism, not the goal of America's Constitution, or its Founding Fathers.

> "America's abundance was created not by public sacrifices to the common good, but by the productive genius of free men who pursued their own personal interests and the making of their own private fortunes. They did not starve the people to pay for America's industrialization. They gave the people better jobs, higher wages, and cheaper goods with every new machine they invented, with every scientific discovery or technological advance- and thus the whole country was moving forward and profiting, not suffering, every step of the way."
> Ayn Rand

Federal Land Use Control
Through Ecosystem Management

By Henry Lamb

Private ownership of land

The hope of land ownership is the compelling force that brought people to America from the oppression of governments around the world. The right to own property is one of those "inalienable rights" described by Jefferson in the Declaration of Independence. The right to own land is a "natural right" demonstrated throughout nature. The term "own" land must be defined as the power to control the use of land. Throughout nature, every member of every species "owns" land. That is, every species in the universe controls the use of the space, and the resources contained therein, it requires to sustain its life. It controls that space until it is usurped by another. Such is the law of nature.

As early as 1651, Thomas Hobbes decried the plight of man living under the theory of natural law as "solitary, poore, nasty, brutish, and short." His solution: "The control of power must be lodged in a single person, and no individual can set their own private judgments of right and wrong in opposition to the sovereign's commands."[1] The sovereign, according to Hobbes, with absolute authority and power, could delegate land and resource use for the benefit of all.

John Locke countered the Hobbesian thought in 1690 with the idea that unowned things (resources) are not owned in common under the authority of the sovereign, but that ownership of any unowned thing belongs to its first possessor.[2] Locke says: "...every man has a property in his own person; this nobody has any right to but himself. The labour of his body and the work of his hands we may say are properly his."[3]

Man has no less natural right to space, and the resources contained therein, than any other species. Man, however, created a mechanism to minimize the constant conflict among humans for the use of land. The mechanism that evolved is called government. With few exceptions in all of history, government became the usurper, and granted land use to favored citizens and denied land use to others, which Hobbes recognized and described in Leviathan. It was just such a system of government-granted favors and denials that motivated oppressed people to challenge the vast oceans and untamed wilderness of the new continent, in hopes of securing land under the Lockean concept of "ownership by first possession."

There can be no question that the founding fathers held private ownership of land to be a natural right co-equal to the right of free speech, and the right to worship freely. Nor can there be any question that the first purpose of the government created by the founding fathers was to protect those "inalienable rights," including the right of individuals to own, and control the use of, private property, whether acquired by "first possession" or by contract from first possessors.

The Northwest Ordinance of 1785 set the procedure for distributing lands acquired by the federal government to private ownership.

A minimum price of $1 per acre was stipulated. By 1862, not enough land had been transferred to private ownership, so Congress implemented the Homestead Act, which gave 160 acres to anyone who would live on the land for five years. The Act also provided for the purchase of land for $1.25 per acre after a six month residency.

The Timber Culture Act of 1873 and the Desert Land Law of 1877, both provided for free transfer of government land to private ownership. For the first 150 years, the objective of American land policy clearly was to get government land into private ownership. Progressive forces, as early as 1871, urged Congress to set aside forest land for protection from "robber barons." Twenty years later, Congress obliged with the Forest Reserve Act of 1891. By 1908, Theodore Roosevelt, and his natural resources advisor, Gifford Pinchot, extended forest protection to more than 132,000,000 acres, 88% of today's reserves.[4]

The distribution of government land to private ownership ended with the Taylor Grazing Act of 1934. The official policy of "public domain" lands was set in concrete in 1976 with the Federal Land Policy and Management Act. Throughout much of this century, and particularly since 1970, federal land policy has shifted a full 180 degrees. Originally, the policy was to promote private land ownership to the extent of giving land to individuals. Then the policy shifted to locking up the remaining federal lands for the "public domain." Then the policy shifted to acquiring more land to expand the "public domain." And now, the policy is rapidly shifting toward absolute government control of all lands, both public and private.

Driving Public Policy

American land policy has been driven by a parade of identifiable people who see free enterprise and private property rights as an obstacle to be overcome rather than as a value to be protected. The idea of "conservation" had emerged by 1900, when both political parties endorsed the concept. The concept, though, was not clearly defined. To John Muir, who founded the Sierra Club in 1892, conservation meant preservation. To Gifford Pinchot, conservation meant federally regulated use of resources on public land. The battle between Muir's preservation ideas and Pinchot's federally regulated conservation ideas came to a head over the Hetch Hetchy Dam. Pinchot won in 1909, and the dam was built.

For the next fifty years, the federal government pursued a land policy of federally regulated use of resources on public lands. The Sierra Club led the growth of the preservation movement which became the modern environmental movement, dominated by three international NGOs (non-governmental organizations): the International Union for the Conservation of Nature (IUCN); the World Wide Fund for Nature (WWF); and the World Resources Institute (WRI).

Robert Marshall, Aldo Leopold, and Benton Mackaye founded The Wilderness Society. Mackaye was a member of the Socialist Party that supported Eugene V. Debs. Marshall joined the Socialist Party of Norman Thomas which was more radical than the Debs group.[5] In 1933, Robert Marshall published The People's Forests, which advocated the confiscation of privately owned forest land.

Another dam project in Echo Park in Western Colorado and Eastern Utah unified a growing number of preservation groups in the 1950s. The Wildlife Management Institute, the National Audubon Society, and the Izaak Walton League joined the Sierra Club and the Wilderness Society to defeat the construction project. Howard Zahniser of the Wilderness Society was the primary lobbyist in Washington.

Howard Zahniser was also the driving force behind the Wilderness Act of 1964.[6] The Act set aside nine million acres to be forever preserved as wilderness. Since then, more than 100 million acres have been added to the wilderness inventory. The preservationists gained more strength with the 1970 "Earth Day" organized by Senator Gaylord Nelson (D-WI), who left the Senate to become an advisor to The Wilderness Society.

The preservation movement came together to produce a series of documents, funded by the Rockefeller Brothers Fund, which set forth the preservationists' agenda. The first, The Use of Land: A Citizen's Policy Guide to Urban Growth, published in 1972, was edited by William K. Reilly, who served as EPA Administrator under George Bush. The document begins with a quote from Aldo Leopold:

"It is time to change the view that land is little more than a commodity to be exploited and traded. We need a land ethic that regards land as a resource which, improperly used, can have the same ill effects as the pollution of air and water, and which therefore warrants similar protection."[7]

The second document, entitled The Unfinished Agenda, was published in 1977 to "enlist the collective expertise of sixty-three leading environmentalists...to identify and describe the most critical problems...."[8] The final document in the series, Blueprint for the Environment, was 1500 pages containing 730 specific recommendations delivered to President-elect, George Bush on November 30, 1988. The document was prepared by:

The Wilderness Society, Sierra Club, National Audubon Society, The Nature Conservancy, National Wildlife Federation, Izaak Walton League, Friends of the Earth, Zero Population Growth, Environmental Defense Fund, and other NGOs, all affiliated with one or more of the three international NGOs.

The 1972 document was accompanied by a five-year effort in Congress to adopt the "Land Use Policy and Planning Assistance Act." Led by Morris Udall, and supported by NGOs, the effort to achieve federal land use control was defeated primarily through the efforts of David A. Witts, attorney for the Texas and Southwest Cattle Raisers Association.[9]

The proponents of federal land use control didn't abandon their dream. They simply fell back to regroup and plan another strategy to achieve absolute control of private property in America.

Administrative expansion of the Clean Water Act of 1972, and the Endangered Species Act of 1973 have served as effective federal land use control devices. Both land use policies came about as the result of conforming American laws to meet the requirements of UN treaties. Ocie Mills, John Poszgai and Bill Ellen, all served prison sentences for minor infringements of wetland policy, to serve as examples to other land owners who dared to use their own property which the federal government declared to be "waters of the United States." Thousands of other land owners have been prevented from using their own land because a usurping government invoked the federal land use control device - wetlands.

The Endangered Species Act has had a similar chilling effect on the use of both federal and private lands. The spotted owl has never been in danger of extinction. Andy Stahl, of the Sierra Legal Defense Fund, told a conference at the University of Oregon, in 1988, that the spotted owl was just a "surrogate" to stop timber harvests until "Congress [has] a chance to provide specific statutory protection for those forests."[11] The National Audubon Society, the Wilderness Society and other NGOs initiated litigation that has prevented any use of millions of acres of prime timberland.

Stephen McCabe, chairman of a California NGO, opposed the expansion of Quail Hollow quarry. To block the company's expansion, he has proposed that the Mount Hermon June beetle be listed as an endangered species. He readily admits: "My goal is to protect the habitat...The best route at present is to try to get individual species listed and by doing that get protection for the habitat."[12]

In Orange County California, the Natural Resources Defense Council used the Gnatcatcher to stop a highway project and other development on 400,000 acres until Judge Stanley Sporkin ruled that the Gnatcatcher had to be removed from the endangered species list because it was not endangered.[13] Nevertheless, continued negotiations between environmental NGOs and local government resulted in a "Multiple Species Conservation Plan" that locks up 172,000 acres "of meaningful open space."[14]

The hind legs on Tipton Kangaroo rats are one one-hundredth of an inch longer than the hind legs of a Herman's Kangaroo rat. The Tipton is listed as "endangered;" the Hermon is not. Taung Ming-Lin had never heard of either when he bought a 720 acre farm near Bakersfield, California. Mary Mason knew both species well. When she saw a tractor discing land owned by Ming-Lin, but used by the Tipton rat, she brought down a covey of 20 state and federal regulators on the Ming-Lin farm, took the tractor and disc into custody, and threatened Ming-Lin with a $300,000 fine - whereupon he had a stroke.[15]

The federal government, driven by NGOs, has found inventive ways to control the use of private land and private property - jailing land owners and suing tractors. The Ecosystem Management Plan, adopted by federal government agencies, eliminates the need to identify wetland or endangered species as an excuse to control land use. It will empower NGO-spawned federal bureaucrats to control every square inch of land in America.

The objective

The ultimate objective of the NGOs is to implement the policies of the United Nations as published in the Convention on Biological Diversity, the Global Biodiversity Assessment, Agenda 21, and other treaties and documents. The objective is so bizarre, so foreign to the ideas of Jefferson and Madison, the ideas on which America was founded, that free market property rights advocates have discounted their ideas as the lunatic fringe of the environmental movement.

The preservationist objective is only suggested by Aldo Leopold in his 1949 Sand County Almanac. He says: "We are only fellow-voyagers with other creatures in the odyssey of evolution." An awareness of which "changes the role of Homo sapiens from conqueror of the land-community to plain member and citizen of it."[16]

Dave Foreman, father of the Wildlands Project, sheds more light on the ultimate objective of the preservationists:

"We should demand that roads be closed and clearcuts rehabilitated, that dams be torn down, that wolves, grizzlies, cougars, river otters, bison, elk, pronghorn, bighorn sheep, caribou and other extirpated species be reintroduced to their native habitats. We must envision and propose the restoration of biological wildernesses of several million acres in all of America's ecosystems, with corridors between them for the transmission of genetic variability. Wilderness is the arena for evolution, and there must be enough of it for natural forces to have free rein."[17]

He also says:

"...it boils down to the question of whether private property (and those dollars or jobs the property represents) or natural ecosystems are more valuable. Although most people in this country (myself included) respect the concept of private property, life - the biological diversity of this planet - is far more important."[18]

Foreman's dream of massive wilderness in America is not a private fantasy. Bill Devall says, in Deep Ecology, "The entire continent of Antarctica should be zoned as wilderness. In the United States, tens of millions of acres should be zoned wilderness with rigid restrictions on industrial developments."[19]

David Brower, former director of the Sierra Club and founder of Friends of the Earth, says:

"Man needs an Earth International Park, to protect on this planet what he has not destroyed and what need not be destroyed. In this action, all nations could unite against the one real enemy - Rampant Technology."[20]

Philosopher, John Phillips says:

"The biosphere as a whole should be zoned, in order to protect it from the human impact. We must strictly confine the Urban-Industrial Zone, and the Production Zone (agriculture, grazing, fishing), enlarge the Compromise Zone and drastically expand the Protection Zone, i.e. wilderness, wild rivers. Great expanses of seacoast and estuaries must be included in the Protection Zone, along with forests, prairies, and various habitat types. We must learn that the multiple-use Compromise Zone is no substitute, with its mining, lumbering, grazing, and recreation in the national forests, for the scientific, aesthetic, and genetic pool values of the Protection Zone. Such zoning, if carried out in time, may be the only way to limit the destructive impact of our technocratic industrial-agri-business complex on earth."[21]

Gary Snyder, Pulitzer Prize winning poet, says:

"If man is to remain on earth he must transform the five-millennia-long urbanizing civilization tradition into a new ecologically-sensitive harmony-oriented wild-minded scientific/spiritual culture...nothing short of total transformation will do much good."[22]

The wilderness objective is promoted throughout the literature of the environmental movement. Dave Foreman, one of the more articulate spokesmen for the movement, has substantially advanced his dream.

Until 1980, Foreman was a lobbyist for The Wilderness Society. Unhappy with the progress being made, he resigned and created Earth First! He published Ecodefense: a Field Guide to Monkeywrenching, and Confessions of an Eco-Warrior. His next venture was the creation of the Cenozoic Society, which publishes Wild Earth. In an 88-page special issue, entitled "The Wildlands Project", published with funds from the Hati Foundation for Deep Ecology, Foreman distributed 75,000 copies of his vision for land use in America. The mission of The Wildlands Project is:

"To stem the disappearance of wildlife and wilderness we must allow the recovery of whole ecosystems and landscapes in every region of North America. Allowing these systems to recover requires a long-term master plan. Our vision is simple: we live for the day when Grizzlies in Chihuahua have an unbroken connection to Grizzlies in Alaska; when Gray Wolf populations are continuous from New Mexico to Greenland; when vast unbroken forests and flowing plains again thrive and support pre-Columbian populations of plants and animals; when humans dwell with respect, harmony, and affection for the land; when we come to live no longer as strangers and aliens on this continent."[23]

The plan itself was devised by Reed F. Noss, who holds a Ph.D. in wildlife ecology from the University of Florida, who is a research scientist at the University of Idaho, a research associate at Stanford University, and is a member of the Board of Directors of The Wildlands Project. Noss says:

"Most conservation biologists agree that compatible human uses of the landscape must be considered...However, the native ecosystem and the collective needs of non-human species must take precedence over the needs and desires of humans."[24]

The plan calls for a biological survey to identify and catalog plant and animal populations. It calls for the designation of "at least 50% of the land area" as "core reserves" surrounded by an "inner buffer zone" and surrounded again by an "outer buffer zone," almost exactly like that described by John Phillips above. The reserve areas are to be connected by corridors that could be several hundred miles wide. Noss says: "Eventually, a wilderness network would dominate a region and thus would itself constitute the matrix, with human habitations being the islands." He says that specific actions to be taken include:

"...land and mineral rights acquisitions, Wilderness or other reserve designations on public lands, road closures, cancellation of grazing leases and timber sales, tree planting, dam removals, stream dechannelization, and other restoration projects. In many cases, private lands will need to be acquired and added to national forests and other public lands in order to serve as effective buffers."

Noss acknowledges that his work was prepared under contract with the National Audubon Society and The Nature Conservancy.[25]

The Global Biodiversity Assessment, an 1140-page document published by Cambridge University Press for the United Nations Environment Program (UNEP), for those concerned with the implementation of the Convention on Biological Diversity, explicitly identifies the "Wildlands Project," as central to the preservation of biodiversity required by the Convention.[26]

John Davis, Editor of Wild Earth, and a Director of The Wildlands Project, says wilderness advocates must face squarely such problems as "private property, local versus state or federal control, and appropriate human roles in natural areas." He says people would not be required to relocate if they would "...refrain from any use of motors, guns, or cows. The problem here is not so much people as it is their damnable technologies."

To achieve this massive objective, Michael E. Soule, a member of The Wildlands Project Board and a teacher in the Environmental Studies Department at the University of California, preaches a policy of patience. Rather than take a rancher's land, he suggests getting the rancher involved in a watershed council, or similar local group and "teach" him the tax benefits of donating his land to a conservancy after his death. He says:

"...we must hurry to plan the system and the strategy. Some protective actions cannot wait. Some pieces and parts can wait as long as the plan is well conceived and is being implemented systematically. The goal should be staying the course, not setting a speed record."

The plan: Ecosystem Management

After the flop of the FLUP (Federal Land Use Planning) Acts in the mid 1970s, NGOs realized that seduction might be more effective than rape. A new strategy was devised: go to the U.N. for help, and infiltrate the government. The Carter administration provided the opportunity for implementation of both initiatives. The President's Council on Environmental Quality sponsored a "Forum on Preservation of Farmland," which determined that:

"The greatest need is to create a federal policy. This can be done by various tax and regulatory schemes. Another way is for the community to become part-owner in the land. A third way, well tested in Europe, is for the community to intervene in the actual market of land buying and selling."[27]

Stanley D. Shift, head of the U.S. Delegation to the U.N. Habitat Conference, participated in the Forum, and in the U.N. Habitat Conference. The Conference report begins:

"Private land ownership is a principal instrument of accumulating wealth and therefore contributes to social injustice. Public control of land is therefore indispensable."

The Conference recommended:

"Public ownership of land is justified in favor of the common good, rather than to protect the interests of the already privileged."[28] (See eco•logic, January/February, 1997 for a complete report of the UN Conference on Human Settlements in Vancouver, BC, 1976.)

The Carter administration welcomed the environmental seducers into policy-making positions. In the Department of Interior, Under Secretary, Barbara Heller, and water specialist, Joe Browder came from Ralph Nader's Environmental Policy Center. Assistant Secretary, Cynthia Wilson came from the National Audubon Society. Assistant Secretary, Robert Herbat came from the Izaak Walton League. Attorney James Moorman came from the Sierra Club, Solicitor John Leshey, from the Natural Resources Defense Council.[29]

The Reagan administration cleaned house and replaced the Carter policy-makers with people such as James Watt from Mountain States Legal Foundation. The environmental community organized a national campaign against Watt, even before his confirmation, and eventually forced his resignation.

The ground lost by NGOs to the Reagan administration was recovered in part during the Bush years, most notably through the appointment of William Reilly as EPA administrator, who came directly from his position as head of the World Wildlife Fund. (The man he replaced, Russell Train, became Chairman of the World Wildlife Fund). The Clinton administration reopened the doors to NGOs, and in marched an army of enviromentalists. Bruce Babbitt,

Secretary of the Department of Interior, formerly headed the League of Conservation Voters. Assistant Secretary, George Frampton, formerly presided over The Wilderness Society, the same Wilderness Society founded by avowed Socialists Robert Marshall and Benton MacKaye. Several others in the Clinton administration were recruited directly from NGOs.[3]

This formidable array of environmental buraucrats is commanded by Vice President, Al Gore, not President Clinton. Gore immediately named his former assistant, Carol Browner, to head the EPA, and another assistant, Katie McGinty, to head the White House Office on Environmental Policy. Gore initiated the National Performance Review (NPR) which was sold as the "reinvention of government." Gore, as Senator, apologized at the Earth Summit in Rio de Janeiro for President Bush's failure to sign the Biodiversity Treaty, and then as Vice President, applauded Bill Clinton's signature binding America to a world wide environmental agenda under the control of the United Nations. Despite the U.S. Senate's refusal to ratify the Convention on Biological Diversity, the administration's Ecosystem Management Policy is implementing the Convention's requirement to control of the use of all land, both public and private, to achieve the objectives of the United Nations.

Endnotes

1. Richard A. Epstein, Takings: Private Property and the Power of Eminent Domain, Harvard University Press, Cambridge, Massachusetts, p.2f.

2. Ibid, p.10. Epstein's discussion of emerging philosophies provides an excellent foundation for tracking the continuing conflict of philosophies which underlie land use policies.

3. Ibid, p.11.

4. Jo Kwong Echard, Protecting the Environment: Old Rhetoric, New Imperatives, Capitol Research Center, Washington DC, p.7.

5. Ibid, p.13, 203.

6. Dave Foreman, Confessions of an Eco-Warrior, Harmony Books, New York, 1991, p. 179.

7. Ron Arnold and Alan Gottlieb, Trashing the Economy, Free Enterprise Press, Bellevue, Washington, p.20.
8. Echard, Op Cit., p.20.

9. Hearings before the Subcommittee on Economic Growth and Stabilization of the

Joint Economic Committee, Ninety-fifth Congress, June 7 and 13, 1977, p. 154ff.

10. Gregg Easterbrook, "The Spotted Owl Scam: Was industry destroyed for a bird in no danger?" The Sacramento Bee, April 24, 1994.

11. Andy Stahl, Sierra Legal Defense Fund, Transcript of speech presented to Western Public Interest Conference, University of Oregon School of Law, Eugene, Oregon, March 5, 1988.

12. John Bessa, "Expert bugged by proposed listing," Santa Cruz County Sentinel, June 27, 1994.

13. "Straining at a gnatcatcher," Sacramento Bee, May 20, 1994.

14. Dianne Jacob, Supervisor, San Diego County, "MSCP: Balancing Economic Growth & The Environment," September 1997.

15. United States of America v. One Ford Tractor, Model 8630 #A927242, One Towner Offset Disc, Model A248 #24C665, Eastern District, U.S. District Court, #CV-F-94-5315.

16. Bill Devall and George Sessions, Deep Ecology, Peregrine Smith Books, Salt Lake City, 1985, p. 85.

17. Dave Foreman, Op Cit., p.7.

18. Ibid, p.121.

19. Devall, Op Cit., p. 30.

20. David Brower, Introduction to Galapagos: The Flow of Wilderness, 1968.

21. Devall, Op Cit., p. 124.

22. Ibid, p.171.

23. "The Wildlands Project," Wild Earth, Special Issue, 1992, p.3.

24. Ibid, p.13.

25. "The Wildlands Project," Op Cit, p.21.

26. Global Biodiversity Assessment, (Cambridge University Press, 1995,) p. 993.
27. David A. Witts, Theft, La Verne University Press, La Verne, California, 1982, p. 15.

28. Report of the UN Conference on Human Settlements, Agenda Item 10, "Preamble," Vancouver, BC, May 31-June 11, 1976.

29. Environmental organizations represented in the Carter administration also include: Sheldon Novick, publisher of Environment Magazine, David Hawkins, from the Natural Resources Defense Council (NRDC), Gustave Speth from NRDC, Gerald

Barney from Environmental Agenda, Marion Edey, from the League of Conservation Voters, Kathy Fletcher, from the Environmental Defense Fund (EDF), Rupert Cutler, from The Wilderness Society, George Davis, from The Wilderness Society, Dennis Hayes, Earth Day organizer, and EPA Administrator, Doug Costle, from Connecticut's Environmental Protection Department, who said:

"The fervor of the sixties has evolved into the environmental institution of today. Environmentalists today carry calculators instead of pickets. The street leaders of Earth Day have become the institution leaders of today. In fact, many of them are now EPA administrators."

Source: David A. Witts, Theft.

30. Clinton administration policy-makers from environmental organizations include:

Office of Management and Budget Deputy Director Alice Rivlin served as Chair of the Wilderness Society.

Scientific Advisor at the Department of Interior Thomas E. Lovejoy was an official at the World Wildlife Fund. (Lovejoy is the mastermind who created "debt-for-land" swap that let American environmental organizations buy foreign debt for as little as fifteen cents on the dollar, then give the purchased notes to a sister organization in the debtor country to be redeemed at face value, with interest, for the purpose of purchasing land and expanding the influence of the organization).

Rafe Pomerance, Senior Associate for Policy Affairs at the World Resources Institute, has been appointed Deputy Assistant Secretary of State for Environment, Health and Natural Resources.

Former World Resources Institute Vice President Jessica Tuchman Mathews has been appointed Deputy Undersecretary of State for Global Affairs.

Former World Resources Institute President Gus Speth has been chosen by the White House to head the United Nations Development Programme.
Former Sierra Club Legislative Director David Gardiner is the Assistant Administrator for Policy Planning and Evaluation at the Environmental Protection Agency.

Brooks Yeager, Former National Audubon Society Vice President for Government Relations and Advisory Committee member for the MacWilliams Cosgrove Snider report, is Director for Policy Analysis at the Department of Interior.

Former Natural Resources Defense Council official John Leshy is Solicitor of the Department of Interior.

Source: Organization Trends, published by the Capital Research Center, September, 1993.

Mr. Lamb's treatise was penned over a decade ago. It is exactly what is happening in America today, as the Environmental Movement grows stronger and richer by the day. The goals are truly scary. This excerpt, reiterated from Henry Lamb's article, states the frightening objective:

"We should demand that roads be closed and clearcuts rehabilitated, that dams be torn down, that wolves, grizzlies, cougars, river otters, bison, elk, pronghorn, bighorn sheep, caribou and other extirpated species be reintroduced to their native habitats. We must envision and propose the restoration of biological wildernesses of several million acres in all of America's ecosystems, with corridors between them for the transmission of genetic variability. Wilderness is the arena for evolution, and there must be enough of it for natural forces to have free rein."

He also says:

"...it boils down to the question of whether <u>private property (and those dollars or jobs the property represents) or natural ecosystems are more valuable.</u> Although most people in this country (myself included) respect the concept of private property, life - the biological diversity of this planet - is far more important."

Please read the above statement very carefully, because it summarizes very succinctly the viewpoint of the Environmental Movement. Are jobs (and therefore food, shelter, clothing, transportation, recreation, and all other human activities which require a medium of exchange, i.e. money) or natural ecosystems more important? **"Biological Diversity is far more important."**

Important to whom? As a Homo sapien, it is my biological duty to preserve my species, to compete with other species, for limited space on this planet. If biological diversity is important to the Government Canyon Cave Bat Spider, or the Appalacian Monkeyface Pearly Mussel, then let them fight for that concept. I am much more interested in growing food for my grandchildren, keeping them warm in the winter, and dry in the summer. And yes, watching them open presents under the Christmas tree, swimming in our swimming pool, teaching them to fly fish and otherwise enjoying the fruits of my labors as I so choose. I absolutely refuse to apologize for my humaness.

What good does biological diversity do Homo sapiens, if we are to perish in the process, and more importantly, if our liberties are to perish in the process?

"Man cannot survive except through his mind. He comes on earth unarmed. His brain is his only weapon. Animals obtain food by force. man had no claws, no fangs, no horns, no great strength of muscle. He must plant his food or hunt it. To plant, he needs a process of thought. To hunt, he needs weapons,and to make weapons - a process of thought. From this simplest necessity to the highest religious abstraction, from the wheel to the skyscraper, everything we are and we have comes from a single attribute of man -the function of his reasoning mind."
Ayn Rand (The Fountainhead)

Government run amok*

Posted: June 05, 2001
By Linda Bowles
© 2011 Linda Bowles

In his 1992 best-seller, "The Way Things Ought To Be," Rush Limbaugh wrote: "With the collapse of Marxism, environmentalism has become the new refuge of socialist thinking. The environment is a great way to advance a political agenda that favors central planning and an intrusive government. What better way to control someone's property than to subordinate one's private property rights to environmental concerns."

At the time, this sounded like hyperbole. But it wasn't. Limbaugh's warning was worthy and prophetic. I realized this a few years ago when I came across a story concerning Taiwanese immigrant Taung Ming-Lin, a farmer in Kern County, Calif., who was arrested for allegedly running over an "endangered" kangaroo rat while tilling his own land. His tractor was seized and held for over four months, and he faced a year in jail and a $200,000 fine.

A U.S. Fish and Wildlife agent asserted, "We're the caretakers and the stewards of the land, and we have no right to deny the existence of these endangered species."

As time has passed, it is now clear that what happened to the farmer in Kern County was not an anomaly, but part of a developing pat-

*http://o.wnd.ha-hosting.com/index.php?fa=PAGE.printable&pageId=9508

tern of government invasion of private rights. What the Fish and Wildlife agent said was not just a misguided personal opinion – he was stating official U.S. government policy.

On April 7, 2001, the federal government's Bureau of Reclamation cut off irrigation water to 1,500 family farms in the Klamath Basin on the Oregon-California border. Based on "citizen lawsuits" filed by environmental activists, all the available water will go to save fish, primarily the sucker fish. A federal judge denied an appeal by the farmers saying, "Congress has spoken in the plainest of words, making it abundantly clear that the balance has been struck in favor of affording endangered species the highest of priorities."

While the farmers are going bankrupt, the legal bills of the environmentalists are paid for by the American taxpayers under the "citizen lawsuit" provisions of the Endangered Species Act.

Meanwhile, based on a successful lawsuit filed by the Earth Justice Legal Defense Fund, the U.S. Fish and Wildlife Service has just designated 4.1 million acres as critical habitats for the endangered California red-legged frog. Nearly 70 percent of the acres are private property.

The protected habitats hopscotch across 28 California counties, including key agricultural counties, adding layers of new regulations on already over-regulated private land. No activity of any kind on this land will be permitted until it has been proven that such activity will in no way affect the well-being of the beloved red-legged frog.

Another endangered critter wreaking damage in California is the fairy shrimp, which thrives in what environmentalists call "vernal pools" and what ordinary folk call standing water or mud puddles. Anyway, when these puddles evaporate, the fairy shrimp eggs nest in the mud until the next seasonal rains hatch them.

Apparently the deal is this: If you drain or spray standing water, you get an award from the mosquito-control people and a summons from the fairy-shrimp police.

The protection of these "vernal pools" is a nightmare to California farmers, developers, and even local governments. For example, environmental concerns for the shrimp cost Fresno County a six-month, $250,000 delay in the construction of an important freeway. However, that's cheap compared to the undisclosed cost of moving the site of a major new University of California campus in Merced, Calif., because there are too many vernal pools on it.

California is the nation's largest producer of food crops and commodities, including fruits, nuts, vegetables, melons, livestock and dairy products. This massive agricultural industry depends entirely on irrigation for water. In California, rainfall is slight or non-existent from early May to mid-October.

Land regulations, fuel costs and electrical shortages are disastrous to farmers. But the most critical issue for them and for all Californians is water. The eco-inspired ban on the construction of dams and water storage facilities to catch the runoff from winter rains and spring snow melts is limiting the supply of water even as demand for it is surging. It is a disaster in the making. Deja vu!

While there is local outrage in California and elsewhere over these abuses, there is little national outrage. One hopes this is due to a lack of coverage by the mainstream media, rather than a fatalistic American submission to state socialism. One fears that only in retrospect, when it is too late to resist, will it be understood that freedoms have been irretrievably forfeited and the Constitution irreversibly abandoned.

As an avid reader of history, abandoning the United States Constitution holds no excitement for me. And, it appears to me, abandoning it we are, slowly but surely. Where is the protection of property rights, clearly stated in our Bill of Rights, and made stronger following the Civil War by the 14th Amendment? If farmers all across the country have to give up their land for Endangered Species, doesn't the rest of America have an obligation to write these people a check? If farming is too intrusive for an endangered species, than certainly higher forms of man's activities, such as manufacturing and housing, will not be permitted. Hence, the land is rendered useless for virtually any human activity, and thus expropriated. Ostensibly, this expropiation, in the opinion of U.S. Fish and Wildlife Service, is for the greater good of the American public, since the intrinsic value of that particular Endangered Species trumps any possible human endeavors.

Once the American people, already fed up with our National Debt, have to start writing checks for this expropriated land, they will start to wake up. Until now, U.S.F.W.S. has been pretty careful about hiding the actual damage it does to our economy, which is billions of dollars annually. Environmentalism has become a huge industry; an industry that produces nothing and prevents others from producing anything. How much, and to whom, are these Environmental Extremists contributing, and how does it affect their votes? As an American people, we need to turn up the lights a bit brighter, and watch the cockroaches scatter.

> "It becomes evident that while discussing climate we are not witnessing a clash of views about the environment, but a clash of views about human freedom.
>
> As someone who lived under communism for most of my life I feel obliged to say that the biggest threat to freedom, democracy, the market economy and prosperity at the beginning of the 21st century is not communism or its various softer variants," said Klaus, responding to questions posed by the two lawmakers. "Communism was replaced by the threat of ambitious environmentalism."
> Vaclac Klaus, President of the Czech Republic

How unfortunate is it that Americans have to hear this wisdom from the President of Czecholavakia? Where is our national leadership? Where are the politicians, both Republicans and Democrats? Does offending the "Greenies", and the possible loss of their votes come before the welfare of our nation?

> "In matters of style, swim with the current;
> In matters of principle, stand like a rock."
> Thomas Jefferson

Where are our rocks?
"Green is the New Red" has been slow to be recognized, primarily be-

cause the liberal press refuses to accept such a blasphemous concept. Instead, America and much of the world, has embraced the Chicken Little-like mantra of Global Warming. Activist judges have used the Endangered Species Act of 1973 to shut down logging, mining, outfitting, petroleum production, fishing, farming, hospitals, college campuses, and a host of other economic activities, all under the guise of protecting the environment. Hollywood piled on the idea by awarding Al Gore an Oscar, for his propaganda laced film "An Inconvenient Truth". The film had little to do with the truth, and much to do with conveniently lining the former vice-president's pockets.

Protecting the environment is, or at least should be, everyone's concern. No reasonable person can argue that point. The good works of the early environmental movement, the cleaning up of our waterways, and the reduction in air pollutants, are all tremendous examples of the good work accomplished, and Americans today enjoy the fruits of the early environmentalists' labors.

The Endangered Species Act of 1973, I have no doubt, was passed with great and honest intentions. It passed the Senate by verbal acclimation and the House of Representatives by a vote of 355 to 4. The new law distinguished threatened from endangered species, allowed listing of a species that is in danger in just part of its range, allowed listing of plants and invertebrates, authorized unlimited funds for species protection, and made it illegal to kill, harm, or otherwise "take" a listed species. "In effect, the law made endangered species protection the highest priority of government."

However well intentioned, the troubles with the new law began almost immediately. A University of Tennessee biologist discovered a snail darter in the Tennessee River, thus halting the construction of the virtually completed Tellico Dam. The Supreme Court found in favor of the snail darter, and against the dam builders, the Tennessee Valley Authority. (Congress eventually passed an exception, allowing the dam to be completed, but it was clear from the beginning that the Environmental Movement had a huge new weapon in its arsenal.)

Over the last 40 years, the environmentalist movement has evolved, changing from the "save the planet" idealism of th 1960s, to "stop all capitalist projects wherever possible" of the 21st century. Even Patrick Moore, the founder of the iconic environmental group Greenpeace, has seen enough.

http://www.ti.org/ESAHistory.html, The History of the Endangered Species Act.

"Patrick Moore, Greenpeace co-founder, has become a harsh critique abruptly leaving it after leading the group from 18-years because of what he calls "pop-environmentalism." Specifically he cites fellow directors who without any formal science training labeled nuclear energy "evil" while going on to chemicals and biology and genetics. He calls it "pop-environmentalism" that uses misinformation, fear and sensationalism to deal with people on the emotional level rather than intellectual level.

Moore favors nuclear power because of its low cost ($1.68 per kilowatt hour) and reliability. Moore says natural gas cost three times as much (and where most of the electrical cost increases have come from); wind cost five times as much and solar ten times as much. Moore calls solar power completely ridiculous.

Moore explains nuclear waste recycling reduced it by 90% making it disposal manageable. He wonders how many Americans know half of the U. S. nuclear energy comes from dismantled Russian nuclear war heads? He speaks of a nuclear renaissance to replace coals fired power plants, and debunking the misbegotten idea nuclear reactors produce weapons which they do not. Moore labels the environmental movement an "obstacle.""

Excerpted and edited from NEWSWEEK, April 21, 2008, page 42.

If the Environmental Movement has evolved into a well funded, well organized anti-capitalist movement, than citizens, voters, and our elected officials, must also evolve to combat this threat to our freedoms and ways of life. If the liberal press does not sound the alarm, than others must. (Hence, the writing of this book.) Politicians are too busy getting elected, and think a "green mantra" will accomplish that, regardless of the consequences to our economy and our nation. After all, only an axe-murderer doesn't want to "save wildlife, enhance habitat, protect our fisheries, clean up toxic waste sites, reduce air pollution, save the polar bear", etc. It gets votes, but, when taken to the extreme, which is exactly what is happening, it destroys economic viability of a country.

In 2008, the greatest recession/depression experienced in the United States since the 1930s began. For the average man on the street, in 2011, that depression continues. The building business is virtually non-existent. Real estate sales are abysmal. Home foreclosures are at an all time high. Personal debt and public debt are at unprecendented levels.

Our balance of payments to foreign nations remains a huge problem. We have no clearly delineated energy policy, despite new technologies that provide incredible amounts of clean energy, found right here at home and in Canada. We have a president that still thinks windmills are the answer. It is not a pretty picture.

Small businessmen, such as myself, make up a huge part of the American economy. The following are the statistics from the United States Small Business Administration:

How important are small businesses to the U.S. economy?

Small firms:
- **Represent 99.7 percent of all employer firms.**
- **Employ half of all private sector employees.**
- **Pay 44 percent of total U.S. private payroll.**
- **Generated 65 percent of net new jobs over the past 17 years.**
- **Create more than half of the nonfarm private GDP.**
- **Hire 43 percent of high tech workers (scientists, engineers, computer programmers, and others).**
- **Are 52 percent home-based and 2 percent franchises.**
- **Made up 97.5 percent of all identified exporters and produced 31 percent of export value in FY 2008.**
- **Produce 13 times more patents per employee than large patenting firms.**

Many small businessmen today are under attack. Not by the vagaries of the free market, or increasing oil prices, or labor unions, or foreign imports, or immigration laws, or the myriad of other obstacles Americans willingly accept when they venture out on their own to build themselves a better life. The attack is comes from within, from the "Fifth Column", found within our own government, the U.S. Fish & Wildlife Service.

> "There's a lot of small business people across this country who don't have the opportunity to stand up for themselves; can't afford to stand up for themselves."
> Clint Eastwood

What is the Role of the U.S. Fish & Wildlife Service?

The following is a statement listed as the **Number One Objective of** the U.S. Fish & Wildlife, on its website:

"Objective One: Assist in the development and application of an environmental stewardship ethic for our society, based on ecological principles, scientific knowledge of fish and wildlife, and a sense of moral responsibility."

Environmental Stewardship Ethic for our Society??? Moral Responsibility???? With all due respect, in a free nation, ethics and responsibility are up to the individual to develop, in conjunction with his family, friends, clergyman, mentors, etc. Societal development is most certainly not be the role of anyone within any government, and most certainly is not the role of unelected bureaucrats working for the U.S. Fish & Wildlife Service!!!!

"Some writers have so confounded society with government, as to leave little or no distinction between them; whereas they are not only different, but have different origins ... Society is in every state a blessing, but Government, even in its best state, is but a necessary evil; in its worst state, an intolerable one."
Thomas Paine

Czech President Klaus, quoted earlier, writes:

"The environmentalists' attitude toward nature is analogous to the Marxist approach to economics. The aim in both cases is to replace the free, spontaneous evolution of the world (and humankind) by the would-be optimal, central or-using today's fashionable adjective-global planning of world development. Much as in the case of Communism, this approach is utopian and would lead to results completely different from the intended ones. Like other utopias, this one can never materialize, and efforts to make it materialize can only be carried out through **restrictions of freedom, through the dictates of a small, elitist minority over the overwhelming majority. In short, we will not only lose our freedom but economic progress and human advancement will be stifled.** And more people will inevitably die."

Klaus adds, "In the past 150 years (at least since Marx), the socialists have been very effectively destroying human freedom under humane and compassionate slogans, such as caring for man, ensuring social equality, and fostering social welfare. The environmentalists are doing the same under equally noble-minded slogans, expressing concern about nature more than about people (recall their radical motto 'Earth first'). In both cases, the slogans have been (and still are) just a smoke-screen. In both cases, **the movements were (and are) completely about power, about the hegemony of the 'chosen ones' (as they see them-selves) over the rest of us, about the imposition of the only correct worldview (their own), about the remodeling of the world."**

Why, you ask, hasn't this been brought to the American judicial system? Isn't the Supreme Court the final arbiters of right and wrong in this country? How can these people have their lives destroyed, their property taken away, by lying government officials, and no recourse taken? How, in America, the land of the free, could this happen?

The answer to that, is simple. It takes an incredible amount of money to fight the United States government. Many of the people in this book are "just" small businessmen. Some are well educated, and some are not. All are hard working, honest, patriotic people. But the fact is, with their businesses already destroyed, **they don't have the time, or the money, to fight the government, which has endless time, and endless money.**

Ellis Washington, posted this in his column "The Report from Washington" on Octobeer 16, 2010, Entitled:

Is green the new red (communism)?

Global warming is the greatest and most successful pseudo-scientific fraud I have seen in my long life.
~ Dr. Harold Lewis

Ten days ago, Harold Lewis, Ph.D., emeritus professor of physics at the University of California, Santa Barbara, tendered his letter of resignation to Curtis G. Callan Jr., Princeton University, president of the American Physical Society, because Dr. Lewis finally realized that he could no longer support what he called the "successful pseudo-scientific fraud" of global warming.
Remember, to the Democratic Party and RINO Republicans, truth doesn't matter, because to them truth is relative. All that matters to liberals and progressives is Nietzsche's "Will to Power" and control over the people. Like the Islamic doctrine Taqiyya, which sanctions

deceit to further Islam, to progressives the end justifies the means; therefore, lying, stealing, killing and perverting the Constitution and science is acceptable to utopian socialists as long as they "change the world."

Recall the words of New Deal brain-truster Stuart Chase who, after visiting the Soviet Union in the 1920s, asked with incredulity, "Why should Russians have all the fun remaking the world?" Progressives are very resilient, so when Soviet communism finally collapsed after 70 years of world wide tyranny, progressives and liberal Democrats pushed the existential green movement to the forefront, which was in reality the same old exhausted red communism in a new disguise.

Green is now the new red (communism).
I realize it's hard to accept that progressives and liberals, our fellow Americans, or anti-Americans, are so hell-bent on remaking the world while destroying society and allowing our minds, intellect, soul and spirit to degenerate into the abyss of socialism.

See the full documentation explaining how your life could be changed by climate-related laws, taxes and regulations: "Climategate: A Veteran Meteorologist Exposes The Global Warming Scam"

Leon Trotsky called this tactic "perpetual revolution." Always keep the revolution going; always have a crisis before the face of the people; always keep society in a controlled state of chaos. Saul Alinsky, Hillary Clinton and Obama's intellectual mentor, furthered Trotskyite tactics in his book, "Rules for Radicals"(1971), and now President Obama is forcing America to live out the Democrats' green socialist nightmare, which stopped the Reagan economic revolution dead in its tracks while plunging America into a second Great Depression.

Liberalism isn't new. It's been called by different names over time. Note some of the sophistic ideas liberal Democrats and progressives have used to control and denigrate society over the past 250 years:
•The Age of Enlightenment (humanism, atheism, skepticism)
•Karl Marx (socialism, communism)
•Charles Darwin (evolution, eugenics, separation of Christianity and science)
•Jeremy Bentham, John Austin (advent of positive law, end of nat-

ural law)
- Sigmund Freud, Alfred Ki   y, Benjamin Spock (sexual promis-
cuity, family deconstruction)
- Woodrow Wilson, FDR, LB   Obama (welfare state)
- Walter Lippmann, Herbert   oly, John Dewey, H.G. Wells, Mar-
garet Sanger, George Bernar Shaw (education propaganda, pro-
gressivism, moral relativism)
- Lenin, Stalin, Hitler, Mao (st e socialism, totalitarianism)
- Rachel Carson ("Silent Spri   [1962]), Ira Einhorn, Al Gore, Van
Jones ("Green New Deal")

Why did it take 40 years for D Lewis, a man of superior academic
credentials, who has dedicat his entire life to the pursuit of scientifically verified truths, to   eak out publicly against the radical
environmentalist movemen   id the Big Lie of manmade global
warming, a diabolical collus n between science and politics that
dates back to the first Earth D , April 16-22, 1970, the advent of the
modern environmentalist mo ement?

Could the reason Dr. Lewis remained a member of the American
Physical Society for 67 years be because as a young scientist in the
1940s he didn't want to rock the boat or ruin the career he had
worked so hard to achieve by speaking against the fraudulent col-
lusion between science and government in its myriad forms, which
always produces bad science and terrible policy? After all, Dr. Lewis
could have rationalized, "I am just one man." What difference could
I make? Who would believe my ideas about the numerous factual
errors of climate change verses the peer-reviewed studies by thousands of scientists all over the world attesting to manmade global
warming?

Green is now the new red (communism).

I don't know Dr. Lewis personally, and I'm not attacking him. I simply am using him as a metaphor against green lobbying groups, like
Al Gore's Alliance for Climate Protection, which are making millions peddling lies to useful idiots – people who are too cowardly to
stand up and speak truth to power.

Thank God for Martin Niemoller (1892-1984), that great German
Protestant minister who for ars suffered in Nazi concentration

camps for his outspoken Christian beliefs in the face of Hitler's genocidal madness and Aryan supremacy. Recalling the cowardice of silence from his fellow clergymen as Hitler's Nazism progressed, Niemoller wrote these poignant lines for the ages:

When the Nazis came for the communists,
I remained silent;
I was not a communist.

Then they locked up the social democrats,
I remained silent;
I was not a social democrat.

Then they came for the trade unionists,
I did not speak out; I was not a trade unionist.

Then they came for the Jews,
I did not speak out;
I was not a Jew.
When they came for me,
there was no one left to speak out for me.

During the Age of Obama and FDR's welfare state, part 2, Niemoller is one of my heroes, and that's why we must speak out against this 40-year-old green movement, which is fascist in conception and a cynical backdoor attempt by the Democratic Party to destroy liberty of contract, free-market capitalism and to subvert society gradually through Fabian socialism.

I appeal to you Dr. Harold Lewis, and to the entire academy to follow Niemoller's courageous stance against Nazism, tyranny and socialism in all its guises. Don't wait until you are an old man, financially secure with tenure from the university; sacrifice careerism and speak truth to power! If you don't, then the new green movement, which is the old red communist menace, will continue to eradicate our natural rights to the downfall of liberty, truth and civilization.

Environmentalism, Eco-Terrorism and Endangered Species

25 January 1999 Glenn Woiceshyn

While mainstream environmental groups may try to distance themselves from ELF and its "eco-terrorist" methods, the truth is that ELF did directly what mainstream environmentalists have been doing indirectly for years via the U.S. government's Endangered Species Act (ESA).

An underground environmental group called Earth Liberation Front (ELF) claimed responsibility for incinerating four ski lifts (October 1998) and three buildings worth 12 $million at Vail, Colorado. Vail's plans to expand its ski area apparently clashed with environmentalists' plans to re-populate the "endangered" lynx in Colorado. ELF destroyed this property "on behalf of the lynx" and warned skiers to ski elsewhere this winter.

While mainstream environmental groups may try to distance themselves from ELF and its "eco-terrorist" methods, the truth is that ELF did directly what mainstream environmentalists have been doing indirectly for years via the U.S. government's Endangered Species Act (ESA).

Since becoming law in 1973, the ESA has been used in countless ways to inflict harm on people in the name of protecting endangered species and their habitats. The Northern Spotted Owl became famous when timber production was virtually halted in the Pacific Northwest to protect the species.

In Oregon in 1992, the water regularly supplied to several Oregon farmers from the Klamath Irrigation Project near the Oregon-California border was cut off by government to protect the shortnose sucker and the Lost River sucker, causing severe damages to crops and livestock.

In California, construction was halted on the San Bernardino Medical Center and, later, on a neighboring subdivision to protect the Delhi Sands flower-loving fly. Near Bakersfield, Calif., a farmer was arrested in 1994 by Fish and Wildlife officers for inadvertently killing five Tipton kangaroo rats while plowing his own soil. His tractor and plow were seized as "murder weapons." Under the ESA he faced heavy fines and three years in prison.

What motivates environmentalists to protect endangered species with so much zeal that they are oblivious to the harm inflicted on people?

Some environmentalists assert that "species diversity" is beneficial to humans. Yet, environmentalists are among the staunchest opponents of genetic engineering, which has vast potential for creating new species. Some assert that an endangered species could hold beneficial medical secrets. But in 1991 when Taxol -- processed from the bark of the Pacific Yew tree -- was discovered to be highly effective in treating certain forms of cancer, environmentalists blocked people from harvesting the tree. It seems that whenever human needs conflict with the "protection" of nature, environmentalists invariably put nature first.

The real motive behind environmentalism is stated by David Graber (a biologist with the U.S. National Park Service): "We are not interested in the utility of a particular species, or free-flowing river, or ecosystem to mankind. They have intrinsic value ...."

This "intrinsic value" philosophy means that man must value nature -- not for any benefit to man, but because nature is somehow a value in and of itself. Hence, nature must be kept pristine despite any harm caused to humans. We must halt activities beneficial to us, such as farming, forestry, cancer treatment, in order to safeguard fish, birds, trees, and rats.

Throughout history, people were told that they must sacrifice their lives to God, the king, the proletariat, the nation, or the Fuhrer -- all with deadly consequences. And environmental legislation, such as the ESA, provides government with massive powers to enforce such sacrifices. What disasters could such power lead to?

It's difficult to predict but certain environmentalists have expressed their preference. "Until such time as Homo sapiens should decide to rejoin nature," writes biologist Graber, "some of us can only hope for the right virus to come along." City University of New York philosophy Professor Paul Taylor adds: "[T]he ending of the human epoch on Earth would most likely be greeted with a hearty 'Good Riddance.'"

While extreme, these anti-human sentiments are logically consistent with environmentalism's "intrinsic value" philosophy: Since man survives only by conquering nature, man is an inherent threat to the "intrinsic value" of nature and must therefore be eliminated. **Environmentalism makes man the endangered species.**

The only antidote to these anti-human types is to reject their anti-human philosophy and uphold man's right to pursue his own life and happiness as his nature demands -- by improving his environment via technology, production and development.

Because governments are supposed to protect individual rights, not violate them, we should stop handing government the power to sacrifice people to nature, and demand that it relinquish any such power it currently wields. (This is especially urgent given that Canada's Environment Minister Christine Stewart -- facing intense lobbying from environmentalists -- recently announced plans to introduce endangered species legislation next spring.)

As for the eco-terrorists who destroy property and (in the case of the Unabomber) even harm and kill people, they would not be so brazen in committing terrorism were in not for the moral sanction they currently derive from the anti-human philosophy underlying environmentalism. Furthermore, governments stripped of its power to sacrifice people to nature would have more resources and resolve to track these criminals down and bring them to justice.

"A government big enough to give you everything you want, is strong enough to take everything you have."
Thomas Jefferson

Jobs or Endangered Species?

The loss of jobs correlated with endangered species is not a theory, it is a fact. Nevada, California, Michigan, and South Carolina have the highest rates of unemployment in America, averaging, as of August 23, 2011, **an unemployment rate of 11.7 per cent. On average, they have listed 105 endangered species.**

The four states with the lowest unemployment rates are North Dakota, Nebraska, South Dakota, and New Hampshire. **Their unemployment** rate is 4.3%. On average, they have listed 14 endangered species.

Ask the man in 2011 who can't feed his family, or the mother who has to pay for groceries with food stamps, or the family having their home foreclosed. Ask the guy with a PhD., working at McDonald's. Ask the Real Estate agent who can't give property away. Ask the banker, who has to foreclose on his friends and neighbors. Ask a logger how he likes Spotted Owls. Ask the builder how he likes laying off loyal employees of twenty years. Ask the farmer how he likes watching his crops wither away from lack of water. Ask the flooded out Missouri homeowner what he thinks of protecting the Piping Plover. Ask Taung Ming-lin how he likes the sound of helicopters hovering overhead.

Is a Tipton's Kangaroo Rat, or a Puritan Tiger Beetle, or a Government Canyon Bat Cave Spider more important than the hungry child, living down the street? As an American, I think we need to put that concept to a vote. Congress needs to look past the special interest groups, and think about what is right for America, American jobs, and America's future. Man is part of the ecosystem, not its enemy. And American liberty represents the hope of men everywhere. If that liberty is extinguished, then who will remain to give a damn about biological diversity and the Appalacian Monkeyfaced Pearly Mussel?

Environmentalism is not going to make man the endangered species. It is going to make "life, liberty, and the pursuit of happiness" the endangered species.

"The Constitution is not an instrument for the government to restrain the people, it is an instrument for the people to restrain the government - lest it come to dominate our lives and interests."
Patrick Henry

Conclusion

> "What good fortune for governments that the people do not think."
> Adolph Hitler

It is time for the American people to start thinking.

> "You can avoid reality, but you cannot avoid the consequences of avoiding reality."
> Ayn Rand

On December 23, 1776, less than six months after the Declaration of Independence, one of America's great thinkers, Thomas Paine, penned the following words in The American Crisis:

"These are the times that try men's souls: The summer soldier and the sunshine patriot will, in this crisis, shrink from the service of his country; but he that stands by it now, deserves the love and thanks of man and woman...... If there must be trouble, let it be in my day, that my child may have peace."

Just two days later, on a stormy Christmas night, General George Washington, hoping to cheer his troops, read these same words to a group of weary, discouraged, American patriots. It was so cold, that two soldiers would freeze to death that very night. Inspired by Paine's words, these brave men crossed the ice clogged Delaware River, and, at dawn's early light, defeated the Hessian army at Trenton. The infant American nation, poised at the precipice of defeat, was preserved.

Will this be the American generation that squanders the freedoms bequeathed to us by those brave patriots? Will we throw away our rights and freedoms, and instead, give those rights and freedoms, to rats, bats, scorpions, flies, and fungus? It is one thing to claim America is a great nation. It is altogether another thing to **be** a great nation.

Freedom has a momentum to it. The generation that grew up in the 1960s and 1970s, my generation, enjoyed the momentum of freedom created by our parents, that sacrificed so much in the Second World War. Tyranny, vanquished (but never destroyed) back in 1945, also has momentum. The two are intertwined. As freedom loses momentum, tyranny gains ground. And that is where we are in America today, October of 2011.

Like the generation that suffered through the Great Depression, and fought a great war spawned by that depression, America can emerge from this current economic debacle stronger and more free. But that is not a given. Now it's our turn to stand up to the tyranny of the Environmental Movement, that has spun out of control.

It is up to Americans as individuals. We can't afford to wait for the other guy to stand up. Each and every one of us must do our part, as best we can. That may just mean working a little harder. Saving a little more for the future. Making sure we vote. Using our critical thinking skills. Saying a prayer for our country. Speaking up against injustices, wherever, and whenever, we see them. Earning our own way, and not seeking government handouts. Reading to our children. It may actually mean fighting, but one prays it doesn't come that. But if it does, then fight we must.

> "If ye love wealth greater than liberty, the tranquility of servitude greater than the animating contest for freedom, go home from us in peace. We seek not your counsel, nor your arms. Crouch down and lick the hand that feeds you; and may posterity forget that ye were our countrymen."
> Samuel Adams

We can't all be great men, but we can all be good men. And if we are all good men, then, together, as a nation, we will all be free men.

"We, the People," have the power to change what is happening in our country. The Endangered Species Act of 1973 must be repealed. Not amended, not tweaked, but repealed. Start over again, with something that makes sense and that works for our country. Let the legislators hammer out a bill that protects private property rights, and allows the proper use of America's abundant natural resources, many of which are renewable. If we want to get our economy revitalized, we must get this gorilla, the E.S.A., off the backs of American businessmen and entrepeneurs. Remember this. Businesses that are making money have more money to spend on creating clean air and clean water. People liv-

Conclusion

ing in poverty create more pollution, not less.

The Environmental Movement will cry foul, and rant and rave about the doomsday of drowning polar bears, wolf pups losing their mothers, caribou calves dying of global warming, etc. The fact is, the moment the act is repealed, not a single species will be lost. Not a single animal will die. Americans are not going to run out their back doors and start slaughtering Hungerford's crawling waterbeetles or Coachella Valley fringe-toed Lizards. Americans have better things to do, like getting back to work. And the wildlife around us will learn to adapt to humans, as they have for the past 200,000 years.

Common sense must be returned to our governance. Command and control of America's property, private and public, dictated by unelected bureaucrats in the Federal Government, must end. Environmentalists and their attorneys, bent on stopping all human progress, will lose one of their primary legal tools, which is critical. Farmers will start farming again, and producing food for the nation's hungry. Trees will be harvested, used for rebuilding our country, and, believe it or not, new trees will be replanted and grow back, to be harvested by future generations of Americans. Firemen will not die, because they feared taking water from a nearby stream. Wolf and Grizzly Bear numbers will be controlled, under the direction of local wildlife offices, and elk, moose, deer, and bighorn sheep populations will recover. Yellowstone National Park will once again be alive with abundant wildlife for all to enjoy. Predator-Prey balance will be restored for the benefit of all species, including humans, which are part of the eco-system, not its enemy. The valleys of the west will not be choked with smoke every summer, because forests will be managed, not allowed to simply grow old, die, and burn. Children will still play with California Red Legged Frogs. Hospitals will be built, and the Delhi Sand Flower Loving Fly will adapt to the changing environment. It will still rain, and the Fairy Shrimp will still find mud puddles in which to make love, and have their babies. Hard working, honest Americans, will no longer fear a knock on the door, or the finding of Appalacian Monkeyface Pearly Mussels, in a nearby stream, or a Coffin Cave Mold Beetle in their backyard landscaping.

The following is a true story. *

In the summer of 1708, a young Scottish lad, James Anderson, ambled down the gangplank of a sailing ship, and onto the busy wharf at the fledgling city of Philadelphia, then only a mere town of 4400 people.

*"Notes of Family History: The Anderson, Schofield, Pennypacker, Yocum, Crawford, Sutton, lane, Richarson, Bevan, Aubrey, Bartholomew, DeHaven, Jermain, and Walker Families. Isaac C. Sutton,Esq, Philadelphia, 1948

James had come to America to seek his fortune. Only eighteen years of age, he had left the Isle of Skye, Scotland, alone, and penniless. All he possessed was a willingness to work, a quick smile, intelligence, and a fierce determination.

Unable to pay for his passage, James, as was the fashion of the time, indentured himself to a Welsh miller, for a period of five years. The miller, Thomas Jermain, had acquired the first license from William Penn to operate a gristmill, in what is now Great Mill, Pennsylvania. At that time, it was on the frontier border between civilization, and the forested haunts of the Lenni-Lenape Indians. Today, it is shopping centers, malls, factories, and housing developments.

Following the five year period of indentured servitude, the handsome and industrious young man eloped with the miller's daughter, Elizabeth. Elizabeth had been promised to another, Enoch Walker, whose father owned the pretentious estate, Rehobeth. Her heart, however, belonged to the Scotsman. The young couple traveled west, on foot, under the moonlight, and lived, at first, in a cave, along the Pickering Creek. They were befriended and helped by their Indian neighbors. It was a dangerous place, "for each night, wolves prowled in the neighborhood. Even later, when Anderson had bought sheep, the snow about the tight-walled sheepfold was trampled by packs of hungry wolves." Their first child, Patrick, was the first white child born in what later became known as Valley Forge, Pennsylvania.

The Andersons worked hard, and prospered. They moved from the cave, to a log cabin, and eventually to a large stone home, which still stands. Patrick grew to manhood, and eventually inherited the family farm. But under British rule, they were not truly free. Patrick Anderson and his family had much to lose, but were willing to risk all, so that future generations of Andersons would be truly free.

With the events at Lexington and Concord, war finally came. Having served as a captain in the French and Indian War, Patrick mortgaged his farm so that he could outfit a regiment of American patriots, his friends and neighbors. He and his sons served ably in the battles of Long Island, Fort Washington, Brandywine, and Germantown. Patrick's son, Isaac, serving as an army scout, slipped behind enemy lines, and stole a beautiful white horse from a British officer, and gave it to his commanding officer, General George Washington. That same horse is often pictured with Washington in paintings from that era. Isaac Anderson would later serve in the United States Congress.

This was not a war fought on some foreign land, but in the Anderson's own backyard, the fields and forests of eastern Pennsylvania. One can still today see the bloodstains on the wooden floor of their home, where the Hessian soldiers ransacked their house, and slaughtered their livestock.

If you visit the little Valley Forge Memorial Chapel in Valley Forge National Park, Pennsylvania, there is a plaque in Patrick Anderson's memory on one of the simple wooden pews. It states:

> **To the Glory of God and in memory**
> **of Patrick Anderson**
> **July 24, 1719-1793**
> **Captain in the French and Indian War,**
> **1755**
> **Member of the Chester County Committee**
> **of Safety, 1774**
> **Major in Wayne's Battalion of Minute**
> **Men 1775**
> **Senior Captain in Command of the Penn-**
> **sylvania Battalion of Musketry 1776**
> **Member of the Assembly of Pennsylvania,**
> **1778,1781**

Patrick Anderson was my great-great-great-great-great grandfather.

I owe this book to him, to my grandchildren, and the dozens of generations in between, that helped build this great nation: the farmers, the millers, the legislators, the shop keepers, the frontiersmen and women, the lawyers, the small businessmen, the entrepeneurs, the college professors, the teachers in the one room schoolhouses, and the citizen soldiers.

America can return to greatness, the greatness envisioned by that young Scottish lad, stepping off a sailing ship in Philadelphia, over 300 years ago. But it cannot, and will not, return to greatness as long as the Endangered Species Act of 1973 remains in place. The law simply gives too much power to those that would destroy the American dream.

Acknowledgements

Acknowledgements

I would like to thank all of the many authors that have contributed to this book. Whether current political pundits, or Founding Fathers, I feel a kindred spirit with their love of America and individual freedom.

I would especially like to thank Amy Ridenour, of the National Center for Public Policy Research, who graciously allowed me to use the stories from "Shattered Dreams." It saved me a lot of time, which I appreciated, as I felt it important to get this work into print.

There are dozens of Americans with whom I spoke, that had similar stories to the ones discussed in this book. They did not make the final cut, but their stories inspired me to push forward with the project.

I must, of course, acknowledge my family, which has tolerated my obsessiveness with this project. I am an outfitter and hunting consultant, not a professional writer, and so they have encouraged me through my writing frustrations. The fact is, if my businesses had not been expropriated by environmentalists in Canada, I would never had had the time to write this book, so perhaps some good will eventually come of that event. I know it helped me understand the frustrations Americans are feeling at the treatment they are receiving from their own government, a government which is clearly overstepping the bounds envisioned by our Founding Fathers.

This book is 439 pages long. It could have easily been a thousand pages longer, were I to include everyone's tragic story that I heard. I live in a small town in rural Montana. If I can discover these stories, surely so can Congress. All they need to do is listen to the people.

John Andre
October 21, 2011

Made in the USA
Lexington, KY
09 December 2011